Realizing the UN Declaration on the
Rights of Indigenous Peoples

Realizing the UN Declaration on the Rights of Indigenous Peoples

Triumph, Hope, and Action

◇

edited by

Jackie Hartley, Paul Joffe,
and Jennifer Preston

PURICH
PUBLISHING
LIMITED
SASKATOON, SK. CANADA

Purich Publishing Ltd.
Box 23032, Market Mall Post Office, Saskatoon, SK, Canada, S7J 5H3
Phone: (306) 373-5311 Fax: (306) 373-5315 Email: purich@sasktel.net
www.purichpublishing.com

Library and Archives Canada Cataloguing in Publication

Realizing the UN Declaration on the Rights of Indigenous Peoples : triumph, hope, and action / edited by Jackie Hartley, Paul Joffe & Jennifer Preston.

ISBN 978-1-895830-38-5

1. United Nations. General Assembly. Declaration on the Rights of Indigenous Peoples. 2. Indigenous peoples — Legal status, laws, etc. 3. Indigenous peoples (International law).
1. Joffe, Paul II. Hartley, Jackie, 1978– III. Preston, Jennifer, 1965–

K3246.4 2007 R43 2010   341.4'852   C2010-901443-X

Edited, designed, and typeset by Donald Ward.
Cover design by Duncan Campbell.
Index by Ursula Acton.
Cover image courtesy of Grand Chief Edward John.

Printed and bound in Canada at Houghton Boston Printers & Lithographers, Saskatoon.
Printed on 100 per cent post-consumer, recycled, ancient-forest-friendly paper.

Purich Publishing gratefully acknowledges the assistance of the Government of Canada through the Canada Book Fund, and the Creative Industry Growth and Sustainability Program made possible through funding provided to the Saskatchewan Arts Board by the Government of Saskatchewan through the Ministry of Tourism, Parks, Culture and Sport for its publishing program.

Contents

III: TREATY RIGHTS AND FREE, PRIOR, AND INFORMED CONSENT:
ESSENTIAL ASPECTS OF SELF-DETERMINATION

IV: DIMENSIONS OF COLLECTIVE AND INDIVIDUAL SECURITY

CONCLUSION

APPENDICES

A Living Instrument

◯

Phil Fontaine

former National Chief of the Assembly of First Nations, Canada

For the world's 370 million Indigenous people, 13 September 2007 was an historic day for the advancement and recognition of their human rights. The *United Nations Declaration on the Rights of Indigenous Peoples* was adopted on that day by the General Assembly after more than two decades in the making. As Indigenous peoples, we should be proud of how far we have come. Not that long ago, the United Nations was closed to us. Today, the visibility of Indigenous peoples in the international human rights system is astonishing. This is owing to the collective efforts of Indigenous peoples from all over the world, and their representative organizations working with the United Nations.

Since the adoption of the *Declaration*, many people have remarked to me about the breadth of the work — the preparation, the years of commitment, and the level of co-ordination among the Indigenous peoples' organizations in Canada and abroad — that was involved in making the *Declaration* a reality. This declaration is the work of thousands of people who never gave up. I would like to acknowledge, in particular, the years of professional commitment that former Assembly of First Nations Regional Chief Wilton Littlechild and Grand Chief Edward John of the First Nations Summit have contributed to representing the rights and interests of our people internationally. They have served us well, they have conducted themselves with honour, and they have made us proud. I also thank all those champions of the *Declaration* who are no longer with us, but whose efforts and commitment are embodied in the *Declaration*. We know they are with us in spirit to celebrate this achievement and inspire us to move forward. I also acknowledge all the supporters of Indigenous rights, individual human rights champions, non-governmental organizations, and supportive nation-states who worked alongside us for many years. Meegwetch.

The *Declaration* has its roots in the efforts of our ancestors, who fought to be heard and to have our perspectives and our rights recognized at both the domestic and the international level. The *Declaration* is the only international instrument in which Indigenous peoples' representatives played a key role in the United Nations standard-setting and decision-making processes.

To see how far we have come, we can look back to 1923 when Chief Deskaheh of the Haudenosaunee went to Geneva to speak to the League of Nations and defend the rights of his people to live on their land, under their own laws and customs. Around the same time, in 1924, Maori Chief Ratana made the journey to Geneva for the same reasons. Even though they were not allowed to speak to the international body, their vision and perseverance inspired the generations that have followed in their footsteps.

In the 1970s, Indigenous peoples from all over the world again travelled to Geneva, demanding representation at the international level. Thirty years later, we see Indigenous people speaking in the United Nations General Assembly.

It has taken a long time for us to make this journey. But each step was a step for our rights, for self-determination, for our voices, for our future.

The *Declaration* bridges the global and the local. It is a response to the human rights abuses suffered by Indigenous peoples everywhere. It is an expression of the local experiences of Indigenous peoples all over the world. But it is also an expression of the global partnerships and solidarity of Indigenous peoples.

The *Declaration* is fundamentally about building meaningful relationships with Indigenous peoples across the globe, and with nation-states and with Indigenous rights supporters. It is about our relationships with each other, our lands, natural resources, our laws, our rights, our languages, our spiritualities, our ways of life.

In important ways, the *Declaration* is our declaration. We can build on it in the coming years. Our growing participation at the global level has led to the creation of new political spaces that hold the potential for transformation and empowerment.

Our challenge is to harness this potential. This is the hope and the opportunity of the *Declaration*. It represents what can be and what should be. The adoption of the *Declaration* by the United Nations was not an endpoint; it is the beginning. The work to see it fully implemented at home and internationally is now upon us.

So what does the *Declaration* do? It sets out best practices that nation-states should implement. Consistent with principles of equality and diversity, it enshrines our right to be different as peoples. It affirms minimum standards for the survival, dignity, security, and well-being of Indigenous peoples worldwide. In practical terms, in the global context, the provisions of the document can influence and inform the interpretation of existing international human rights instruments. It can also help shape the political priorities, programs, and policies of the United

Nations and other international agencies. These changes are already beginning to take place.

In the domestic context, it can inform public opinion, influence public policy, and guide future jurisprudence. As Indigenous peoples, we can use it in our pursuit for the full recognition, respect, and implementation of our rights at home. Human rights institutions and courts can use the *Declaration* as a standard to measure how Canada behaves toward our peoples, our communities, and our nations. The same is true — or can be made a reality — in other countries where Indigenous peoples occupy and use their ancestral lands.

In short, the *Declaration* is a living instrument that contains hope for change and a promise of social justice for Indigenous peoples around the world.

We have a significant challenge to ensure that this promise is realized in Canada. Canada played an important leadership role in building consensus and bridging positions between states and Indigenous peoples in the standard-setting processes that led to the *Declaration*. Unfortunately, Canada did not fulfill its promise as a human rights leader when it voted against the *Declaration* in the Human Rights Council in June 2006 and in the General Assembly in September 2007. Canada decided that it was going to pick and choose which human rights it was prepared to support. Clearly, it was not prepared to support the rights of Indigenous peoples.

Canada's refusal to endorse and implement the *Declaration* is a stain on the country's human rights record. The nation has failed to uphold its international obligations. It can no longer credibly claim to be a defender of human rights in the international community.

But this does not have to be a lost opportunity. Canada can still do the right thing. It is only lack of political will that prevents Canada from declaring its support for the *Declaration*. The *Declaration* should be viewed as a chance for states to build new relationships with Indigenous peoples, based on the principles of justice, democracy, respect for human rights, equality, non-discrimination, sharing, co-operation, and mutual respect. It opens the door for the meaningful expression of Indigenous rights in Canada and abroad.

Our task now is to breathe life into the *Declaration* so that it will be implemented and the principles it embodies become a reality for our people and for Indigenous peoples everywhere. Our cultures, our hope, our determination, and our vision for justice and self-determination are still strong, even though we face difficult challenges in many of our communities. We are determined to take control over our circumstances, our lives, and our future. The *Declaration* can help us chart new paths for the present and future. It can help us assert our right to self-determination.

The promise and hope of the *Declaration* is shaped by our ability to use it creatively. We will continue to listen to all our communities so that the *Declaration* can have meaning and effect at home. We will be guided, in particular, by our elders, our youth, and women in developing priorities and solutions.

The fight against the ongoing violations of our human rights continues. We must refer to the *Declaration* in our dealings with the courts, in our negotiations with governments, in all our work. It needs to be part of everything we do to assert our rights. We must never forget that the *Declaration* is not an abstract idea that is out of reach of our communities and nations, but a living document that reflects the inherent human rights of Indigenous peoples.

On 19-20 February 2008, the Assembly of First Nations, the British Columbia Assembly of First Nations, the First Nations Summit and the Union of BC Indian Chiefs hosted an international symposium on "Implementing the *United Nations Declaration on the Rights of Indigenous Peoples.*" Indigenous peoples and supporters gathered to determine how we can make the *Declaration* a reality. Over these two days, we heard people remind us that it is up to us to use the *Declaration* and make it a key part of our decision-making and problem-solving in building a better future.

I warmly thank the presenters at the symposium for sharing their wisdom and experience with us. I also thank the organizers for their hard work in ensuring the success of the event.

This publication draws on the lessons from the symposium. It is a collection of many voices — Indigenous leaders, academics, legal counsel, representatives of states and non-governmental organizations — united in their commitment to ensure that the *Declaration* is fully implemented. It is an important reference not only for Indigenous peoples in Canada, but for Indigenous peoples and supporters worldwide. I congratulate the editors on the production of an excellent resource for human rights education and advocacy.

I encourage Indigenous people to take the *Declaration* home to their communities. Read it with your people. Discuss it with them. Discuss it with your children. Listen to what our people have to say, and share that wisdom with others. We have a continuing responsibility to ensure that the hard work of our people fighting for justice, equality, and self-determination can be fully realized for present and future generations.

From Development to Implementation

An Ongoing Journey

○

Jackie Hartley, Paul Joffe, and Jennifer Preston

Today, by adopting the Declaration on the Rights of Indigenous Peoples, we are making further progress to improve the situation of indigenous peoples around the world . . . we are also taking another major step forward towards the promotion and protection of human rights and fundamental freedoms for all.

Her Excellency Sheikha Haya Rashed Al Khalifa
President, 61st Session of the United Nations General Assembly[1]

The *United Nations Declaration on the Rights of Indigenous Peoples*[2] is a unique instrument in the field of international human rights. It is also a powerful symbol of triumph and hope.

The human rights of the world's Indigenous peoples are routinely trampled, even when entrenched in national laws. Indigenous peoples urgently require international affirmation and protection of their human rights. Developed in response to the deep injustices and extreme human rights violations that they suffer, the *Declaration* affirms the "minimum standards for the survival, dignity and well-being of the indigenous peoples of the world."[3] These standards develop and promote a human rights-based approach to addressing issues faced by Indigenous peoples. The *Declaration* provides a principled legal framework for achieving reconciliation, redress, and respect.

The *Declaration* makes a much-needed contribution to global understanding and the promotion of human rights through its emphasis on inherent collective rights, which are indispensable to the survival and well-being of Indigenous peoples and their development as peoples.[4] These include treaty rights, land and resource rights, and the right to self-determination.

INTRODUCTION

The *Declaration* has achieved widespread international support. One hundred and forty-four[5] states supported the *Declaration* in the General Assembly. Only four nations — Australia, Canada, New Zealand, and the United States — voted against it. Eleven abstained.

Support for the *Declaration* continues to grow. Declarations of the General Assembly are universally applicable upon their adoption, and do not require states to become signatories. States that did not vote in favour of the *Declaration* at the time of its adoption can later endorse or express their support for it at any time. Following a change of government, Australia issued a formal statement of support for the *Declaration* on 3 April 2009.[6] New Zealand and the United States are reconsidering their position.[7] Colombia and Samoa, two of the 11 abstaining members, have now also endorsed the *Declaration*.[8]

Canada's vote in the General Assembly was disappointing to Indigenous peoples, human rights organizations, and many member states. Canada had played a leading role during the final years of negotiations, but with the election in 2006 of the minority Conservative government led by Prime Minister Stephen Harper, the country's supportive position was reversed. The Harper government had come to power just before the text of the draft declaration was released. From that time onward, Canada has opposed the *Declaration* in an unsubstantiated manner (see Chapter 5). With support for the *Declaration* growing across the world, Canada is increasingly isolated.

As the authors in this collection recount, the journey toward the adoption of the *Declaration* in the General Assembly was long and difficult. However, the triumph of 13 September 2007 was the beginning of a new era — the era of implementation. As Victoria Tauli-Corpuz, chair of the United Nations Permanent Forum on Indigenous Issues, stated, "effective implementation of the Declaration will be the test of commitment of States and the whole international community to protect, respect and fulfill indigenous peoples collective and individual human rights."[9]

Implementation of the *Declaration* began immediately after its adoption, and remains ongoing. It is occurring in international forums, domestic courts, and in treaty and other negotiations with governments. It is also being realized through Indigenous peoples' exercise of the rights affirmed in the *Declaration*.

On 19-20 February 2008, less than six months after the adoption of the *Declaration*, the Assembly of First Nations, the British Columbia Assembly of First Nations, the First Nations Summit, and the Union of British Columbia Indian Chiefs hosted an international symposium, "Implementing the *United Nations Declaration on the Rights of Indigenous Peoples*," at the Chief Joe Mathias Centre of the Squamish Nation in North Vancouver.

More than 300 delegates from across Canada and the United States attended, including Indigenous leaders and community members, legal counsel, academics, students, representatives of non-governmental organizations, and parliamentarians. Speakers included experts in Canadian and international human rights law from Canada, the United States, Australia, New Zealand, Guatemala, and the Philippines, many of whom had been instrumental in the development and adoption of the *Declaration*.

The symposium celebrated the adoption of the *Declaration*, raised awareness of its provisions, and urged its full implementation. Participants overwhelmingly expressed their desire to learn more about the *Declaration*: what it is, where it came from, what it means, and how to use it. The idea of preparing this book was conceived at the symposium by Grand Chief Edward John as a means of building on and sharing more widely the information presented over those two days.

To ensure that the *Declaration* is a living document, meaningful for the world's Indigenous peoples, it should be discussed, used, and implemented internationally, nationally, and locally. The history of the development of the *Declaration* and the long road travelled by Indigenous peoples to secure its adoption should not be forgotten. An appreciation of the history and nature of the standard-setting process that led to the *Declaration* may also provide important insights for the further evolution of human rights standards and processes.

The aim of this collection is to foster this ongoing dialogue. The various chapters explore the history and significance of the *Declaration*, drawing on the personal experience of the authors. A central and unifying theme is that the *Declaration* needs to be implemented in Canada and internationally as a matter of urgency.

In Part I, Kenneth Deer and Les Malezer review the history of the processes leading to the development and adoption of the *Declaration*, and reflect on the steps necessary for implementation. Both authors have spent years immersed in United Nations processes, and both have served as chair of the Indigenous Peoples' Caucus — Deer in the earlier years and Malezer in the final year at the General Assembly in New York. They draw on their personal experiences, both in the global Indigenous rights movement and at the grassroots level.

Grand Chief Edward John, who is both a hereditary chief and an elected leader, focuses on the *Declaration* as a framework for reconciliation between First Nations and Canada. He elaborates on concrete examples to show how First Nations in British Columbia are implementing the *Declaration* in asserting their rights.

Part II explores the roles, responsibilities, and perspectives of states, civil society, and Indigenous peoples in the creation, adoption, and ongoing implementation of the *Declaration*. Connie Taracena, a permanent state representative at the General Assembly, discusses Guatemala's support for the *Declaration*, illustrating how the document is being integrated into the work of the United Nations and other international bodies. This is a significant form of implementation.

Paul Joffe critiques the Canadian government's arguments against the *Declaration*, concluding that the government's position is motivated by ideology rather than justice and international law. He highlights the importance of adopting a human rights-based approach to Indigenous peoples' issues, and analyzes the legal status of the *Declaration*, noting the potential for its application by Canadian courts.

Jennifer Preston, a representative of a non-governmental organization (NGO) with a long history at the United Nations, examines the importance of partnerships between Indigenous peoples and NGOs. She describes their involvement, both in the years leading to the adoption of the *Declaration* and in ongoing human rights initiatives in Canada. Undertaken in partnership among Indigenous peoples and civil society, these initiatives are a further form of implementation.

In Part III, the authors consider the relationship between the *Declaration* and Indigenous peoples' treaty rights. Chief Wilton Littlechild, who has been a significant force at the United Nations for over three decades, explains how the desire to ensure respect for and enforcement of treaties influenced the development of the *Declaration*. Chief Littlechild played a critical role in developing and securing state support for the treaty provisions in the final *Declaration*.

Andrea Carmen, who also participated for many years in the development of the *Declaration*, focuses on the right of free, prior, and informed consent, arguing for a new framework for redress and reparation based on the minimum standards affirmed by the *Declaration*.

Romeo Saganash and Paul Joffe jointly consider the significance of the *Declaration* for the James Bay Cree, a treaty nation. Their chapter discusses the importance of Indigenous peoples' collective rights, including the right of self-determination, of which treaty making is an important dimension. The authors conclude that the *Declaration* is crucial in interpreting treaty rights and in filling any gaps from a human rights-based perspective.

Finally, Part IV analyzes the fundamental importance of the *Declaration* as a standard for ensuring the security and well-being of Indigenous peoples and individuals.

Celeste McKay and Craig Benjamin articulate a vision for implementing the rights affirmed in the *Declaration* as they relate to Indigenous women. Their examination is based on the indivisibility and interconnectedness of human rights, with a focus on economic, social, and cultural rights as well as the provisions in the *Declaration* that address the issues of violence and discrimination.

The Honourable Mary Ellen Turpel-Lafond explores how the *Convention on the Rights of the Child*[10] and the *Declaration* can work together to protect the rights of Indigenous children in Canada. She further describes how international standards can play a role in advocacy, interpreting domestic law and focusing political will to support better outcomes for Indigenous children.

The editors thank the First Nations Summit, including its Executive Director, Howard E. Grant, and staff for the initiative and support for this project. Special appreciation goes to the Grand Council of the Crees (Eeyou Istchee) and the Canadian Friends Service Committee (Quakers) for their commitment to and support of this work.

The editors thank the contributors for their dedication to this project over many months, and for their generosity in sharing their knowledge and experience. We especially acknowledge the leadership of Grand Chief Edward John, whose vision and determination have made this book possible.

We honour the efforts of Indigenous peoples worldwide and the human rights advocates who contributed to the realization of the *Declaration,* and who are striving for its full and effective implementation. As Michael Dodson underlines, "[t]he value of human rights is not in their existence; it is in their implementation. That is the challenge for the world with this Declaration. The standards are set. It is up to us to meet them."[11]

This book is intended to contribute to this pressing and crucial goal.

POSTSCRIPT

As this book was in the final stages of production, the government of Canada announced that it will take steps to endorse the *Declaration* "in a manner fully consistent with Canada's Constitution and laws."[12] An endorsement by Canada is long overdue. However, a qualified endorsement is likely to pose serious problems. The government has previously claimed that there are incompatibilities between the Canadian Constitution and the *Declaration* (see Chapter 5). This argument has been refuted by constitutional and international law experts (see Appendix 11). The government would miss an important opportunity to advance reconciliation should it seek to rely on such flawed arguments to qualify its support of the *Declaration.* In addition, to require full consistency with Canada's laws would simply perpetuate the status quo.

We join with Indigenous peoples and human rights and faith based organizations in urging the government to embrace the *Declaration* without conditions or limitations. We also encourage the government to work in genuine partnership with Indigenous peoples to craft its statement in support of the *Declaration,* in a way that honours the *Declaration's* spirit and intent.[13]

Publisher's note: at the time of going to press, New Zealand has announced its support for the *UN Declaration on the Rights of Indigenous Peoples.*

◯

PART I

Development, Adoption,
and
Implementation

Reflections on the Development, Adoption, and Implementation of the UN Declaration on the Rights of Indigenous Peoples

○

Kenneth Deer

1. INTRODUCTION

I was fortunate to have been involved in all stages of the standard-setting process relating to the *United Nations Declaration on the Rights of Indigenous Peoples* (*Declaration*). I also participated in strategic meetings that preceded this process. For many years I had the honour of serving as co-chair of the Indigenous Peoples' Caucus. In this chapter, I share my recollections and personal views. I recount what I consider the defining moments in the development and adoption of the *Declaration*, and highlight some key provisions of the document. Finally, I offer perspectives on its implementation.

2. DEFINING MOMENTS IN THE DEVELOPMENT OF THE DECLARATION

The events that led to the development of the *Declaration* were initiated in the 1970s. Following the standoff at Wounded Knee, South Dakota in 1973 — a 71-day occupation that ended with two dead and 300 Indians under indictment[1] — elders and traditional leaders in the Americas concluded that there was no way we could get justice in the domestic situations in which we found ourselves. In 1974, the International Indian Treaty Council was created. The council held its first meeting in Standing Rock Sioux territory in North Dakota. It was decided at this meeting to take the issues of Indigenous peoples to the international level. A campaign began to get Indigenous issues onto the agenda of the United Nations (UN).

After a good deal of lobbying, some 250 Indigenous people from the Americas travelled to Geneva in 1977 to attend the International NGO Conference on Discrimination against Indigenous Populations in the Americas, organized by the UN NGO Subcommittee on Racism, Racial Discrimination, Apartheid and Decolonization. There was considerable apprehension among certain states about this meeting, not least because the chair of the meeting, Edith Ballantyne (a Canadian), was a communist. She was general secretary of Women's International League for Peace and Freedom, and president of the Conference of NGOs in Consultative Relationship with the United Nations.

The presence of "Red Indians" caused a stir in Geneva and the UN itself, and there was talk that the Indigenous representatives might not be allowed into the building. Undeterred, they walked through the gates in groups. UN staff watched from the windows as delegation after delegation in full regalia walked by their offices and entered the meeting room. These delegations were the ones that opened the doors of the UN to let other peoples follow.[2]

One of the objectives of this international effort was to convince the UN that the rights of Indigenous peoples were not being protected by international law, and that Indigenous peoples had no adequate means of access to the UN. At that time, the only avenue for Indigenous peoples was through bodies that dealt with minorities, such as the UN Sub-Commission on Prevention of Discrimination and Protection of Minorities (Sub-Commission).

The UN had to be convinced that Indigenous rights are different from minority rights. Minorities have a right to their language, culture, education, and religion, as Indigenous peoples do, but there is a fundamental difference, in that Indigenous peoples, as peoples, have a right to self-determination[3] and a profound relationship with traditional lands and territories. Our rights to lands, territories, natural resources and all other rights flow from or are interdependent with self-determination.

In 1982, the Sub-Commission created the Working Group on Indigenous Populations (WGIP) to "review developments pertaining to the promotion and protection of the human rights and fundamental freedoms of indigenous populations,"[4] giving special attention to the evolution of standards. The word "populations" was used in the title of the WGIP rather than "peoples," as the latter term implies the right to self-determination under international law. Thus, this right was denied from the outset of this working group.

The WGIP was a working group of the Sub-Commission. This Sub-Commission reported to the Commission on Human Rights, which was itself a subsidiary body of the United Nations Economic and Social Council. The WGIP was therefore at the bottom level of the UN hierarchy. Yet, this is how we gained access.

The WGIP began the standard-setting process that ultimately led to the *Declaration* following the recommendations of the report by Special Rapporteur José Martínez Cobo.[5] The purpose of this report was to make a complete and comprehensive study of the problem of discrimination against Indigenous populations.

Special Rapporteur Martínez Cobo was tasked with recommending national and international measures for eliminating such discrimination. His report helped open the doors of the United Nations to serious consideration of Indigenous peoples' inherent rights. It also contributed to the start of a substantive dialogue at the WGIP in the context of international human rights.

There were many pivotal points in the development of the *Declaration*, but four major events ultimately led to its adoption.

2A The Adoption of the Original Draft Declaration by the WGIP

The WGIP was made up of human rights experts — one from each of the five regions into which the UN divides itself — but none of these experts was an Indigenous person. Although we greatly influenced the drafting of the original WGIP text, the authors of this first draft declaration will go down in history as being non-Indigenous. The members of the WGIP initially knew little about Indigenous peoples, and we had to educate them over the years. I give tribute to Erica-Irene Daes, chair of the WGIP, who ably steered the working group for many years, and Miguel Alfonso Martinez, who also played a pivotal role. They engaged with Indigenous representatives and brought strong leadership to the WGIP.

Indigenous peoples were active in the WGIP sessions, drafting articles for the draft declaration that we subsequently submitted to the WGIP and pressured it to adopt. We were a part of this standard-setting process along with member states, who also proposed text. Canada was a major player in this process and generally had the largest delegations.

From 1985 to 1993, the WGIP's text grew in size and scope. Except for 1986, the group met each year for a week in July or August, when new articles were added and refined. From 1990 to 1993, the WGIP met for two weeks in order to speed up the drafting process. The draft was finally completed in 1993. One of the last articles to be added was article 3: the right to self-determination. This right is the key and the basis for equality and respect from the rest of the world. In 1994, the Sub-Commission, the parent body of the WGIP, adopted the draft declaration without changes.[6]

2B The 1996 Walk Out

The Sub-Commission and the WGIP were made up of independent human rights experts. Their parent body, however, was the Commission on Human Rights, which was comprised of government delegates. After the Sub-Commission adopted it, the draft declaration advanced to the Commission on Human Rights. The state representatives at the Commission on Human Rights were not willing to adopt the draft declaration in the form in which it had been submitted.

Some states had found the WGIP process frustrating, while others had simply not participated. In 1995, the Commission on Human Rights created an open-ended inter-sessional working group to consider the Sub-Commission's draft text.[7] We called it the "Open-Ended Inter-Sessional Working Group on the Draft Declaration on the Rights of Indigenous Peoples," but it was officially known as the Working Group on Resolution 95/32. State governments again avoided the use of the term "Indigenous peoples" or "peoples." The annual meeting became known as the Working Group on the Draft Declaration (WGDD).

The WGDD was comprised of representatives of states. During its sessions, Indigenous peoples again fought to be included in the international processes. Indigenous peoples' organizations were invited to participate in the WGDD's sessions, but by 1996 we still felt that we were not being included in the process. The then-chair of the WGDD, Ambassador Urrutia of Peru, would not recognize us when we raised our hands to speak, so we eventually walked out of the session. We demanded respect from the chair before we went back. We had some leverage in this because without Indigenous participation, the WGDD lacked credibility.

The challenge, then, was how to get back into the room. There were negotiations with states as to the possibility of establishing an Indigenous co-chair, for instance, and other processes that would level the playing field between states and Indigenous representatives were discussed. The chair eventually agreed to accept the Indigenous representatives along with the states as part of the consensus in the informal sessions of the WGDD.

This solution informally gave us free, prior, and informed consent in the process. It meant that the states and Indigenous representatives had to come to a consensus on the various provisions in the draft declaration before the chair would agree to call a vote. This was a significant victory for Indigenous peoples, which those who entered the process after 1996 may not fully appreciate: if we had not been part of the consensus, we would not have the *Declaration* we have today. This level of Indigenous participation was unprecedented. It does not exist in any other forum in the United Nations.

2C The Strategy of "No Change"

The work of the Working Group on the Draft Declaration lasted from 1995 to 2006. Initially, we had hoped that a declaration would be approved in five years, during the first International Decade of the World's Indigenous People — again, note the lack of an "s" on "People" — and we could turn our attention to the implementation of the *Declaration* during the second part of the decade. That did not happen.

During the WGDD sessions, there was tremendous state resistance to the WGIP's text, particularly toward the right to self-determination and lands, territories, and resources. Surprisingly, some states objected to seemingly non-controversial articles that addressed such things as education and health.

Rather than accepting the unfair or discriminatory objections of states, Indigenous peoples adopted a "no change" strategy. For years, this strategy was a major factor in maintaining the integrity of the draft declaration. Our position was that the text of the draft declaration as adopted by the WGIP in 1993 was what we wanted. We would not settle for anything less. If we had allowed governments to make changes to the WGIP text, we would not have achieved the *Declaration* we have today, because they were hostile to many of its provisions.

The longer we delayed agreeing to changes to the draft declaration, the more time we had to educate governments, engage them in dialogue, and begin to make them feel comfortable with the wording. Through this dialogue, it was hoped that governments would become better educated about the inherent rights of Indigenous peoples and be less threatened by the wording of the text. For this strategy to work, we needed to remain part of the consensus. The agreement that was reached after the walk-out built on our "no change" strategy.

We maintained this strategy until the early 2000s. By 2004, however, even the most supportive states made it clear that the strategy could not be continued, and that some amendments would have to be made in order for the draft declaration to be adopted. During intensive discussions with states between 2004 and 2006, we cautiously proposed some amendments ourselves — amendments that would not weaken the existing text, but rather clarify its provisions to answer concerns raised by states. A key achievement of this process was the agreement by the United Kingdom and a number of other resistant states to the affirmation of our collective rights in the draft declaration. This generated significant momentum in the approval of dozens of provisions in the draft text.

While some changes were eventually made to the WGIP text, our persistence in holding to our "no change" strategy granted us time to convince states to agree to the core right of self-determination. This was a significant achievement, one we would not have been able to reach in the 1990s.

2D Finalization of the Text of the Draft Declaration by the WGDD Chair

To me, the most critical point in the history of the *Declaration* was not its adoption by the Human Rights Council in 2006 or by the General Assembly in 2007. Rather, it was the submission to the Commission on Human Rights of a revised text by the chair of the WGDD in March 2006.[8]

By 2006, governments and Indigenous peoples had informally reached consensus on the greater part of the draft declaration. In his report that accompanied the revised text, the chair of the WGDD described the scope of informal consensus:

The representative of Norway informed the working group on the outcome of the informal consultations she facilitated during the week. She identified the articles that could be considered as a basis for provisional agreement. In this regard, she stated that no further discussion was required regarding [sixteen] preambular paragraphs ... as well as [twenty-one] articles. ... The representative of Norway also reported that [three additional] articles were close to consensus.[9]

By the end of the final meeting of the WGDD, however, it was clear there was insufficient time to reach consensus on the wording of some of the contentious issues, such as those regarding lands and territories. Based on the proposals that had been made in the WGDD by states and Indigenous peoples, the then-chair, Luis-Enrique Chávez of Peru, revised the articles on which there had been disagreement, based on what he judged was the closest to an achievable consensus. He made strategic changes to existing provisions, basing them on previous proposals by states and Indigenous peoples. He submitted this text to the Commission on Human Rights as an annex to in his final report. Chávez had indicated that he would make revisions in this manner at the final meeting of the WGDD.[10]

We were not happy with every aspect of this final text, but it was a compromise. The revised text kept intact the provisions relating to self-determination; our rights to our lands and territories; our collective rights; free, prior, and informed consent; and treaties. These were the major provisions that we wanted affirmed.

Owing to UN restructuring — the Human Rights Council replaced the Commission on Human Rights in June 2006[11] — the chair's report was presented to the first meeting of the Human Rights Council.[12] It is owing to the work of Luis-Enrique Chávez in finalizing the text that we have the *Declaration* today. The WGDD had run out of time, and there was no guarantee that its mandate would have been extended.[13] Therefore, in the absence of a final text as presented by the chair, the future of the draft declaration would have been put in serious jeopardy. It was a "now or never" situation for the submission of a product of the WGDD.

Had we not had a final text, the draft declaration would not have gone before the Human Rights Council in 2006. If the draft declaration had not been adopted by the Human Rights Council, it would not have been adopted (with a few changes) by the General Assembly in 2007. The fact that most states and Indigenous peoples ultimately accepted the compromises made by the chair shows that his actions were neither extreme nor unreasonable overall.

3. The Adoption of the Declaration

The Indigenous Peoples' Caucus and our supporters were hoping the text finalized by Chávez would be adopted by consensus in the Human Rights Council. Then Canada called for a vote. Canada had been active in promoting the draft declaration in the WGDD, and had been expected to support the final text. Unfortunately, the Harper government came to power a month before the final text was released, and decided, without consultation, not to support the draft declaration.

The vote in the Human Rights Council was one of the most exciting events I have ever witnessed — more exciting even than the final vote in the General Assembly in 2007. When the issue came to a vote, members were supposed to push a button on their desk and an electronic board would indicate the votes. But the buttons did not work, so an old-fashioned roll-call was held. The Chair of the Council drew the state of Cuba to begin the vote, and other states followed in alphabetical order.

We were not sure how the vote would go. Minutes before the meeting, Argentina had informed us that they had instructions to abstain. This infuriated Indigenous representatives from Latin America, and we did not know if more unpleasant surprises awaited us. Because it was a roll-call vote, each of the 47 member-countries, in turn, had to state its position, so the drama was strung out over several minutes. Most states voted yes, some abstained, a few were absent. When Russia voted no, there was a murmur in the crowd. Argentina abstained, as expected. One of the last states to vote was Canada. We waited silently for the response: "No." The murmur turned to an audible groan. It was sad to see Canada disown the process it had done so much to facilitate. The country was on the wrong side of the issue and it was an embarrassment to all Canadians.

When the result became clear, however, the room exploded in applause. People stood and hugged one another. A tremendous weight had been lifted from our shoulders, and all the hard work and sacrifice had been justified — at least at that time.

The declaration then needed to be adopted by the United Nations General Assembly in New York. That was a different battle, with a different atmosphere. New York is not about human rights, New York is about power and politics and we were behind the eight ball.

Following the adoption of the text by the Human Rights Council, the African governments, many of whom had not participated in the WGDD process, expressed concerns about it.[14] In December 2006 they succeeded in obtaining a delay of about nine months for further consultations. The General Assembly adopted the resulting resolution on 20 December 2006, and also decided that consideration of the declaration would be concluded before the end of its 61st session in September 2007.[15]

This hiatus came as a surprise. Many state representatives in New York were uninformed about the history of the development of the draft declaration in Geneva. They were unaware of the extent of Indigenous participation and the need for Indigenous peoples to support the text. At the same time, states opposed to the declaration were spreading misinformation, and it was again important to educate governments and their representatives about our rights.

Canada engaged in heavy lobbying against the declaration, more so than any other nation, including Australia, New Zealand, and the United States. Canada invested political capital to try to bring other governments on side and make radical changes to the text. Late in the consultation process — 13 August 2007 — Canada, Colombia, New Zealand, and the Russian Federation proposed amendments. These failed to attract support among other states.

In May 2007, the African Group of States raised a number of specific concerns with the declaration and submitted to the President of the General Assembly an initial proposal for far-reaching changes. What they suggested was unacceptable to Indigenous representatives as well as to human rights organizations, as many of their proposals were not compatible with international law or African regional human rights law.[16] Following this development, there were some hard negotiations among the African states, headed by Namibia, and the many states that supported the adoption of the declaration, led by Mexico, Peru, and Guatemala. All parties knew that a solution had to be reached or the General Assembly might fail to adopt the declaration. Politically it would have been an extreme embarrassment and a failure for the General Assembly to demonstrate to the world that, after more than two decades of negotiations, the international community could not agree on human rights for Indigenous peoples.

As an outcome of these negotiations, one week before the deadline imposed by the General Assembly, nine changes were made to the text that had been adopted by the Human Rights Council. They were not welcome, but after careful analysis the Indigenous caucus concluded that they did not alter or weaken the text to the extent that they could not be accepted. Some, in fact, strengthened the text, while others were neutral. Some indeed weakened the declaration, but we knew that we had to show some flexibility or risk losing the declaration completely. In New York we were not part of the consensus, as we had been in Geneva, but supportive states indicated that they would not proceed with the adoption of the declaration if the Indigenous Peoples' Caucus was not in agreement.

The global Indigenous Peoples' Caucus had a matter of days to review the changes and accept going forward to a vote in the General Assembly, or refusing, and ending the journey there. Each geographic region had co-ordinators who were responsible for circulating the revisions and providing feedback to our representatives in New York. Quickly, Indigenous peoples around the globe agreed that we wanted the revised text to go forward to the General Assembly.

Canada continued to lobby, but its concerns were not endorsed by the states involved in the final negotiations, and the country's credibility was severely damaged as a result. It had completely changed its approach to the declaration. Canada had sponsored the resolution that created the WGDD. Especially in the last few years of that body's deliberations, Canadian representatives spent much time and energy promoting the draft declaration. When Paul Martin was Prime Minister, Canada's contributions in the WGDD were positive and in good faith. In October 2006, Martin confirmed that his government "would have unequivocally signed the document leading to the UN declaration on indigenous rights."[17]

Many governments were upset at Canada, including those that had changed their position on the declaration because Canada had convinced them to support it. The Canadians had previously persuaded fellow states not to be afraid of the draft declaration. They had convinced other states that the affirmation of Indigenous peoples' collective rights was a central element of the draft declaration, convincing them that self-determination was not a threat, but a reflection of an existing right in the two human rights covenants.[18]

When Canada voted against the declaration in the Human Rights Council, some governments felt betrayed. Others privately described Canada's actions as disingenuous. Some state representatives privately expressed profound dismay. When the time came to vote on the *Declaration* in the General Assembly, 13 September 2007, at least we knew where Canada stood. The question now was, who else would vote no?

Supportive states had reached an agreement with the African states so we knew there would be solid support from Africa. Most of Latin America would vote in favour, and the European Union was expected to follow suit. We expected most of the Asian governments to follow Africa's lead, since they tend to vote in a bloc. We were not sure of the Eastern European group, since Russia had voted against the declaration at the Human Rights Council. But we did not know what was going to happen. I predicted that there would be 11 or 12 votes against. I knew we would win, but I did not know by how much.

The vote was called in the General Assembly. This time the buttons worked. There was no suspenseful roll call. Instead, the voting board was displayed and all the lights came on. In seconds, we knew the result. There were many green lights, each one a yes vote. There were some yellow lights for abstentions. There were only four red lights: Canada, the United States, Australia, and New Zealand. Russia abstained, as did Colombia, which had voiced concerns about the *Declaration*.

Perhaps these voices of dissent will eventually fade. Following a change of government, Australia has now endorsed the *Declaration*.[19] Indigenous peoples are also hopeful that the Obama administration will lead the United States to endorse and implement the *Declaration*.

Such a large vote in favour of the *United Nations Declaration on the Rights of Indigenous Peoples* ushers in a new era in Indigenous and state relations.

4. KEY PROVISIONS OF THE DECLARATION

From the start of our international work, Indigenous peoples sought recognition of our right to self-determination. This right has been key from the beginning. The *Declaration* affirms in article 3 that "Indigenous peoples have the right to self-determination. By virtue of that right they freely determine their political status and freely pursue their economic, social and cultural development."

All our rights either flow from or are linked to our right of self-determination. These include our right to land, our right to natural resources, our right to our language and culture, our right to our songs. We believe these are collective rights. The only right that certain countries believe exists as a collective human right is the right to self-determination. The United Kingdom, for example, stated in its explanation of its vote: "With the exception of the right to self-determination, we . . . do not accept the concept of collective human rights in international law."[20] Yet the *Declaration* recognizes that we possess and enjoy inherent rights as "peoples." Article 26 affirms that "Indigenous peoples have the right to the lands, territories and resources which they have traditionally owned, occupied or otherwise used or acquired." After generations of being regarded as minorities and populations, the *Declaration* finally recognizes us as peoples.

"Free, prior, and informed consent" (FPIC) also flows from the right to self-determination. FPIC is noted in many articles of the *Declaration*. Article 19, for example, states, "States shall consult and cooperate in good faith with the indigenous peoples concerned through their own representative institutions in order to obtain their free, prior and informed consent before adopting and implementing legislative or administrative measures that may affect them."

In explanation of its negative vote, Canada stated that it had concerns about "free, prior and informed consent when used as a veto."[21] But free, prior, and informed consent is not automatically a veto, since our human rights exist relative to the rights of others. Nor is there any reference to a veto in the *Declaration*. Free, prior, and informed consent is a means of participating on an equal footing in decisions that affect us.

The *Declaration* also affirms our rights to peace and security, and affirms our cultural integrity. Article 7 states: "Indigenous individuals have the rights to life, physical and mental integrity, liberty and security of person." Article 7 further states: "Indigenous peoples have the collective right to live in freedom, peace and security as distinct peoples and shall not be subjected to any act of genocide." In article 8, the *Declaration* affirms that "Indigenous peoples and individuals have the right not to be subjected to forced assimilation or destruction of their culture."

REALIZING THE UN DECLARATION

These and other articles address the historical efforts of the dominant society to destroy our culture and weaken our nations. In Canada, such actions have been exemplified by the Indian Residential Schools system and the extinguishment of our rights in land claims negotiations. If you destroy our culture, you take away our language, our identity, and our right to self-determination.

The draft declaration approved by the Working Group on Indigenous Populations stated that "Indigenous peoples have the collective and individual right not to be subjected to ethnocide and cultural genocide."[22] This provision was removed by objecting states that claimed that the terms "ethnocide" and "cultural genocide" were not recognized in international law. This is not accurate.[23] As William A. Schabas explains: "Although the Genocide Convention does not recognize cultural genocide as a criminal act falling within its scope, proofs of attacks directed against cultural institutions or monuments, committed in association with killing, may prove important in establishing the existence of a genocidal rather than merely a homicidal intent."[24] The Spanish jurist and historian Bartolomé Clavero further emphasized that cultural genocide "must be prevented both by itself for rights' sake and for the prevention of [genocide]. The better they are identified, the better they are prevented."[25]

Articles 7 and 8 of the *Declaration* essentially contain provisions that are useful in preventing ethnocide or cultural genocide. Indigenous peoples should therefore consider using these articles carefully when challenging any action, activity, or legislation advanced by governments that may have an impact on our peoples.

5. CONCLUSION: IMPLEMENTING OUR RIGHTS

After years of struggle, we have a *United Nations Declaration on the Rights of Indigenous Peoples*. The challenge now is full and effective implementation.

Implementation of the *Declaration* is about implementing our rights. You do not ask for rights; you assert them. When rights are asserted, they grow. No state will "give" rights to Indigenous peoples, and no state will "offer" them. Indigenous peoples must assert and exercise our inherent rights. Exercising our rights is what makes us who we are.

Canada's attitude toward the *Declaration* cannot prevent its implementation. Canada is a member of the United Nations. The United Nations held a vote on the *Declaration* and Canada lost that vote. If Canada believes in democracy, it must recognize the *Declaration*. If Canada continues to object to this universal human rights instrument, it will continue to be criticized internationally, and its reputation will continue to diminish. In the meantime, Indigenous peoples will continue to exercise our rights in a spirit of justice, equality, and non-discrimination for the benefit of present and future generations.

CHAPTER TWO

Dreamtime Discovery

New Reality and Hope

◇

Les Malezer

1. Rights for Indigenous Peoples

The *United Nations Declaration on the Rights of Indigenous Peoples* (*Declaration*) is a significant benchmark in human rights history — an instrument pursued and achieved by Indigenous peoples out of necessity.

In the modern era, Indigenous peoples have vigorously sought status in the international community to address the colonization and exploitation of their communities, territories, and resources. In 1923, Haudenosaunee Chief Deskaheh travelled to Geneva to address the League of Nations as a peer to affirm and defend the right of his people to live under their own laws, on their own land, and in accordance with their own values and beliefs. Although the League of Nations denied the request, Chief Deskaheh did attract attention to the cause of Indigenous peoples. He was the first in a continuous line of delegations to campaign in global forums for the equality and freedoms of Indigenous peoples.

The *Declaration* has been a long time coming. Adopted 60 years after the *Universal Declaration of Human Rights* was proclaimed, the *Declaration on the Rights of Indigenous Peoples* comes at the tail end of human rights standard-setting. It may well be one of the last significant standards on human rights established by the United Nations (UN).

It was not until the United Nations decided in 1982 to establish a Working Group on Indigenous Populations (WGIP)[1] that Indigenous peoples established a foothold in the struggle for a global voice and identity. It did not take long for an international human rights standard to emerge as the top priority for Indigenous peoples.

By 1995, a completed draft declaration was presented to the Commission on Human Rights, and the General Assembly set the key objective of adopting it as part of the International Decade of the World's Indigenous People.[2] For the next decade, however, the draft declaration became engulfed in debate, dividing Indigenous peoples and states.

Indigenous peoples insisted that the right to self-determination must be affirmed in the draft declaration, while powerful states opposed any references that suggested the sovereignty of Indigenous peoples. Certain states also opposed Indigenous peoples' rights to territory, development, autonomy, and restitution on the basis that such rights threatened the interests of other parties.

These disagreements were ultimately settled through the developing comprehension of the issues and the compromise, multipart final text of the *Declaration*. The resultant *Declaration* emerges as a mechanism that encourages partnerships between Indigenous peoples and states.

The interpretation of rights elaborated in any one article in the *Declaration* depends very much on an understanding and respect for the entire *Declaration* as a summation document. Articles 43 and 45 affirm that the rights contained in the *Declaration* "constitute the minimum standards for the survival, dignity and well-being of the indigenous peoples of the world," and that nothing in the document "may be construed as diminishing or extinguishing the rights indigenous peoples have now or may acquire in the future."

Despite the importance of the *Declaration* to international human rights law, it does not create new human rights. The rights contained in the *Declaration* already exist. The *Declaration* identifies rights that are particularly important for Indigenous peoples — rights that are historically and currently denied to Indigenous peoples, and rights and freedoms that are generally taken for granted by others.

As the *Declaration* elaborates the rights of Indigenous peoples that have been denied, particularly rights to property and development, it exposes and addresses the potential conflicts between Indigenous peoples and those parties that have pursued interests in Indigenous peoples' territories without respect for the rights of Indigenous peoples. The *Declaration* identifies the rights of Indigenous peoples to obtain redress and restitution, and has precise language requiring the fair and independent adjudication or arbitration of such conflicts.

One of the major achievements of the *Declaration* is to generate better awareness and appreciation of the rights already embodied in international human rights law as they apply to Indigenous peoples, and the obligations of states to respect, protect, and fulfill these rights. The first preambular paragraph of the *Declaration* refers to the "good faith in the fulfilment of the obligations assumed by States in accordance with the Charter" of the United Nations. There are five references to states in the preambular paragraphs. Twenty-six of the 46 articles identify actions for, and responsibilities of, states.

In this chapter, I first consider the roles of the Indigenous Peoples' Caucus, states, and the United Nations in the standard-setting process that led to the *Declaration*. I then examine the key components of the *Declaration*. Finally, I analyze the obligations arising from the *Declaration* and the responsibilities of the UN, Indigenous peoples, and states to realize the vision of the *Declaration*.

2. INDIGENOUS PEOPLES' CAUCUS

Immediately after the United Nations formally adopted the *Declaration*, I attended a session of the Human Rights Council in Geneva. In a "side-event," involving non-governmental organizations (NGOs), I listened to a delegate appeal for unity and more cohesive actions by NGOs, citing the Indigenous Peoples' Caucus as an exemplar for successful campaigning. These NGOs had been impressed by the determination and strategy of Indigenous peoples as they worked for more than two decades to achieve the *Declaration*.

Through unity and determination, it was seen, non-state parties could be successful and influential at the highest levels of the United Nations. This describes the success and strength of the Indigenous Peoples' Caucus — as an open, inclusive, informal, unstructured assembly for delegations participating in United Nations and related forums.

For almost a quarter of a century, delegations of Indigenous peoples have been able to participate in UN meetings on Indigenous issues. The Economic and Social Council has taken the view that it is not only correct that Indigenous peoples be heard in these forums, but critical that they have influence over the deliberations.

The Indigenous Peoples' Caucus has been an important part of the interaction between the United Nations and Indigenous peoples. In the early days, the caucus served to inform and instruct delegates who were new to the UN system. It also served to support communications among delegations and help members prepare for pending UN business. In these roles, it also served to widen the representation of delegations from all parts of the world.

This caucus is usually convened on the weekend before a UN meeting and meets regularly for the period of the meeting. It has become an important mechanism for UN officials who seek feedback on matters of protocol. It can also function as a steering mechanism to guide UN chairpersons and experts. However, it does have its shortcomings.

Because the Indigenous Peoples' Caucus functions as an open, inclusive, and egalitarian forum, it is limited in its capacity for reaching consensus on complex policy or strategy positions. These positions of critical concern need the caucus to operate with a level of expertise, experience, and diplomacy that is difficult to achieve, particularly in brief meetings.

The caucus may well be able to inform and influence individual Indigenous delegations and the positions they take in UN forums, but that influence may not always be appropriate or wise, depending on delegate participation, quality of information, objectivity, and strategic focus during a particular meeting. Because participation is open, delegations come and go on a regular basis, and records are not kept, it is difficult for the caucus to maintain "hard line" positions from meeting to meeting.

In spite of these constraints, the Indigenous Peoples' Caucus served as a rallying point during the later stages of the negotiations on the draft declaration. The text prepared in the WGIP was adopted by the Sub-Commission on the Prevention of Discrimination and Protection of Minorities and forwarded to the Commission on Human Rights in 1994.[3] When the Commission on Human Rights established the Working Group on the Draft Declaration (WGDD) in 1995[4] to examine the recommended text for the declaration, the process became bogged down as Indigenous peoples sought to prevent the erosion of the text. They were resolved to protect the text, which had been brought to this stage by human rights experts, not government officials, and they were opposed to changes that might be made by states at the level of the Commission on Human Rights.

By 2004, no substantial progress had been made and no end was in sight when a group of states — Denmark, Finland, Iceland, New Zealand, Norway, Sweden, and Switzerland — presented an amended text for the draft declaration. This new draft was labelled CRP.1, or Conference Room Paper 1[5] and soon became the new focus for discussion.

Of the Indigenous delegations, the Saami Council took the lead in supporting the discussion of the CRP.1 text, thus breaking with the "no change" position of the Indigenous Peoples' Caucus. The Saami were was soon joined by other delegations who felt that, without a more elaborate strategy that allowed alternative texts to be considered, the draft declaration would move no further toward adoption. From that point, the position of the Indigenous peoples' delegations became divided among the original text, the CRP.1 text, and alternative text presented in the negotiations. The result of this, however, was that states also altered their positions, and a better accord developed between states and Indigenous peoples' delegations. A majority of delegations — states and Indigenous peoples alike — were able to enter into negotiation and, for the most part, agree on the text for the draft declaration.

Dissent diminished until only a few opponents to the majority positions were left. Unfortunately, this led them to become more intransigent.

The Indigenous Peoples' Caucus was no longer presenting the prevailing positions on the draft declaration; the most influential statements and documents regarding the text of the draft declaration were now appearing in the form of joint statements signed by large numbers of Indigenous delegations. These statements presented sound legal advice and compelling human rights examples to influence the negotiations on the text.

At the beginning of 2006, the chair of the WGDD presented a final version of the draft declaration.[6] This version, based on the chair's own evaluation of the positions expressed by the various delegations, was presented for endorsement as a complete document by the WGDD.

To determine a caucus position on this final text, it was agreed that the Indigenous delegations would divide into their regional caucus groups to consider and make decisions on this proposal. By this time, most Indigenous delegations were operating in regional groups, as this was a more effective process for functioning than in the global caucus.

The regional caucus groups — covering the seven regions of Asia, the Pacific, North America, Latin America and the Caribbean, the Arctic, the Russian Federation, and Africa — were quick to develop their positions, communicate with their constituents, and respond to developments. All regions reported that they could accept the final text, and, thus, the way was cleared for the adoption of the draft declaration by the United Nations.

The Human Rights Council, based in Geneva, held its first session in June 2006. One important matter of business for this new body was the adoption of the declaration. Canada, one of the 47 members of the Human Rights Council, was opposed to the declaration and called for a vote, thus ending the possibility that the declaration might be adopted by consensus. Only Canada and the Russian Federation voted against the declaration, however, and the document was adopted by the Human Rights Council on 29 June 2006.[7]

The Indigenous Peoples' Caucus established a steering group to monitor the progress of the declaration as it moved to the final stage before the General Assembly at UN Headquarters in New York. The steering group consisted of two skilled representatives from each of the regional caucus groups. Their role was to ensure that the text of the declaration was not altered, and to keep the Indigenous community informed of developments.

In December 2006, the General Assembly voted to defer consideration of the declaration to allow time for further consultations. The General Assembly also decided to conclude consideration of the declaration before the end of its 61st session.[8] This gave the African states, which had expressed concerns about the declaration, time to review the text. However, this delay increased the risk that the text might be altered, so the steering group commenced a continuous campaign at UN Headquarters to build support from all member states of the United Nations. This campaign focused attention on the African states, and included a panel of African human rights experts to discuss human rights concerns with the African state representatives. The campaign also brought wide public attention to the declaration and the delays within the system, emphasizing the political opposition being generated against the declaration at UN Headquarters and around the world by particular states.

The structure of the steering group worked well to streamline the campaigning while at the same time ensuring that constituents around the world were kept informed of the issues and developments. Their most critical task came in September 2007 when a proposal was finally negotiated between Mexico, acting on behalf of states that supported the declaration, and Namibia, acting on behalf of the African group, agreeing on nine minor amendments to the text of the declaration.

Many states vowed that they would not support any amendments without support from the Indigenous peoples. The steering group considered the amendments carefully and sought feedback from the regions. The regions all supported the proposition that the declaration be adopted on the terms of the Mexico/Namibia proposal. The revised text was given the green light by Indigenous peoples.

After nine months of intense campaigning at UN Headquarters, the *Declaration on the Rights of Indigenous Peoples* was finally adopted by the United Nations General Assembly on 13 September 2007. The final vote of 144 votes in favour and four votes against, represented an outstanding level of support for the *Declaration*. The Indigenous Peoples' Caucus had succeeded in establishing a substantial human rights standard addressing the rights of Indigenous peoples.

3. STATES

While we have reason to criticize the CANZUS group — Canada, Australia, New Zealand, and the US — for trying to prevent the adoption of the *Declaration*, we should first acknowledge the many states that worked with Indigenous peoples in the United Nations to see *Declaration* adopted and proclaimed by the General Assembly. But for the commitment of those nations, I doubt we would have succeeded and there would be no *Declaration on the Rights of Indigenous Peoples* now or in the foreseeable future.

The Nordic countries were consistent supporters of the declaration from the beginning. They played important roles at critical stages to ensure that the document continued to be developed and that negative forces did not overcome the process. Sometimes they were at the forefront of the process and other times they were in the background, but it is not possible to doubt their resolve throughout the long period of negotiations.

States from Latin America, led by countries such as Guatemala, Mexico, Peru, and Bolivia, were committed to the declaration and the positions of the Indigenous Peoples' Caucus. These countries took the lead in promoting the declaration and negotiating with other states for their support. Peru, in the first instance, was the sponsor of the resolution to adopt the declaration in Geneva at the Human Rights Council and in New York at the General Assembly, and therefore took the lead role in convening any meetings on the declaration. In New York, Mexico assumed a leading role in negotiating with representatives of the African Group of States to obtain support.

The European Union remained steadfast in its support of the declaration once the final text had been given wide support at the beginning of 2006, and remained unswayed by the concerns of the African Group of States at UN Headquarters.

There were times when it looked as if the declaration might fail at the General Assembly. The situation in New York was indeed precarious, and, because of the opposition of a few powerful states, much heavy-handed political bargaining came into play during 2006 and 2007.

Ambassador Luis Alfonso de Alba from the Permanent Mission of Mexico in Geneva, became the first president of the Human Rights Council in 2006, and gave clear indications to the Indigenous Peoples' Caucus that the declaration would be on the agenda of the Human Rights Council. De Alba continued to play a leadership role when the declaration came under scrutiny at UN Headquarters by advocating immediate adoption of the declaration by the General Assembly. His commitment to the declaration was in part motivated by his determination to see that the new Human Rights Council was taken seriously as the new "third pillar" (human rights) of global well-being, alongside the Security Council (security) and the Economic and Social Council (development).

At its first session the position was advanced that the Human Rights Council should have the autonomy to establish human rights standards without the ratification of the General Assembly. This view was not supported by many of the states at UN Headquarters, on the grounds that the Human Rights Council was limited to 47 members while at the General Assembly in New York, all 192 members of the United Nations could take part in making a decision on the declaration.

Of most concern to the Indigenous Peoples' Caucus was the view, expressed on more than one occasion by a few state delegations, that the adoption of the declaration was ultimately a political decision, and that Indigenous peoples had no right to participate in this final stage.

When the General Assembly decided in December 2006 to defer consideration of the declaration, it effectively gave the African states nine months in which to formulate amendments to address their concerns. States in support of the declaration were uneasy about this, not only because of the potential for the African states to propose changes to the text of the declaration, but also because they were aware that their own political regimes might change and the new regimes might not support the declaration.

There were 54 states in the African Group. Opposition by these states was a real threat to the success of the declaration. A number of them were concerned that the declaration would have negative consequences for the people and governments of Africa, as "indigenous" can refer to almost all Africans on the continent, and confusion would exist as to those who would be deemed "indigenous peoples." They also argued that certain groups claiming the status of Indigenous peoples would be seen to have more rights, or primary rights, over other groups in a particular country, causing discrimination. The most alarming concern, fuelled by the lobby of the CANZUS group, was that Indigenous peoples, under the right to self-determination, would have a mandate to secede from the state.[9]

The African Group continued to study the text and look for ways to resolve their concerns, but within the group it was difficult to reach full agreement on what the key issues were and how to address them. Indigenous peoples' delegations from Africa and a panel of human rights experts commenced a strong lobby in New York and in the African countries to address the myths and fears surrounding the declaration. Pressure also came from human rights advocates and other states.

The African states were not of the same mind. A number did support the declaration as adopted by the Human Rights Council, but no clear position emerged and ultimately the African Group agreed on nine minor amendments to the text. These amendments did not, in the view of the supporting states and the Indigenous peoples' delegations, adversely affect the integrity of the declaration, so an agreement was formed among the African Group, the Latin American group, and the European Union to vote in favour of the declaration with the agreed amendments.

Canada, speaking on behalf of the CANZUS group, objected to the agreed position on the basis that not all states had been privy to these negotiations. However, the CANZUS group had ample time to promote their position during the nine-month period granted by the General Assembly for further consultations. When the resolution was put on 13 September 2007, Canada, Australia, New Zealand, and the US voted against the *Declaration* — the only states to do so. One hundred and forty-four states voted in favour, thus sending a message of overwhelming support for the human rights of Indigenous peoples.

4. THE UNITED NATIONS

Much has been recorded about the infringement of the human rights of Indigenous peoples. It is rarely seen that states advocate in favour of the rights of Indigenous peoples within their own jurisdictions. Now the United Nations has clearly demonstrated its willingness, as a global body, to uphold the interests of Indigenous peoples. Given that it is states that make up the membership of the United Nations, it is clear that states are collectively aware of the global situation of Indigenous peoples, but they seem reluctant to rectify injustices within their own borders. This reluctance was examined by the then United Nations Special Rapporteur on the situation of human rights and fundamental freedoms of indigenous people in his 2006 report, in which he identifies the "implementation gap" in states' actions, emerging from a lack of political will to address Indigenous issues:

> The main problem, however, is the "implementation gap" that is, the vacuum between existing legislation and administrative, legal and political practice. This divide between form and substance constitutes a violation of the human rights of indigenous people. To close the gap and narrow the divide is a challenge that must be addressed through a programme of action for the human rights of indigenous people in the future.[10]

Since the Working Group on Indigenous Populations was established in 1982, the United Nations has been inundated with reports that elaborate continuing human rights abuses against Indigenous peoples. The treaty bodies, too, have presented conclusions and recommendations, in relation to individual states and in the form of general comments, which highlight the situations of Indigenous peoples and expose the extent of state discrimination.

The United Nations has responded by developing a number of mechanisms to address the problems:

1982: Working Group on Indigenous Populations (terminated in 2006)

1993: International Year of the World's Indigenous People

1995: International Decade of the World's Indigenous People

2001: Special Rapporteur on the situation of human rights and fundamental freedoms of indigenous people

2002: First session of the United Nations Permanent Forum on Indigenous Issues

2005: Second International Decade of the World's Indigenous People

2007: *United Nations Declaration on the Rights of Indigenous Peoples*

2008: First session of the Expert Mechanism on the Rights of Indigenous Peoples.

Indigenous individuals are now appointed as experts to the Permanent Forum on Indigenous Issues, the Expert Mechanism on the Rights of Indigenous Peoples, and to the position of Special Rapporteur. In addition, there are special accreditations for Indigenous peoples' delegations to participate in these new mechanisms. "Indigenous peoples" are also included on the agendas of meetings of most of the relevant bodies in the UN; the Human Rights Council, the Economic and Social Council, and the General Assembly each maintain separate agenda items to address Indigenous issues.

Despite this range of mechanisms to address the human rights of Indigenous peoples, the situation of Indigenous communities around the world remains largely unchanged. The United Nations needs to develop a more direct interest in the situation of Indigenous peoples in individual states. This is likely to occur over the coming decade, as the case for direct action is supported by the *Declaration* itself, which states that "the United Nations has an important and continuing role to play in promoting and protecting the rights of indigenous peoples."[11]

5. Key Components of the Declaration

Although the *Declaration* has been adopted, it is not yet well known or understood at the national and local levels. If it is going to be effectively used in the promotion and protection of human rights, it will need to be clearly understood by states and Indigenous peoples. These parties will need to design and execute strategies to ensure Indigenous peoples enjoy the benefit of those rights.

The *Declaration* is a carefully constructed instrument, intended to address specifically those rights that have been historically denied to Indigenous peoples and yet are taken for granted by others. The *Declaration* is also a collection of component rights that should be considered in relation to each other and the overall context of the *Declaration*. But there are several key principles on which the document is founded.

5A The Rights of Peoples

Indigenous peoples are "peoples" in the meaning of international human rights law. The *Declaration* affirms that "indigenous peoples are equal to all other peoples,"[12] and, "Indigenous peoples and individuals are free and equal to all other peoples and individuals and have the right to be free from any kind of discrimination, in the exercise of their rights, in particular that based on their indigenous origin or identity."[13]

These statements are central to the *Declaration,* as much of the *Declaration* is focused on the collective rights of peoples. These collective rights are taken for granted by many, but denied to Indigenous peoples, including the right to an identity, to a culture, to a system of beliefs and values, to a society, to forms of governance, to social institutions, and to a territory. Without respect for such collective rights, Indigenous peoples are exposed to the assimilation policies of states that assume adaptations of individual rights to promote formal equality and sameness.

Article 3 of the *Declaration* states that Indigenous peoples "have the right to self-determination. By virtue of that right they freely determine their political status and freely pursue their economic, social and cultural development." This is almost identical to article 1 of the *International Covenant on Civil and Political Rights* (ICCPR)[14] and article 1 of the *International Covenant on Economic, Social and Cultural Rights* (ICESCR).[15] The covenants carry additional text in these articles:

> All peoples may, for their own ends, freely dispose of their natural wealth and resources without prejudice to any obligations arising out of international economic co-operation, based upon the principle of mutual benefit, and international law. In no case may a people be deprived of its own means of subsistence.

Some states argue that Indigenous peoples have a form of self-determination which is internal, or subject to national law.[16] This interpretation creates a lower standard for Indigenous peoples' right of self-determination, but as Indigenous peoples point out, the *Declaration* only affirms the same right of self-determination that exists under international law for all peoples.

Article 4 of the *Declaration* asserts that Indigenous peoples "have the right to autonomy or self-government in matters relating to their internal and local affairs, as well as ways and means for financing their autonomous functions." Articles 18 and 19 refer to collective rights in decision-making: "Indigenous peoples have the right to participate in decision-making in matters which would affect their rights .. as well as to maintain and develop their own indigenous decision-making institutions" and "States shall consult and cooperate in good faith with the indigenous peoples concerned . . . in order to obtain their free, prior and informed consent before adopting and implementing legislative or administrative measures that may affect them."

The right to self-determination includes a right to economic development and the utilization of natural wealth and resources. This right is elaborated in article 26 of the *Declaration,* which states: "Indigenous peoples have the right to own, use, develop and control the lands, territories and resources that they possess by reason of traditional ownership. . . ."

Another relevant right, belonging to Indigenous peoples as a collective, is the right to Indigenous institutions. Article 34 states: "Indigenous peoples have the right to promote, develop and maintain their institutional structures and their distinctive customs, spirituality, traditions, procedures, practices and, in the cases where they exist, juridical systems or customs, in accordance with international human rights standards."

5B The Need for Redress

The *Declaration* gives attention to the rights of redress, restitution, and compensation. Indigenous peoples continue to experience the effects of the invasion of their territories, the exploitation of their natural resources, social segregation, and political isolation. Simply ending acts of discrimination and promoting cultural identity is not sufficient to overcome their disadvantages and marginalization.

Indigenous peoples cannot enjoy and exercise their rights and freedoms without compensation, redress, and restitution. This applies to traditional territories, natural resources, and means for economic development. Compensation is needed for past injustices to address concerns of poverty and the lack of infrastructure, education, and skills training.

Articles 8, 10, 11, 20, 28 and 32 of the *Declaration* each identify rights to redress, restitution, or compensation. The *Declaration* also contains, in article 40, a provision for the adjudication of disputes between states and Indigenous peoples. It states that Indigenous peoples have "the right to access to and prompt decision through just and fair procedures for the resolution of conflicts and disputes with States or other parties."

The rights of Indigenous peoples cannot be implemented without these provisions.

6. Toward a New Reality

6A The United Nations

Now that the *Declaration* has been adopted, the task is to develop strategies to promote it and ensure that positive changes arise out of the implementation of the rights it contains. As has been indicated above, much has happened in the United Nations during the past 25 years to empower Indigenous peoples at the international level. Significant structures and mechanisms have been developed, and Indigenous experts are now part of the UN system.

The United Nations Permanent Forum on Indigenous Issues is now able to advise the Economic and Social Council on a broad range of issues under its mandate, and has the advantage of an independent secretariat. The Permanent Forum is able to co-ordinate with the many UN bodies and agencies to ensure that Indigenous issues are receiving close and specialized attention.

The Human Rights Council has established the Expert Mechanism on the Rights of Indigenous Peoples and appointed Indigenous experts as its members. The Expert Mechanism is well placed to work within the wider human rights network of the United Nations and civil society.

Both these structures have the opportunity to guide the United Nations in its actions and strategies to meet the needs of Indigenous communities. But these structures do not have the capacity to investigate human rights abuses or comment adversely on a situation in any particular state. This limitation is not well understood by inexperienced Indigenous delegations, many of whom have travelled to UN meetings to express grievances on behalf of their communities. At one meeting, about four years ago, the Foundation for Aboriginal and Islander Research Action recorded 44 separate human rights complaints made by Indigenous peoples.

The Special Rapporteur on the situation of human rights and fundamental freedoms of Indigenous people does, however, have the mandate to examine national situations and report to the Human Rights Council. The General Assembly formally requested the 2009 reports of the Special Rapporteur.[17] The Special Rapporteur reported to the Third Committee of the General Assembly for the first time in 2009.[18] The Special Rapporteur therefore has the potential to be a key source of information on the various states' implementation of the *Declaration*.

The work of the Special Rapporteur can be closely related to the operations of the human rights treaty bodies. The following bodies have mandates to interpret and monitor the implementation of the particular human rights for which they have responsibility. These mandates are highly relevant to the rights and interests of Indigenous peoples, including those contained in the *Declaration*:

- Committee on the Elimination of Racial Discrimination (*International Convention on the Elimination of All Forms of Racial Discrimination*[19]);
- Human Rights Committee (ICCPR);
- Committee on Economic, Social and Cultural Rights (ICESCR); and
- Committee on the Rights of the Child (*Convention on the Rights of the Child*[20])

There is significant potential for the reports of the Special Rapporteur and these human rights treaty bodies to inform the international community and promote the implementation of the *Declaration*.

For example, in August 2009 the Committee on the Elimination of Racial Discrimination issued a general recommendationon on "special measures" to guide states at risk of breaching the rights of Indigenous peoples through the misunderstanding of what constitutes a special measure.

While the Special Rapporteur and the treaty bodies have the capacity to investigate complaints of human rights abuses, it is likely that their work will be more effective if they are able to engage states in a positive manner that can inform them how to fulfill their human rights obligations.

It should be noted that the Special Rapporteur has a better opportunity to engage the states in a positive dialogue. Unlike the treaty bodies, the Rapporteur does not need to wait for five-yearly reports to engage with states, nor does he have formalized and complex procedures to receive and send communications on Indigenous issues. His interest can be invoked relatively simply, by a letter, so Indigenous groups who feel that their rights are being threatened and who have exhausted domestic remedies to resolve their disputes can request the Special Rapporteur to intervene or investigate. The Special Rapporteur has the ability either to visit a country to investigate complaints or to correspond with states on matters of concern. Of course, his ability is limited by the attitude of the state and the Rapporteur's capacity for the volume of work generated.

The Special Rapporteur presents his actions and findings in an annual report to the Human Rights Council. These reports are scrutinized by the members of the Council and must be objective, factual, and consistent with the mandate.

The UN has implemented a new mechanism to ensure that states are meeting their human rights obligations under the *Charter of the United Nations*. The Human Rights Council has established the Universal Periodic Review to examine all 192 member states of the United Nations and their human rights record once every four years. It is an examination of states by their peers, who evaluate performances using reports generated by the UN special mechanisms — i.e., from human rights treaty bodies and Special Rapporteurs, as well as from civil society and other sources.

It will be interesting to see if the Universal Periodic Review has any "teeth" to hold states accountable for the rights of Indigenous communities within their borders.

Little attention has been given to the Second International Decade of the World's Indigenous People, and the Programme of Action (POA) adopted by the General Assembly on 16 December 2005.[21] The POA contains specific actions and strategies that provide an authoritative approach, sanctioned by the General Assembly, and a robust medium in which to pursue the implementation of the *Declaration*. It recommended, for instance, that "tripartite committees should be established at the country level composed of governments, indigenous peoples and United Nations country offices to promote implementation of the objectives of the Second Decade."[22] The POA also proposed that the Permanent Forum on

Indigenous Issues might call for meetings "at which indigenous peoples, governments and the United Nations country teams can exchange experiences with national institutions at the country level."[23]

Additionally, the Permanent Forum is requested to hold "regional meetings on indigenous issues with existing regional organizations with a view to strengthening cooperation and coordination."[24] The most interesting component in the POA is perhaps the call for Indigenous organizations to establish committees at the national and local levels to monitor the implementation of the POA.[25]

6B Implementation Challenges

I recall discussions with Vicky Tauli-Corpuz, executive director of Tebtebba (Indigenous Peoples' International Centre for Policy Research and Education), a few years ago about the possibility that an Indigenous peoples' tribunal or commission might be established at the international level to intercede or mediate where disputes exist between states and Indigenous peoples. The idea was not yet ready to go forward, but it may be something to revisit in the future.

It does not take much effort to understand that, as Indigenous peoples seek to enjoy the rights contained in the *Declaration,* they are likely to come into conflict with the state and other interests within the state. Generally speaking, states worldwide have the reputation of opposing the rights of Indigenous peoples, for political and prejudicial reasons, and established justice systems are inherently biased against the rights of the Indigenous peoples. Indigenous peoples are inevitably going to run into political and legal barriers. Before even addressing the immediate needs of the Indigenous communities, therefore, advocates are going to face the problem of confronting, and changing, the political and legal systems of the state. This seems an almost impossible task because, in most instances, Indigenous peoples do not have sufficient influence or power to alter the political and economic organization of the state. Also, through the course of history, communications and interactions between the state and Indigenous peoples have led to predictable, predetermined results — i.e., results that undermine Indigenous peoples' interests. Indigenous peoples must consider how to deal with these issues, and consider the advantages of advocating for an international authority of the world's Indigenous peoples that is not couched within the UN framework.

As stated previously, the *Declaration* is clear in affirming that Indigenous peoples have the right to "just and fair procedures for the resolution of conflicts and disputes with States," and a "fair, independent, impartial, open and transparent process ... to recognize and adjudicate the rights of indigenous peoples pertaining to their lands, territories and resources."[26]

Of further relevance here is the status of historical treaties between Indigenous peoples and states. The *Declaration* acknowledges that these treaties "are, in some situations, matters of international concern, interest, responsibility and character,"[27] and that Indigenous peoples have the right to the enforcement of these treaties.[28] The identification of independent processes to resolve treaty disputes is vital.[29]

The achievement of fair and independent processes will not be easy. States may rely on their sovereign status and territorial integrity to restrict international involvement in these disputes, but Indigenous peoples can take heart in the UN's continuing commitment to the promotion and protection of the rights of Indigenous peoples as a matter of international concern.[30]

6c Partnerships between Indigenous Peoples and States

During the final stages of reviewing the draft declaration, Denmark requested that the document conclude with a strong, motivating message that would stress the significance of the *Declaration* and the importance of its implementation. This request became lost in the complex arrangement of article 46, as vested interests pushed for additional words to qualify the document. As a result, the final article became a scramble of oratory rather than an inspiring conclusion.

A positive result, however, was achieved at the end of the preamble, where the text reads: The General Assembly "*Solemnly proclaims* the following United Nations Declaration on the Rights of Indigenous Peoples as a standard of achievement to be pursued in a spirit of partnership and mutual respect." This text reflects the theme of the Second Decade of the World's Indigenous People: "Partnership for action and dignity."[31]

The message of partnership is clear: states are encouraged to act, cognizant of UN concerns for the human rights of Indigenous peoples, and to undertake initiatives to make change. The *Declaration* reminds states to "comply with and effectively implement all their obligations as they apply to indigenous peoples under international instruments, in particular those related to human rights, in consultation and cooperation with the peoples concerned."[32]

As noted, the Special Rapporteur has highlighted the "implementation gap" where even good intentions, in the form of legislative and administrative changes, have failed to deliver benefits for Indigenous peoples. States should take note of and treat seriously the five objectives of the POA for the Second Decade of the World's Indigenous People:

1) Promoting non-discrimination and inclusion of Indigenous peoples in the design, implementation, and evaluation of processes regarding laws, policies, resources, programs and projects;

2) Promoting full and effective participation of Indigenous peoples in decisions, considering the principle of free, prior, and informed consent;

3) Redefining development policies, showing respect for the cultural and linguistic diversity of Indigenous peoples;

4) Adopting targeted policies, programs, projects, and budgets for the development of Indigenous peoples;

5) Developing strong monitoring mechanisms and enhancing accountability.[33]

The Programmes of Action for the First and Second Decades of the World's Indigenous People both called upon states to review their constitutions and laws to ensure the identity and rights of Indigenous peoples are recognized.[34] States are also called upon to ratify the International Labour Organization's (ILO) *Indigenous and Tribal Peoples Convention, 1989*,[35] an international treaty supporting the human rights of Indigenous peoples. Such reforms are necessary and can demonstrate the willingness of a state to meet its human rights obligations.

But the first step is clear: states must establish a partnership relationship with Indigenous peoples for the purpose of creating national and local plans and addressing the capacity requirements within the populations, both Indigenous and non-Indigenous, to achieve the necessary changes.

I am hopeful that the journey toward partnership has begun in Australia. On 13 February 2008, Prime Minister Kevin Rudd formally apologized "for the laws and policies of successive Parliaments and governments that have inflicted profound grief, suffering and loss," apologizing "especially for the removal of Aboriginal and Torres Strait Islander children from their families, their communities and their country."[36] On 3 April 2009, the Rudd government issued a formal statement in support of the *Declaration*. In the words of the Minister for Families, Housing, Community Services and Indigenous Affairs, Jenny Macklin: "Today, Australia changes its position. Today, Australia gives our support to the Declaration. We do this in the spirit of re-setting the relationship between Indigenous and non-Indigenous Australians and building trust."[37]

The government has presented an open and honest position, stating "[w]e show our faith in a new era of relations between states and Indigenous peoples grounded in good faith, goodwill and mutual respect."[38] As Tom Calma, then the Aboriginal and Torres Strait Islander Social Justice Commissioner, recognized, this statement was a "watershed moment in Australia's relationship with Aboriginal and Torres Strait Islander peoples."[39] The government has decided to accept the rights of Indigenous peoples as the basis for building understanding and trust.

Of course, there is much to be done. This is part of a long journey, and there is no way the government is going to find a way forward without positive assistance from Indigenous communities and their leaders. It is a time to listen, learn, and contribute. Most of all, it is a time to encourage better policies and practices through real engagement. As human rights defenders, it is time for us to change from wielding weapons of attack to using our building tools.

7. A Vision of the Future

Martin Luther King, Jr., in his famous speech of 3 April 1968, said, "I've been to the mountaintop. . . . And I've looked over. And I've seen the promised land."[40] He was able to see a vision of what the future looked like in a different world and time. Many who worked on the *Declaration on the Rights of Indigenous Peoples* also had a dream, and a vision of a possible new reality filled with hope.

As each session of the Working Group- on the Draft Declaration ended, we would travel home and be confronted with the reality of our people's daily tribulations — the racism, the helplessness, the social dysfunction. But by analyzing the text of the *Declaration*, musing on what this *Declaration* is about, and being able to see and anticipate a better future — a real future — we can see the other side.

Those who can see have, in some crucial ways, already reached the other side. The *Declaration* carries with it a framework for partnership and development in the context of Indigenous self-determination. Self-determination, a prerequisite to the exercise and enjoyment of all other human rights, is now reaffirmed as a right of Indigenous peoples throughout the world.

CHAPTER THREE

Survival, Dignity, and Well-Being

Implementing the Declaration in British Columbia

◌

Grand Chief Edward John

1. INTRODUCTION

13 September 2007 was the day Indigenous peoples took Manhattan. On this historic day, the United Nations General Assembly adopted the *United Nations Declaration on the Rights of Indigenous Peoples* by an overwhelming majority of 144 states in favour, four against, and 11 abstaining. Indigenous peoples, with the assistance of supportive states and non-Indigenous non-governmental organizations, worked and fought for the *Declaration*. Its adoption marked a triumphant moment for the "survival, dignity and well-being of the indigenous peoples of the world."[1] As UN Secretary-General Ban Ki-moon stated in a message for the 2008 International Day of the World's Indigenous People, the *Declaration* "provides a momentous opportunity for States and indigenous peoples to strengthen their relationships, promote reconciliation and ensure that the past is not repeated."[2]

Only Canada, the United States, Australia, and New Zealand voted against the *Declaration*. Canada, which formerly possessed a proud reputation as a champion of human rights, turned its back on us on the day we most needed its support. But in some ways, Canada's vote does not matter. This is a United Nations declaration. This is *our* declaration. It provides a supportive framework for the assertion of our inherent rights.

In this chapter, I offer a perspective on the *Declaration* from British Columbia. First, I examine how, for over 150 years, the rights of First Nations in BC have been, and continue to be, ignored or denied by the Crown. I next argue that the *Declaration* provides the inspiration for a new way forward — that is, a process of reconciliation based on the recognition of the inherent human rights of Indigenous peoples. Finally, I consider the ways that First Nations leaders in BC are already engaging in initiatives to implement the *Declaration*. We are drawing strength from the *Declaration* as we assert our rights. We invite Canada and the Province of British Columbia to work with us to endorse the *Declaration* and ensure the survival, dignity, and well-being of Indigenous peoples.

2. THE DENIAL OF ABORIGINAL TITLE AND RIGHTS IN BRITISH COLUMBIA

Canada's actions in opposing the *Declaration* and the rights of Indigenous peoples have attracted worldwide criticism. The then UN High Commissioner for Human Rights, Louise Arbour, registered her "profound disappointment" at Canada's actions.[3] Amnesty International Canada warned that Canada's "position as a global human rights champion may be slipping" due to its opposition to the human rights of Indigenous peoples.[4]

First Nations in the territory now known as British Columbia have experienced this opposition first-hand. Unlike other parts of Canada, few treaties were entered into between First Nations and colonial authorities in BC. Our territories have been colonized and treated as *terra nullius* — "empty land" "belonging to no one." In the 1858 *Act to Provide for the Government of British Columbia,* the British Parliament referred to our lands as "certain wild and unoccupied Territories on the North-West Coast of North America . . . to be named British Columbia."[5] On 14 February 1859, James Douglas (the first Governor of British Columbia) proclaimed that "[a]ll the lands in British Columbia, and all the Mines and Minerals therein, belong to the Crown in fee,"[6] disregarding our rights to our lands, territories, and resources.

The doctrine of *terra nullius* should have no place in Canadian law or policy. Section 35 of the *Constitution Act, 1982*[7] recognizes and affirms the existing Aboriginal and treaty rights of the Aboriginal peoples of Canada. The Supreme Court of Canada has held that section 35 is directed toward "the reconciliation of pre-existing aboriginal claims to the territory that now constitutes Canada, with the assertion of British sovereignty over that territory."[8] The Supreme Court has found that section 35 recognizes and affirms communal Aboriginal title — meaning that title holders have the right to the exclusive use and occupation of the land, and to choose the uses to which the land is put.[9]

Despite this, the rights of First Nations in British Columbia continue to be denied today. Governments come to negotiating tables and to court armed with the same strategy of denying the existence and rights of our peoples, instead of advancing reconciliation based on rights recognition. While courts do not question the validity of Canada's title and sovereignty, Canada constantly puts First Nations to proof and forces them into expensive litigation to defend their inherent rights. This creates an "implementation gap" in Canada regarding Aboriginal title and rights — that is, there is a vacuum between constitutional rights, Canada's human rights obligations, and Canada's administrative, legal, and political practice.[10]

In 2007, the UN's Committee on the Elimination of Racial Discrimination expressed concern that, in Canada, "claims of Aboriginal land rights are being settled primarily through litigation, at a disproportionate cost for the Aboriginal communities concerned due to the strongly adversarial positions taken by the federal and provincial governments."[11]

The efforts of the Tsilhqot'in Nation in seeking judicial protection of their title and rights in response to forestry activities in their traditional territory indicate that Canada and the province have maintained their "strongly adversarial positions" toward the rights of Indigenous peoples. The *Tsilhqot'in Nation* v. *British Columbia* trial was one of the longest civil trials in the history of Canada, lasting 339 days over five years, at enormous cost.[12] At one point in the trial, Justice Vickers of the Supreme Court of British Columbia "looked out at the legions of counsel and asked if someone would soon be standing up to admit that Tsilhqot'in people had been in the Claim Area for over 200 years, leaving the real question to be answered [which was — what were the consequences that would follow such an admission?]."[13] He was "assured that it was necessary to continue the course" that the court and counsel were set upon.[14]

Rather than recognize Aboriginal title to the traditional territory of the Tsilhqot'in Nation, Canada and the province sought to limit any declaration of Aboriginal title to small sites where specific activities or practices took place. In his decision of 20 November 2007, Justice Vickers regarded this as an "impoverished view of Aboriginal title."[15] Although the Tsilhqot'in Nation had satisfied the legal test for Aboriginal title to almost half the area claimed, as well as certain other lands, Justice Vickers was unable to issue a declaration of title owing to a legal technicality. He did hold, however, that the Tsilhqot'in Nation possessed certain Aboriginal rights throughout the claim area.

Justice Vickers acknowledged that, in "an ideal world, the process of reconciliation would take place outside the adversarial milieu of a courtroom," and that courts were "ill equipped to effect a reconciliation of competing interests. That must be reserved for a treaty negotiation process."[16] Similarly, the Supreme Court of Canada has repeatedly stated that negotiation, rather than litigation, is the preferred method of achieving the reconciliation of the pre-existence of Aboriginal societies with the sovereignty of the Crown.[17]

Many First Nations share this view and have, since 1992, entered into modern treaty negotiations with Canada and the province. I am a political executive member of the First Nations Summit (FNS), which speaks on behalf of First Nations involved in treaty negotiations in British Columbia. Currently, 60 First Nations in BC are at various stages of negotiations,[18] but modern-day treaty negotiations have yet to achieve reconciliation owing to the unreasonable negotiating mandates of Canada and the province.

Only two agreements negotiated with Canada and British Columbia pursuant to this process have been ratified by First Nations.[19] The FNS respects and supports the decisions of these First Nations to ratify their agreements. However, it also recognizes the growing frustration expressed by most First Nations regarding the inflexible and insufficient mandates pursued by Canada and the province in treaty negotiations. First Nations have been raising these concerns for years.[20]

In particular, they object to the Crown's requirement that their rights be "exhaustively" set out in agreements made pursuant to the treaty negotiation process in BC, thereby achieving a "full and final settlement" of their claims to Aboriginal title and rights. To achieve "certainty," Canada insists that Aboriginal title and rights can continue only as "modified" and set out in the agreement. Further, the First Nations parties must agree to indemnify Canada and British Columbia in respect of legal claims regarding the existence of Aboriginal rights, including title, that are other than, or different in attributes or geographic extent from, the rights as set out in the agreement.[21]

In the recent past, Canada explicitly required the extinguishment or surrender of inherent Aboriginal rights in return for the rights granted by a treaty.[22] Canada has asserted to the international community that it no longer requires the extinguishment or surrender of rights in treaty negotiations.[23] Instead, it demands the "modification" of Indigenous rights. However, international human rights bodies have repeatedly found that there is no distinction in practical effect between the "extinguishment" and "modification" of Aboriginal title and/or rights, and have recommended that there be no extinguishment of rights regardless of the form or wording adopted in agreements.[24] Canada has failed to implement these recommendations.

Other elements of the negotiating mandates of Canada and British Columbia exacerbate the problems associated with a "full and final settlement" of rights, including: the quantum of land on offer at treaty negotiating tables is a small percentage of the traditional territories of First Nations — far too small to sustain their distinct societies; Canada will not consider restitution, including compensation, for land unilaterally taken and transferred to third parties, significantly reducing the land base that is available for treaty settlements; the treaty negotiations must be forward-looking political processes (thereby precluding any negotiation of compensation for rights violations); and Aboriginal title must be "modified" into the fee simple lands set out in a final agreement.

Further, the Crown's approach is for 80 per cent of treaty negotiation support funding for First Nations to be advanced as loans to be drawn against final treaty settlements. First Nations in British Columbia have borrowed $371 million to prepare for and negotiate treaties,[25] and many now find their growing debt burden too onerous to remain in negotiations. Indigenous peoples have the right to have access to financial and technical assistance from states for the enjoyment of rights contained in the *Declaration*.[26] It is a fundamental breach of the rights of Indigenous peoples that First Nations need to borrow money from governments to resolve issues created by the governments' historic and present denial of Aboriginal title and rights.

Treaty-making and the rules that accompany it must be fair and balanced — not unilaterally imposed by the Crown. It is only by way of an honourable process that negotiations can lead to a just settlement. As the Supreme Court of Canada makes clear:

> Where treaties remain to be concluded, the honour of the Crown requires negotiations leading to a just settlement of Aboriginal claims. . . . Treaties serve to reconcile pre-existing Aboriginal sovereignty with assumed Crown sovereignty, and to define Aboriginal rights guaranteed by s. 35 of the *Constitution Act, 1982*.[27]

The Supreme Court has further emphasized that "[s]ection 35 represents a promise of rights recognition, and '[i]t is always assumed that the Crown intends to fulfil its promises'. . . . This promise is realized and sovereignty claims reconciled through the process of honourable negotiation."[28] Self-serving rules that favour the Crown do not meet the constitutional objectives of "rights recognition" and "honourable negotiation."

In *Tsilhqot'in Nation* v. *British Columbia*, Justice Vickers urged the parties that the "time to reach an honourable resolution and reconciliation is with us today."[29] We cannot continue the *status quo* of rights denial and interminable litigation. We must work toward reconciliation based on recognition and respect for the fundamental human rights of Indigenous peoples, guided by the minimum standards affirmed by the *Declaration*.

3. THE WAY FORWARD

The *Declaration* is framed "as a standard of achievement to be pursued in a spirit of partnership and mutual respect."[30] As James Anaya, the UN Special Rapporteur on the situation of human rights and fundamental freedoms of indigenous people, has observed, the "spirit of cooperation and mutual understanding between States and indigenous peoples is a theme throughout the Declaration."[31]

In this spirit, governments should no longer attempt to extinguish or deny our rights, subjecting our people to long, expensive, and acrimonious litigation. Nor should they come to the negotiating table with unreasonable conditions that do not meet the standards of Canadian and international law. For reconciliation to progress, there must be a systemic shift in the positions and policies of governments. We are prepared to work with governments to achieve reconciliation, provided that our inherent rights are recognized and respected. A shared understanding of the human rights of Indigenous peoples is an essential prerequisite for ongoing, harmonious relationships between Indigenous peoples and Canada.

The *Declaration* provides a principled framework, based on co-operation and mutual understanding, to guide the reconciliation process in Canada. It affirms that "Indigenous peoples and individuals are free and equal to all other peoples."[32] We have "the right to be free from any kind of discrimination"[33] and "the right to the full enjoyment, as a collective or as individuals, of all human rights and fundamental freedoms."[34] We do not seek to deny the human rights of other Canadians: the provisions of the *Declaration* are to be "interpreted in accordance with the principles of justice, democracy, respect for human rights, equality, non-discrimination, good governance and good faith."[35]

At the heart of the *Declaration* is the affirmation that Indigenous peoples have the right to self-determination.[36] Closely tied to this right is the obligation upon states to "consult and cooperate in good faith with the indigenous peoples concerned through their own representative institutions in order to obtain their free, prior and informed consent before adopting and implementing legislative or administrative measures that may affect them."[37]

The *Declaration* affirms our rights to our lands, territories, and resources.[38] In conjunction with Indigenous peoples, states are to "give legal recognition and protection to these lands, territories and resources . . . with due respect to the customs, traditions and land tenure systems of the indigenous peoples concerned."[39] Furthermore, Indigenous peoples have the right to redress for their lands, territories, and resources which have been confiscated, taken, occupied, used, or damaged without their free, prior, and informed consent.[40]

Our right to practise and revitalize our customs and traditions is a further key element of the *Declaration*. We have the right to revitalize, use, and develop our histories, languages, and oral traditions, and transmit these to future generations. We also have the right to manifest, practise, develop, and teach our spiritual and religious traditions, customs, and ceremonies.[41] Particular attention is to be paid to the rights and special needs of Indigenous elders, women, youth, children, and persons with disabilities in the implementation of the *Declaration*.[42] The *Declaration* therefore provides the imperative for Canada to break from, and atone for, the past, and to forge a new path in partnership with Indigenous peoples that is respectful of our cultures and traditions.

4. From Apology to Action

In recent times, there have been some signs that Canada has the potential to re-examine its past as part of the reconciliation process. On 11 June 2008, Prime Minister Stephen Harper delivered an historic apology on behalf of Canada and all Canadians for the nation's role in the Indian Residential Schools system. Harper asked the forgiveness of Aboriginal people and recognized that "this policy of assimilation was wrong, has caused great harm, and has no place in our country."[43]

The entire residential schools system was underpinned by a fundamentally racist and genocidal policy — "to kill the Indian in the child." I was sent to Lejac Indian Residential School at a very young age. As children, we all felt deeply our removal from our siblings, from our parents and grandparents, and from our people, communities, languages, and cultures. We grew up in brutal atmospheres devoid of the recognition of, and respect for, who we were as Indigenous children with distinct languages and cultures. In 1996, the Royal Commission on Aboriginal Peoples reported that Indian residential schools were aimed at "severing the artery of culture that ran between generations and was the profound connection between parent and child sustaining family and community."[44] The *Indian Act* was amended in 1920 to make it mandatory for Indian children to attend these schools.[45] In many cases, two, three, and up to four generations of children from the same families were moved to these schools. Some of these children were as young as four and five.

Many survivors of this system could not cope with their pain and suffering, and died prematurely. A high school friend of mine who attended the residential school in Williams Lake, BC, took his own life, unable to find his way out of the trauma arising from sexual abuse at the hands of those to whom his care had been entrusted.

On 11 June 2008, the FNS (in partnership with the Indian Residential Schools Survivors' Society) arranged for eight "live" sites across BC, linked by teleconference, for First Nations people to gather to view the apology and offer their response. The largest gathering was held at the Chief Joe Mathias Centre, Squamish Nation (North Vancouver). Against the backdrop of a banner reading "Survival, Dignity, Well-being," Chief Gibby Jacob and other members of the Squamish Nation led the gathering in song and prayer to honour our loved ones — those who have passed, those of the present, and those of future generations.

Media reports of the event stated that the North Vancouver gathering was attended by up to 1500 people.[46] Prime Minister Harper's apology and the responses by Stéphane Dion of the Liberal Party, Jack Layton of the New Democratic Party, and Gilles Duceppe of the Bloc Québécois were viewed largely in silence. Of all the statements by leaders of political parties, the crowd reserved its loudest applause for the acknowledgement by the leaders of the New Democratic Party and the Bloc Québécois that, by endorsing the *Declaration*, Canada can demonstrate its "commitment to never again allow such a travesty of justice and transgression against equality to occur,"[47] and that it has "learned from past mistakes and is making a solemn promise to the victims that their children and grandchildren will have respect and dignity."[48]

For individual survivors and their families, the acceptance of an apology is a highly personal matter. The giving of forgiveness is an essential element of an apology; this, too, is personal. Survivors and their families continue to respond to the apology in their own way. Apology, acceptance, and forgiveness are essential parts of the grieving process and of letting go. They cannot be rushed.

However well-intentioned, the apology cannot wipe away history, nor can it wipe away the deep effects of cultural and linguistic genocide. Apologies should be more than words. Action is a significant part of any apology.

As Romeo Saganash, Grand Council of the Crees (Eeyou Istchee), has recognized, "[i]t is inconsistent with a meaningful apology for the Canadian government to actively oppose the *UN Declaration*. . . . The *Declaration* explicitly denounces the very policies and practices of superiority that were a rationale for the forced assimilation in residential schools."[49] The *Declaration* provides many safeguards against a repeat of the residential schools tragedy, including the affirmation that "Indigenous peoples and individuals have the right not to be subjected to forced assimilation or destruction of their culture."[50] We possess "the collective right to live in freedom, peace and security as distinct peoples," with the *Declaration* affirming the prohibition on "any act of genocide or any other act of violence, including forcibly removing children of the group to another group."[51] Furthermore, the preamble to the *Declaration* recognizes "the right of indigenous families and communities to retain shared responsibility for the upbringing, training, education and well-being of their children, consistent with the rights of the child."

This apology provides us with a unique, historic, and monumental opportunity to move forward, recognizing and building on respect for fundamental human rights. As an integral part of the reconciliation process, it is critical that Canada demonstrate unequivocal respect for the human rights of our peoples by endorsing and implementing the *United Nations Declaration on the Rights of Indigenous Peoples*. The *Declaration* presents Canada with clear directions on what must be done to ensure that racist policies and violations of human rights truly have no place in Canada. It is time for all Canadians to work together, to move from apology to action, to reconciliation, guided by the framework the *Declaration* provides.

5. Implementation of the Declaration by First Nations Leaders in BC

While we call on the Canadian government to endorse and implement the *Declaration*, we know from experience that we cannot wait for governments to implement our rights. These rights are inherent — they do not depend upon the *imprimatur* of the state. First Nations leaders in BC are taking positive steps to implement the *Declaration* by ensuring that respect for the rights it affirms is at the forefront of our work.

The FNS, either as a single organization or with the Union of British Columbia Indian Chiefs and the British Columbia Assembly of First Nations, holds province-wide forums on specific issues, and/or negotiates with governments, with the aim of creating action plans endorsed by resolution at First Nations Summit meetings. We work to establish bodies mandated with implementing those action plans, as necessary. From time to time, the FNS also adopts, by resolution, plans created by partner organizations and works with those partners to ensure effective implementation.

Since its adoption, First Nations leaders in BC have united in solidarity to declare our support for the *Declaration* and to work together to ensure that it is implemented. The FNS Chiefs in Assembly adopted a resolution on 28 September 2007 to support and endorse the full implementation of the *Declaration*.[52]

In November 2007, First Nations leaders gathered to celebrate the victory of the Tsilhqot'in Nation and the many Indigenous nations and individuals that have brought court cases resulting in significant contributions to the advancement and protection of Aboriginal title and rights. Over 120 leaders signed "All Our Relations: A Declaration of the Sovereign Indigenous Nations of British Columbia," affirming Aboriginal title to our respective territories.[53]

In this declaration, First Nations leaders endorsed "the provisions of the *UN Declaration on the Rights of Indigenous Peoples* and other international standards aimed at ensuring the dignity, survival and well-being of Indigenous peoples." The "All Our Relations" declaration is a strong example of the ways that the *Declaration* is empowering Indigenous peoples. Many of the provisions of the "All Our Relations" declaration reflect the language of the minimum standards affirmed by the *Declaration*. We have Aboriginal title and rights to our lands, waters and resources. We will exercise our collective, sovereign, and inherent authorities and jurisdictions over these lands, waters and resources. We respect, honour, and are sustained by the values, teachings, and laws passed to us by our ancestors. We have the right to manage and benefit from the wealth of our territories.

We have the inalienable sovereign right of self-determination. By virtue of this right, we are free to determine our political status and free to pursue our economic, social, health and well-being, and cultural development. We have diverse cultures, founded on the ways of life, traditions, and values of our ancestors, which include systems of governance, law, and social organization. We have the right to compensation and redress with regard to our territories, lands, and resources which have been confiscated, taken, occupied, used, or damaged without our free, prior, and informed consent. We will only negotiate on the basis of a full and complete recognition of the existence of our title and rights throughout our entire lands, waters, territories and resources.[54]

First Nations leaders have confirmed in the "All Our Relations" declaration that we will accept no less than the full recognition of, respect for, the minimum standards for the survival, dignity and well-being of our peoples.

Support for the *Declaration* is also recognised in the declarations and protocols of "Recognition, Support, Cooperation and Coordination" that the British Columbia Assembly of First Nations, the First Nations Summit and the Union of British Columbia Indian Chiefs have entered into with other First Nations and Aboriginal organizations. These organizations include the First Nations Health Council, the First Nations Forestry Council, the First Nations Fisheries Council, and the Aboriginal Tourism Association of British Columbia. These protocols have been developed to co-ordinate technical and political strengths toward the objectives of unity and advancing First Nations inherent rights of self-determination, title and treaty rights, and improving the socio-economic conditions of First Nations people and communities.[55]

At a nation-to-nation level, the *Declaration* inspired the signing of a Treaty of Peace and Friendship on 7 October 2008 between my own Carrier Sekani Tribal Council, the Kaska Nation, and the Tsay Keh Dene First Nation. The nations have committed to work together to protect our Aboriginal title and rights, to joint efforts to protect our lands, resources, cultures, and languages, and to strengthen our historic ties of culture, friendship, and kinship. I believe that, in this treaty, the nations are "living the spirit and intent of the *UN Declaration*."[56]

First Nations leaders in BC are being further guided by the *Declaration* in our efforts to improve the quality of life of our people, including endeavours directed toward ensuring the survival, dignity, and well-being of our children. The situation of First Nations children in British Columbia requires urgent attention. Fifty per cent of children in care in BC are Aboriginal. In some parts of the province, such as the north, up to 76 per cent of children in care are Aboriginal.[57] To address this, the British Columbia Assembly of First Nations, the First Nations Summit and the Union of British Columbia Indian Chiefs convened provincial-wide "Child at the Centre" forums in January and July 2008. In accordance with the provisions of the "All Our Relations" declaration, the *Declaration* and the

Convention on the Rights of the Child,[58] First Nations leaders at the January "Child at the Centre" forum committed to work together to develop a "coordinated social justice framework that promotes a holistic approach to resolving the systemic disadvantages experienced by Indigenous children in British Columbia."[59]

On 23 July 2008, First Nations leaders issued the "One Heart, One Mind: Statement of Solidarity & Cooperation," in which we asserted our inherent right of self-determination, including jurisdiction in relation to the children and families of our nations. We affirmed that Indigenous families and communities retain shared responsibility for the upbringing, training, education, and well-being of their children, consistent with the *Declaration* and the *Convention on the Rights of the Child*. Taking the initiative to ensure the implementation of our rights, we committed "to work in Solidarity and Cooperation to design, deliver and evaluate programs and services for our children, families, and communities, and Indigenous Nations in a way that is consistent with our common cultural beliefs and systems that improves our overall quality of life."[60]

In furtherance of this commitment, First Nations leaders have established an Interim Chiefs' Child and Family Wellness Council to develop plans to advance the welfare of First Nations children. The "One Heart, One Mind: Statement of Solidarity & Cooperation" was endorsed by resolution of the province-wide FNS Chiefs in Assembly on 26 September 2008. Further, the British Columbia Ministry of Children and Family Development and the political executive of the British Columbia Assembly of First Nations, the First Nations Summit, and the Union of British Columbia Indian Chiefs signed a Recognition and Reconciliation Protocol on 30 March 2009 to establish a political relationship and dialogue process regarding First Nations child and family wellness in BC.[61]

The rights affirmed by the *Declaration* provided a framework and a context for the development of other sector-specific action plans, even as we worked toward the final adoption of the *Declaration* by the UN General Assembly. In the First Nations Energy Action Plan, for instance, one of the key items to ensure healthy and self-sufficient communities is to "respect and promote United Nations declarations and conventions (e.g., UN Declaration on the Rights of Indigenous Peoples, UN Convention on Biodiversity)."[62] Since its adoption, the *Declaration* has formed an important part of the political and legal context against which we have developed other action plans, including the BC First Nations Forestry & Land Stewardship Action Plan.[63]

In addition to these political efforts, we have worked hard to educate our peoples about their rights and to empower them to assert them. Our education initiatives have included the symposium on "Implementing the *United Nations Declaration on the Rights of Indigenous Peoples*," co-hosted by the Assembly of

First Nations, the British Columbia Assembly of First Nations, the First Nations Summit, and the Union of British Columbia Indian Chiefs on 19 - 20 February 2008 on the territory of the Squamish Nation. At this historic event, Indigenous peoples from across North America gathered to learn about the *Declaration* in order to bring the language of human rights home to our communities.

Through these actions, and many others, First Nations leaders in British Columbia are exercising our right to self-determination. We are united in our support for the *Declaration*. We are not waiting for governments to endorse the *Declaration* — we are engaging in our own collective work toward its full implementation.

6. CONCLUSION

In 2008, the Province of British Columbia celebrated its 150th anniversary. Throughout BC, people participated in events marking dates relating to the anniversary. It is critical that the public understand that some of these dates represent a dark time in the history of First Nations.

We have struggled for generations for recognition of our rights. We have fought for our survival, dignity, and well-being, and the struggle continues.

Canada's denial of First Nations' land rights falls well short of the minimum standards affirmed by the *Declaration* and demonstrates a clear failure by Canada to implement its human rights obligations. Prime Minister Harper's apology for Canada's role in the Indian Residential Schools acknowledged that the policy of assimilation was wrong and has no place in our country. Yet, Canada's policy of denying Aboriginal title and rights is premised on the same attitude of assimilation. It is time for this attitude and the policies flowing from it to be cast aside.

The *Declaration* calls for the development of new relationships based on recognition and respect for the inherent human rights of Indigenous peoples. With the *Declaration*, we have international recognition of, and support for, the human rights of Indigenous peoples. Neither governments nor courts can ignore this *Declaration* or the rights recognized by it.

As Indigenous peoples, we also have responsibilities to breathe life into the *Declaration*. We must ensure that it is well-known and understood, and that it is carried forward by our young people for the benefit of future generations.

◌

PART II

States and Civil Society

Implementing the Declaration

A State Representative Perspective

◇

Connie Taracena

1. INTRODUCTION

When the *United Nations Declaration on the Rights of Indigenous Peoples* (*Declaration*) was adopted by the United Nations (UN) General Assembly on 13 September 2007, it was a day of triumph for Indigenous peoples around the world. It was also a day of historic significance, with political, legal, moral, and symbolic implications.

The *Declaration* embodies a legitimate and long-standing demand of Indigenous peoples throughout the world. There is now an urgent need for governments and societies to recognize the unique heritage and contributions of Indigenous peoples and to protect and promote their human rights, if we are to achieve societies based on justice and equality. The *Declaration* provides a framework for harmonious and co-operative relations between states and Indigenous peoples, based on the principles of justice, democracy, respect for human rights, non-discrimination, and good faith. Painful histories, an essential part of our collective memory, should now be left behind in order to move forward together on the path of human rights, justice, and development for all.

Guatemala was a co-sponsor of the resolution to adopt the *Declaration*, and continues to be a strong supporter. As Minister Counsellor of the Mission of Guatemala to the UN, I have represented Guatemala for over seven years at the Third Committee of the General Assembly. This work has included attending sessions of the UN Permanent Forum on Indigenous Issues, engaging with Indigenous peoples and others before, during, and after the adoption of the *Declaration*, and working to mainstream the *Declaration* within the work of the UN.

Drawing on this experience, this chapter considers some of the ways that the *Declaration* is being implemented throughout the UN system, other international agencies, and regional bodies. My focus is on recent General Assembly resolutions, guidelines developed by international agencies, and, within the Organization of American States (OAS), the efforts of states and Indigenous peoples to draft an American Declaration on the Rights of Indigenous Peoples. Through such initiatives, we can demonstrate and strengthen international commitment to the *Declaration* and the standards it affirms.

2. THE UNITED NATIONS GENERAL ASSEMBLY

The United Nations was established in 1945. As the preamble to the *Charter of the United Nations* affirms, the organization was born out of the international determination "to reaffirm faith in fundamental human rights, in the dignity and worth of the human person, in the equal rights of men and women and of nations large and small."[1] One of the main purposes of the UN is the achievement of international co-operation "in promoting and encouraging respect for human rights and for fundamental freedoms for all without distinction as to race, sex, language, or religion."[2]

Membership in the UN is open to all "peace-loving states."[3] There are currently 192 members. Guatemala became a member on 21 November 1945.

The General Assembly is the main deliberative body of the United Nations. It is comprised of all 192 members of the United Nations. Each member state has one vote in the General Assembly. While the recommendations of the General Assembly are not binding on member states, it can have a powerful influence on states and encourage international pressure.

The General Assembly clusters its agenda items around the work of six committees:

First Committee	Disarmament and International Security Committee;
Second Committee	Economic and Financial Committee;
Third Committee	Social, Humanitarian and Cultural Committee;
Fourth Committee	Special Political and Decolonization Committee;
Fifth Committee	Administrative and Budgetary Committee; and
Sixth Committee	Legal Committee.

The responsibilities of the Third Committee, which is comprised of state representatives, include human rights issues. It considers matters pertaining to human rights and develops draft resolutions and decisions for consideration by the General Assembly.

The General Assembly performs much of its work by adopting decisions or resolutions. In this way, member states are encouraged to promote international co-operation or development in economic, social, cultural, and related fields. This is, in part, how the UN assists in the realization of human rights and fundamental freedoms for all peoples and individuals without discrimination. Indeed, the adoption of the *Declaration* was achieved by means of a General Assembly resolution. The actual text of the *Declaration* was included as an Annex to the resolution.

The government of Guatemala was a strong supporter of the *Declaration* during the standard-setting process and the ultimate adoption of the *Declaration* by the General Assembly. Guatemala continues to advocate for the implementation of the *Declaration* throughout the United Nations system.

3. Guatemala's Support for the Declaration

For many years, the government of Guatemala has been committed to working globally to support the human rights of Indigenous peoples. In May 2006, in its Pledges and Commitments to the newly formed UN Human Rights Council, the government stated:

> Guatemala has permanently and actively supported initiatives to promote the human rights of Indigenous Peoples in various international fora. Within the Organization of American States (OAS), the Alternate Ambassador of Guatemala to the OAS is presiding over the drafting of the American Declaration on the Human Rights of Indigenous Peoples. At the Human Rights Commission, Guatemala engaged constructively in the drafting of the United Nations Declaration on the Rights of Indigenous Peoples. . . . Guatemala fully commits to support the advancement of the rights of Indigenous Peoples and in particular to promote the swift adoption of the United Nations Declaration on the Rights of Indigenous Peoples.[4]

During the long history of development of the draft declaration in Geneva, the government of Guatemala played an active and positive role, and indeed supported the Indigenous Peoples' Caucus in the often challenging negotiations with member states. Early in the standard-setting process, Guatemala was one of the few states that recognized the necessity of the active role Indigenous representatives had in the development of the text. Guatemala supported the position that this draft declaration must reflect the human rights and needs of Indigenous peoples, such that language that was not supported by the Indigenous Peoples' Caucus was unacceptable.

During the early years of the Working Group on the Draft Declaration in Geneva, the Indigenous Peoples' Caucus was united in its efforts not to change the text that had been formulated by the Working Group on Indigenous Populations and approved by the UN Sub-Commission on Prevention of Discrimination and Protection of Minorities (Sub-Commission) in 1994.[5] After several years of debate, the majority of the Indigenous Peoples' Caucus moved from a position of "no change" to the Sub-Commission text, to the position of being willing to engage with states on changes that would clarify or strengthen the text. At this time, Guatemala worked with Indigenous representatives to propose a package of provisions to the Working Group on the Draft Declaration relating to the right of self-determination, consistent with the human rights covenants.[6] This helped to create a dynamic of Indigenous and state representatives working together, and it provided a launching point for the constructive dialogue that brought us to a compromise text that almost all parties were willing to support.

This compromise text was adopted by the UN Human Rights Council on 29 June 2006.[7] The final step was for the text to be adopted by the UN General Assembly. In a development that took many by surprise, representatives of the African Group of States, many of whom had not participated in the Geneva process, requested more time to consider the text. Members of the African Group raised several concerns about the declaration, including the definition of "Indigenous peoples" and a concern that the declaration "can be misrepresented as conferring a unilateral right of self determination and possible secession upon a specific subset of the national populace, thus threatening the political unity and the territorial integrity of any country."[8]

A resolution to adopt the declaration was presented to the Third Committee on 28 November 2006. The committee resolved, on the initiative of Namibia, which was acting on behalf of the African group, to defer consideration of the declaration. In December 2006, the UN General Assembly resolved to defer final consideration of the declaration so as to allow for further consultations.[9]

In the final months before the General Assembly adopted the *Declaration*, Guatemala worked with Mexico and other states to negotiate with representatives of the African Group of States. Guatemala was deeply committed to seeing the *Declaration* successfully pass with a text that was supported by the Indigenous Peoples' Caucus. The efforts by supportive states and Indigenous representatives were critical in overcoming the negative actions of a few states.

Guatemala's Deputy Permanent Minister José Alberto Briz Gutiérrez spoke at the General Assembly after the vote to adopt the *Declaration* on 13 September 2007. He noted that the 20-year struggle to draft the *Declaration* had ended with the adoption of a text that would strengthen the dignity of people around the world. He highlighted that the *Declaration* was a balanced, useful instrument that would serve as a genuine guide for improving the living conditions of Indigenous peoples. Great care had been taken to ensure that the *Declaration* was consistent with the principles of international law.

REALIZING THE UN DECLARATION

Gutiérrez said he had been sure that the text would have been adopted by consensus. However, that proved idealistic. The reality was different, and the text had been changed. While he would rather have not seen it amended, he was satisfied that member states' concerns had been considered.

The *Declaration*, he continued, did not create new rights, but reaffirmed the rights of Indigenous peoples, recognizing the collective right to live in freedom, peace, and security. Guatemala reaffirmed its conviction that the full realization of human rights was a prerequisite for attaining peaceful and harmonious existence. While the *Declaration* could not make up for the past, it could prevent discrimination and intolerance. The *Declaration* was the expression of the international community's political will to respect the rights of Indigenous peoples. As the first UN instrument for the promotion and protection of Indigenous peoples' human rights, the *Declaration* would open the door for a better future for Indigenous peoples worldwide.[10]

4. Implementing the Declaration throughout the UN System

The United Nations has an important responsibility to promote the implementation of the *Declaration* worldwide. Article 42 of the *Declaration* states:

The United Nations, its bodies, including the Permanent Forum on Indigenous Issues, and specialized agencies, including at the country level, and States shall promote respect for and full application of the provisions of this Declaration and follow up the effectiveness of this Declaration.

Article 41 of the *Declaration* provides:

The organs and specialized agencies of the United Nations system and other intergovernmental organizations shall contribute to the full realization of the provisions of this Declaration through the mobilization, *inter alia*, of financial cooperation and technical assistance. Ways and means of ensuring participation of indigenous peoples on issues affecting them shall be established.

One practical way of promoting the implementation of the *Declaration* is to ensure that it is referenced in the work of the General Assembly. Resolutions of the General Assembly can be used to "mainstream" the *Declaration* to ensure that respect for, and protection of, the rights of Indigenous peoples are incorporated into the work of all relevant UN bodies.

Resolutions are divided into two parts. Preambular paragraphs (PPs) contain the foundations and context for the resolution. Operative paragraphs (OPs) call for specific actions. When a resolution is adopted by vote, the language is generally stronger than when it is adopted by consensus.

Guatemala has worked to ensure that references to Indigenous peoples and the *Declaration* are included in diverse resolutions adopted by the General Assembly, thereby promoting Indigenous peoples and their rights and striving to end their marginalization.

Following the adoption of the *Declaration*, during its 62nd session, the General Assembly adopted resolutions that specifically mention the *Declaration* in relation to such key issues as the elimination of racism, the rights of the child, the right to food, the rights of women, and the right to development. For example, the General Assembly has:

- Emphasized "its commitment to indigenous peoples in the process of realization of the right to development," and stressed "the commitment to ensure their rights in the areas of education, employment, vocational training and retraining, housing, sanitation, health, and social security recognized in international human rights obligations and highlighted in the United Nations Declaration on the Rights of Indigenous Peoples";[11]

- Stressed "its commitments to promote and protect, without discrimination, the economic, social and cultural rights of indigenous peoples, in accordance with international human rights obligations and taking into account, as appropriate, the United Nations Declaration on the Rights of Indigenous Peoples";[12]

- Reaffirmed "the commitment to promote the rights of indigenous peoples in the areas of education, employment, housing, sanitation, health and social security," and noted "the attention paid to those areas in the United Nations Declaration on the Rights of Indigenous Peoples";[13]

- Reaffirmed "its commitment to eliminating all forms of racism, racial discrimination, xenophobia and other forms of related intolerance against indigenous peoples," and noted "the attention paid to the objectives of combating prejudice and eliminating discrimination and promoting tolerance, understanding and good relations among indigenous peoples and all other segments of society in the United Nations Declaration on the Rights of Indigenous Peoples";[14] and

- Noted with appreciation "the attention paid to children in the United Nations Declaration on the Rights of Indigenous Peoples."[15]

Regarding the rights of women, the General Assembly has:

- Encouraged the United Nations Development Fund for Women, "within its mandate, to continue to assist Governments in implementing the rights of indigenous women, in accordance with international human rights obligations and taking into account, as appropriate, the United Nations Declaration on the Rights of Indigenous Peoples";[16]
- Reaffirmed "the commitment to protect and promote the human rights of all women, including, without discrimination, indigenous women who migrate for work," and noted "the attention paid in the United Nations Declaration on the Rights of Indigenous Peoples to the elimination of all forms of violence and discrimination against indigenous women, as appropriate";[17] and
- Noted "the attention paid to the improvement of the situation of indigenous women in rural areas in the United Nations Declaration on the Rights of Indigenous Peoples."[18]

Indigenous peoples have also been mentioned in General Assembly resolutions regarding the importance of co-operatives in social development,[19] human rights and cultural diversity,[20] policies and programs involving youth,[21] and implementation of the World Programme of Action concerning Disabled Persons.[22]

The *Declaration* can also be "mainstreamed" into the work of the General Assembly through existing mechanisms and mandates, such as the Special Rapporteur on the situation of human rights and fundamental freedoms of indigenous people (Special Rapporteur) and the Second Decade of the World's Indigenous People (Second Decade).

The Special Rapporteur is appointed by the Human Rights Council. The mandate of the Special Rapporteur includes the promotion of "the United Nations Declaration on the Rights of Indigenous Peoples and international instruments relevant to the advancement of the rights of indigenous peoples, where appropriate."[23] The Special Rapporteur has made it clear in his reports that he is using the *Declaration* as the normative framework in his mandate.[24]

The Second Decade was proclaimed by the General Assembly to commence on 1 January 2005. The General Assembly decided that the

goal of the Second Decade shall be the further strengthening of international cooperation for the solution of problems faced by indigenous people in such areas as culture, education, health, human rights, the environment and social and economic development, by means of action-oriented programmes and specific projects, increased technical assistance and relevant standard-setting activities.[25]

On 18 December 2008, the 63rd General Assembly adopted an important resolution dealing with Indigenous issues. In this resolution, the GA resolved to request

the Secretary-General, in consultation with Member States, relevant United Nations organizations and mechanisms and other stakeholders, including indigenous organizations, to submit to the Assembly at its sixty-fifth session a midterm assessment report that evaluates progress made in the achievement of the goal and objectives of the Second International Decade of the World's Indigenous People.[26]

The General Assembly also resolved to request the Special Rapporteur to report on the implementation of his mandate to the General Assembly at its 64th session. This resolution signals the importance placed on the Second Decade and the work of Special Rapporteur by the General Assembly. The Special Rapporteur reported to the Third Committee of the General Assembly for the first time in 2009.[27]

The preamble to the December 2008 resolution on Indigenous issues refers to the adoption of the *Declaration*. This is especially noteworthy, as the four states that originally voted against the *Declaration* all co-sponsored this resolution in the Third Committee. By incorporating consideration of the *Declaration* and the rights of Indigenous peoples into the work of the General Assembly, states can convey the international community's commitment to implementing the *Declaration* throughout the UN system. This is important because implementation at the international level can encourage states to engage constructively at the domestic level.

5. IMPLEMENTATION BY INTERNATIONAL AGENCIES, PROGRAMS, AND FUNDS

Another important way of implementing the *Declaration* is to ensure that Indigenous peoples' issues are incorporated into the work of international agencies, programs, and funds. The Inter-Agency Support Group on Indigenous Peoples (IASG) supports the work of the UN Permanent Forum on Indigenous Issues and other intergovernmental bodies and entities. The IASG consists of 31 members, including the World Bank, the European Union, and the World Health Organization.[28] Its terms of reference include advising and assisting in the mainstreaming of Indigenous peoples' issues within the international system.[29]

In February 2008, the Secretariat of the UN Permanent Forum on Indigenous Issues, together with the IASG, elaborated guidelines to assist the UN system to mainstream and integrate Indigenous peoples' issues.[30] These guidelines are useful in our collective efforts toward building better societies. The guidelines set out a broad normative policy and operational framework for implementing a human rights-based and culturally sensitive approach to development for and with Indigenous peoples. They also provide lines of action for planning, implementing, and evaluating programs involving Indigenous peoples and for duly integrating the principles of cultural diversity into UN country programs.

These guidelines contain three sections. Section 1 provides an overview of the situation of Indigenous peoples and the existing international norms and standards that have been adopted to ensure the realization of their rights and to resolve some of the crucial issues they face. Section 2 presents a practical table and checklist of key issues and related rights. Section 3 discusses specific programmatic implications for UN country teams for addressing and mainstreaming Indigenous peoples' issues. These guidelines acknowledge that the *Declaration* "provides a universal framework for the international community and States," and "establishes a framework for discussions and dialogue between indigenous peoples and States."[31]

The IASG further expressed its commitment to the *Declaration* at a special meeting on 26-27 February 2008, noting that some agencies are already developing or revising their existing policies to bring them into line with the standards affirmed by the *Declaration*.[32] One of the recommendations that came out of this meeting was for IASG members to "facilitate dialogue between indigenous peoples and governments to promote implementation of the rights of indigenous peoples and promote the integration of indigenous peoples' rights into national accountability mechanisms."[33] These commitments should prove helpful in achieving progress in efforts to recognize and respect the rights of Indigenous peoples worldwide.

6. IMPLEMENTING THE DECLARATION IN THE AMERICAS

The standards affirmed by the *Declaration* must also guide the work of regional organizations. The OAS is currently engaged in efforts to draft an American Declaration on the Rights of Indigenous Peoples (draft American Declaration). Guatemala has actively supported the development of the draft American Declaration in the OAS Working Group to Prepare the Draft American Declaration on the Rights of Indigenous Peoples. This work is of course influenced by the adoption of the *Declaration* by the United Nations. On 26 – 28 November 2007 in Washington DC, representatives of states and Indigenous peoples attended a "Meeting for Reflection." At this meeting:

> The majority of States and all of the indigenous representatives supported the use of the UN Declaration as the baseline for negotiations and indicated that this represented a minimum standard for the OAS Declaration.

ON THE RIGHTS OF INDIGENOUS PEOPLES

Accordingly, the provisions of the OAS Declaration have to be consistent with those set forth in the United Nations Declaration. Moreover, the OAS Declaration should expand on the general concepts of the United Nations Declaration by addressing the particular characteristics of the indigenous peoples of the Americas, while at the same time filling in any gaps or regulatory lacunae in those areas that were insufficiently addressed in the United Nations Declaration.[34]

Representatives of the Inter-American Commission on Human Rights have also supported this approach. On the occasion of the adoption of the *Declaration*, the Inter-American Commission's Rapporteur on the Rights of Indigenous Peoples expressed his belief "that the *UN Declaration* should constitute the minimum standard in the considerations of the Working Group charged with preparing the *Draft American Declaration on the Rights of Indigenous Peoples*," along with the hope that the adoption of the *Declaration* "will facilitate the prompt approval of the OAS Declaration so that the rights of the indigenous peoples of the Americas can be recognized and protected."[35] This approach demonstrates the commitment of the majority of OAS member states, including Guatemala, to use the *Declaration* as a practical instrument in our regional work. In this regard, the OAS Working Group is both respecting and building on the international human rights standards of the United Nations.

7. Conclusion

The *Declaration* is a remarkable achievement, and its implementation will likely continue in many forms. It is vitally important that the *Declaration* be integrated into and guide the work of the United Nations, other international organizations, and regional bodies. As a member state of the UN and the OAS, Guatemala is committed to upholding the standards of the *Declaration* in fulfilling its international obligations. Indigenous peoples are members of the human family, and as the *Universal Declaration of Human Rights* confirmed: "recognition of the inherent dignity and of the equal and inalienable rights of all members of the human family is the foundation of freedom, justice and peace in the world."[36] The dignity and rights of Indigenous peoples should be affirmed and respected throughout the international human rights system.

Canada's Opposition
to the UN Declaration

Legitimate Concerns or Ideological Bias?

○

Paul Joffe

1. INTRODUCTION

As Victoria Tauli-Corpuz, Chair of the UN Permanent Forum on Indigenous Issues, declared, "[t]he 13th of September 2007 will be remembered as a day when the United Nations and its Member States, together with Indigenous Peoples, reconciled with past painful histories and decided to march into the future on the path of human rights."[1]

There are over 370 million Indigenous people in more than 70 countries across the world. The *United Nations Declaration on the Rights of Indigenous Peoples* (*Declaration*) constitutes a major step toward addressing the widespread and persistent human rights violations against them. It is the most comprehensive and universal international human rights instrument explicitly addressing the rights of Indigenous peoples. It responds to the "urgent need to respect and promote the inherent rights of indigenous peoples,"[2] and elaborates international human rights standards for the "survival, dignity and well-being of the indigenous peoples of the world."[3]

An earlier version of this article was published as "UN Declaration: Achieving Reconciliation and Effective Application in the Canadian Context" in *Aboriginal Law Conference – 2008: Challenges and Opportunities on the Road to Reconciliation*, published by the Continuing Education Society of British Columbia. It is adapted from *"UN Declaration on the Rights of Indigenous Peoples:* Canadian Government Positions Incompatible with Genuine Reconciliation" (2010) 26 *National Journal of Constitutional Law* 121. The author is grateful to Jennifer Preston and Suzanne Jasper for their valuable comments on earlier drafts.

The adoption of the *Declaration* has been hailed in every region of the world. United Nations Secretary-General Ban Ki-moon welcomed it as a "triumph for indigenous peoples around the world."[4] The European Union embraced the *Declaration* as "one of the most significant achievements in this field of human rights."[5] The African Group of States described the adoption of the *Declaration* as providing "a new and comprehensive framework," and emphasized the promotion of its "implementation."[6]

The vote was 144 states in favour and four opposed: Canada, the US, New Zealand, and Australia. On 3 April 2009, the Labor government in Australia endorsed the *Declaration*. Canada was the only country on the 47-member Human Rights Council to vote against it in the General Assembly. Against worldwide opinion, the Conservative government of Canada insists that its decision to oppose the adoption "was the right one."[7] The government claims it has "principled and well-publicized concerns"[8] and that it has tackled Indigenous issues "openly, honestly, and with respect."[9]

In this chapter, I conclude that the Canadian government's opposition to the *Declaration* is based on ideological bias rather than on a legitimate, legal rationale. The Canadian government has consistently engaged in exaggerated, absolutist interpretations of the *Declaration* which have generated confusion and opposition both at home and abroad. It has repeatedly violated the rule of law in Canada and internationally, misled the Canadian public, and undermined the human rights of Indigenous peoples. Such conduct fails to uphold the honour of the Crown and is inconsistent with the constitutional objective of reconciliation with Indigenous peoples. As a consequence of its actions, Canada's international reputation on human rights has been severely tarnished.[10]

This chapter will begin by showing why it is critically important to take a human rights-based approach when addressing Indigenous issues. It will then critique the specific arguments of the Canadian government against the *Declaration*. Finally, the chapter analyzes the legal status of the *Declaration* and how it may be used in Canadian courts.

2. Importance of Adopting a Human Rights-Based Approach

The rights of Indigenous peoples and individuals are human rights and are addressed as such by the international system. Article 1 of the Declaration affirms: "Indigenous peoples have the right to the full enjoyment, as a collective or as individuals, of all human rights and fundamental freedoms as recognized in the Charter of the United Nations, the Universal Declaration of Human Rights and international human rights law."

Under a "human rights-based approach," Indigenous issues are addressed within a framework of international human rights law and standards. Indigenous rights are included as an integral part of both policy and law. In practice, state governments often fail to affirm that Indigenous peoples have inherent collective rights that are human rights, including the right of self-determination.

In the absence of a principled human rights framework, violations or denials of Indigenous peoples' rights are likely to continue to be treated casually by governments and the courts. Even when domestic judicial remedies are provided, they have often fallen short. Redress of past dispossessions of Indigenous peoples' lands, territories, and resources or prevention of future injustices has been dependent on discretionary governmental policies or programming. This has led to uneven treatment and results. These situations perpetuate a lack of dignity, security, and well-being among Indigenous peoples.

It is appropriate to draw on international human rights concepts and standards when interpreting and implementing the Aboriginal and treaty rights of Indigenous peoples in Canada. As stated by Chief Justice Beverley McLachlin of the Supreme Court of Canada, emerging international norms guide both governments and the courts, and cannot be ignored:

Aboriginal rights from the beginning have been shaped by international concepts.... More recently, emerging international norms have guided governments and courts grappling with aboriginal issues. Canada, as a respected member of the international community, cannot ignore these new international norms any more than it could sidestep the colonial norms of the past. Whether we like it or not, aboriginal rights are an international matter.[11]

In an era of increasing globalization, major issues relating to Indigenous peoples are being addressed at the international level. This growing trend enhances the significance of international human rights norms for the domestic Canadian context. In a wide range of Indigenous issues in Canada, it can prove very useful to invoke international human rights norms and law in negotiations with governments, corporations, and other third parties. The same is true for Indigenous cases in domestic courts.

The November 2007 *Report of the Special Rapporteur on the situation of human rights and fundamental freedoms of indigenous people* concluded that the "rights and principles enshrined in the Declaration mesh with the general principles of the [human] rights-based approach."[12] Similarly, the United Nations Development Group has accentuated that the *Declaration* is an integral part of a human rights-based approach:

The human rights standards contained in, and principles derived from, the Universal Declaration of Human Rights, the United Nations Declaration on the Rights of Indigenous Peoples and other international human rights instruments, as well as the recognition of indigenous peoples' collective rights, provide the framework for adopting a human rights-based and culturally sensitive approach when addressing the specific situation of indigenous peoples.[13]

Based on almost 30 years of data, there is a well-established practice to address Indigenous peoples' collective rights within international and regional human rights systems. Indigenous peoples' rights are increasingly integrated with such human rights systems.

There are a number of other compelling reasons for maintaining a human rights-based approach to addressing Indigenous issues, especially one that embraces relevant and uplifting international norms. First, it is recognized that Indigenous peoples' collective rights are human rights.[14] As Irwin Cotler states: "A . . . category [of human rights], one distinguishably set forth in the Canadian *Charter* — and increasingly recognized in international human rights law — is the category of *aboriginal rights*."[15] The Canadian Human Rights Commission emphasizes:

[H]uman rights have a dual nature. Both collective and individual human rights must be protected; both types of rights are important to human freedom and dignity. They are not opposites, nor is there an unresolvable conflict between them. The challenge is to find an appropriate way to ensure respect for both types of rights without diminishing either.[16]

In its Agenda and Framework for the Programme of Work, the UN Human Rights Council has permanently included the "rights of peoples" under Item 3, "Promotion and protection of all human rights. . . ."[17] The Office of the High Commissioner for Human Rights has underlined: "The Declaration . . . provides the foundation — along with other human rights standards — for the development of policies and laws to protect the collective human rights of indigenous peoples."[18] Therefore, the position that the Canadian government has taken against recognizing Indigenous peoples' collective rights as human rights is without merit. At the Organization of American States (OAS) negotiations on a draft American Declaration on the Rights of Indigenous Peoples (draft American Declaration), the Conservative government has strongly objected to recognizing Indigenous peoples' collective rights as human rights.[19]

Second, a human rights approach should serve to ensure a more coherent and consistent interpretation and treatment of Indigenous peoples' fundamental rights.

To date, Canadian courts have not engaged in comprehensive human rights analyses in interpreting Aboriginal and treaty rights. Two UN committees concerned with human rights have linked Canada's extinguishment policies to "economic marginalization" and "dispossession."[20] Yet the Supreme Court of Canada continues to apply the discriminatory[21] and anachronistic doctrine of extinguishment to Aboriginal rights, despite far-reaching adverse human rights considerations.[22]

Third, in Canada and internationally, it is recognized that the principles of democracy, the rule of law, and respect for human rights are profoundly interrelated.[23] Therefore, a human rights approach is required to ensure balanced and comprehensive legal analyses. According to Stephen J. Toope, "Canadian legal values concerning human rights are rooted directly in international standards."[24] In *R. v. Demers*, Supreme Court Justice LeBel stated that "a further principle underlying our constitutional arrangement is respect for human rights and freedoms."[25]

An additional reason for adopting a human rights approach relates to the acute poverty facing Indigenous peoples in different regions of Canada. This poverty is closely interconnected with the denial of human rights. Such poverty is not happenstance, but a result of colonialism, dispossession, and discrimination.

Denials of Indigenous peoples' collective human rights, including self-determination, are root causes and major contributors to deep-seated health and other socio-economic problems.[26] As the Canadian Medical Association has concluded, "[i]t is recognized that self-determination in social, political and economic life improves the health of Aboriginal peoples and their communities. Therefore, the CMA encourages and supports the Aboriginal peoples in their quest for resolution of self-determination and land use."[27] Land and resource dispossessions entail highly serious and far-reaching human rights abuses, endangering the survival and well-being of distinct Indigenous peoples and cultures.[28] Both peoples and individuals are affected. Therefore, eradicating poverty is, in essential ways, a human rights challenge that would be aided by the *Declaration*.

As international experts have emphasized, "The adoption of the *Declaration* . . . should be seen as providing impetus for renewed efforts by the international community to address the pressing concerns of the world's 370 million indigenous people, including perhaps the most urgent issue of all: poverty and marginalization."[29]

The adoption of a human rights-based approach should prove beneficial for interpreting and implementing Indigenous peoples' rights and the *Declaration*, but the effective use of such an approach will require ongoing human rights learning and education. The UN General Assembly proclaimed 2009 the International Year of Human Rights Learning in order to "promote a human rights culture worldwide."[30] The significance of human rights education in relation to Indigenous peoples has been described as follows:

Human rights education, if effective, should serve to promote tolerance, re-spect and understanding. . . . [I]t is important for people of all ages to ap-preciate that Aboriginal and treaty rights are human rights that must be re-spected. . . . the sacred nature and historical and contemporary significance of treaties should be an integral part of human rights education.[31]

In the Programme of Action for the Second International Decade of the World's Indigenous People, it is recommended that "programmes of education on the hu-man rights of indigenous peoples should be developed and strengthened . . . and should advocate against stereotypes and ethnic stigmatization."[32] To increase un-derstanding, diversity, equality, and non-discrimination, the *Declaration* and In-digenous peoples' human rights should be integrated into the school curriculum at different grade levels. In regard to Indigenous nations and communities, it would be useful to develop versions of the *Declaration* in various Indigenous languages. This is already taking place in different regions of the world.[33]

National and regional conferences and workshops are also useful in fostering increased understanding and insight in relation to the *Declaration* and international human rights law. It should prove highly beneficial for Indigenous leaders, among others, to gradually integrate a human rights-based approach in addressing their di-verse issues. Such an approach is likely to be particularly relevant in formulating and implementing Indigenous constitutions and in a wide range of governance issues.

Many scholars, lawyers, legislators, and government officials are also in need of human rights education. Increased comprehension of the relationship of interna-tional human rights law to Canadian domestic law is needed.

Education is crucial if Indigenous peoples' human rights are to be protected, respected, and fulfilled. The human rights of Indigenous peoples in the *Declaration* are core considerations in the international and Canadian context. As illustrated in the following sections, the arguments and actions of the government of Canada against the *Declaration* can best be analyzed and countered by embracing a human rights-based approach.

3. CANADIAN GOVERNMENT ARGUMENTS AGAINST THE DECLARATION

It is worth noting that the UN Committee on the Elimination of Racial Dis-crimination has not accepted Canada's reasons for opposing the *Declaration*. The Committee indicated its regret in "the change in the position" of Canada from the previous government and recommended that Canada "support the immediate adoption of the United Nations Declaration."[34]

As a minority government, the Conservatives have also failed to follow the will of Parliament. The three opposition parties — Liberal, New Democrat, and Bloc

Québecois — all support the *Declaration*. On 8 April 2008, Members of Parliament voted 148 to 113 in favour of the following motion:

> That the government endorse the United Nations Declaration on the Rights of Indigenous Peoples as adopted by the United Nations General Assembly on 13 September 2007 and that Parliament and Government of Canada fully implement the standards contained therein.[35]

In formulating its positions on the *Declaration* since early 2006, the government has not engaged in any consultations with Indigenous peoples or made any attempt to accommodate their concerns. Yet the government has a duty under s. 35 of the *Constitution Act, 1982* to consult and accommodate Indigenous peoples. This duty is grounded in the "honour of the Crown."[36] The Crown must act honourably in all its dealings with Aboriginal peoples, including its "historical and future relationship" with Indigenous peoples.[37] In particular, there must be no appearance of "sharp dealing."[38]

The duty to consult arises "when a Crown actor has knowledge, real or constructive, of the potential existence of Aboriginal rights or title and contemplates conduct that might adversely affect them. . . . Responsiveness is a key requirement of both consultation and accommodation."[39] The Supreme Court has stated, further, that "consultation that excludes from the outset any form of accommodation would be meaningless."[40] On questions of pure law, Canada has failed to meet the judicial standard of "correctness"[41] in raising extreme and unsubstantiated concerns relating to the *Declaration*.

3A Balancing of Rights

The Canadian government has claimed that the *Declaration* does not contain any "balancing" of individual and collective rights. At the time of the adoption of the *Declaration*, Indian Affairs Minister Chuck Strahl stated:

> In Canada, you are balancing individual rights vs. collective rights, and [this] document . . . has none of that. . . . By signing on, you default to this document by saying that the only rights in play here are the rights of the First Nations. And, of course, in Canada, that's inconsistent with our constitution.[42]

This statement is contradicted by the *Declaration* itself, in which 17 provisions address individual rights.[43] The *Declaration* also contains some of the most comprehensive balancing provisions that exist in any international human rights in-

76   *Paul Joffe*

strument. According to article 46(3), for example, all provisions in the *Declaration* "shall be interpreted in accordance with the principles of justice, democracy, respect for human rights, equality, non-discrimination, good governance and good faith." It was, ironically, officials of the previous Liberal government, together with representatives of Indigenous organizations, who drafted key aspects of these balancing provisions. The same government encouraged other states to endorse these provisions.

After the change in government, Canada sought to include further balancing provisions in the text. In proposed amendments of 13 August 2007, Canada and three other states proposed that the *Declaration* be also interpreted in accordance with the "constitutional frameworks" of each state.[44] No such qualification is found in the *Universal Declaration on Human Rights*[45] or the two international human rights covenants.[46] In past years, Indigenous peoples have rejected such proposals as constituting a discriminatory double standard and as likely to legitimize state actions to deny them their rights.[47]

3B Effects on the Canadian Charter and Constitution

On 21 June 2006, the Indian Affairs Minister declared to Parliament:

[The *Declaration*] is inconsistent with the Canadian Charter of Rights and Freedoms. It is inconsistent with our Constitution. It is inconsistent with the National Defence Act. It is inconsistent with our treaties. It is inconsistent with all of the policies under which we have negotiated land claims for 100 years.[48]

No government representative has been able to provide an explanation of the minister's rationale. Three months later, the government quietly altered its previous statement and suggested that the *Declaration* "could be interpreted as being inconsistent with" the *Canadian Charter of Rights and Freedoms* and the Constitution.[49]

At the time of the vote at the General Assembly, Indian Affairs Minister Chuck Strahl stated that "the rights of non-native Canadians would have been threatened had the government not opposed" the *Declaration*. Minister Strahl further indicated that the *Declaration* is "inconsistent with Canadian legal tradition," adding that "the document is unworkable in a Western democracy under a constitutional government."[50]

In the absence of any specific factual situation, it is irresponsible for the government to presume that support for the *Declaration* is inconsistent with Canadian law, or that it would threaten the rights of "non-native Canadians."

As the Supreme Court of Canada has ruled, it is "improper" to assess an "alleged collision of rights" without any factual context.[51] The government's vague assertion that the *Declaration* could be interpreted as being inconsistent with the Canadian *Charter of Rights* is again contradicted by the *Declaration* itself. Article 46 states that in the exercise of the rights enunciated in the *Declaration*, the "human rights and fundamental freedoms of all shall be respected."

Furthermore, in concluding that the *Declaration* is "inconsistent with the National Defence Act," the government contradicted its own Department of National Defence, which had recommended that the government support the *Declaration* with a statement of understanding.[52]

3c Military Activities on Indigenous Lands

Article 30 of the *Declaration* states:

1. Military activities shall not take place in the lands or territories of indigenous peoples, unless justified by a relevant public interest or otherwise freely agreed with or requested by the indigenous peoples concerned.

2. States shall undertake effective consultations with the indigenous peoples concerned, through appropriate procedures and in particular through their representative institutions, prior to using their lands or territories for military activities.

The Canadian government incorrectly claimed that the *Declaration* would prevent the military from providing assistance in the event of natural disasters and other emergencies on Indigenous lands.[53] It is a widely accepted international standard that advance preparation with local people regarding natural disasters is necessary.[54]

The proposed amendments of August 2007 would have limited the obligation upon states to consult with Indigenous peoples contained in article 30(2) of the *Declaration*. States would have a duty to consult only "where military activities take place by agreement or upon request" of Indigenous peoples.[55] This would invite unilateral military activities to take place on Indigenous lands with no consultation – clearly a lesser standard than what is required under section 35 of the *Constitution Act, 1982*. The government's amendments ignore the gross atrocities committed with impunity by militaries against Indigenous peoples in various regions of the world. These include: extrajudicial killings, rapes, environmental degradation, burning of homes and forced labour, including prostitution.[56] Such an amendment would have gone well below what is essential to ensure the "survival, dignity and well-being" of the world's Indigenous peoples.

3D Treaties with Indigenous Peoples

The Canadian government argues that 500 treaties have been signed with Indigenous peoples in Canada over the past 250 years, and "[t]he government does not support the declaration because that declaration jeopardizes those treaties, the enforceability and the meaning of them."[57] Under Canadian law, it is not possible for a declaration to upend the treaties that Canada has entered into with Indigenous peoples. The treaty rights of Indigenous peoples are protected by section 35 of the *Constitution Act, 1982*, and the treaties themselves cannot be jeopardized by international human rights instruments. Indeed, Indigenous peoples' treaty rights generally constitute an elaboration of human rights.[58]

Again, the government's statements are contradicted by the *Declaration* itself. The preamble recognizes "the urgent need to respect and promote the rights of indigenous peoples affirmed in treaties." It also affirms that "treaties . . . and the relationship they represent . . . are the basis for a strengthened partnership between indigenous peoples and States."[59] Further, article 37 affirms that "Indigenous peoples have the right to the recognition, observance and enforcement of treaties . . . concluded with States . . . and to have States honour and respect such treaties."[60] All these provisions serve to honour, protect, and enforce treaties with Indigenous peoples as sacred[61] and living agreements.

The former Indian Affairs Minister concluded that the *Declaration* is "inconsistent with all of the policies under which we have negotiated land claims for 100 years."[62] This statement lacks coherence and accuracy. It also ignores that fact that such land claims policies have frequently entailed a denial of Indigenous peoples' human rights. For 24 of the last 100 years (1927-1951), it was an offence under the *Indian Act* for "Indians" to raise funds or retain a lawyer for the advancement and prosecution of land claims.[63] At the Assembly of First Nations (AFN) General Assembly on 16 July 2006, former Indian Affairs Minister Jim Prentice decried the specific claims process: "I have been one of the most outspoken critics in this country over the last 20 years of how the claims process isn't working."[64] Yet he was prepared to cite this process as a reason for not endorsing the *Declaration*.

Domestic laws and policies do not prevail over international law.[65] It is neither necessary nor appropriate for an international human rights instrument to reflect national laws and policies. If it did, the *Declaration* would also have to reflect the laws, treaties, and policies of approximately 70 other countries that include Indigenous peoples, perpetuating the status quo and the regressive laws and policies of countless governments.[66] A key purpose of the *Declaration* is to provide universal and elevating international human rights norms.

3E Lands, Territories, and Resources

The Canadian government has made misleading statements about the nature and effect of the *Declaration's* provisions in relation to lands, territories, and resources. In Parliament, the government has claimed that

> the declaration contemplates those countries that are signatory to it to enter into a scenario that would start the discussions [with Indigenous peoples] from the perspective of a pre-contact state for the indigenous peoples. In light of that . . . [should Canada] simply set aside the historic treaties we have negotiated with our first nations peoples throughout our history, which have built this great country? Should we set aside all the ongoing negotiations that we have with our first peoples? Should we set aside our Constitution, which incorporates Métis, first nations and Inuit people into the very document that binds our country together?[67]

The government perceives that "[a]rticle 26 is the most problematic of the lands and resources provisions, especially the phrase: 'Indigenous peoples have the right to the lands, territories and resources which they have traditionally owned, occupied or otherwise used or acquired'."[68] It has argued that the "declaration suggests that we must return to that pre-contact moment."[69] However, article 26 reflects the criteria used in Canada and elsewhere to establish Aboriginal title and rights to lands and resources. Aboriginal rights are based on traditional occupation and use that are rooted well in the past. These are the criteria required by both the Supreme Court of Canada[70] and federal land claims policies.[71] Further, the land and resource rights affirmed in article 26 of the *Declaration* are relative in nature, not absolute. Article 46 makes clear that the rights in this instrument are balanced with the rights of others.

3F Self-Government

The Conservative government opposes the right of Indigenous peoples to self-government, which is affirmed in article 4 of the *Declaration,* based on the belief that the provision does not recognize the "importance of negotiations."[72] This description does not reveal the far-reaching dimensions of the government's position.

In the proposed amendments of August 2007, Canada appears to convert the right of self-government into a joint or contingent right to be exercised "in co-operation with the State."[73] Yet the inherent right of self-government is a human right that flows from the right of self-determination.[74] In international human rights instruments, human rights are recognized as inherent and inalienable. They are not contingent on state co-operation or joint exercise with the state.

3G Cultural Heritage and Intellectual Property

Article 31(1) of the *Declaration* affirms the right of Indigenous peoples to "maintain, control, protect and develop their cultural heritage, traditional knowledge and traditional cultural expressions." In Canada's proposed amendments, the terms "control" and "protect" were deleted. Also, the "right to maintain, control, protect and develop their intellectual property" was changed to read "may have the right...."[75]

At the OAS negotiations on a draft American Declaration, the Harper government has refused to use the terms "tangible"[76] and "intangible"[77] in relation to cultural heritage, but the two are interdependent and both relate to Indigenous peoples.

Canada's positions in regard to cultural heritage and traditional knowledge are not consistent with the approaches taken by international bodies or instruments.[78] The *Convention on the Protection and Promotion of the Diversity of Cultural Expressions* recognizes "the importance of traditional knowledge as a source of intangible and material wealth, and in particular the knowledge systems of indigenous peoples ... as well as the need for its adequate protection and promotion."[79]

In relation to intellectual property, the Harper government claims:

> Throughout 2006 and 2007, Canada continued to advocate for ... [a] negotiation process in order to achieve changes to the most problematic portions of the Declaration. With respect to substance, our areas of greatest concern relate to the portions of the text having to do with the following: ... intellectual property.[80]

At the time of the vote on the draft declaration at the Human Rights Council on 29 June 2006, the Canadian government raised concerns on other provisions of the draft but was silent on the issue of intellectual property.[81]

On 28 June 2007, Canada indicated that the declaration "goes well beyond current and evolving intellectual property rights regimes and could undermine complex negotiations in other fora."[82] This does not reflect the position of the World Intellectual Property Organization (WIPO) and other international bodies. With regard to the protection of traditional knowledge and cultural expressions against misappropriation and misuse, for example, "WIPO member states have ... emphasized that no outcome of the work of WIPO in this area is excluded. ... They have also emphasized that the work of WIPO should not prejudice developments in other forums."[83]

UNESCO also disagrees with Canada's position, confirming that the *Declaration*

> echoes the principles of the UNESCO Universal Declaration on Cultural Diversity (2001) and related Conventions — notably the 1972 World Heritage Convention, the 2003 Convention for the Safeguarding of the Intangible Cultural Heritage, and the 2005 Convention on the Protection and Promotion of the Diversity of Cultural Expressions.[84]

3H Free, Prior, and Informed Consent

The Canadian government has raised particular concerns regarding free, prior, and informed consent (FPIC). FPIC is affirmed in various provisions of the *Declaration*,[85] including article 19, which affirms that "[s]tates shall consult and cooperate in good faith with the indigenous peoples concerned through their own representative institutions in order to obtain their free, prior and informed consent before adopting and implementing legislative or administrative measures that may affect them."

FPIC is being increasingly used as a standard by international[86] and domestic[87] bodies and mechanisms, including UN treaty monitoring bodies,[88] special rapporteurs and other independent experts,[89] UN specialized agencies,[90] and the Permanent Forum on Indigenous Issues,[91] as well as in the Inter-American human rights system.[92] Further, in the *Programme of Action for the Second International Decade of the World's Indigenous People*, the General Assembly highlighted the objective of promoting "full and effective participation of indigenous peoples in decisions which directly or indirectly affect their lifestyles, traditional lands and territories, their cultural integrity as indigenous peoples with collective rights or any other aspect of their lives, considering the principle of free, prior and informed consent."[93]

The Indian Affairs Minister has indicated that "free, prior and informed consent when used as a veto" is a "core concern" for the government.[94] However, as evident in article 46, the provisions in the *Declaration* are generally relative in nature, and the rights of others must be taken into account in interpreting and implementing it. The scope of all rights and the degree of balancing required can only be determined by examining the facts and law in each situation in a manner consistent with international law.

In many cases, even after the rights of others are fully and fairly considered, the FPIC of Indigenous peoples must prevail. The Supreme Court of Canada has ruled that the nature and scope of the Crown's duty to consult would require the "full consent of [the] aboriginal nation . . . on very serious issues."[95]

31 Opposing the Declaration in the Climate Change Context

At the December 2008 world meeting on climate change in Poznań, Poland,[96] it was reported that Canada, Australia, New Zealand, and the United States had spearheaded the removal of any references to the term "rights" in relation to Indigenous peoples or to the *Declaration*. These same states "used the phrase 'indigenous people' instead of 'indigenous peoples' with an 's' which is the internationally accepted language."[97] At a news conference in Poland, Canada's Environment Minister, Jim Prentice, claimed that the *Declaration* "has nothing whatsoever to do with climate change."[98]

Such actions not only politicize Indigenous peoples' human rights, they also undermine global attempts to respond effectively to climate change. The minister's statement further detracts from a human rights-based approach to climate change.[99]

The *Declaration* includes a wide range of economic, social, cultural, political, spiritual, and environmental rights that may be severely affected by climate change.[100] As Special Rapporteur on the situation of human rights and fundamental freedoms of indigenous people (Special Rapporteur), S. James Anaya, has described, "The *Declaration* further acknowledges indigenous peoples' intergenerational responsibilities, including environmental stewardship, with regard to their traditional lands, territories and resources."[101] The Permanent Forum on Indigenous Issues also emphasizes the importance of the *Declaration* in climate change issues:

> The United Nations Declaration on the Rights of Indigenous Peoples should serve as a key and binding framework in the formulation of plans for development and should be considered fundamental in all processes related to climate change at the local, national, regional and global levels.[102]

In 2008, the World Conservation Congress of the International Union for the Conservation of Nature (IUCN) adopted a resolution to endorse and implement the *Declaration*, recognizing it as "the accepted international mechanism for relieving the tremendous pressures and crises faced by indigenous peoples throughout the world as they endeavor to protect indigenous ecosystems, including biological, cultural and linguistic diversity."[103]

Kyung-wha Kang, UN Deputy High Commissioner for Human Rights, has also called for a human rights approach to climate change: "As climate change will inevitably affect the enjoyment of human rights, safeguarding of human rights should be a key consideration in efforts to address the impact of climate change."[104] In relation to Indigenous peoples, the Office of the High Commissioner for Human Rights urges "greater integration of human rights in climate change discussions."[105] The UN Development Group cautions that the "direct and indirect impacts of climate change may threaten the very existence of the peoples of the Arctic, of small islands, high altitude areas, dry lands and other vulnerable environments."[106]

In light of the growing effects of climate change, the Canadian government should be adopting a principled approach in collaboration with Indigenous peoples.

3J Failure to Substantiate Specific Arguments

The arguments of the Government of Canada do not justify its opposition to the adoption and implementation of the Declaration. As over 100 scholars and experts in Canada concluded in an open letter,

> No credible legal rationale has been provided to substantiate these extraordinary and erroneous claims. . . . We are concerned that the misleading claims made by the Canadian government continue to be used to justify opposition, as well as impede international co-operation and implementation of this human rights instrument.[107]

The Canadian government has consistently refused to provide any written legal analysis to substantiate its claims regarding the *Declaration*. It invokes solicitor-client privilege to justify the non-disclosure of the legal implications of its various positions on Indigenous peoples' rights. Representatives of Indigenous organizations, however, have made clear that no requests have been made for access to any privileged documents prepared by Canada's legal counsel. In view of the real and potential adverse effects of Canada's positions on the rights of Indigenous peoples, the government has an obligation to substantiate in legal terms its positions and disclose their legal implications. In the absence of relevant legal information,[108] meaningful consultations on Indigenous peoples' rights are, in effect, precluded. This approach offends the principles of accountability and transparency.

3K Failure to Uphold International Obligations

Canada's opposition is also inconsistent with its international obligations. As a member state of the UN, Canada has a duty to respect the purposes and principles of the *Charter of the United Nations* (*UN Charter*), which require actions "promoting and encouraging respect" for human rights and not undermining them.[109] In Canada, this duty is reinforced by the underlying constitutional principle of respect for human rights and freedoms.[110]

84   *Paul Joffe*

As an elected member of the Human Rights Council, Canada accepted the commitment to "uphold the highest standards in the promotion and protection of human rights . . . [and] fully cooperate with the Council."[111] This co-operation includes supporting the Council in carrying out its responsibility "for promoting universal respect for the protection of all human rights . . . for all, without distinction of any kind and in a fair and equal manner."[112] As a Council member, Canada should not have politicized human rights. A key reason for the creation of the new Council was the need to ensure "objectivity and non-selectivity in the consideration of human rights issues, and the elimination of double standards and politicization".[113]

In relation to the *Declaration* and Indigenous peoples' human rights, the Canadian government has failed to respect the purposes and principles of the *UN Charter* and has reneged on its commitment to "uphold the highest standards in the promotion and protection of human rights." Indigenous peoples and human rights organizations have called for Canada's conduct in relation to the Declaration to be reviewed by the Human Rights Council.[114]

Canadian government opposition to the *Declaration* adversely impacts Indigenous peoples in Canada and elsewhere across the globe. As emphasized by the High Commissioner for Human Rights, "[r]especting human rights is not only a legal obligation. It is also a precondition for our societies to grow and prosper in peace and security."[115]

Similarly, the UN General Assembly and its member states have affirmed that "development, peace and security and human rights are interlinked and mutually reinforcing."[116] This has been articulated by the UN Secretary-General as follows: "we will not enjoy development without security, we will not enjoy security without development, and we will not enjoy either without respect for human rights."[117]

Despite Canada's ongoing opposition, the *Declaration* has an important role to play in promoting and protecting the rights of Indigenous peoples in Canada and internationally.

4. LEGAL STATUS OF THE DECLARATION AND ITS APPLICATION BY CANADIAN COURTS

A central aspect of the Canadian government's strategy against the *Declaration* is exemplified by the following statement: "[T]his Declaration has no legal effect in Canada, and its provisions do not represent customary international law. It is therefore inappropriate for the Special Rapporteur to promote the implementation of this Declaration with respect to Canada."[118]

This appears to be the first time that Canada has vigorously opposed a human rights instrument adopted by the General Assembly. In its December 2007 report,

Amnesty International Canada cautions that Canada's position "attempts to set a very dangerous precedent for UN human rights protection":

> The proposition that governments can opt out . . . by simply voting against a Declaration, resolution or other similar document, even when an overwhelming majority of states have supported the new standards, dramatically undercuts the integrity of the international human rights system. . . . It is impossible to recall a similar example of Canada taking such a harmful position on the basic principles of global human rights protection.[119]

"Canada's position, in many ways, drives a stake through the very integrity of the international human rights system, for indigenous peoples and everyone," underlined Amnesty International Canada's Secretary-General, Alex Neve. "The essence of Canada's position is that states should feel free to disregard a UN decision, such as the adoption of an important human rights declaration . . . if they have not voted in favour of it."[120]

4A Legal Effect

The government is incorrect in declaring that the *Declaration* has no legal effect in Canada. Canadian courts are free to rely on declarations in interpreting the human rights of peoples and individuals. The government has also declared that its actions will be based "not on the UN Declaration, but on Canada's international human rights obligations and our existing domestic framework, including Canadian constitutional provisions and other laws, and treaties between the government and Aboriginal groups."[121] Such statements profoundly misrepresent the relationship between international and domestic law, as well as the *Declaration* itself.

The *Declaration* does not create any new rights,[122] but affirms a wide range of inherent rights, and reflects a diverse range of international obligations that apply to Canada. One cannot wholly separate the *Declaration* from other international human rights instruments and law. As Special Rapporteur S. James Anaya explains,

> Given the complementary and interrelated character of international human rights law, as well as the existing and developing jurisprudence on various human rights treaties by international bodies and mechanisms, it is clear that the provisions of the Declaration should factor into the interpretation of States' international human rights obligations. . . .[123]

A state's opposing vote at the General Assembly cannot prevent international treaty monitoring bodies from recommending that the *Declaration* "be used as a guide to interpret the State party's obligations" under human rights treaties.[124] Within their respective mandates, international and regional bodies are free to rely on the *Declaration* in interpreting the rights of Indigenous peoples in Canada and elsewhere. The *Declaration* itself, at article 42, requires that the "United Nations, its bodies ... and specialized agencies ... promote respect for and full application of the provisions of this Declaration and follow up the effectiveness of this Declaration." The *Declaration* is already being used by the OAS as "the baseline for negotiations and ... a minimum standard" for the draft American Declaration.[125]

The *Declaration* was adopted as an Annex to a General Assembly resolution. Such resolutions, including declarations, are generally considered to be non-binding, but they may have diverse legal effects both now and in the future:

> General Assembly resolutions do not *per se* create binding international law. That said, they may either influence or reflect international law in several ways. First, as the [International Court of Justice] concluded in the *Nicaragua Case*, they may be *evidence* of *opinio juris* which confirms the existence of a rule of customary international law. Second, they may be invoked as an authoritative interpretation of a binding treaty obligation, such as those set out in the UN Charter. Third, they may be regarded as assessments of general principles of law accepted by states, a third source of international law anticipated in Article 38 of the Statute of the International Court of Justice.... And in all of these various ways, they may influence the practice and *opinio juris* of states and, thus, the future content of customary international law.[126]

The value of "hard" law instruments, such as international conventions or treaties, should not be underestimated. At the same time, it is important to appreciate that "soft" law instruments, such as resolutions and declarations adopted by the General Assembly and other multinational forums, can have diverse uses and benefits. This may well be the case, both domestically and internationally. In various situations, their use may prove more advantageous than resorting to hard law instruments:

> Soft law offers many of the advantages of hard law ... and has certain advantages of its own. Importantly because one or more of the elements of legalization can be relaxed, softer legalization is often easier to achieve than hard

legalization. . . . Soft law also provides certain benefits not available under hard legislation. It offers more effective ways to deal with uncertainty, especially when it initiates processes that allow actors to learn about the impact of agreements over time. In addition, soft law facilitates compromise, and thus mutually beneficial cooperation, between actors with different interests and values . . . and different degrees of power.[127]

The *Declaration* affirms Indigenous peoples' human rights, highlights international and national obligations, and elaborates universal standards. It also provides for the implementation of all its provisions, with the collaboration of Indigenous peoples, by international institutions and states. These elements of the *Declaration* are highly beneficial, especially since it did not seem feasible to negotiate a convention during the past 25 years.[128] Regardless of whether the *Declaration* constitutes the first step toward the realization of a convention, it has diverse merits in its own right.[129]

At the international level, soft law is utilized much more than traditional lawmaking, and clearly outpaces the latter's ability to generate international norms.[130] Further, as Dinah Shelton indicates:

The line between law and not-law may appear blurred. Treaty mechanisms are including more "soft" law obligations, such as undertakings to endeavor to strive to co-operate. Non-binding instruments in turn are incorporating supervisory mechanisms traditionally found in hard law texts. Both types of procedures may have compliance procedures that range from soft to hard. . . . In fact, it is rare to find soft law standing in isolation. . . . Soft law can be used to fill in gaps in hard law instruments or supplement a hard law instrument with new norms.[131]

These characteristics are particularly relevant to the *Declaration*. A declaration *per se* allows for a great deal of flexibility. It is not limited in terms of purposes, subject matter, language, or implementation. In this regard Christine Chinkin generally states:

There is a wide diversity in the instruments of so-called soft law which makes the generic term a misleading simplification. Even a cursory examination of these diverse instruments inevitably exposes their many variables in form, language, subject matter, participants, addressees, purposes, follow up and monitoring procedures.[132]

In assessing the overall status and value of the *Declaration*, Mauro Barelli recently concluded:

> ... the use of soft law has actually enhanced the value of the Declaration in a number of important respects, particularly its universality and legitimacy, and does not prevent the Declaration from having important legal effects with regard to international treaty-making and customary international law.[133]

As discussed further below, the *Declaration* can have legal effect when it reflects customary international law. In September 2006, Canada's Indian Affairs Minister restated the government's position that the *Declaration* does not represent customary international law. At the same time, he conceded that it does reflect international standards that are binding on Canada:

> With respect to provisions of the *Draft Declaration*, such as those against racial discrimination, to the extent that they reflect standards that Canada has already accepted, such as the *Convention for the Elimination of Racial Discrimination*, Canada will continue to be bound by its international obligations.[134]

The prohibition against racial discrimination is binding on Canada as both a conventional treaty obligation and as customary international law. This is also true for a number of other international obligations, rights, and principles.

In cases where norms exist both in a treaty and in customary international law, the treaty norm and the customary international norm each have a "separate applicability."[135] As Malcolm Shaw explains,

> Parties that do not sign and ratify the particular treaty in question are not bound by its terms. This is a general rule. . . . However, where treaties reflect customary law then non-parties are bound, not because it is a treaty provision but because it reaffirms a rule or rules of customary international law."[136]

Such rules have important implications for the application of the *Declaration*. The existing norms of customary international law affirmed by the *Declaration* apply to Canada, regardless of its opposition.

4B The Declaration and Customary International Law

A norm of customary international law has binding effect when: (1) most countries adhere to the norm in practice, and (2) those countries follow the norm because they feel obligated to do so by a sense of legal duty (*opinio juris*).[137] No state can exercise a veto over the emergence of a customary norm.[138]

Absolute adherence by all states is not necessary to establish a customary rule, but the conduct of states should generally be consistent with such rules. Thus, instances of state conduct inconsistent with a given rule should be treated as breaches of the rule, not as indications of the recognition of a new rule.[139]

Evidence of state practice supporting the rights of Indigenous peoples may be found at both the international and domestic level. Internationally, examples of relevant practices include international judicial decisions, provisions in treaties and other international instruments, and official governmental conduct, as well as the practice of international and regional governmental organizations, such as the UN and the OAS and their organs. At the domestic level, examples of relevant practices include judicial decisions, and constitutional and other laws that affirm and safeguard Indigenous rights.[140] Different levels of proof may be found in UN resolutions and declarations,[141] as well as in the writings of prominent jurists. Ratification of international human rights treaties "provides compelling evidence of both state practice and *opinio juris*."[142] Defining the scope of customary international norms can still prove highly difficult, particularly in relation to human rights.[143]

It is inaccurate for the Canadian government to declare that the provisions of the *Declaration* do not represent customary international law. In his report to the Human Rights Council, Special Rapporteur S. James Anaya states:

> Albeit clearly not binding in the same way that a treaty is, the Declaration relates to already existing human rights obligations of States.... In addition, insofar as they connect with a pattern of consistent international and State practice, some aspects of the provisions of the Declaration can also be considered as a reflection of norms of customary international law."[144]

Various rights, obligations, and principles affirmed in the *Declaration* are considered to be customary international law, if not also peremptory norms. As Ian Brownlie explains, peremptory norms or *jus cogens* "are rules of customary law which cannot be set aside by treaty or acquiescence but only by the formation of a subsequent customary rule of contrary effect."[145]

Examples in the *Declaration* of customary international law include, *inter alia*, the general principle of international law of *pacta sunt servanda* (treaties must be kept);[146] the prohibition against racial discrimination;[147] the right to self-determination;[148] the right to one's own means of subsistence;[149] the right not to be subjected to genocide;[150] the obligation of states under the *UN Charter* to promote "universal respect for, and observance of, human rights and fundamental freedoms for all";[151] and the requirement of good faith in the fulfillment of the obligations assumed by states in accordance with the *UN Charter*.[152] Some prominent jurists have noted that the rule banning gender discrimination is now customary international law as well.[153]

4c Application of the Declaration in Canadian Courts

Canadian courts have the legal capacity to take the *Declaration* into account in interpreting Indigenous peoples' rights.[154] For example, Chief Justice Dickson of the Supreme Court of Canada has stated:

> The various sources of international human rights law — declarations, covenants, conventions, judicial and quasi-judicial decisions of international tribunals, customary norms — must, in my opinion, be relevant and persuasive sources for interpretation of the Charter's provisions.[155]

For interpretative purposes, Canadian courts can invoke any human rights instrument, regardless of whether Canada has approved, acceded to, or ratified it.[156] The judiciary has cited international declarations on numerous occasions.[157]

The provisions of the *Declaration* should not be interpreted in isolation as simply a list of Indigenous rights and related state obligations.[158] To maintain its integrity, the *Declaration* should be read as a whole and its various provisions combined so as to construct strong and cohesive legal positions. Other international human rights instruments, particularly those ratified by Canada, should also be cited, using the *Declaration* to ensure more relevant, contextual interpretations.

Generally, it may not prove effective to raise legal arguments based solely on the *Declaration* since it is, *per se*, a non-binding instrument. However, in a number of instances this comprehensive human rights instrument is declaratory[159] of customary international law. It may also provide evidence of *opinio juris* which confirms the existence of customary international law.

Customary international human rights norms reflected in the *Declaration* can be directly invoked in Canadian courts and independently provide the basis for a remedy.[160] These norms can be of assistance in interpreting and applying domestic law.[161] Also, the *Declaration* may be used to further the development or crystallization of new customary international law standards. Judicial interpretations of the Aboriginal and treaty rights of Indigenous peoples in Canada may thus be significantly strengthened.

4D Persistent Objector Doctrine

To avoid being bound by the *Declaration* or its provisions, the government of Canada is attempting to use the "persistent objector" doctrine. As illustrated below, the government is incorrectly applying this doctrine.

A persistent objector is "a state that has actively and consistently denied the existence or applicability to it of a rule of customary international law prior to and since the crystallization of that rule. The effect of this is to escape the binding effect of the rule."[162]

The persistent objector doctrine would apply only to norms that may be in the process of becoming customary international law. The doctrine has no application to existing customary international law, including peremptory norms.[163] It has already been demonstrated, above, that the *Declaration* contains provisions that are declaratory of existing customary international law. Therefore, the Canadian government cannot rely on the persistent objector doctrine in all instances.

For example, Canada has raised objections relating to the self-government provisions in the *Declaration*. Yet, as reflected in article 4, the right to self-government is a political dimension of the right to self-determination. Since the latter right is widely accepted as a customary international norm, Canada cannot invoke the "persistent objector" doctrine in relation to the right of self-government.

While many writers support the persistent objector rule, the legal precedents in its favour are weak. As Antonio Cassese explains, "there is no firm support in state practice and international case law for a rule on the 'persistent objector'."[164] Jonathan L. Charney similarly concludes that "the proponents of the persistent objector rule have not put forward persuasive evidence of state practice or even judicial opinions that would definitively establish the persistent objector rule."[165]

Indeed, there appear to be no cited cases in which an objector effectively maintained its status after the rule became well accepted in international law.[166] Commentators suggest that opposing states may have the effect of slowing down the formation of new customary international law, but this does not amount to any legal entitlement to be exempted, once the rule has crystallized.[167] The customary rule prohibiting racial discrimination, for example, matured during the period that South Africa consistently objected to it, yet the persistent objector rule did not prevent the application of the rule prohibiting racial discrimination to South Africa.[168]

The persistent objector rule gives rise to additional considerations in the context of human rights, which are recognized internationally as universal in nature. As Holning Lau explains, "[t]he human rights regime's universalist assumption is at odds with the effects of the persistent objector doctrine. By allowing individual states to exempt themselves from international human rights law, the human rights regime's universalist nature is necessarily compromised."[169] Thus, Lau concludes that the persistent objector doctrine is not compatible with international human rights and the principle of universality.[170] The *UN Charter*, which obliges member states to promote "universal respect for, and observance of, human rights and fundamental freedoms for all," reinforces this conclusion.

Although the Canadian government takes the position that it has persistently objected to the *Declaration*, the facts reveal the opposite. In the proposed amendments of August 2007, Canada and three other states submitted proposed revisions to 13 articles in the *Declaration*. Therefore, Canada did not object to the 24 preambular paragraphs and 33 other articles.

Previous Canadian governments raised concerns over certain draft articles in the two working groups that considered the draft declaration, but these concerns varied over the years and, in any event, did not constitute persistent objections. Former Prime Minister Paul Martin indicated in a press conference in October 2006 that his government "would have unequivocally signed the declaration."[171]

The objections of the Conservative government evolved slowly. On 29 June 2006, it indicated to the Human Rights Council without elaboration that Canada had objections in the areas of lands, territories, and resources; the land claims process; the balancing of the rights of "Aboriginal peoples and other Canadians"; free, prior, and informed consent; and self-government.[172] Further concerns relating to language, education, Indigenous legal systems, conservation, environmental protection, and intellectual property were not publicly raised until late September of that year when the government issued a document entitled "Canada's Position."[173] There is also the question as to whether the minority Conservative government can claim to be a "persistent objector," since the Canadian Parliament formally indicated its endorsement of the *Declaration* by majority vote in April 2008.

As an elected member of the Human Rights Council, Canada accepted the commitment to "uphold the highest standards in the promotion and protection of human rights ... [and] fully cooperate with the Council."[174] This co-operation included Canada supporting the Human Rights Council in carrying out its responsibility "for promoting universal respect for the protection of all human rights ... for all, without distinction of any kind."[175] Such consent, explicitly given, contradicts the notion that Canada can subsequently claim to act as a "persistent objector" to a universal human rights standard.

5. Conclusions: Moving Toward Effective Implementation

There is no turning back. The *United Nations Declaration on the Rights of Indigenous Peoples* is a living instrument that has universal application in over 70 countries. It is broadly crafted to address a wide range of circumstances both now and in the future. It provides a framework for ensuring justice, dignity, and security for the world's Indigenous peoples.

A vast range of UN bodies including the Human Rights Council, UN specialized agencies,[176] as well as regional and domestic courts, states, and Indigenous peoples all over the world have already taken initiatives to use and implement the *Declaration*. A growing number of UN General Assembly resolutions are making specific reference to this international human rights instrument, and the Secretary-General has urged the Permanent Forum on Indigenous Issues to "translate the Declaration into a living document at the national and international levels."[177]

In its May 2008 report, the Permanent Forum on Indigenous Issues called for the "promotion, use and implementation of the Declaration as the most universal, comprehensive and fundamental instrument on indigenous peoples' rights." It affirmed that the *Declaration* "will be its legal framework," therefore ensuring that the Declaration is integrated in all aspects of its work.[178]

In contrast to these positive developments, the Conservative government in Canada, guided by ideology rather than international law, continues to counter the *Declaration*. The government has accorded little or no consideration to its ongoing violations of Canadian constitutional and international law. Instead of honouring the nation's commitment to reconciliation, justice, and international co-operation, the politicization of human rights remains the preferred option. As a result, Canada's international reputation and credibility increasingly suffer.[179] Such government strategies are antithetical to the interests of the world's Indigenous peoples and to Canada as a whole.

With or without the support of the government, significant steps are being taken by Indigenous peoples and others to ensure implementation of the *Declaration*. By invoking the *Declaration* in a wide range of domestic and international issues, Indigenous peoples and their supporters can ensure a crucial and dynamic future for the *Declaration*.

Clearly, much remains to be done. The *Declaration* is like a tapestry, carefully woven over many years with countless interrelated and mutually reinforcing strands. These fibers are based on the thousands of interventions of Indigenous peoples worldwide who repeatedly travelled to Geneva to recount the legacy of colonization and injustice they continue to suffer.

This tapestry of human rights remains a work in progress, since their significance and interrelationships are always evolving. It is the responsibility of present and future generations to continue to weave new strands in this tapestry and collectively reinforce its indelibility and relevance.

CHAPTER SIX

Realizing the Human Rights of Indigenous Peoples

Partnerships with Non-Indigenous NGOs

○

Jennifer Preston

1. INTRODUCTION

The *United Nations Declaration on the Rights of Indigenous Peoples* (*Declaration*) is a vital and progressive contribution to the international human rights system. Its adoption was globally celebrated in recognition of the extraordinary achievement it represents, and the need that it fills. The development of the *Declaration* was a unique and democratic process that took place over more than two decades.

A critical element was that, for the first time, a United Nations (UN) human rights instrument was developed with the rights holders themselves as active participants. Indigenous peoples' representatives participated in both working groups that developed the text, first with the Working Group on Indigenous Populations (WGIP)[1] and then the intersessional Working Group on the Draft Declaration (WGDD) set up by the Commission on Human Rights.[2]

For many years, Indigenous and state representatives dialogued, providing essential information, exchanging views, and ultimately negotiating to create a common basis for the final text. During the majority of this time, only a few human rights non-governmental organizations (NGOs) participated, and then mainly as observers and funders.

The UN continues to use the general category of "non-governmental organization" to accredit a wide range of non-state actors to participate in UN forums. Indigenous peoples and their governments may be non-state actors, and some Indigenous peoples' organizations are NGOs. However, Indigenous peoples are not, in fact or in law, simply NGOs or "civil society." The UN practice may primarily relate to article 71 of the *Charter of the United Nations* (*UN Charter*): "The Economic and Social Council may make suitable arrangements for consultation

95

with non-governmental organizations which are concerned with matters within its competence."

For the purposes of this chapter, the term NGOs generally refers to non-Indigenous organizations, many of whom have supported Indigenous peoples in their quest for justice in international forums. For many years I have represented the Society of Friends, or Quakers, in international and domestic forums, in relation to Indigenous peoples and the *Declaration*. In this chapter, I will provide a Quaker perspective, bearing in mind that not all NGOs have the same priorities or positions, and many may have their own interesting viewpoints to add.

The Quakers are faith-based, and participate at the UN as an NGO in General Consultative Status with the Economic and Social Council (ECOSOC). General Consultative Status is the highest level of engagement that NGOs can attain at the United Nations. It is accorded to large, established international NGOs whose area of work has a broad geographical reach and encompasses most of the issues on the agenda of the ECOSOC.

Since the inception of the UN in 1945, NGOs have played an increasingly active and effective role in issues of global concern. In the *2005 World Summit Outcome*, the General Assembly and its member states recognized the "positive contributions" of NGOs in the promotion and implementation of development and human rights programs, and stressed the "importance of their continued engagement with Governments, the United Nations and other international organizations in these key areas."[3]

In 2000, former Secretary-General Kofi Annan declared, "I see a United Nations which recognizes that the NGO revolution — the new global people-power — is the best thing that has happened to our Organization in a long time."[4] More recently, Professor José Alvarez indicated that "no one questions today the fact that international law — both its contents and its impact — has been forever changed by the empowerment of NGOs."[5] These buoyant views have been echoed by others, notably Professor Steve Charnovitz, who wrote: "Nongovernmental Organizations . . . have exerted a profound influence on the scope and dictates of international law. NGOs have fostered treaties, promoted the creation of new international organizations (IOs), and lobbied in national capitals to gain consent to stronger international rules."[6]

In light of challenging global issues, one cannot assume that NGOs will necessarily remain effective or successful. As will be illustrated, it takes considerable effort and collaborative engagement to contribute to a beneficial outcome.

In this chapter I will explore how, in the final years of development of the *Declaration*, human rights representatives, acting in partnership with Indigenous peoples, played a role in educating state representatives and lobbying for support.

NGOs relied on their existing relationships, expertise, and position as defenders of the international human rights system to engage with states. From a perspective of human rights, NGOs worked to persuade states of the urgent need for the *Declaration*, emphasizing its legitimacy and credibility.

I will also elaborate on an *ad hoc* coalition currently working in Canada, detailing some of our initiatives. Based on our experience to date, there is a need for NGOs to continue to work in partnership with Indigenous peoples, especially in the area of human rights education and advocacy. To ensure that the *Declaration* is a living instrument, it is essential that it is fully implemented, in partnership with Indigenous peoples, by states, and by international and regional institutions.

2. The Role of NGOs at the Working Groups

A number of NGOs closely followed the development of the *Declaration* through the standard-setting process in Geneva. Some were organizations whose work is directed to Indigenous peoples, notably the International Work Group on Indigenous Affairs (IWGIA), the Netherlands Centre for Indigenous Peoples (NCIV), and the Indigenous Peoples' Center for Documentation, Research and Information (doCip). They, along with the Canada-based Rights and Democracy, which was created by an Act of Parliament,[7] played critical support roles by providing travel funding and other resources such as translation, interpretation, and technical support. These resources made it possible for many Indigenous representatives to travel annually to Geneva to participate in the two working groups.

In order for the Indigenous Peoples' Caucus in Geneva to function effectively, it was necessary to provide interpretation in several languages. doCip provided technical support — including a room of computers, available every day — and the translation of caucus documents. This quiet background support over the life of the two working groups made a significant contribution in assuring that Indigenous peoples' voices were heard at the table, both by each other and by states.

Quakers participated at the WGDD under the auspices of the Quaker United Nations Office (QUNO), with staff from the American Friends Service Committee and the Canadian Friends Service Committee (CFSC).[8] Major human rights organizations with permanent offices at the United Nations — Amnesty International, International Service for Human Rights, and the International Federation of Human Rights Leagues (FIDH) — also participated as observers. All these organizations have longstanding existing relationships in the UN system and with each other, and collaborated on support for the *Declaration*.

NGOs were generally cautious in their participation in the WGDD, because it was essential that non-state involvement be led by representatives of Indigenous peoples. The NGOs therefore worked in a manner that complemented the strategies established by the Indigenous Peoples' Caucus. While NGO representatives were not part of the caucus, we were included by many as partners, and over time relationships grew. It was clear that the NGOs would engage in the direction set by the Indigenous Peoples' Caucus, but would not speak on its behalf. Like all good relationships, this one took time to develop and time for trust to grow.

In the first years of the WGDD, the NGOs were mainly silent observers. Their attendance was, in part, to "bear witness" to the process, and ensure that state representatives knew that the human rights community was monitoring developments. As negotiations moved into the final stages, after the majority of the Indigenous Peoples' Caucus decided to move past the "no change"[9] position, the NGO role began to grow.

Many Indigenous peoples' representatives recognized that human rights NGOs could play a role in convincing state representatives to engage more collaboratively with Indigenous peoples. Those that came to be involved, such as the Quakers and Amnesty International, were seen by states as defenders of the human rights system rather than advocates for Indigenous rights. The support of these NGOs helped remove objections by states that were based on the misguided claim that the system of universal rights required protection against "special interests." The fact that these organizations have a global membership base was important in demonstrating that there was strong public interest in seeing a timely and positive resolution of the debates.

A major contribution that the Quakers and Amnesty brought to the work was their long-standing relationships at the UN. These organizations have ongoing interactions with many government representatives and an international reputation as human rights defenders.[10] Both the Quakers and Amnesty International are past recipients of the Nobel Peace Prize — the Quakers in 1947 and Amnesty in 1977 — for international peace, justice, humanitarian, and human rights work.

In engaging state representatives, we spoke as human rights defenders. Our existing relationships facilitated access to state representatives to discuss human rights. It was clear that the NGOs were not trying to speak as experts on Indigenous rights. We were careful not to take a position on issues of process or substance where the Indigenous Peoples' Caucus itself was still working to achieve a common position.

Substantive discussions with Indigenous representatives enabled some NGOs to show how the arguments that were being presented by Indigenous representatives fit into the broader human rights system and existing international human rights law. This was an issue for many states. It was important to clarify that the *Declaration* was not about creating new rights, but ensuring that international human rights law was inclusive of "all members of the human family."[11] The process creating the *Declaration* examined the international human rights system and elaborated Indigenous rights within it. Human rights NGOs often had the credibility to make that argument because of their mandates and prior achievements. Professor Steve Charnovitz explains in more general terms:

> What made international law susceptible to being influenced by NGOs? One of the earliest insights was the NGO advantage in being independent. NGOs can be more creative than government officials because NGOs are not burdened with the need to champion a particular national or governmental interest.[12]

In effect, NGOs adopted a different approach to achieve a common goal. The work complemented that of the Indigenous Peoples' Caucus and, at every stage, was carried out in dialogue with Indigenous partners. During the final years of negotiations, the majority of the Indigenous Peoples' Caucus presented joint positions on critical issues, and human rights NGOs were invited to add their names to these written submissions. Many NGOs endorsed these documents, which were consistent with international human rights law and its progressive development.[13]

Many states in the WGDD adopted a neutral position and were willing to engage with human rights NGOs. Some states had little knowledge of the issues and little experience working with Indigenous peoples. Certain states were hindered by assumptions that human rights dealt almost exclusively with individuals. Others seemed to perceive Indigenous peoples' cultures, identities, and traditions as either irrelevant or possibly a threat. As protectors and advocates of human rights, NGOs could reiterate to states the credibility and legitimacy of Indigenous peoples' positions. An issue of central significance in the draft declaration, for example, was that the collective rights of Indigenous peoples are human rights.[14]

3. NGO INITIATIVES TO SUPPORT THE DECLARATION

NGOs sought to use their influence in a number of ways, both publicly and privately. In addition to the dialogue with state representatives, this included issuing press releases, developing educational materials, making statements to the working group, convening informal meetings of states and Indigenous representatives, and hosting side events at related UN meetings.

NGOs organized a side event in 2005 at the Commission on Human Rights. The event featured the then High Commissioner for Human Rights, Louise Arbour, as well as the then Special Rapporteur on the situation of human rights and fundamental freedoms of indigenous people, Professor Rodolfo Stavenhagen. The panel was completed by three key representatives from the Indigenous Caucus: Dalee Sambo Dorough of Alaska, Mililani Trask of Hawai'i, and Wilton Littlechild of Canada. The panel was chaired by Rachel Brett of the Quaker United Nations Office.

This was the first time that Louise Arbour, as High Commissioner, spoke publicly on Indigenous peoples' rights, and there was high anticipation for her speech. It was the only NGO event during the six-week session of the Commission on Human Rights to feature the High Commissioner. Arbour accepted our invitation to speak because she felt the draft declaration and Indigenous peoples' human rights were important and the working group was at a critical period in terms of negotiating the text.

The event created a high level of visibility for the draft declaration in the Commission on Human Rights, among other human rights organizations working at the Commission on various issues, and among the state representatives that were not engaged in the *Declaration* process. A publication was subsequently produced in English, French, and Spanish, containing the speeches of all the panelists.[15] The booklet proved useful in our ongoing discussions with state representatives. The views of the High Commissioner on the draft declaration and the rights of Indigenous peoples were influential with numerous states.

At the request of our Indigenous partners, NGOs assisted in facilitating key meetings among Indigenous peoples themselves, between sessions of the working group. Logistical and financial support were provided to bring Indigenous representatives from all regions of the globe, conduct meetings in several languages, and assist with producing and circulating documentation. This gave practical assistance to our Indigenous partners in the development of caucus positions.

Another contribution the Quakers made throughout the process was to facilitate dialogue between representatives of the Indigenous Peoples' Caucus and states. In both Geneva and New York, Quaker House was frequently used to host informal, off-the-record meetings. State representatives know that the space is hospitable and safe, a place where people are looking to resolve disputes and move the conversation forward.

Some of these meetings focused on a geographical region. Many African states, for example, were not following the WGDD; at the request of African Indigenous organizations, we hosted gatherings with representatives of African states and African Indigenous peoples. The first one was held in Geneva. One of the African Indigenous participants later remarked that it was the first time that African state and Indigenous representatives had engaged at that level in Geneva.

The many meetings at Quaker House wer e about creating an inviting and reflective space for dialogue, encouraging a level of substantive conversation and engagement that was not easily attained within the UN. Such events fostered new understandings and good will that frequently extended into the future. On various levels, significant progress was achieved.

Human rights NGOs also co-ordinated to produce joint statements and press releases.[16] The objective was to raise the visibility of the draft declaration as a critical element in the larger international human rights system. Human rights representatives were continually stressing the fact that the draft declaration was not "just" about Indigenous rights, but constitutes a vital contribution to international human rights law. It is the most comprehensive, universal international instrument expressly devoted to the human rights of Indigenous peoples. If states were to deny Indigenous peoples' rights, they would be undermining the international human rights system itself. This would be inconsistent with the purposes and principles of the *UN Charter* and would violate corresponding state obligations.[17]

4. PARTNERSHIPS DURING THE FINAL YEAR IN NEW YORK

After the declaration was adopted by the Human Rights Council in June 2006,[18] the final step was adoption by the General Assembly in New York, expected in the fall of 2006. When the General Assembly agreed to a nine-month delay to allow for "further consultations,"[19] it came as quite a shock. There was a real possibility that, if states were allowed to re-open negotiations, the text would be so diminished as to be lost.

In this last crucial stage, states appeared to gain control over the fate of the declaration. The Indigenous Peoples' Caucus urgently strategized on how best to manage this unexpected development. The caucus met in January 2007 in New York, and a few NGOs were invited to that meeting. The conclusion was a firm commitment to the Human Rights Council text, and initiatives were planned to garner the number of states needed to win the vote in the General Assembly. Les Malezer of Australia was appointed chair of the Indigenous Peoples' Caucus, and took up temporary residence in New York. Regional co-ordinators were appointed as focal points for information-sharing with Indigenous peoples around the globe.

During the period from January 2007 until the final adoption in September 2007, the Quakers and Amnesty International used our respective bases in New York to work in support of the caucus. During this period I worked in New York with Renzo Pomi of Amnesty International and international human rights lawyer, Paul Joffe. New York was different from Geneva in various ways. State representatives in New

York had little or no history with Indigenous representatives and their unique role in the UN, and some did not appear to have the necessary knowledge of international human rights law, especially in relation to Indigenous peoples.

At the same time, NGOs were in a beneficial position, as state representatives generally regarded us as neutral parties devoted to human rights. As a result, many responded more openly to Quakers and Amnesty International than to the Indigenous Peoples' Caucus. The NGO work was carried out in close contact with the caucus chair, but clearly distinguished from that of the caucus.

As the Quakers and Amnesty have worked on countless issues in New York, there was again liberal access to state representatives owing to pre-existing relationships with them. And again, we presented the voice of human rights in support of the positions of Indigenous peoples and of the international human rights system. We had individual meetings with dozens of state representatives, carefully explaining how the declaration strengthened the existing human rights system and answering questions about the meaning and effect of the declaration.

NGOs shared the concern that attempting to weaken the Human Rights Council text would lead to the failure of the UN to realize a meaningful declaration on the rights of Indigenous peoples. States needed to know that, although the Indigenous Peoples' Caucus could not vote in the General Assembly, supportive states had made a commitment that a text would not go forward if the caucus was not supportive. Several human right organizations also made it clear to states that, if the final text were rejected by the Indigenous Peoples' Caucus, the human rights community would also reject it.

Owing to the critical role of the African Group of States, many meetings were held with African state representatives. As well as discussing the declaration, we also respectfully explained how it was wholly compatible within the regional African human rights system. When the African Group of States produced a document in May 2007 that proposed wide-ranging changes to the declaration, we respectfully illustrated how these changes violated existing international human rights law, as well as regional African standards. The document, which bears neither date nor name, includes over 30 amendments to the text adopted by the Human Rights Council. Several African ambassadors took a keen and principled interest in these arguments, and we were informed in due course that the May 2007 document should be viewed as an "initial" proposal that was open to revision.

Representatives from the Indigenous Peoples of Africa Co-ordinating Committee (IPACC), an umbrella organization consisting of about 155 Indigenous organizations in 22 African countries, could not be present in New York for extended periods. IPACC nevertheless supported and encouraged our diplomatic dialogues, sending useful information on developments in the African continent.

We collaborated closely with IPACC and shared its substantive materials with African states.[20]

Regretfully, many state representatives appeared not to take a human rights approach to the declaration. New York is very political, and it often appeared that positions were being taken based on "horse trading" rather than respect for the human rights of Indigenous peoples. Greater progress was made with state representatives who were well-versed in human rights and used their knowledge and experience to increase support for the declaration.

5. PARTNERSHIPS IN CANADA

If one took at face value the public positions of the Conservative government of Canada, one would conclude that there is a strong and healthy engagement between the government and NGOs. For example, in 2007, then Foreign Affairs Minister Peter MacKay declared that "civil society has made Canada grow to become strong and free. . . . Civil society and NGOs have the credibility, and the singularity of purpose, that can allow them to succeed where governments cannot."[21]

Similarly, the Canadian government took a highly positive position when its human rights record was reviewed in the Human Rights Council's Universal Periodic Review (UPR) in February 2009. In Canada's opening statement, Deputy Minister of Justice John Sims stated that, in Canada "respect for human rights has become very much a part of our national discourse. This public discussion of human rights is on-going. . . . It is a prominent theme in civil society initiatives. . . . We view the participation of civil society as an important aspect of the UPR process."[22]

The reality is that the government failed to consult NGOs and Indigenous peoples in Canada in preparing its National Report for the UPR,[23] despite the fact that "states are encouraged to prepare the information through a broad consultation process at the national level with all relevant stakeholders."[24] The government failed even to mention the *Declaration*, likely because of its international and domestic strategy to oppose it.

The actions of the Canadian government against the *Declaration* reinforced the need for co-ordinated strategies among Indigenous and human rights NGOs. In Canada there is a small and active *ad hoc* coalition which has collaborated for several years on the *Declaration*. It consists of most national Aboriginal organizations (NAOs), some regional Aboriginal organizations, Indigenous nations, human rights and faith-based organizations. This *ad hoc* coalition was built over several years, as trust developed in relationships based on a common goal. Now that the *Declaration* has been adopted, the coalition is working on implementation, including human rights education, and initiatives to have Canada endorse and implement it.

Individuals in the *ad hoc* coalition bring different skills and assets to the work. By working together, coalition members are collectively much stronger. The coalition's work influenced the previous Liberal government in a positive direction, with daily meetings with Canadian representatives during the WGDD sessions. There were also meetings domestically between sessions. Unfortunately, those relationships were damaged by the Conservative government that came to power in 2006. Collaborative meetings with officials ended. In the few meetings called by the government, human rights and faith-based organizations were deliberately excluded. Some representatives of Indigenous peoples and organizations that had been actively involved in the UN standard-setting process on the *Declaration* for over two decades were abruptly excluded from meetings with the government on the premise that they were not representing NAOs. In response, NAO partners invited the excluded NGO and Indigenous representatives to attend the meetings as part of their own delegations.

The position of the government moved Canada from being a strong supporter of Indigenous rights to being an opponent, and resistance to the *Declaration* did not stop with the resounding vote in favour of the *Declaration* in the UN General Assembly. The government's ideological approach created a considerable amount of domestic work for the *ad hoc* coalition.

The coalition has positively influenced and gained the support of the three opposition parties and the Parliamentary Standing Committee on Aboriginal Affairs. This support was solidified in January 2008 with a breakfast briefing in Parliament for members of Parliament and senators to learn about the *Declaration* and its importance. These relationships contributed to the successful adoption of the April 2008 motion in the House of Commons to endorse the *Declaration* and implement the minimal standards it requires. Only Conservative MPs in Canada's minority government opposed the motion.[25]

In May 2008 the *ad hoc* coalition released an open letter,[26] endorsed by more than 100 experts in the fields of Indigenous rights and constitutional and international law, disputing Canada's arguments for not supporting the *Declaration*. Some of our organizations also issued a joint press release to accompany the letter.[27] All these materials were then used in international forums, such as the UN Permanent Forum on Indigenous Issues, the UN Expert Mechanism on the Rights of Indigenous Peoples, the UN Human Rights Council's Working Group on Universal Periodic Review, and the Organization of American States' Working Group to draft an American Declaration on the Rights of Indigenous Peoples.

Other states proved very interested in the open letter and the motion adopted by Parliament, particularly in the UPR process concerning Canada. In the February 2009 UPR meeting on Canada, a number of states questioned Canada on its opposition to the *Declaration* and recommended that it reconsider its position.[28] Norway stated:

We believe the UN Declaration on the Rights of Indigenous Peoples is unique as a universal framework for improving implementation of existing rights of indigenous peoples in all countries of the world. We would therefore recommend the Government of Canada to reconsider its position and endorse the UN Declaration on the rights of indigenous peoples....[29]

In September 2009, to mark the second anniversary of the adoption of the *Declaration*, the *ad hoc* coalition released a comprehensive report detailing the global progress on implementation as well as the ongoing challenges.[30] The press release announcing the report stated:

The report shows that in the two years since the adoption of the *Declaration*, governments, UN agencies, and regional and national courts and human rights bodies have increasingly turned to the *Declaration* for guidance in implementing measures to protect the rights of Indigenous peoples....

"The *UN Declaration on the Rights of Indigenous Peoples* is the best available tool to address the longstanding human rights violations facing Indigenous Peoples worldwide," says Assembly of First Nations National Chief Shawn Atleo. "It's time for the government of Canada to follow the example of other governments and institutions around the world and support its implementation."[31]

In both domestic and international settings, the *ad hoc* coalition prepares joint statements, holds press conferences, organizes events, and produces educational materials. The information sharing among all the organizations is invaluable. The partnerships work because they are based on mutual trust and respect. It is understood that we all have different roles to play. These roles complement each other and strengthen the work of all participants. This co-operation took time and energy to build, and we are mutually supportive in maintaining these partnerships.

6. IMPLEMENTATION OF THE DECLARATION

The implementation of UN human rights declarations occurs in various ways at both the domestic and international levels. Internalization of the instrument is critical in Canada and other states. As affirmed in the *UN Declaration on Human Rights Defenders*, "Each state has a prime responsibility and duty to protect, promote, and implement all human rights and fundamental freedoms."[32] Internalization occurs as we use the *Declaration* in many ways. The more it is referenced and used, the more internalization and implementation increase.

In contrast to treaties or conventions, the *Declaration* is generally considered to be a non-binding instrument. However, as confirmed by the former Chief Justice of the Supreme Court of Norway, Carsten Smith, "this does not mean that the Declaration is without any legally binding effect."[33] Such "soft law" instruments are increasingly a primary form of standard-setting at the international level, and can have far-reaching significance. This is especially true in regard to the *Declaration*, since it was adopted overwhelmingly by the General Assembly.[34]

The partnerships between Indigenous peoples and non-Indigenous NGOs are engaged with implementation in many ways. Human rights education is an important aspect of implementation. In July 2008, the *ad hoc* coalition produced an illustrated pocket-sized booklet of the *Declaration* in both French and English. The booklet has received wide distribution and is immensely popular. The thought behind it was that for people to support the *Declaration*, they have to know what it is. We encourage people to take it, read it, share it, and engage with it.[35]

The *ad hoc* coalition has been trying to work with the media, which we find quite difficult. Repeatedly, we are startled to see the negative spin of the Canadian government represented in the mainstream media. The persistence of the government's spin illustrates the need for continued solidarity and collaboration. When politicians and the media can portray the protection of human rights as a threat to Canadian values or the public[36] because the rights holders are Indigenous, human rights organizations need to speak out. Letters to the editor are often not printed, and press statements go unnoticed. Continued efforts are needed on a number of fronts.

More public events, such as the symposium that kindled this publication, are needed across the country. Members of the *ad hoc* coalition have had opportunities to speak in various forums which are essential for engaging the public. We are working on engaging churches, trade unions, other NGOs, human rights bodies, professional organizations, and educational institutions. Partners from the *ad hoc* coalition are presenting workshops in Indigenous communities to discuss the *Declaration*. We are filming the workshops to produce an educational DVD which will be widely distributed for people to learn about what the *Declaration* is, where it came from, why it is important and how we can use it.

The *Declaration* needs to be understood and respected by all Canadians. As Louise Arbour has emphatically stated, "Canada's vote against a United Nations declaration of aboriginal rights was an 'astonishing' move for a country that claims to be a model of tolerance and diversity."[37]

In November 2008, Craig Benjamin of Amnesty International Canada and I were part of a Presidential Panel organized by the Centre for Economic and Social Aspects of Genomics, University of Lancaster, UK, at the annual meeting of the American Anthropological Association (AAA) in San Francisco. This is a major professional gathering, with more than 5,000 participants. The panel also included Les Malezer and Mililani Trask. We all spoke to our involvement and to the implementation of the *Declaration*. We also offered suggestions as to how this academic professional association could integrate the document in meaningful ways to promote the rights in the *Declaration*.

The organizers of the AAA panel expressed their satisfaction with the turnout and level of engagement of the participants. They plan to follow up with specific suggestions, including examining the code of ethics used by their membership, with a view to integrating the *Declaration* as a standard in their work.

National faith-based bodies, such as the Quakers, are formally endorsing the *Declaration* and encouraging members to familiarize themselves with it, and to use the standards therein in all their engagements with Indigenous peoples.

It would be beneficial to teach the *Declaration* in schools, at all levels. We know this is happening in various settings, and now it needs to be formally included in curriculum development. Teachers' and students' federations have contacted us for copies of the *Declaration* booklet and resources to educate their members. Policy makers in diverse disciplines should familiarize themselves with the rights affirmed in the *Declaration* and work to ensure that current policies are in line with them.

7. IMPLEMENTATION OF THE SPECIAL RAPPORTEUR'S RECOMMENDATIONS

In October 2006, members of the *ad hoc* coalition organized a two-day forum in Ottawa on the implementation of the work of the UN Special Rapporteur on the situation of human rights and fundamental freedoms of indigenous people. Immediately following, in Montreal, there was a three-day international expert seminar on the implementation of the Special Rapporteur's work on a global scale.

The Canadian Forum, whose theme was "Closing the Implementation Gap," looked at the Special Rapporteur's recommendations in his official report on Canada following his visit in 2004.[38] The forum was organized by the Assembly of First Nations, the Native Women's Association of Canada, the Grand Council of the Crees (Eeyou Istchee), Amnesty International Canada, the Canadian Friends Service Committee, and Rights and Democracy, with the co-operation of the UN Special Rapporteur on the situation of human rights and fundamental freedoms of indigenous people.

The forum examined whether the recommendations are being implemented and, if not, how they should be realized. The organizers produced a report, which contains text from the presentations as well as recommendations on how to move forward.[39] One recommendation is to establish a permanent agenda item for the federal standing committees in Parliament that focus on foreign affairs, human rights, and Aboriginal affairs. This agenda item would be to examine UN reports that contain recommendations on Indigenous peoples and discuss their implementation in Canada. The adoption of the *Declaration* by the General Assembly adds a new and essential dimension to this recommendation. Clearly, these recommendations must be implemented in the spirit and context of the *Declaration*. This is one important means of implementation at the national level.

The international expert meeting on the global implementation of the Special Rapporteur's work led to the production of a book, *The UN Special Rapporteur: Indigenous Peoples Rights: Experiences and Challenges*, available in English, French, and Spanish.[40] The book addresses a number of questions:

- What is the mechanism of the Special Rapporteur?
- What is the nature and scope of his or her work?
- How can Indigenous peoples gain access to and benefit from this mechanism?
- How can one implement the recommendations of the Special Rapporteur?

This, again, was a joint project among human rights and Indigenous organizations. The major recommendation that came from the seminar was that one cannot just expect the implementation of Indigenous peoples' rights. State governments need to be engaged, and they must honour their international obligations. A key conclusion drawn from the work of the Special Rapporteur is that the greatest level of implementation must take place at the grassroots levels. It must occur in Indigenous communities and with NGOs in the society of each state.

These findings are consistent with those of international jurists. In regard to the persistent and pervasive human rights violations taking place in different regions of the world, Professor Antonio Cassese concludes:

Collective efforts must be made at all levels — not only by governments, but also, and above all, unofficially, by individuals, groups, associations, and other non-governmental bodies. To be sure, gross breaches of human rights will not cease overnight. What matters, however, is that one should not stop being indignant at such violations. As long as officials responsible for those breaches are called to account and other governments are prodded to react forcefully to oppression and injustice, there may be some hope of stemming inhumanity.[41]

In addressing human rights issues globally and in states, the conclusions from both the "Closing the Implementation Gap" forum and the international expert seminar translate easily to the implementation of the *Declaration*. The *Declaration* elaborates the economic, social, cultural, political, and spiritual rights of Indigenous peoples. Such rights are indivisible from and interrelated with the rights under other international human rights instruments. The *Vienna Declaration* put it succinctly: "All human rights are universal, indivisible, interdependent, and interrelated. The international community must treat human rights globally in a fair and equal manner, on the same footing, and with the same emphasis."[42]

In addressing this challenging work, it is beneficial to build on the partnerships that have been forged between Indigenous peoples and human rights organizations. Indigenous partners continue to take the lead, with the NGO partners playing a supportive role, engaging in solidarity in the promotion and protection of human rights, and helping to ensure compliance. Based on past experiences, such efforts produce tangible results.

8. Conclusion

The *United Nations Declaration on the Rights of Indigenous Peoples* is an essential catalyst for achievement and well-being. On a global basis, it is also generating renewed hope. As Victoria Tauli-Corpuz eloquently states:

The Declaration is an important instrument for indigenous peoples for their liberation from discrimination and oppression. Its implementation, however, will be an uphill struggle. Edmund Burke's exhortation that the "price of freedom is eternal vigilance" very much applies to us, indigenous peoples, and to our supporters. Indeed, the price for our assertion to be recognized as distinct peoples, and to have our rights, as contained in the UN Declaration on the Rights of Indigenous Peoples, protected, respected, and fulfilled is eternal vigilance.[43]

Such vigilance requires strategic and co-ordinated networks. Dynamic and challenging goals need to be constantly renewed and fulfilled. The international human rights of the world's Indigenous peoples must be exercised and enjoyed freely and fully at the grassroots level.

It is an honour to work with Indigenous partners on the advancement of the rights of Indigenous peoples. The *Declaration* reinforces the international human rights system as a whole, benefitting all states, peoples, and individuals. In the global Indigenous context, a human rights-based approach should be an integral part of any objective or strategy. Experience shows that, in order for the *Declaration* to have genuine meaning and effect concrete change, NGOs should continue to work in partnership with Indigenous peoples.

In a joint statement on the day of the adoption, human rights organizations emphasized:

> Adoption of the Declaration sends a clear message to the international community that the rights of Indigenous peoples are not separate from or less than the rights of others, but are an integral and indispensable part of a human rights systems dedicated to the rights of all. . . . These organizations call on all states to seize the historic opportunity presented by adoption of the Declaration to enter into a new relationship with Indigenous peoples based on a principled commitment to the protection of human rights.[44]

Our partnerships are about realizing these aspirations.

○

PART III

Treaty Rights and Free, Prior, and Informed Consent

Essential Aspects of Self-Determination

Consistent Advocacy
Treaty Rights and the UN Declaration

◇

Chief Wilton Littlechild

For many Indigenous peoples, the need for our treaty rights to be recognized and respected was key to our involvement in the international arena. After years of effort, the spirit and intent of our treaties, as understood by our elders, is now reflected in the *United Nations Declaration on the Rights of Indigenous Peoples* (*Declaration*). In this chapter, I provide an overview of the history of the treaty provisions in the document, and pay tribute to those who paved the way for the adoption of the *Declaration* by the UN General Assembly on 13 September 2007.

This chapter is dedicated to the warriors, particularly the law warriors, whose advocacy for our rights led to the adoption of the *Declaration*. I would especially like to honour the work of the late Chiefs Joe Mathias and George Manuel. In the 1970s, when we used to have annual meetings of Indian lawyers, we could have met in any restaurant in Canada at a table for five. There are now over 1,000 lawyers working as Indigenous professionals.

In 1975, my cousin the late Ed Burnstick said to me, "Willie, get packing because we're going to Wounded Knee." I was in the middle of my law exams and was unable to attend. However, the seeds of the *Declaration* were sown there, at Wounded Knee, where Indigenous peoples began drafting their first statement of principles which was the forerunner to the *Declaration*.[1]

My involvement in international advocacy began in July 1977. The Executive Director of the office of the late Chief George Manuel contacted me and said, "Willie, there's going to be a meeting in Sweden, and we're looking for a chairman to convene a session on ILO Convention 107.[2] But you don't have to tell us right away, we'll give you a couple of weeks to think about it and we'll phone you back." When they phoned back, I said, "Yeah, I'd love to go to Sweden. I don't know about this chairman thing, and what the heck is Convention 107?"

"Don't worry about it," they said. "We'll fax it to you."

So there I was on a plane to Sweden with a Maskwacîs delegation. Our elders had told us to be always mindful of treaty principles. They reminded us that "the sun, the water, and all the grasses, in particular, sweet grass" are treaty principles.

The elders gave us the fundamental principles on which we were to go into the international arena. I am not sure how to say in English what those mean in terms of treaty making, but we have a word for it in Cree: *kakitipahakek*. In 1979, for the first time, the elders started writing down the rights based on the spirit and intent of treaty as they understood it.

When I look back to those first ceremonies where the elders gave us their advice, I look fondly on the *Declaration* because it incorporates all the principles they had given us.

Treaties, in particular Treaty No. 6, were the reason we turned our attention to international advocacy.[3] Our elders convened us before the Elders Council at Panee Agri Plex, Hobbema, and said, "We're very, very disappointed at how readily our treaties are being violated, almost on a daily basis." So, it was with a mission not only to protect and maintain our treaties, but to strengthen them, that we embarked on this journey in the international arena over 30 years ago.

We took every opportunity to assert our rights. In 1982, Canada patriated its constitution, which gave us an early venue in which to assert our rights. We went to Britain's High Courts in London, accompanied by legal consultants Sharon Venne and Rodney Soonias. I remember days in court when there were 27 lawyers on one side defending Canada and five of us on the other side defending our treaty rights. Our treaty had been negotiated and concluded with the Queen's representativ es, and we did not believe this relationship could be unilaterally severed. We were also trying to make sure that, before the constitution was patriated, the treaties were going to be entrenched in it.[4]

Back then, ILO Convention 107 was the only international law explicitly relating to Indigenous peoples. However, its assimilationist language was out-dated and "destructive."[5] When I studied the document, I realized that it did not contain one word about treaties. It focused mainly on economic, social, and cultural rights, while civil and political rights were largely omitted.

The International Labour Organization (ILO) adopted another convention in 1989: *Indigenous and Tribal Peoples Convention, 1989* (ILO Convention No. 169).[6] However, we were told when the convention was being drafted that we could not include the right to self-determination because that responsibility belonged with the UN. As the ILO explained, it had

worked for three years during the adoption of the Convention to decide whether or not to change the term "populations" in Convention No. 107

to the term "peoples" in the new Convention. . . . It was finally agreed that the only correct term was "peoples," because this term recognizes the existence of organized societies with an identity of their own rather than mere groupings sharing some racial or cultural characteristics. . . . It was also decided that it was outside the competence of the ILO to determine how the term "self-determination" should be interpreted in general international law. It was understood, however, that the Convention does not impose any limitation on self-determination nor take any position for or against self-determination.[7]

The limitations of the ILO conventions inspired us to focus our efforts at the UN. To us, Treaty No. 6 was evidence of our right to self-determination. This is a crucial point for Canada and other states to understand. As an inherent part of our right to self-determination, we freely determined our relations in Treaty No. 6 with the Queen's representatives.[8] A central purpose of our treaty was to ensure the security[9] and well-being[10] of the Maskwacîs Cree citizens, for present and future generations. An essential element of our right of self-determination is a right to choose — a right to determine our own future. As the Royal Commission on Aboriginal Peoples confirmed, "[s]elf-determination refers to the collective power of choice; self-government is one possible result of that choice."[11]

If we did not have the inherent right of self-determination, we could not appear before international bodies as distinct peoples defending our treaty and treaty rights. As a 2009 Report of the Office of the High Commissioner for Human Rights affirms, "[w]hile the right to self-determination is a collective right held by peoples rather than individuals, its realization is an essential condition for the effective enjoyment of individual human rights."[12]

For diverse reasons, then, it was important that we concentrated on developing a UN declaration. It was especially important that our treaties and our right of self-determination were affirmed and protected in international and domestic law. In 1985, the Working Group on Indigenous Populations (WGIP) began to develop a draft declaration on the rights of Indigenous peoples.[13] In 1986, the meetings were cancelled for budgetary reasons. Indigenous peoples around the world recognized that this could cause the drafting process to lose momentum, or even give states a chance to terminate the work of the WGIP.

So we convened our own meeting, paid for it ourselves, and rented rooms at the UN in Geneva. I had the honour of co-chairing that meeting, and it was there that we consolidated our previous work into one text, including the principles that came out of the 1975 meeting at Wounded Knee. Indigenous representatives presented a joint statement that included treaty principles to the chair of the WGIP.

We argued that the WGIP should begin with these articles, especially those that represented an Indigenous declaration on treaties. We did not succeed, unfortunately, and the WGIP began to draft from scratch.

In 1987, we again presented our statements of principles to the UN, and our efforts began to be noticed. In 1989, the UN Commission on Human Rights commissioned a study on treaties. Based on the recommendations of the final report of this study,[14] two treaty seminars were held, one in Geneva and one on the Maskwacîs Cree territory in the Treaty No. 6 area.[15]

We sought to raise treaty issues in other UN expert meetings. In 1990 an Expert Meeting on Indigenous Self-Government was held in Nuuk, Greenland, where our treaties were explicitly considered.[16] Further UN expert seminars were held on various key issues, such as public administration of justice (Spain),[17] health (Geneva),[18] and secondary education (Paris).[19] At each of those meetings, the Maskwacîs Cree delegation presented interventions to ensure that there was a reference to treaties in the reports of the meetings, because our elders had said, "these are treaty rights."

In 1995, the Commission on Human Rights established another working group to further consider the draft declaration.[20] In the last years of this intersessional working group, I was co-chair of the meetings on the provisions relating to treaties, especially article 37 (at the time it was article 36). A Canadian government representative was the other co-chair.

Our efforts, and those of many other Indigenous peoples and state representatives, ultimately resulted in significant provisions on treaty rights in the *Declaration*. Virtually all the provisions of the *Declaration* can be related to treaties.

Preambular paragraph 7 contains a reference to "recognizing the urgent need to respect and promote the inherent rights of indigenous peoples." It was important that the *Declaration* recognize our inherent rights. In addition, preambular paragraph 14 states, "the rights affirmed in treaties, agreements and the constructive arrangements between States and indigenous peoples are, in some situations, matters of international concern, interest, responsibility and character." Again, our elders believed that the treaties signed in the 19th and early 20th centuries were international in nature, made with Queen Victoria on behalf of the Crown of Great Britain and Northern Ireland. So it was important for us to make sure that the *Declaration* referred to the "international character" of treaties, and that it recognized "also that treaties, agreements and other constructive arrangements, and the relationship they represent, are the basis for a strengthened partnership between indigenous peoples and States."[21]

Article 37 of the *Declaration* is the key article on treaties. Article 36 of the text approved by the Sub-Commission on Prevention of Discrimination and Protection of Minorities on 24 August 1994 contained a reference to "the right to the recognition, observance and enforcement of treaties, agreements and other constructive arrangements concluded with States or their successors, according to their original spirit and intent."[22] The Indigenous Peoples' Caucus removed the reference to "original spirit and intent" because we were concerned that states too often considered that the "original spirit and intent" of treaties was to steal our land.[23]

We looked at the original spirit and intent of treaties based on the principles our elders had conveyed to us regarding Indian government and nationhood. Our elders referred to the spirit and intent of treaties in terms of such things as Indian institutions and administration, lands and water and other resources, education and health, social assistance, police protection, economic development, hunting, fishing, trapping and gathering, as well as the right to cross international boundaries, to meet in council, and the right to shelter, mutual consent, and implementation.

As adopted, the *Declaration* contains an article or a preambular paragraph relating to each of these elements. We felt that removing the reference to the "spirit and intent" of treaties did not disadvantage us, because this understanding could be read into all the articles. Such an interpretive approach would be consistent with the report from the first seminar on treaties, held in December 2003, which concluded, "that historic treaties, agreements and other constructive arrangements between States and indigenous peoples should be understood and implemented in accordance with the spirit in which they were agreed upon."[24]

The report emphasizes what is at stake: "historic treaties, agreements and other constructive arrangements between States and indigenous peoples have not been respected, leading to loss of lands, resources and rights, and that non-implementation threatens indigenous peoples' survival as distinct peoples."[25]

Although Canada, the United States, New Zealand, and Australia opposed the *Declaration*, not one state took the floor of the General Assembly to argue against article 37. The current Conservative government of Canada has not opposed the treaty provisions. In the last years leading to the conclusion of the working group in 2006, a Canadian government representative and I together led the informal consultations with states and Indigenous peoples on the draft declaration's treaty provisions. These consultations led to overwhelming agreement in the working group.

We tend to focus attention on the disagreements, but we should not ignore the agreement on a substantial number of articles, including articles relating to treaties, for there is widespread agreement among states on article 37 of the *Declaration*. The United States appeared to be the only country to oppose this article at the conclusion of the discussions in the intersessional working group in 2006. However, there are clear indications that President Barack Obama intends to take a supportive position on treaties:

> My Indian policy starts with honouring the unique government-to-government relationship between tribes and the federal government and ensuring that our treaty obligations are met, and ensuring that Native Americans have a voice in the White House. I'll appoint an American Indian policy advisor to my senior White House staff to work with tribes. . . . So let me be clear. I believe that treaty commitments are paramount law.[26]

First Lady Michelle Obama has further confirmed on the president's behalf:

> Barack has pledged to honor the unique government-to-government relationship between tribes and the federal government. And he'll soon appoint a policy advisor to his senior White House staff to work with tribes and across the government on these issues such as sovereignty, health care, education — all central to the well-being of Native American families and the prosperity of tribes all across this country. So there is a lot of work to do — a lot of work.[27]

These statements are promising. I am hopeful that there will be positive changes in the position of the United States in relation to Indigenous peoples' treaties.

In December 2003, the Canadian government acknowledged the importance of implementing treaties and resolving related disputes. At the first UN seminar on treaties, Canada concluded:

> Treaties establish ongoing relationships that require implementation planning, dispute resolution mechanisms and other ongoing mechanisms within the state to manage and sustain the treaty relationships. . . . Canada's negotiation policies and processes will need to continue to evolve to achieve workable treaties in different parts of the country.[28]

Yet the government frequently does not honour its treaties with Indigenous peoples, regardless of whether the treaties have been entered into in historic or modern times. Recently, Indigenous signatories of all of the 21 modern treaties made in Canada since 1975 — known as the Land Claims Agreements Coalition — have emphasized to the UN:

the ongoing failure of the Government of Canada to fully, meaningfully and universally implement the modern treaties between it and the members of the Coalition. . . . This failure is inconsistent with the Constitution of Canada, many judgments of the Supreme Court of Canada, and Canada's human rights obligations in international law, including the right of self-determination, the right to economic, social and cultural development and well-being, and other particular collective rights belonging and applying to indigenous peoples.[29]

Canada's highest court has emphasized that the treaties with Indigenous peoples are sacred.[30] Yet, in relation to our own Treaty No. 6, the court has set a very low standard for the Crown when it is managing our revenues in trust.[31] The Supreme Court of Canada held that the Crown had the obligation to guarantee that the trust funds of the Samson and Ermineskin Nations would be preserved and would increase, but this did not mean there was any duty to invest the funds so as to obtain a higher return. Under Treaty No. 6, the court ruled, there was no treaty right to investment by the Crown. As a result, the interest paid by the federal government on the monies of the two nations was well below the returns generated through diversified trust portfolios, long-term bond portfolios, or the pension plan of the federal government's own public servants.

In such challenging times, we recall the wisdom of our elders, and will persevere with our advocacy to safeguard our treaty rights for present and future generations. We must ensure that the standards of the *Declaration* are applied in a manner that honours our treaties and ensures the full and effective enjoyment of our treaty rights.

Article 42 of the *Declaration* is a critical provision dealing with the international and domestic implementation of our rights: "The United Nations, its bodies, including the Permanent Forum on Indigenous Issues, and specialized agencies, including at the country level, and States shall promote respect for and full application of the provisions of this Declaration and follow up the effectiveness of this Declaration."

The Permanent Forum on Indigenous Issues, an advisory body to the UN Economic and Social Council, has begun to examine how it can best fulfill its responsibilities to promote the implementation of the *Declaration*, including those provisions relating to treaties. In January 2009, the UNPFII Permanent Forum hosted an International Expert Group Meeting on the implementation of article 42 of the *United Nations Declaration on the Rights of Indigenous Peoples*. The implementation of the provisions relating to treaty rights was a focus of the meeting. Participants emphasized that the UN system "should continue its work on the treaties between

States and indigenous peoples," and "suggested that a seminar or conference on this subject be undertaken, to be hosted by a tribal nation or assembly in North America."[32]

The Permanent Forum can play an important role in promoting the implementation of the *Declaration* in the context of treaties and agreements between Indigenous nations and states. I suggested at the expert meeting that "perhaps the UN Permanent Forum could call on Treaty parties to jointly work on an implementation mechanism(s) for Treaties given the preambular paragraphs 8, 14, 15 and article 37 of the UN Declaration."[33]

Article 42 holds a great deal of promise for the full implementation of Indigenous peoples' rights, but implementation can only be achieved in conjunction with Indigenous peoples, at both the national and international level.

In the preamble, the *Declaration* is described as "a standard of achievement to be pursued in a spirit of partnership and mutual respect." This applies equally to our treaties. A principled implementation of the treaties can only encourage harmonious and co-operative relations with states. Implementation of both the *Declaration* and the treaties is a crucial element for the full and effective realization of our human rights.

The Right to Free, Prior, and Informed Consent

A Framework for Harmonious Relations and New Processes for Redress

◯

Andrea Carmen

1. FREE, PRIOR, AND INFORMED CONSENT: AN OVERVIEW

For Indigenous peoples, the right of free, prior, and informed consent (FPIC) is a prerequisite for the exercise of their fundamental right to self-determination as defined in international law. It underpins their ability to exert sovereignty over their lands and natural resources, to redress violations, and to establish the criteria for negotiations with states on matters affecting them.

Respect for Indigenous peoples' consent is essential for the implementation and ongoing viability of treaties and agreements among Indigenous peoples and other parties. As affirmed by experts at a 2003 UN seminar on treaties, agreements, and other constructive agreements between states and Indigenous peoples, "treaties, agreements and other constructive arrangements constitute a means of promoting harmonious, just and more positive relations between States and indigenous peoples because of their consensual basis and because they provide benefits to both indigenous and non-indigenous peoples."[1]

The failure of state parties to respect the right of FPIC of Indigenous nations is a principal cause of treaty contraventions and abrogations, and results in a wide range of human rights violations. The continuing validity of treaties under both national and international law reaffirms the ongoing nature of the nation-to-nation relationship between treaty parties, based on equal standing, mutual recognition, respect, and the fundamental principle of consent.

The adoption of the *United Nations Declaration on the Rights of Indigenous Peoples* by the General Assembly on 13 September 2007 was an historic step forward for Indigenous peoples. As article 43 states, the rights contained in the *Declaration* "constitute the minimum standards for the survival, dignity and well-being of the indigenous peoples of the world." The *Declaration* is applicable to all UN member states, even the four that voted against it. In its 2008 Concluding Observations on the United States, the Committee on the Elimination of Racial Discrimination recommended that the *Declaration* be used as a guide to interpret the obligations of the United States under the *International Convention on the Elimination of All Forms of Racial Discrimination*[2] relating to Indigenous peoples, notwithstanding that the US voted against the adoption of the *Declaration*.[3]

The *Declaration* includes numerous provisions affirming the right or principle of FPIC, as well as related state obligations. These provisions address such key issues as relocation of Indigenous peoples; redress (including restitution) for violations of Indigenous peoples' rights to lands, territories, and resources; development activities; environmental protection; redress pertaining to cultural, intellectual, religious, and spiritual property; and legislative or administrative measures that may affect Indigenous peoples.

The right of FPIC is an essential element for concluding nation-to-nation treaties, as well as for negotiations between Indigenous peoples and states pertaining to new agreements and constructive arrangements. It also provides a framework for Indigenous parties and states to establish, in partnership, the processes and criteria for settling disputes arising from the failure to respect and implement treaties.

2. BEYOND THE FAILED MODELS OF THE PAST

The desire of states and private interests to access Indigenous peoples' lands for mineral and other resource development has been a primary force behind the illegal acquisition and appropriation of many of the treaty lands in the United States and elsewhere. As underscored generally by the Special Rapporteur on the situation of human rights and fundamental freedoms of indigenous people,

> Wherever large-scale projects are executed in areas occupied by indigenous peoples, it is likely that their communities will undergo profound social and economic changes that the competent authorities are often incapable of understanding, much less anticipating. Sometimes the impact will be beneficial, very often it is devastating, but it is never negligible. . . . Indigenous peoples bear a disproportionate share of the social and human costs of resource-intensive and resource-extractive industries, large dams and other

infrastructure projects, logging and plantations, bio-prospecting, industrial fishing and farming, and also eco-tourism and imposed conservation projects.[4]

One example of such abuse was the confiscation of treaty lands in the Black Hills of South Dakota in response to the discovery of gold. This occurred less than a decade after the sacred Black Hills were recognized in the 1868 Fort Laramie Treaty between the United States and the Sioux Nation as belonging to the Lakota (Sioux) in perpetuity. In 1980, the US Supreme Court noted that the Court of Claims had concluded that "[a] more ripe and rank case of dishonorable dealing will never, in all probability, be found in our history."[5] The Court of Claims had also stated, "The duplicity of President Grant's course and the duress practiced on the starving Sioux, speak for themselves."[6] Despite clear acknowledgement of wrongdoing, these illegally-confiscated treaty lands have not been returned, and gold mining continues in the Black Hills.

Processes purporting to provide redress or to settle treaty violations, unilaterally established by states, frequently — and overwhelmingly — favoured state interests at the expense, and over the objections, of the Indigenous claimants. Even when Indigenous lands had been appropriated in direct violation of treaties, the rules governing claims processes almost never resulted in the return of any lands, although this was the primary or only form of acceptable redress called for by the Indigenous peoples concerned. Such processes clearly violated the rights of Indigenous peoples freely to withhold or give their consent either to the process for redress or its outcome. The Indian Claims Commission (ICC) in the United States is a key example of a failed settlement process.[7] Remedies for land and resources dispossessions were limited by Congress to monetary damages. As Professor Nell Jessup Newton emphasized, "The determination that money damages can be the only remedy for ancient wrongs inevitably shapes the kinds of wrongs that can be remedied. Ironically then, the worst crimes against tribes were the least remediable."[8]

Established by the US government in 1946 and active until it was dissolved in 1978, the ICC was a blatant example of a unilateral decision-making process by which the state party that had violated treaty rights was also the sole arbiter of the resulting claims. This had disastrous effects for Indigenous treaty nations in the US, whose rights were doubly violated by this process — first, through the confiscation of their traditional lands and resources, then through an imposed settlement process in which Indigenous treaty nations had little voice in decision-making. Their consent was not a factor in either the process or the result.

In the case of *Mary and Carrie Dann* v. *United States*,[9] submitted to the Inter-American Commission on Human Rights, Western Shoshone people contested the propriety and validity of the decision by the ICC that Western Shoshone land and treaty rights had been "extinguished" through acts of "gradual encroachment" by settlers, miners, and other non-Indians.[10] In 1974, the ICC had authorized a monetary payment to the Western Shoshone claimants based on the estimated value of the land in July 1872, the date when the ICC decided the encroachment had occurred. This amounted to 15¢ an acre plus the estimated value of mineral rights and the gold and other resources extracted before 1872.[11] However, the land and minerals had never been offered for sale by the Western Shoshone. Because the ICC authorized this payment, which was then accepted unilaterally by the US government as "trustee" for the Western Shoshone, the United States has continued to claim that the case was settled — despite the fact that the funds have been refused by most Western Shoshones.[12]

The Inter-American Commission examined the Western Shoshone land title claims as well as the settlement process, and concluded that "these processes were not sufficient to comply with contemporary international human rights norms, principles and standards that govern the determination of indigenous property interests."[13] The UN Committee on the Elimination of Racial Discrimination also expressed concern that the US's position was "made on the basis of processes before the Indian Claims Commission, 'which did not comply with contemporary international human rights norms'... as stressed by the Inter-American Commission on Human Rights."[14]

Self-serving policies and practices have been the norm in most countries that have concluded treaties with Indigenous peoples. New Zealand's Treaty of Waitangi Settlements Process, for example, established to redress violations of the 1840 Treaty of Waitangi, resulted mostly in monetary settlements rather than the return of lands appropriated from the Maori in violation of the treaty. Most Maori land claims remain outstanding, with Maori land ownership in 2008 totaling only five per cent of the country's land.[15]

In all these countries, including Canada, the state treaty parties or their successor states have continued to assert that they have sole jurisdiction to determine and control the process of redress for treaty violations. They unilaterally establish procedures and timelines, decide if any violations have occurred, and set the terms and parameters (referred to as "fiscal caps" in New Zealand) for compensation when and if violations are recognized.

Maori scholar Craig Coxhead writes:

When we think of negotiation, words such as compromise, bargaining, competition and cooperation come to mind. However, there is a lack of negotiation in the Direct Negotiations process. The Government has set the procedures to be followed. . . . This is not negotiable and . . . was essentially imposed on Maori. The Government has set the total pool of money that it is prepared to spend. This means that, once the first claim is settled, other claims that follow are not negotiated on the basis of loss of land or loss of lives but on relativity to other claims.[16]

The right to FPIC of the concerned Indigenous treaty party is, once again, not a primary factor in these procedures. Yet "consent" and "good faith" of all parties are the two most essential elements in treaty-making.[17] Following the adoption of the *Declaration*, the call upon states and Indigenous peoples to work together to implement remedial processes consistent with international human rights standards is clear and compelling. This is especially crucial in relation to the international norm of FPIC.

3. Indigenous Peoples' Understanding of the Right to Free, Prior, and Informed Consent

Indigenous peoples have often been informed, after the fact, of someone else's decision about what will be done with their lands and resources, despite relevant existing treaty rights. In many cases, they have been forcibly moved off their lands, out of the way of so-called "progress." The term "consultation" is too often interpreted by states in a self-serving manner that involves an exchange of views, but excludes decision-making on the part of the Indigenous peoples concerned.

Free, prior, and informed consent, in contrast, may best be described as a broad and comprehensive right, with attendant state obligations:

1) "Free" necessarily includes the absence of coercion and outside pressure, including monetary inducements (unless they are mutually agreed on as part of a settlement process), and "divide and conquer" tactics. Indigenous peoples must be able to say "no," and not be threatened with or suffer retaliation if they do so.

2) "Prior" means that there must be sufficient lead time to allow information-gathering and sharing processes to take place, including translations into traditional languages and verbal dissemination as needed, according to the decision-making processes of the Indigenous peoples in question. This process must take place without time pressure or time constraints. A plan or project must not begin before this process is fully completed and an agreement with the Indigenous peoples concerned is reached.

3) "Informed" means that all relevant information reflecting all views and

positions must be available for consideration by the Indigenous peoples concerned. This includes the input of traditional elders, spiritual leaders, traditional subsistence practitioners, and traditional knowledge holders. The decision-making process must allow adequate time and resources for Indigenous peoples to find and consider impartial, balanced information as to the potential risks and benefits of the proposal under consideration. Consistent with the "precautionary principle," information regarding potential threats to health, environment or traditional means of subsistence must be available. This principle "advocates taking pro-active, anticipatory action to identify and prevent biological or cultural harms resulting from research activities and development, even if cause-and-effect relationships have not yet been scientifically proven."[18]

4) "Consent" involves the clear and compelling demonstration by the Indigenous peoples concerned of their agreement to the proposal under consideration. The mechanism used to reach agreement must itself be agreed to by the Indigenous peoples concerned, and must be consistent with their decision-making structures and criteria (for example, traditional consensus procedures). Agreements must be reached with the full and effective participation of the leaders, representatives, or decision-making institutions authorized by the Indigenous peoples themselves.

A process or activity which does not meet these or other criteria put forth by the affected Indigenous peoples as requirements for obtaining their FPIC must cease. From the perspective of Indigenous peoples, this consent is an essential prerequisite for the ongoing legality and validity of treaties, agreements, and other arrangements, whether concluded in the past or to be negotiated in the future.

When deciding whether to enter into treaties, agreements, and arrangements, Indigenous peoples must not be subjected to coercion, including threatened or actual starvation, small pox epidemics, cuts to or elimination of basic human services, forced removals, or annihilation under the gun. Further, any new agreement or process for settlement or redress cannot be carried out under an implied threat or with the stated denial of other options. For example, it is inconsistent with the right to FPIC for Indigenous peoples to be told by a state, "This is your only choice, you better take it or you'll be left with nothing at all," or, "We're going to do this on your land whether you like it or not, so you better agree so you can at least get a share of the jobs/cut of the profits/a little piece of your land back."

These considerations also apply to any changes in the terms, interpretations, or implementation of the original treaty provisions as understood by the Indigenous peoples when they were first agreed upon. The *Vienna Convention on the Law of*

Treaties states that termination of or withdrawal from a treaty requires the consent of all parties.[19] Indeed, the unilateral termination of a treaty or the non-fulfillment of obligations contained therein "has been and continues to be unacceptable behaviour according to both the Law of Nations and more modern international law."[20]

Many Indigenous peoples also apply what could be called the principle of FPIC to ask for permission from the animals, plants, minerals, and spirits living in places that they have traditionally used. The traditional peoples of Indigenous nations still practise this when they harvest plants to eat or water to drink, cut trees for building or making fires, hunt animals, catch fish, gather medicines for healing, or before digging into the earth for any reason.

Indigenous peoples are taught to ask for and obtain permission when they are contemplating any activity that might disrupt the equilibrium of a place where any of their natural world relations are living, including when they make agreements with outside parties about plans for development that may affect not only their lives but the lives and survival of other living things. Indigenous peoples have been instructed to defend them and be responsible for them, not just as resources to use but as living beings who themselves have rights to survive and prosper, and to give their consent.

4. The Declaration and the Right to Free, Prior, and Informed Consent

The *Declaration* was the product of over 20 years of negotiations and lobbying by Indigenous peoples and their supporters, working with UN member states and UN experts. The right to FPIC was one of the pivotal points of debate at meetings of the inter-sessional Working Group on the Draft United Nations Declaration on the Rights of Indigenous Peoples (WGDD).[21]

Indigenous peoples from around the world consistently reiterated that they could accept no less than the full recognition of this essential right in the *Declaration*. In the end, they prevailed. The *Declaration* is now the primary international instrument explicitly addressing the rights of Indigenous peoples. The *Declaration* affirms that Indigenous peoples are "peoples" with the right to self-determination[22] and the "right to the full enjoyment, as a collective or as individuals, of all human rights and fundamental freedoms as recognized in the Charter of the United Nations, the Universal Declaration of Human Rights and international human rights law."[23]

This full and unqualified recognition leaves no room for doubt. Although the *Declaration* is not legally binding in the same way as a convention, the standards set out in legally binding instruments such as the *International Covenant on Economic, Social and Cultural Rights* (ICESCR),[24] the *International Covenant on Civil and Po-*

litical Rights (ICCPR),[25] and the *International Convention on the Elimination of All Forms of Racial Discrimination* (ICERD)[26] also apply to Indigenous peoples.

The *Declaration* affirms "that treaties, agreements and other constructive arrangements, and the relationship they represent, are the basis for a strengthened partnership between indigenous peoples and States."[27] Many provisions of the *Declaration* directly refer to, imply, or underscore the importance of FPIC in the context of treaties, agreements, and other arrangements between states and Indigenous peoples.[28]

Article 10 affirms that Indigenous peoples shall not be forcibly removed from their lands or territories, and that "[n]o relocation shall take place without the free, prior and informed consent of the indigenous peoples concerned and after agreement on just and fair compensation and, where possible, with the option of return." Article 32(2) specifically requires states to "consult and cooperate in good faith with the indigenous peoples concerned through their own representative institutions in order to obtain their free and informed consent prior to the approval of any project affecting their lands or territories and other resources." These provisions are vitally important, as lands and resources are central issues in most situations involving violations of treaty rights in different regions of the world.

The *Declaration* also clearly sets out terms and criteria for redress, including restitution and compensation, when violations of rights to lands, territories, and resources occur. Article 27 requires that

> States shall establish and implement, in conjunction with indigenous peoples concerned, a fair, independent, impartial, open and transparent process, giving due recognition to indigenous peoples' laws, traditions, customs and land tenure systems, to recognize and adjudicate the rights of indigenous peoples pertaining to their lands, territories and resources, including those which were traditionally owned or otherwise occupied or used. Indigenous peoples shall have the right to participate in this process.

Where lands, territories, and resources traditionally owned or otherwise occupied or used by Indigenous peoples have been "confiscated, taken, occupied, used or damaged without their free, prior and informed consent," according to article 28(1), the Indigenous peoples in question "have the right to redress, by means that can include restitution or, when this is not possible, just, fair and equitable compensation." Article 28(2) states that such compensation is to "take the form of lands, territories and resources equal in quality, size and legal status or of monetary compensation or other appropriate redress" — "[u]nless otherwise freely agreed upon by the peoples concerned."

These provisions affirm the specific rights of Indigenous peoples and call upon states to respect the relationships with Indigenous peoples that are enshrined and recognized in treaties. They also highlight some of the most critical ways in which treaty rights as well as the related right to FPIC are systematically violated, both historically and in contemporary contexts. The *Declaration* therefore provides clear direction for the ongoing recognition and respect of treaty rights, consistent with the right to FPIC. It also provides impetus for the development of new processes to remedy violations of treaty rights.

5. FREE, PRIOR, AND INFORMED CONSENT AS RECOGNIZED IN OTHER INTERNATIONAL INSTRUMENTS AND JURISPRUDENCE

The *Declaration* does not create any new rights. Craig Mokhiber of the New York Office of the High Commissioner for Human Rights calls it a "harvest" from existing "fruits," including "a number of treaties, and declarations, and guidelines, and bodies of principle, but, importantly, also from the jurisprudence of the Human Rights bodies that have been set up by the UN and charged with monitoring the implementation of the various treaties."[29] These additional sources serve to reinforce the inherent rights in the *Declaration*, as well as its overall significance.

The International Labour Organization's *Indigenous and Tribal Peoples Convention, 1989* (ILO Convention No. 169), provides that "[s]pecial measures shall be adopted as appropriate for safeguarding the persons, institutions, property, labour, cultures and environment" of Indigenous and tribal peoples, and that "[s]uch special measures shall not be contrary to the freely-expressed wishes of the peoples concerned."[30]

In addition, ILO Convention No. 169 states that Indigenous and tribal peoples shall not be removed from the lands they occupy. Where the relocation of Indigenous or tribal peoples "is considered necessary as an exceptional measure, such relocation shall take place only with their free and informed consent."[31]

ILO Convention No. 169 also recognizes that Indigenous peoples have the "right to decide their own priorities for the process of development as it affects their lives, beliefs, institutions and spiritual well-being and the lands they occupy or otherwise use,"[32] and requires states to consult with Indigenous peoples and ensure their informed participation in decisions pertaining to development, national institutions and programs, cultural protections, and lands and resources.[33] Consultations carried out must be undertaken in good faith and in a form appropriate to the circumstances, with the objective of achieving agreement or consent.[34]

The UN General Assembly's *Programme of Action for the Second International Decade of the World's Indigenous People* also highlights the importance of FPIC.[35] One of the five objectives of the Second Decade is "promoting full and effective participation of indigenous peoples in decisions which directly or indirectly affect their lifestyles, traditional lands and territories, their cultural integrity as indigenous peoples with collective rights or any other aspect of their lives, considering the principle of free, prior and informed consent."[36]

The committees of independent experts that monitor state implementation of international human rights treaties have also stressed the obligation on states to respect these rights of Indigenous peoples. In its General Recommendation XXIII on the Rights of Indigenous Peoples, the Committee on the Elimination of Racial Discrimination (CERD) called on states to "ensure that members of indigenous peoples have equal rights in respect of effective participation in public life and that no decisions directly relating to their rights and interests are taken without their informed consent."[37]

Consistent with this General Recommendation, the CERD has examined state compliance with this right to FPIC in considering periodic reports submitted by parties to the ICERD. For example, in 2008 the Committee recommended that the United States "recognise the right of Native Americans to participate in decisions affecting them, and consult and cooperate in good faith with the indigenous peoples concerned before adopting and implementing any activity in areas of spiritual and cultural significance to Native Americans."[38] Further, the CERD recommended that the US "take all appropriate measures, in consultation with indigenous peoples concerned and their representatives chosen in accordance with their own procedure — to ensure that activities carried out in areas of spiritual and cultural significance to Native Americans do not have a negative impact on the enjoyment of their rights under the Convention."[39]

The CERD had previously noted with concern that, in the United States, treaties made with Indigenous peoples "can be abrogated unilaterally by Congress," and the land possessed or used by Indigenous peoples "can be taken without compensation by a decision of the Government."[40] The CERD called on the US to "ensure effective participation by indigenous communities in decisions affecting them, including those on their land rights, as required under article 5(c) of the Convention." The CERD drew the attention of the US to General Recommendation XXIII, which stresses "the importance of securing the 'informed consent' of indigenous communities."[41]

The ICESCR and the ICCPR both affirm, in common article 1, the right of all peoples to self-determination. By virtue of this right, all peoples "freely determine their political status and freely pursue their economic, social and cultural development." In monitoring state compliance with the ICESCR, the Committee on Economic, Social and Cultural Rights (CESCR) has highlighted the need for states to obtain Indigenous peoples' consent in matters of resource exploitation.

For instance, in its 2001 Concluding Observations on the periodic report of Colombia, the CESCR noted "with regret that the traditional lands of indigenous peoples have been reduced or occupied, without their consent, by timber, mining and oil companies, at the expense of the exercise of their culture and the equilibrium of the ecosystem."[42] The Committee recommended that Colombia ensure the participation of Indigenous peoples in decisions affecting their lives, and particularly urged the country "to consult and seek the consent of the indigenous peoples concerned prior to the implementation of timber, soil or subsoil mining projects and on any public policy affecting them, in accordance with ILO Convention No. 169 (1989)."[43] Likewise, in 2004 the CESCR stated in relation to Ecuador that it was "deeply concerned that natural extracting concessions have been granted to international companies without the full consent of the communities concerned."[44]

In relation to "measures which substantially compromise or interfere with the culturally significant economic activities" of an Indigenous community, the Human Rights Committee has provided the following view:

> participation in the decision-making process must be effective, which requires not mere consultation but the free, prior and informed consent of the members of the community. In addition, the measures must respect the principle of proportionality so as not to endanger the very survival of the community and its members.[45]

The obligation on states to obtain the FPIC of Indigenous peoples prior to undertaking development, when designing measures to protect against and to redress rights violations, and when entering into agreements with Indigenous peoples, has been repeatedly recognized by UN studies, seminars, and processes.[46] For example, in its 2008 "Guidelines on Indigenous Peoples' Issues," the United Nations Development Group highlights that the "principle of free, prior and informed consent is an integral part of the human rights based approach" to development.[47] Also, Rodolfo Stavenhagen, then the Special Rapporteur on the situation of human rights and fundamental freedoms of indigenous people, concluded in his 2006 report that "[f]ree, prior and informed consent is essential for the human rights of indigenous peoples in relation to major development projects, and this should involve ensuring mutually acceptable benefit sharing, and mutually acceptable independent mechanisms for resolving disputes."[48]

Further, FPIC is the standard underlined in the 2000 *Report of the World Commission on Dams*:

In a context of increasing recognition of the self-determination of indigenous peoples, the principle of free, prior, and informed consent to development plans and projects affecting these groups has emerged as the standard to be applied in protecting and promoting their rights in the development process.[49]

A similar standard is emphasized in the Final Report of the Extractive Industries Review (EIR): "The EIR concludes that indigenous peoples and other affected parties do have the right to participate in decision-making and to give their free, prior and informed consent throughout each phase of a project cycle."[50]

The right to FPIC has also been recognized within the Inter-American human rights system. In *Case of the Saramaka People* v. *Suriname*, the Inter-American Court of Human Rights stated that it:

considers that, in addition to the consultation that is always required when planning development or investment projects within traditional Saramaka territory, the safeguard of effective participation that is necessary when dealing with major development or investment plans that may have a profound impact on the property rights of the members of the Saramaka people to a large part of their territory must be understood to additionally require the free, prior, and informed consent of the Saramakas, in accordance with their traditions and customs.[51]

Further, the Inter-American Commission on Human Rights found that, pursuant to the "general international legal principles applicable in the context of indigenous human rights," the "permanent and inalienable title of indigenous peoples" with respect to historically occupied lands, territories, and resources can be "changed only by mutual consent between the state and respective indigenous peoples when they have full knowledge and appreciation of the nature or attributes of such property."[52]

The Commission further stated that international human rights law requires

special measures to ensure recognition of the particular and collective interest that indigenous people have in the occupation and use of their traditional lands and resources and their right not to be deprived of this interest except with fully informed consent, under conditions of equality, and with fair compensation.[53]

Respect for the right of Indigenous peoples to FPIC is already an important focus of UN and regional human rights bodies. Conventions or international treaties are legally binding on state parties, and the recommendations of the various treaty monitoring bodies cannot be lightly ignored. The *Declaration* now provides the most comprehensive statements on FPIC. Human rights bodies will use its provisions to guide their interpretation of human rights treaties as they apply to Indigenous peoples.

6. The UN Declaration as a Framework for a "New Jurisdiction" for Redress

In 1989, the UN Economic and Social Council and the Commission on Human Rights appointed Miguel Alfonso Martínez as Special Rapporteur to conduct a study on treaties, agreements, and constructive arrangements between states and Indigenous populations. Special Rapporteur Martínez submitted his final report in 1999. One of his most important recommendations — and the least developed to date — was that, owing to the failures of existing mechanisms in resolving conflicts arising from treaty violations, "an entirely new, special jurisdiction" should be established within states "to deal exclusively with indigenous issues."[54] The Rapporteur affirmed that this "new jurisdiction" or mechanism for conflict resolution must be "independent of existing governmental . . . structures."[55]

The Special Rapporteur presented some of the criteria he believed necessary for this new jurisdiction to be a successful and viable tool to resolve disputes and redress violations, including "those related to treaty implementation." A key component would be a "body to draft, through negotiations with the indigenous peoples concerned . . . new juridical, bilateral, consensual, legal instruments with the indigenous peoples," as well as legislation "to create a new institutionalized legal order applicable to all indigenous issues and that accords with the needs of indigenous peoples."[56] To effectively replace the outmoded and ineffective processes for the redress of treaty violations, Indigenous peoples must participate fully and effectively.[57]

In 2007, the International Indian Treaty Council, the Confederacy of Treaty 6 First Nations, and the Aotearoa Indigenous Rights Trust co-sponsored a side event on "Treaty Rights and International Standards" during the sixth session of the UN Permanent Forum on Indigenous Issues. The event was attended by representatives of treaty nations from the United States, Canada, Hawaii, Aotearoa (New Zealand), Nicaragua, Chile, and Kenya. A consensus emerged among the participants that there was an urgent need to address the Special Rapporteur's call for the establishment of this new jurisdiction. Participants began to discuss what an effective and just new legal framework might look like, one in which both treaty parties have an equal role and decision-making authority based on FPIC. A central focus of the discussion, one on which all participants were agreed, was the need to develop just, equitable, and transparent mechanisms with the equal participation and consent of all parties before the actual issues under dispute began to be adjudicated. Recommendations included equal participation by each treaty party in the selection of tribunal judges (i.e., one judge selected by each party and one more selected by agreement of the other two judges). Participants also agreed on the need to continue their discussions in the light of the *Declaration*, which was then awaiting adoption by the General Assembly.

The *Declaration*, as finally adopted, does in fact provide a minimum standard that can be used as the basis for transforming Special Rapporteur Martínez' recommendation into reality. There is now an historic opportunity to bring the procedures for redressing treaty violations in line with international human rights standards.

This "new jurisdiction" would serve as a bilateral mechanism for redress and restitution of the violation of treaty rights, conflict resolution, and the adjudication and recognition of land rights. To be consistent with the *Declaration*, a new mechanism must:

1) Be fair, independent, impartial, open, and transparent, providing a just and fair process for the resolution of conflicts and disputes among Indigenous peoples, states, and other parties;[58]

2) Be established and implemented in conjunction with the Indigenous peoples concerned;[59]

3) Recognize the right of Indigenous peoples to participate in, and have access to, this process;[60]

4) Give due recognition to Indigenous peoples' laws, traditions, customs and land tenure systems and/or give due consideration to the customs, traditions, rules and legal systems of the Indigenous peoples concerned and international human rights;[61]

5) Provide effective remedies for all infringements of the individual and collective rights of Indigenous peoples;[62]

6) Arrive at decisions promptly;[63] and

7) Provide redress for the confiscation, taking, occupation, use, or damage of Indigenous peoples' lands, territories, and resources, including those which they traditionally owned or otherwise occupied or used, without their free, prior, and informed consent.[64] Redress can include restitution of traditionally owned or otherwise occupied or used lands and resources. If this is not possible, compensation shall take the form of lands, terri-

tories, and resources equal in quality, size, and legal status, unless otherwise freely agreed to by the peoples concerned. Monetary compensation or other appropriate redress can also be provided, but only with the free agreement of the affected peoples. Compensation shall be just, fair and equitable.[65]

Any such process must be underpinned by respect for article 37 of the *Declaration*, which affirms the right of Indigenous peoples "to the recognition, observance and enforcement of treaties, agreements and other constructive arrangements concluded with States or their successors and to have States honour and respect such treaties, agreements and other constructive arrangements."

7. CONCLUSION

Now that the *Declaration* has been adopted by the General Assembly, processes developed by Indigenous peoples and states to redress the violation of treaty, land, and other rights must not fall below the basic, minimum standards elaborated in this universal human rights instrument.

The provisions of the *Declaration* are integral to any framework for implementing the objectives of the Second International Decade of the World's Indigenous People. The *Declaration* is an essential reference point and standard for developing just models for reaching agreements, upholding treaties, recognizing and implementing land and resource rights, settling disputes, and providing redress and restitution for rights violations.

Indigenous treaty nations are currently engaged in international dialogues to develop and expand on proposals for a new framework for dispute resolution and redress which can be applied and adjusted to various situations, countries, and areas. With the *Declaration*, we have an historic opportunity to step away from the injustices of the past and undertake a new way forward.

For all our relations.

CHAPTER NINE

The Significance of the UN Declaration to a Treaty Nation

A James Bay Cree Perspective

◌

Romeo Saganash and Paul Joffe

1. Introduction

For thousands of years, the James Bay Cree have occupied their traditional territory, Eeyou Istchee, in what is now Quebec, Canada and the adjacent offshore area. We continue to do so. We are a distinct people and nation. We are also a treaty nation.

Since the early 1980s, the Grand Council of the Crees (Eeyou Istchee) has been actively involved in international issues. Our experiences with federal and provincial governments in Canada have convinced us of the need to protect and advance our status and human rights both domestically and internationally.

The legacy of colonial policies remains evident in all parts of the world. Indigenous peoples suffer from widespread discrimination, marginalization, exclusion, poverty largely resulting from dispossession of lands and resources, cultural genocide, and other human rights violations. It has been well-established that countries around the world have sought to exploit, dominate, assimilate, and dispossess Indigenous peoples on the basis of presumed racial and cultural inferiority. Under English and Canadian law, theories of dispossession were founded in doctrines of European superiority. Indigenous peoples were considered primitive, dismissed as heathens and infidels, and therefore disqualified from owning or controlling lands, territories, and resources.[1] Such racist rationales as the "doctrine of discovery" — which is still a part of the case law in Canada and other countries — purportedly provided European powers with a rationale for claiming jurisdiction and sovereignty over traditional Indigenous territories.[2] It is a legal fiction that inhabited land can be subject to discovery.[3]

In light of this legacy, it is especially important to celebrate the General Assembly's adoption of the *United Nations Declaration on the Rights of Indigenous Peoples*. This human rights instrument affirms that all such "doctrines, policies and practices based on or advocating superiority of peoples or individuals ... are racist, scientifically false, legally invalid, morally condemnable and socially unjust."[4] It affirms that "Indigenous peoples have the right to the lands, territories and resources which they have traditionally owned, occupied or otherwise used or acquired."[5] Further, Indigenous peoples have the "right to redress" in cases of past dispossessions.[6] These aspects are of particular relevance to treaty-making, but in its entirety, the *Declaration* signifies a great deal more.

In this chapter, we will address the overall significance of the *Declaration* from a treaty perspective. Indigenous peoples' treaties embrace a diverse range of human rights. The *Declaration* is especially useful in interpreting treaty rights in the contemporary context and in filling any gaps from a human rights-based perspective.

2. The Significance of the UN Declaration

The *Declaration* is the most comprehensive international instrument on the human rights of Indigenous peoples, including a wide range of political, economic, social, cultural, spiritual, and environmental rights. As such, it has potentially far-reaching effects for some 370 million Indigenous people globally. Widely affirmed as universal in nature,[7] it elaborates international human rights standards for the "survival, dignity and well-being of the world's Indigenous peoples."[8]

The *Declaration* strengthens the international human rights system by addressing the status and collective rights of Indigenous peoples in a wide-ranging normative instrument. It provides an Indigenous context to facilitate the just interpretation and application of other human rights instruments to Indigenous peoples globally. Indigenous peoples now have a principled international legal framework that affirms our human rights.

The 2008 Report of the Commission on Social Determinants of Health underlines the importance of separately addressing a wide range of human rights issues:

Colonization has deterritorialized and has imposed social, political, and economic structures upon Indigenous Peoples without their consultation, consent, or choice. . . . Indigenous People continue to live on bounded or segregated lands and are often at the heart of jurisdictional divides between levels of government. . . . As such, Indigenous Peoples have distinct status and specific needs relative to others. Indigenous Peoples' unique status must therefore be considered separately from generalized or more universal social exclusion discussions.[9]

The *Declaration* does not create any new rights, but affirms and elaborates the inherent[10] or pre-existing rights of Indigenous peoples.[11] It provides a global context for elaborating on the universal human rights of Indigenous peoples. As described in the August 2008 report of the Special Rapporteur on the situation of human rights and fundamental freedoms of indigenous people:

> The Declaration does not affirm or create special rights separate from the fundamental human rights that are deemed of universal application, but rather elaborates upon these fundamental rights in the specific cultural, historical, social and economic circumstances of indigenous peoples. These include the basic norms of equality and non-discrimination, as well as other generally applicable human rights in areas such as culture, health or property, which are recognized in other international instruments and are universally applicable.[12]

A predominant characteristic of the *Declaration* is its affirmation of the collective rights of Indigenous peoples, which are "indispensable for their existence, well-being and integral development as peoples."[13] As a 1989 UN report on racism and racial discrimination concluded, [t]he effective protection of individual human rights and fundamental freedoms of indigenous peoples cannot be realized without the recognition of their collective rights."[14] The denial of collective rights generally results in a denial of the rights of individuals.[15] Systematic violation of Indigenous peoples' collective rights has had particular adverse impacts on Indigenous women:

> [F]or Indigenous women, the systematic violation of their collective rights as Indigenous Peoples is the single greatest risk factor for gender-based violence — including violence perpetrated in their communities. Indigenous women's anti-violence strategies are therefore rooted in defending the collective rights of their Peoples.[16]

In assessing the *Declaration*, it is important to recall that the international human rights system since its inception has predominantly focused on individual human rights.[17] A key exception is the right of "all peoples" to self-determination, which is affirmed in the two international human rights covenants.[18] But even this has been denied to Indigenous peoples in most countries, despite states' obligations to "promote the realization ... and ... respect" of this right.[19]

In 1948, the United Nations adopted the *Universal Declaration of Human Rights*.[20] No consideration was given to the human rights of the world's Indig-

REALIZING THE UN DECLARATION

enous peoples during this historic process. Jurists have described this as a significant omission and failure. As Richard Falk commented:

> Undoubtedly, the most vulnerable of all categories of vulnerable peoples is
> that of "indigenous peoples." . . . The specific identities and grievances of in-
> digenous peoples played literally no role in the influential formulations of
> the provisions of the Universal Declaration of Human Rights. Amazing as
> it may seem, indigenous peoples were simply not treated as "human" by the
> Universal Declaration, despite its drafters being among the most eminent
> idealists of their day.[21]

Sixty years later, the collective rights of the world's Indigenous peoples have been
elaborated in the *Declaration* and formally acknowledged by the international
community as an integral part of international human rights standards and law. In
its Agenda and Framework for its programme of work, the Human Rights Council included the "rights of peoples" under Item 3, "Promotion and protection of all
human rights."[22] This Agenda and Framework were approved by consensus in a
Human Rights Council resolution in June 2007. For the past three decades, the
collective rights of Indigenous peoples have been addressed by diverse UN human
rights bodies, so it is exceedingly difficult for any member state to argue that the
collective rights of Indigenous peoples are not human rights.

Yet the United Kingdom and the United States have indicated that they do not
accept that the collective human rights of Indigenous peoples are human rights.[23]
In the standard-setting process of the Organization of American States (OAS),
the Canadian government "has vigorously opposed any characterization of the
collective rights of Indigenous peoples as human rights."[24] The only collective human right explicitly recognized by the Conservative government of Canada is the
right of self-determination: "Canada is aware that collective rights to self-determination stem from human rights instruments. . . . For Canada, collective rights
to lands and resources are reflected in other sources, such as *The Royal Proclamation, 1763*, the *Constitution Act, 1982*, and historic and modern treaties."[25]

These positions are ideological in nature and cannot withstand serious human
rights analysis. Further, they run counter to the *Charter of the United Nations* and
international state obligations.[26]

These positions also ignore the long-standing practice in the UN and OAS
human rights systems[27] in which Indigenous peoples' collective rights are regularly
considered.[28] Such government perspectives are not shared by domestic human
rights bodies, such as the Canadian Human Rights Commission:

[H]uman rights have a dual nature. Both collective and individual human rights must be protected; both types of rights are important to human freedom and dignity. They are not opposites, nor is there an unresolvable conflict between them. The challenge is to find an appropriate way to ensure respect for both types of rights without diminishing either.[29]

The commission's objective of safeguarding both collective and individual rights is reflected in the *Declaration*, which contains some of the most comprehensive balancing provisions that exist in any international human rights instrument. For example, in exercising the rights elaborated in the *Declaration*, the "human rights and fundamental freedoms of all shall be respected."[30] This obligation refers to both collective and individual human rights. Further, all the provisions in the *Declaration* "shall be interpreted in accordance with the principles of justice, democracy, respect for human rights, equality, non-discrimination, good governance and good faith."[31]

Indigenous peoples' rights are generally of a political, economic, social, cultural, and spiritual nature. While Indigenous rights are predominantly collective, these are the same categories of rights that are included in other international human rights instruments. Even when existing international instruments focus on individual human rights, the collective rights of Indigenous peoples are generally an essential part of the analysis in any Indigenous context. In Indigenous communities, "the health of the individual is often linked to the health of the society as a whole and has a collective dimension."[32] In considering violations of the right to property under the *American Convention on Human Rights*,[33] the Inter-American Court of Human Rights has ruled that Indigenous peoples' collective notion of

> ownership and possession of land does not necessarily conform to the classic concept of property, but deserves equal protection under Article 21 of the American Convention. Disregard for specific versions of use and enjoyment of property, springing from the culture, uses, customs, and beliefs of each people, would be tantamount to holding that there is only one way of using and disposing of property, which, in turn, would render protection under Article 21 of the Convention illusory for millions of persons.[34]

For the world's Indigenous peoples, the *Declaration* can be effectively used as an interpretative guide in relation to a wide range of international human rights instruments. For instance, in regard to the *Indigenous and Tribal Peoples Convention, 1989* (ILO Convention No. 169),[35] the International Labour Organization has concluded: "The provisions of *Convention No. 169* and the *Declaration* are compatible and mutually reinforcing."[36]

As the August 2008 Report of the Special Rapporteur on the situation of human rights and fundamental freedoms of indigenous people explains:

> The United Nations Declaration reflects the existing international consensus regarding the individual and collective rights of indigenous peoples in a way that is coherent with, and expands upon, the provisions of ILO Convention No. 169, as well as with other developments, including the interpretations of other human rights instruments by international bodies and mechanisms. As the most authoritative expression of this consensus, the Declaration provides a framework of action towards the full protection and implementation of these rights.[37]

The adoption of the *Declaration* is significant also in terms of reinforcing Indigenous peoples' status as "peoples" with the right of self-determination under international law. For years, we have been the victims of discrimination in the UN system because some states refused to adopt any resolution or other instrument that would refer to us as Indigenous "peoples." Until recently, the term "populations" or "people" was repeatedly used to suggest that we were simply a group of individuals of Indigenous origin, rather than distinct peoples with the right of self-determination and other collective human rights.[38]

A further positive consequence of the adoption of the *Declaration* is that it reinforces the status of Indigenous peoples as "subjects of international law" who have legal personality, rights, and duties. In other words, Indigenous peoples are not simply objects of international concern but have a recognized status and capacity in the international context.

Subjects of international law need not all have the same capacities, and this status is not reserved solely for states. This is especially the case in modern international law. As subjects of international law, Indigenous peoples are playing an increasingly prominent role at the international level: "Indigenous peoples have not only gained recognition of their collective legal status in the decisions and reports of United Nations treaty bodies, but have gained direct access to aid programs and a greater role in United Nations decision-making."[39]

Our diverse contributions as international actors have been widely acknowledged. The preamble of the ILO Convention No. 169 underscores the "distinctive contributions of indigenous and tribal peoples to the cultural diversity and social and ecological harmony of humankind and to international co-operation and understanding."

The *Declaration* reinforces the international juridical personality of Indigenous peoples. This is evident from their unprecedented role at all stages of the standard-setting process leading to the adoption of the *Declaration* and its affirmation of their status and rights as peoples. Moreover, it requires an ongoing participatory role for Indigenous peoples in a wide range of international bodies and forums.[40]

The treaty-making capacity of Indigenous peoples also enhances our international legal personality. As James (Sa'ke'j) Youngblood Henderson has written, "[t]reaty-making with indigenous peoples was not a uniquely North American phenomenon. It was a global, rather than a regional order. Indigenous Nations' agreements with European kings and states were considered as proper subjects of international law."[41] Although countless efforts have been made to diminish the status of Indigenous peoples and the overall importance of our treaties,[42] such treaties are matters of international concern. Consequently, these solemn instruments have at least some form of international character.[43] As S. James Anaya describes,

> whether or not treaties or agreements with indigenous peoples have the same juridical status as interstate treaties is not in itself an issue of much practical importance. What matters is the respect accorded such agreements and the availability of mechanisms to ensure their effectiveness. Even if not of the same character as interstate treaties, agreements with indigenous peoples increasingly are acknowledged to be matters of international concern and hence, in their own right, can be said to have an international character.[44]

The right of Indigenous peoples to an effective remedy for violations of treaty rights should therefore not be limited to domestic forums. Whether procedures to resolve conflicts are of a domestic or international nature, the *Declaration* makes clear that international human rights must be given due consideration.[45]

Irrespective of whether Indigenous peoples have entered into treaties with states, all Indigenous peoples can benefit from the legal framework the *Declaration* provides.

3. THE BENEFICIAL NATURE OF THE DECLARATION FROM A TREATY PERSPECTIVE

The right of Indigenous peoples freely to determine their own relationships is an inherent part of the right of self-determination. Such relationships are often formalized through treaties.[46]

By addressing treaty issues on a principled basis, the *Declaration* serves to highlight the solemn and sacred nature of Indigenous peoples' treaties. "It must be remembered," wrote Justice Cory, "that a treaty represents an exchange of solemn promises between the Crown and the various Indian nations. It is an agreement whose nature is sacred."[47] Similarly, in the United States, as Robert A. Williams, Jr. has written, Indians have fought

> scores of legal battles.... to protect their rights to their lands and other important legal interests guaranteed in literally hundreds of treaties with the United States.... Indians still regard these treaties and their ancient promises as solemn and perpetual pledges of peace and protection between two peoples, pledges that create a sacred relationship of trust.[48]

The *Declaration* underlines the urgency of respecting and promoting Indigenous peoples' rights in treaties.[49] It affirms Indigenous peoples' rights and state obligations in recognizing, honouring, and enforcing treaties. Article 37 provides, in particular:

1. Indigenous peoples have the right to the recognition, observance and enforcement of treaties, agreements and other constructive arrangements concluded with States or their successors and to have States honour and respect such treaties, agreements and other constructive arrangements.

2. Nothing in this Declaration may be interpreted as diminishing or eliminating the rights of indigenous peoples contained in treaties, agreements and other constructive arrangements.

The *Declaration* also reinforces such core international principles as justice, respect for human rights, and good faith, all of which are especially significant in the treaty context.[50] Ted Moses describes the role of treaties as being consistent with self-determination and other core rights and principles:

> Treaties between indigenous peoples and States confirm the sovereign government to government relationship between States and indigenous peoples. They are in principle ideal instruments to resolve conflict and achieve reconciliation; but they must be conceived and implemented in good faith, and in full recognition of all of the human rights of indigenous peoples, including self-determination.[51]

Treaties between states and Indigenous peoples generally contain a wide range of human rights considerations, including those relating to land[52] and resource rights. As Paul Joffe and Willie Littlechild describe:

> Whether in general or specific terms, Indigenous peoples' treaties constitute an elaboration of arrangements relating to the political, economic, social, cultural or spiritual rights and jurisdictions of the Indigenous peoples concerned. These treaties also often include important dimensions relating to the collective and individual security of Indigenous peoples and individuals.[53]

By elaborating diverse arrangements relating to our collective and individual rights, these treaties also provide for our collective and individual security. The *Declaration* affirms in broad terms that "Indigenous individuals have the rights to life, physical and mental integrity, liberty and security of person,"[54] and "the collective right to live in freedom, peace and security as distinct peoples."[55]

The *Declaration* and other international human rights instruments can help ensure progressive and contemporary interpretations of Indigenous treaty rights for present and future generations. This approach is completely compatible with Canada's Constitution, the provisions of which are flexibly interpreted according to the "living tree doctrine" defined in 1930 by Lord Sankey, who stated, "[t]he British North America Act planted in Canada a living tree capable of growth and expansion within its natural limits."[56] This is consistent with Indigenous peoples' understanding of treaties constituting dynamic, "living" agreements. At both international and domestic levels,[57] human rights are dynamic concepts whose interpretations continue to evolve over time.

In addition, by providing a global context relating to Indigenous peoples, the *Declaration* can serve to fill in any gaps in existing treaties. This is especially important in respect to older treaties that may not have the same detailed provisions found in contemporary "land claims" agreements.[58]

This is also consistent with Canada's Constitution. According to the Supreme Court of Canada, underlying constitutional principles may be used "in the filling of gaps in the express terms of the constitutional text."[59] An underlying constitutional principle and value is the "protection of existing Aboriginal and treaty rights"— whether looked at in its own right[60] or as part of the larger concern with minorities.[61]

The *Declaration* also affirms that Indigenous peoples and individuals have the right to an effective legal remedy,[62] which is widely recognized as a human right.[63] This is particularly significant in relation to treaties, since treaty violations frequently occur without legal recourse. "The problem of discrimination," wrote Special Rapporteur Erica-Irene A. Daes, "arises when the state later abrogates or violates the treaty. In the typical case, the injured Indigenous nation or tribe has no legal remedy against the state either in domestic law or under international law."[64]

The *Declaration* can act as a catalyst to ensure honour, justice, and good faith in regard to Indigenous peoples' treaties. To date, the absence of a principled legal framework for respecting Indigenous peoples' rights has had far-ranging adverse impacts on treaty making and implementation. Treaties and other agreements between Indigenous peoples and states generally have not been respected in different parts of the world. As Senator Daniel Inouye reported to the US Congress in 1993:

I am chairman of the Indian Affairs Committee, Mr. President. ... This committee has to act on 800 treaties — 800 treaties — entered into by sovereign Indian nations and the sovereign Government of the United States. But, shamefully, 430 of these treaties were not even considered by this body. And of the 370 that we did consider and ratify, we violated provisions in every one of them.[65]

In Africa, there have been irregularities to such an extent that the African Commission on Human and Peoples' Rights has characterized agreements between the British and the Maasai people in the early 20th century as "fake treaties."[66]

In negotiating with the governments of Canada and Quebec, the James Bay Crees have also experienced difficulties associated with a lack of a principled legal framework for the recognition and respect of Indigenous rights. In 1975, the James Bay Crees and Nunavik Inuit entered into the James Bay and Northern Quebec Agreement (JBNQA).[67] During the negotiations, both the governments of Canada and Quebec denied the existence of our ancestral rights,[68] perpetuating a climate of distrust and making it difficult to arrive at a fair and honourable agreement.

At the same time, the JBNQA and accompanying legislation purported to extinguish Cree and Inuit rights in and to lands in our traditional territories. This discriminatory and outdated doctrine — "another relic of colonialism," as one commentator put it[69] — is the antithesis of human rights. Human rights instruments can provide for the limitation of human rights, but not their destruction. In its 1999 report to Canada, the UN Human Rights Committee recommended "that the practice of extinguishing inherent aboriginal rights be abandoned as incompatible with [the right of self-determination in] article 1 of the International Covenant on Civil and Political Rights."[70] The right of self-determination is a "prerequisite" for the enjoyment of *all* other human rights.[71] Thus, "extinguishment" is also incompatible with the wide range of human rights affirmed by the *Declaration*.

The JBNQA recognizes, among other things, Cree and Inuit land rights in our traditional territories, as well as harvesting rights and an income support program for Cree and Inuit hunters, fishers, and trappers. It establishes regional and local governments, and regional bodies to protect the northern environment. It provides for monetary compensation and the creation of institutions and programs to promote our economic and social development. The agreement also elaborates on remedial and other measures respecting hydro-electric development in our territories.

Regrettably, after the JBNQA came into force, both the federal and Quebec governments failed to fulfill many of their obligations. Over 20 years of litigation helped to generate a different attitude. By 2001, the James Bay Cree people and the Quebec government had opted to establish a much more co-operative and mutually beneficial approach. In February 2002, the Quebec government signed a 50-year "nation-to-nation" agreement — also known as *La Paix des Braves* — with the James Bay Cree.[72]

In *La Paix des Braves*, Quebec and the James Bay Crees have agreed that future development is to be sustainable and compatible with our way of life. It provides for:

- a new Cree-Quebec Forestry Board to review all cutting plans and oversee Cree hunter-company consultations;

- the transfer of Quebec's obligations for Cree economic and community development to the Crees, along with necessary funding;

- jobs and contracts in the forestry industry;

- an annual payment (indexed annually) of $70 million by Quebec to fund the Cree government in respect to economic and community development;

- over $800 million of contracts to be set aside for Cree companies; and

- cancellation of the Nottaway-Broadback-Rupert Project, that would have potentially flooded 8,000 square kilometres.

The Agreement recognizes the James Bay Crees as a "nation" distinct from the "Quebec nation." It also "strengthens the political, economic and social relations between Québec and the Crees, and which is characterized by cooperation, partnership, and mutual respect."[73]

Similarly, after years of litigation, we entered into the Agreement Concerning a New Relationship Between the Government of Canada and the Crees of Eeyou Istchee (the Canada-Cree Agreement) in July 2007. A Cree referendum was held in October 2007, which resulted in the approval of the agreement by over 90 per cent of the voters. The signing ceremony took place on 21 February 2008. The key purposes of this 20-year agreement are:

- to establish the basis for a new relationship between Canada and the Cree Nation;

- to improve implementation of the JBNQA;

- to establish a process for negotiating a Cree Nation Government; and

- to provide for the assumption by the Cree Regional Authority and subsequently by the Cree Nation Government, of certain responsibilities of Canada under the JBNQA.

More than 30 years after the signing of the JBNQA, this latest agreement is a concrete illustration that the parties can jointly commit to strengthening Cree self-governance and other institutions.

A further purpose of the Canada-Cree Agreement is to resolve claims, grievances, and other matters between Canada and Cree entities, and to resolve disputes between the Cree Nation and Canada concerning Canada's past implementation of the JBNQA.

Both *La Paix des Braves* and the Canada-Cree Agreement embrace the basic principles of co-operation, partnership, and mutual respect that are highlighted in the *Declaration*. In particular, the *Declaration* affirms that "treaties, agreements and other constructive arrangements, and the relationship they represent, are the basis for a strengthened partnership between indigenous peoples and States."[74] Both these agreements, however, must be respected in practice by the governments of Canada and Quebec. Recently, Cree Grand Chief Matthew Coon Come expressed concern to the Quebec government about "the danger of the government slipping into its previous pattern of failing to fulfill obligations."[75] Unilateral actions must not replace such key elements as partnership, respect and trust.

4. SECTION 35 AND THE DECLARATION

In regard to Aboriginal and treaty rights, section 35 of the *Constitution Act, 1982* in part provides:

(1) The existing aboriginal and treaty rights of the aboriginal peoples of Canada are hereby recognized and affirmed. . . .

(3) For greater certainty, in subsection (1) "treaty rights" includes rights that now exist by way of land claims agreements or may be so acquired.

(4) Notwithstanding any other provision of this Act, the aboriginal and treaty rights referred to in subsection (1) are guaranteed equally to male and female persons.[76]

The *Declaration* is consistent with Canadian constitutional protections relating to Aboriginal and treaty rights and their progressive interpretation.

International and regional bodies are not bound by the interpretation by domestic courts of a particular term or provision in the *Declaration*. As stated by the Inter-American Commission on Human Rights,

the Commission is not bound by the definition of the "right to culture" as determined by the Canadian courts . . . although the analysis and interpretation of these courts may provide certain useful insights for the Commission's interpretation of the substantive content of Article XIII of the American Declaration [on the Rights and Duties of Man].[77]

As Eric Heinze has explained,

> International human rights law is not intended merely to recapitulate the wishes and practices of States. It arises from the positive consent of nations; yet, once born, it is not necessarily constrained by those nations' individual objectives. It does, so to speak, take on a life of its own.[78]

The jurisprudence arising from international and regional human rights systems will likely gain increasing significance in relation to the *Declaration*. Its adoption by the General Assembly positively contributes to "new social, political and historical realities"[79] worldwide — including Canada, regardless of whether the government chooses to continue its opposition. Canadian courts should fully consider the *Declaration* in their future interpretations of treaty and Aboriginal rights. The courts are free to rely on the *Declaration* in interpreting the rights of Indigenous peoples. As stated by Chief Justice Dickson in the 1987 *Reference re Public Service Employee Relations Act (Alta.)*, "The various sources of international human rights law — declarations, covenants, conventions, judicial and quasi-judicial decisions of international tribunals, customary norms — must ... be relevant and persuasive sources for interpretation of the Charter's provisions."[80]

It is not possible to anticipate every action of successive governments that might adversely affect Aboriginal peoples' rights and interests, so the constitutional recognition and protection of Aboriginal and treaty rights are essential.

In particular, the Supreme Court of Canada has ruled that the government has a constitutional "duty to consult with Aboriginal peoples and accommodate their interests," and this duty is "grounded in the honour of the Crown."[81] The honour of the Crown, in turn, "must be understood generously in order to reflect the underlying realities from which it stems. In all its dealings with Aboriginal peoples, from the assertion of sovereignty to the resolution of claims and the implementation of treaties, the Crown must act honourably."[82] The Canadian government is duty bound to uphold the honour of the Crown in the negotiation, conclusion, and implementation of treaties. Reconciliation is not a "final legal remedy" but "a process flowing from rights guaranteed by s. 35(1) of the *Constitution Act, 1982*."[83]

It is disturbing, therefore, that Canada's minority Conservative government has sought to significantly alter, if not reverse, the Supreme Court's constitutional rulings in relation to Aboriginal peoples who have entered into treaties with the Crown. Rather than promote reconciliation based on respect, the government has argued in court cases that the "duty to consult" is not a constitutional obligation[84] and that the conclusion of treaties achieves reconciliation.[85] These positions contradict the rulings of Canada's highest court[86] and significantly erode good faith and trust.

Currently, the government is seeking to restrict its duty to consult to the terms negotiated in Indigenous treaties, claiming that the duty to uphold the honour of the Crown is satisfied once a treaty is executed and its terms fulfilled.[87] However, treaties may not adequately provide for future circumstances. Unforeseen government actions could lead to prejudicial effects that may not amount to outright infringements, but may still significantly erode treaty rights. Such situations can easily arise, since the unilateral criteria established for treaty negotiations generally favour the federal and provincial governments concerned.[88]

A more honourable course for the Canadian government would be to address the widespread dissatisfaction expressed by 21 Indigenous signatories of modern land claims agreements, especially in regard to implementation. In the experience of these members of the Land Claims Agreements Coalition,

> the ink is barely dry on each land claims agreement before the federal government, and especially its officials, abandons any talk of the broad objectives of the agreement, and proceeds instead on the basis that the government's sole responsibility is to fulfil the narrow legal obligations set out in the agreement.[89]

These fundamental concerns are shared by the Senate Standing Committee on Aboriginal Peoples, which "is troubled by the narrow approach to treaty implementation adopted by the federal government." The committee adds: "Federal practices and policy in this regard have resulted in the diminishment of the benefits and rights promised to Aboriginal peoples under these agreements...."[90]

Another key matter affecting both treaty and Aboriginal rights pertains to major development projects on Indigenous peoples' lands and territories. It is generally acknowledged that such projects are the cause of some of the most severe impacts on Indigenous peoples and their lands, resources, and environment. This issue is underscored in the 2004 report of the Special Rapporteur on the situation of human rights and fundamental freedoms of indigenous people:

> Wherever large-scale projects are executed in areas occupied by indigenous peoples, it is likely that their communities will undergo profound social and economic changes that the competent authorities are often incapable of understanding. ... Indigenous peoples bear a disproportionate share of the social and human costs of resource-intensive and resource-extractive industries, large dams and other infrastructure projects, logging and plantations, bio-prospecting, industrial fishing and farming, and also eco-tourism and imposed conservation projects.[91]

Citing some of the potentially far-ranging social, economic and cultural impacts, the Special Rapporteur continued:

The principal effects of these projects for indigenous peoples relate to loss of traditional territories and land, eviction, migration and eventual resettlement, depletion of resources necessary for physical and cultural survival, destruction and pollution of the traditional environment, social and community disorganization, long-term negative health and nutritional impacts as well as, in some cases, harassment and violence.[92]

It is "essential," the report goes on, "to respect the right of indigenous peoples to be consulted and give their free, informed and prior consent to any development project having such effects."[93]

In regard to proposed development projects, article 32(2) of the *Declaration* requires states to "consult and cooperate in good faith with the indigenous peoples concerned ... in order to obtain their free and informed consent." Article 32 has been cited by the Inter-American Court of Human Rights in a case involving large-scale development affecting the Saramaka people in Suriname.[94] In another case involving development in the territory of the Maya people, article 26, concerning the right to lands, territories, and resources, was cited by the Chief Justice of the Supreme Court in Belize.[95] In both decisions, the court required the free, prior, and informed consent of the peoples concerned.

In Canada, when faced with proposed development projects with potentially major impacts, Indigenous peoples could invoke the *Declaration* and related international precedents to safeguard their rights and interests. To date, Canada's highest court has focused to a large degree on prior consultation with Indigenous peoples and accommodation of their concerns. However, the Supreme Court has also indicated that, for "very serious issues,"[96] the duty of the Crown would go well beyond consultation and require the "full consent of [the] aboriginal nation."[97]

When such issues arise, any evaluation should fully consider Indigenous peoples' perspectives and priorities for development in their own territories. Under international human rights law, Indigenous peoples have the right to development. As article 23 of the *Declaration* affirms: "Indigenous peoples have the right to determine and develop priorities and strategies for exercising their right to development." Article 32(1) reiterates: "Indigenous peoples have the right to determine and develop priorities and strategies for the development or use of their lands or territories and other resources." This right has political, economic, social, cultural, spiritual, and environmental dimensions, but historically it has most often been denied:

Indigenous peoples have suffered from historic injustices as a result of, *inter alia*, their colonization and dispossession of their lands, territories and resources, thus preventing them from exercising, in particular, their right to development in accordance with their own needs and interests.[98]

The Supreme Court of Canada has described the treaties as sacred. By their nature, treaties require the consent of the parties should any changes be contemplated. However, the court has indicated that the tests it set out in *R. v. Sparrow*[99] that could justify infringements of Aboriginal rights would also apply to treaty rights. In *Sparrow*, the criteria for proving a *prima facie* infringement include:

> First, is the limitation unreasonable? Second, does the regulation impose undue hardship? Third, does the regulation deny to the holders of the right their preferred means of exercising that right? The onus of proving a *prima facie* infringement lies on the individual or group challenging the legislation. . . . If a *prima facie* interference is found, the analysis moves to the issue of justification. This is the test that addresses the question of what constitutes legitimate regulation of a constitutional aboriginal right. The justification analysis would proceed as follows. First, is there a valid legislative objective. . . ?[100]

In *R. v. Côté*, the court indicated that "the *Sparrow* test for infringement and justification applies with the same force and the same considerations to both species of constitutional rights."[101] In *R. v. Badger*, Justice Corey stated that the *Sparrow* justification criteria should, "in most cases, apply equally to the infringement of treaty rights."[102] He added that, in comparison to Aboriginal rights, it is "equally if not more important to justify *prima facie* infringements of treaty rights."[103]

These statements of the Supreme Court appear not only to differ in important respects, but they do not respect the consensual nature of treaties and their consensual amendment process. Nor do they sufficiently take into account that treaties with Indigenous peoples already reflect a balancing of interests, as that is inherent in the negotiation process.

Constitutional law expert Peter Hogg has commented on the court's view that the *Sparrow* test for infringement and justification applies with the same force and consideration to both species of constitutional rights:

> With respect, this cannot be right. In the case of a modern land claims agreement, in which the rights and obligations of the Crown and the Indian nation are set out in great detail, and in which there is provision for amendments to be made (invariably by mutual agreement), it seems wrong to me to permit Parliament unilaterally to amend the treaty rights, however strong the justification. At the very least, a higher standard of justification should

be demanded for the infringement of treaty rights than for the infringe-ment of aboriginal rights.[104]

In regard to modern treaties, Ruth Sullivan expresses a similar view:

> The Crown represents the public interest in the course of treaty negotia-tions. The agreement that results is therefore *already* the product of a recon-ciliation of Aboriginal rights and the broader public interest.

> Furthermore, the agreement embodies a mix of rights, obligations, pay-ments and surrenders that have been carefully balanced to produce a fair and reasonable settlement. To read down a right set out in one part of the treaty, while leaving the rest intact, would disrupt the balance and would therefore require a very high threshold.[105]

The *Declaration* could prove of assistance in seeking a more consistent and balanced view from the Supreme Court. Article 37(1) affirms Indigenous peoples' "right to the recognition, observance and enforcement of treaties," and state obligations to "hon-our and respect" them. Article 46(3) generally requires the provisions of the *Dec-laration* to be interpreted in accordance with the principles of "democracy, justice, respect for human rights, equality, non-discrimination, good governance and good faith." The requirement of good faith is critical to the negotiation of treaties, espe-cially when they address a wide range of human rights.

Article 37(2) indicates that nothing in the *Declaration* "may be interpreted as diminishing or eliminating the rights of indigenous peoples contained in treaties." In the preamble, it is underlined that "treaties . . . are the basis for a strengthened partnership between indigenous peoples and States."[106]
These and other provisions in the *Declaration* that relate to treaties serve to underline the importance of treaty-making in promoting harmonious and co-operative relations between states and Indigenous peoples, as well as partnership and mutual respect.[107] Such provisions reinforce the consensual nature of treaties rather than encourage the unilateral actions of states.

In *R. v. Sundown*, the Supreme Court ruled that, in imposing limits on treaty rights, it would

> not be sufficient for the Crown to simply assert that the regulations are "necessary" for conservation. . . . The Crown would also have to demonstrate that the legislation does not unduly impair treaty rights. The solemn prom-ises of the treaty must be fairly interpreted and the honour of the Crown upheld. Treaty rights must not be lightly infringed. Clear evidence of justifi-cation would be required before that infringement could be accepted.[108]

While such judicial statements help to restrict infringements by the Crown, they still leave open the door to unilateral government actions that are not consistent with the consensual nature of treaties. The *Declaration* could be invoked to encourage higher judicial standards, more consistent with a human rights-based approach.

The *Declaration* can be highly effective as a human rights instrument that raises standards globally. It can also ensure progressive interpretations of Indigenous treaty rights for present and future generations. Such an approach is essential, since many of the challenges Indigenous peoples face were not foreseeable when their treaties were signed. Climate change is a case in point, presenting huge challenges in terms of Indigenous peoples' lands, territories, cultures, and rights. As the Office of the High Commissioner for Human Rights (OHCHR) has cautioned, "emerging evidence suggests that the livelihoods and cultural identities of indigenous peoples of North America, Europe, Latin America, Africa, Asia and the Pacific are already being threatened by the impact of climate change."[109]

The treaty rights of the James Bay Cree people include rights relating to environmental protection, but there is no specific mention of climate change since this was not a known threat in 1975. By invoking our treaty rights together with the environmental standards elaborated in the *Declaration* and other international instruments, we can better safeguard the rights and interests of our people, our territory, and our northern environment.

5. Conclusions

Following the historic adoption of the *United Nations Declaration on the Rights of Indigenous Peoples*, it is crucial that it now be fully implemented, taking a human rights-based approach. In the case of treaty nations, this should be done in conjunction with our treaty rights.

Indigenous peoples' rights are human rights and are treated as such at the international level. It is widely accepted internationally that "all human rights are universal, indivisible and interdependent and interrelated."[110] They constitute the "common language of humanity."[111] The *Charter of the United Nations* obliges member states to promote the universal recognition and observance of human rights for all.[112] In addressing present and future challenges, a human rights approach provides a comprehensive, inclusive, and principled framework for analyzing and discussing a wide range of issues relating to the treaty and other rights of Indigenous peoples. After working on it for over 20 years, we are committed to the full and effective implementation of the *Declaration*. The James Bay Cree nation is examining ways of integrating it into our school curriculum and preparing a Cree-language version.

Presently, Canada is one of only three countries that oppose the *Declaration*. Canada was the sole member of the Human Rights Council to vote against it at the General Assembly. The Canadian government's ongoing opposition has not prevented the growing interest in implementing the *Declaration*, which is generating considerable momentum at the international level. Months prior to the adoption of the *Declaration* by the General Assembly, the specialized agencies that are members of the Inter-Agency Support Group on Indigenous Issues had already adopted policies or practices consistent with the main provisions on lands, territories, and resources.[113]

On 28 September 2007, the Human Rights Council extended the mandate of the Special Rapporteur on the situation of human rights and fundamental freedoms of indigenous people, requiring him to "promote the United Nations Declaration on the Rights of Indigenous Peoples and international instruments relevant to the advancement of the rights of indigenous peoples, where appropriate."[114] In November 2007, Special Rapporteur Rodolfo Stavenhagen affirmed:

The Declaration already forms part of the international normative framework that is required to assess the human rights situation of indigenous peoples. . . . The adoption of the Declaration has provided States, international agencies and donors, and civil-society organizations with a clear-cut frame of reference for the formulation and implementation of development policies on behalf of indigenous peoples.[115]

In December 2007, the Human Rights Council created the Expert Mechanism on the Rights of Indigenous Peoples.[116] Since the preamble to the Council's resolution highlights the adoption of the *Declaration* by the General Assembly, it is to be expected that the Expert Mechanism will incorporate it in its work. At its inaugural meeting in October 2008, Chairperson-Rapporteur John Henriksen indicated that the "Expert Mechanism has an important role in promoting the rights affirmed in the *Declaration*, and in mainstreaming them into the Human Rights Council's overall efforts to promote and protect all human rights."[117]

In May 2008, the UN Permanent Forum on Indigenous Issues declared that the *Declaration* will be its "legal framework."[118] This includes the Permanent Forum's seven substantive mandated areas: economic and social development, environment, health, education, culture, human rights, and the implementation of the *Declaration*.

The *Declaration* is also influencing standard-setting at the regional level. In November 2007, the African Commission on Human and Peoples' Rights stated:

The UN Declaration on the Rights of Indigenous Peoples is in line with the position and work of the African Commission on indigenous peoples' rights as expressed in the various reports, resolutions and legal opinion on the subject matter.... [T]he Declaration will become a very valuable tool and a point of reference for the African Commission's efforts to ensure the promotion and protection of indigenous peoples' rights on the African continent.[119]

For over twelve years, the OAS has engaged in standard-setting in order to formulate a draft Declaration concerning Indigenous peoples in the Americas. In April 2008, the OAS Working Group on a draft American Declaration on the Rights of Indigenous Peoples asserted that "[t]he majority of States and all of the indigenous representatives supported the use of the UN Declaration as the baseline for negotiations and indicated that this represented a minimum standard for the OAS Declaration."[120]

In August 2009, the High Commissioner for Human Rights announced, "My Office is committed to be a frontline advocate of universal acceptance and implementation of the Declaration and will continue to support human rights mechanisms dealing with the rights of indigenous peoples."[121] She added that "these rights are, and will remain, a priority area for OHCHR."

On 10 December 2009 (Human Rights Day), the Leader of the Liberal Party of Canada, Michael Ignatieff, reaffirmed "unequivocal support" for the *Declaration*.[122] This further reinforces the motion adopted in April 2008 by the Canadian House of Commons, calling for the Parliament and government of Canada to "fully implement" the standards in the *Declaration*.[123] Only the members of Parliament representing the minority Conservative government voted against this motion.

Indigenous peoples in Canada and across the world should ensure that the *Declaration* flourishes as a living instrument, domestically and internationally. It should be used extensively in Indigenous-related issues and concerns, including those relating to the negotiation, conclusion, and implementation of treaties. Treaties entered into by Indigenous peoples generally entail a wide range of human rights that are essential to the collective and individual security and well-being of present and future generations. In this dynamic context, it is crucial that the ongoing interpretation of our treaties benefit from a human rights-based approach that necessarily includes the *Declaration*.

Indigenous peoples' treaties and the *Declaration* are dynamic instruments that must remain relevant to and effective for all the peoples concerned.

◇

PART IV

Dimensions of Collective
and Individual Security

A Vision for Fulfilling
the Indivisible Rights of Indigenous Women

◌

M. Celeste McKay and Craig Benjamin

1. Introduction

The adoption of the *United Nations Declaration on the Rights of Indigenous Peoples* (*Declaration*) was an historic achievement for the international human rights system. Victoria Tauli-Corpuz, chair of the United Nations Permanent Forum on Indigenous Issues, put it well when she said, "[t]his is a Declaration which makes the opening phrase of the UN Charter, 'We the Peoples . . .' meaningful for more than 370 million indigenous persons all over the world."[1]

The adoption of the *Declaration* was also a heroic accomplishment for the worldwide Indigenous movement and its allies, as well as for all the individuals who carried on the struggle in Geneva and New York for more than two decades. The knowledge and diplomatic skills Indigenous peoples brought to the negotiating table are amply demonstrated by the fact that the document that resulted from this process dramatically advances the international understanding and protection of the human rights of Indigenous peoples.

The *Declaration* covers an extraordinary range of rights and concerns, all of which reflect Indigenous peoples' lived experiences of colonization and genocide as well as their aspirations for a world in which future generations will be able live in dignity and safety. The *Declaration* affirms the right of self-determination. It affirms Indigenous peoples rights to lands, territories, and resources. It affirms the right to maintain and transmit languages, customs, and traditions that have long been under threat. It also affirms the right of Indigenous women to live free from discrimination and violence.[2]

These provisions of the *Declaration* complement and elaborate on human rights protections already available to Indigenous peoples through other international and regional human rights instruments of general applicability to Indigenous and non-Indigenous peoples. The *Declaration* also builds on an important legacy of Indigenous peoples, pressing international and regional human rights bodies to interpret and apply these general instruments in a manner appropriate to Indigenous peoples' specific histories, needs, and aspirations. For example, complaints brought before the UN Human Rights Committee by Sandra Lovelace and the Native Women's Association of Canada[3] and by the Lubicon Cree[4] were each landmarks in the interpretation of the interaction of individual and collective rights under the *International Covenant on Civil and Political Rights* (ICCPR) and the *International Covenant on Economic, Social and Cultural Rights* (ICESCR).[5] To these existing bodies of interpretation, the *Declaration* adds comprehensiveness, specificity, and broad international support.

In this chapter, we wish to highlight the interrelation among a number of the *Declaration*'s provisions on economic, social, and cultural rights as well as the closely related provisions on violence and discrimination. These are vitally important provisions, particularly for Indigenous women, who fought to ensure that protection from gender-based discrimination and violence were an explicit part of the *Declaration*. Using the example of the right to adequate housing, we argue that the economic, social, and cultural rights of Indigenous women are indivisible from their right to be free from violence and discrimination. This reality calls for a new, holistic approach to fulfilling the rights of Indigenous women in Canada.

2. VIOLENCE AGAINST INDIGENOUS WOMEN IN CANADA

Although there are no comprehensive statistical data on violence against Indigenous women in Canada, available information clearly indicates that Indigenous women face a much higher risk of violence than all other women in Canada.[6] According to a 1996 Canadian government statistic, Indigenous women between the ages of 25 and 44 with status under the federal *Indian Act* are five times more likely than all other women of the same age to die as the result of violence.[7] In a 2004 survey, women who self-identified as Inuit, Métis, or First Nations reported rates of violence, including domestic violence and sexual assault, 3.5 times higher than non-Aboriginal women.[8] The Native Women's Association of Canada has compiled an extensive database of cases of missing and murdered Indigenous women in Canada. It has also documented the root causes and trends of violence that have led to the disappearances of more than 520 Indigenous women. This is the most comprehensive compilation of data on Indigenous women who have gone missing or been murdered in the past three decades.[9]

A detailed study of spousal violence in Canada found that that the higher rates of violence against Indigenous women could not be accounted for by differences between the Indigenous and non-Indigenous population such as age, education, the employment status of the victim and the perpetrator, family size, or household alcohol consumption. This study found, further, that many of the social and economic factors commonly associated with increased violence against women in the general population have a significantly different, and sometimes inverse, bearing on Indigenous women's experience of domestic violence. Unlike non-Indigenous women, for example, the study found that the risk of violence for Indigenous women increases with income and higher educational attainment. The author concluded that the history of colonization was a critical factor shaping Indigenous women's experiences.[10]

Amnesty International reached a similar conclusion in 2004 in a report that documented patterns of murder and disappearance of Indigenous women in Canada cities (the *Stolen Sisters* report).[11] The organization argued that long-standing racial stereotypes and prejudices in Canadian society have fostered widespread and brutal acts of violence against Indigenous women by Indigenous and non-Indigenous men alike. The threat is compounded by the vulnerability of women, who, as a consequence of government policies and the dispossession of Indigenous peoples' lands, resources, and territories, have suffered impoverishment, the loss of ties to family and community, and the erosion of their cultural identity. The Amnesty International report also documented the failure of police and other Canadian institutions to respond either appropriately or effectively to this threat.[12]

In its November 2008 Concluding Observations on Canada, the UN Committee on the Elimination of Discrimination Against Women (CEDAW) called on the government of Canada to develop "a specific and integrated plan for addressing the particular conditions affecting aboriginal women, both on and off reserves, and of ethnic and minority women, including poverty, poor health, inadequate housing, low school-completion rates, low employment rates, low income and high rates of violence."[13]

During the February 2009 Universal Periodic Review of Canada at the UN Human Rights Council, a number of states called on Canada to work in collaboration with Indigenous women to institute a comprehensive national plan of action in keeping with the scale and severity of violence faced by Indigenous women.[14]

In September 2009, in a five-year follow-up to the *Stolen Sisters* report, Amnesty International criticized the failure of the government of Canada to establish a comprehensive national plan of action as recommended by Indigenous women and UN human rights bodies and mechanisms. The 2009 report concluded:

The scale and severity of the human rights violations faced by Indigenous women requires a co-ordinated and comprehensive national response that addresses the social and economic factors that place Indigenous women at heightened risk of violence. Such a response needs to address the police response to violence against Indigenous women; the dramatic gap in standard of living and quality of life that increases the risks to Indigenous women; the continued disruption of Indigenous societies by the high proportion of children put into state care; and the disproportionate rate of imprisonment of Indigenous women.[15]

Amnesty International called for a public commitment to implement the standards contained in the *Declaration*.[16]

These findings and recommendations demonstrate the interconnections between the violation of Indigenous women's individual right to security of the person and the way the dominant society has viewed and treated Indigenous peoples as a whole. When the Native Women's Association of Canada worked alongside other Indigenous peoples and representative organizations, including members of the global Indigenous women's caucus, to ensure that explicit provisions on gender-based discrimination and violence were included in the *Declaration*, it was with an awareness that gender-based violence has been and remains a central theme of the relationship between Indigenous peoples and the colonizing state. It was also with an awareness that violations of the collective rights of Indigenous peoples — the imposition of decisions made by the state, the uprooting and dispossession of communities, the assaults on languages and cultures — are often critical factors in creating social strife within Indigenous communities and making Indigenous women vulnerable to violence in their homes and in the larger society. In short, the survival, dignity, and well-being of individuals within Indigenous society and the survival, dignity, and well-being of the society itself cannot be separated but must be protected and advanced together.

3. THE INDIVISIBILITY OF HUMAN RIGHTS

The example of violence against Indigenous women demonstrates the failings of a compartmentalized approach to human rights. It is commonplace to differentiate between rights protecting the security and liberty of the person (civil and political rights) and rights pertaining to identity and development (economic, social, and cultural rights). A similar distinction is often made between the rights of individuals and the collective rights of families, communities, and peoples. The challenge is to understand how these rights interact in the concrete experience of those whose rights are most frequently violated.

It is true that women from all backgrounds and all regions of the world have been subject to violations committed or justified in the name of culture and institutions. It is also true that institutions of diverse cultures and societies throughout the world have failed in their duty to respect and uphold women's rights and to bring to justice those who threaten their lives and safety. This does not mean, as is sometimes claimed, that the individual rights of Indigenous women are distinct from, and at odds with, respect for Indigenous peoples' collective rights of self-determination, culture, and tradition. Systematic violations of the collective rights of Indigenous peoples put the rights of individual Indigenous women at risk. Linkages need to be made between, for example, the sexual exploitation of individual Indigenous women in Vancouver's Downtown East Side and the long term socio-economic marginalization of Indigenous peoples as nations all but stripped of economic, social, cultural, and political power through the operation of the *Indian Act* and other forms of colonization.

This view is consistent with the basic concept of international law: that all human rights are universal, indivisible, interdependent, and interrelated.[17] Rights work together to create the conditions in which all rights can be enjoyed, and the violation of one right puts others in jeopardy. It is not up to governments or other institutions to pick and choose which rights they will respect. All the rights contained in the provisions of the *Declaration* are now part of this larger whole that must be respected and upheld by courts, non-governmental organizations, corporations, states, and the governments of Indigenous peoples themselves. The adoption of the *Declaration* affirms this.

Sadly, some governments appear not to understand or respect this fundamental principle of human rights protection. Four states — Canada, Australia, New Zealand, and the USA — were notorious for their efforts to block the final adoption of the *Declaration*. How many of their objections can be traced to an insistence on reading the provisions of the *Declaration* in isolation from one another other, as though each were absolute and subject to the most extreme and far-fetched interpretation? The Canadian government asserted, for example, that recognition of lands and territories in the *Declaration* would overturn existing treaties between Indigenous nations and the government of Canada,[18] even though article 37 specifically states that "[n]othing in this Declaration may be interpreted as diminishing or eliminating the rights of indigenous peoples contained in treaties."

Now that the *Declaration* has been adopted, one of the critical challenges in moving forward with implementation is to ensure that we give life to the principle of indivisibility at each step of the way. Critical issues facing Indigenous peoples in Canada — poverty, inadequate housing, lack of access to clean water and a healthy environment, and violence against women — must be directly and specifically addressed. To be effective, and not create even greater problems, efforts to address these specific rights violations must be undertaken in tandem with efforts to gain greater recognition of other rights, such as the right of self-determination and rights to lands, territories, and resources.

The interdependence and indivisibility of human rights is something Indigenous women have often remarked on in their own struggles to overcome the multiple forms of discrimination they face on a daily basis.[19] However, from a non-Indigenous perspective, women's equality and the right to live free from violence have often been viewed as priorities which are either best pursued independently of other rights or as directly contradicting collective rights such as the right of self-determination or rights to culture and identity. During the negotiation of the *Declaration*, some states, in fact, tried to argue that the protection of the individual rights of Indigenous women required a weakening of the *Declaration's* protection for collective rights, despite Indigenous women's own insistence that their rights as Indigenous women and the rights of their people needed to be advanced together as part of an inseparable whole.

4. The Rights of Women and the Declaration

The adoption of the *Declaration* affirms that all the rights contained in its provisions are part of the larger body of international human rights laws and standards that states, courts, corporations, non-government organizations, and Indigenous peoples' own governments and institutions must respect and uphold. This body of laws and standards includes:

- the affirmation of the right of self-determination and the right to culture set out in both the ICCPR and the ICESCR;
- the rejection of all discrimination on the basis of race and ethnicity contained in the *International Convention on the Elimination of All Forms of Racial Discrimination*,[20]
- the rejection of all forms of gender discrimination in the *Convention on the Elimination of All Forms of Discrimination against Women*,[21] and
- the concrete program to stop violence against women set out in the *Inter-American Convention on the Prevention, Punishment, and Eradication of Violence against Women* (*Convention of Belem do Para*).[22]

The *Declaration* helps shape the interpretation of these existing norms and standards in relation to Indigenous peoples. In turn, the *Declaration* must be interpreted in the light of these other instruments.

Article 7 of the *Declaration* states both that "Indigenous individuals have the rights to life, physical and mental integrity, liberty and security of the person" and that "Indigenous peoples have the collective right to live in freedom, peace and security as distinct peoples and shall not be subjected to any act of genocide or any other act of violence." In article 44, the *Declaration* affirms the equal rights of Indigenous women and men. It also affirms the need for specific measures to protect the rights and interests of women, elders, people with disabilities, children, and youth. Articles 21 and 22 state:

Article 21

1) Indigenous peoples have the right, without discrimination, to the improvement of their economic and social conditions, including, *inter alia*, in the areas of education, employment, vocational training and retraining, housing, sanitation, health and social security.

2) States shall take effective measures and, where appropriate, special measures to ensure continuing improvement of their economic and social conditions. Particular attention shall be paid to the rights and special needs of indigenous elders, women, youth, children and persons with disabilities.

Article 22

1) Particular attention shall be paid to the rights and special needs of indigenous elders, women, youth, children and persons with disabilities in the implementation of this Declaration.

2) States shall take measures, in conjunction with indigenous peoples, to ensure that indigenous women and children enjoy the full protection and guarantees against all forms of violence and discrimination.

These two articles are preceded and followed by articles affirming the right of Indigenous peoples to have meaningful control over their lives and futures, including by taking part in decision-making, having the right to grant or refuse consent to measures affecting their lives and interests, and maintaining the institutions and practices necessary to their well-being. Articles 18 through 20 state:

Article 18

Indigenous peoples have the right to participate in decision-making in matters which would affect their rights, through representatives chosen by themselves in accordance with their own procedures, as well as to maintain and develop their own indigenous decision-making institutions.

Article 19

States shall consult and cooperate in good faith with the indigenous peoples concerned through their own representative institutions in order to obtain their free, prior and informed consent before adopting and implementing legislative or administrative measures that may affect them.

Article 20

1) Indigenous peoples have the right to maintain and develop their political, economic and social systems or institutions, to be secure in the enjoyment of their own means of subsistence and development, and to engage freely in all their traditional and other economic activities.

2) Indigenous peoples deprived of their means of subsistence and development are entitled to just and fair redress.

Articles 23 and 24 concern the right to development and the provision of health and social services.

Article 23

Indigenous peoples have the right to determine and develop priorities and strategies for exercising their right to development. In particular, indigenous peoples have the right to be actively involved in developing and determining health, housing and other economic and social programmes affecting them and, as far as possible, to administer such programmes through their own institutions.

Article 24

1) Indigenous peoples have the right to their traditional medicines and to maintain their health practices, including the conservation of their vital medicinal plants, animals and minerals. Indigenous individuals also have the right to access, without any discrimination, to all social and health services.

2) Indigenous individuals have an equal right to the enjoyment of the highest attainable standard of physical and mental health. States shall take the necessary steps with a view to achieving progressively the full realization of this right.

In this selection of seven of the 46 articles in the *Declaration*, protection of the specific rights and interests of Indigenous women is embedded in, and is an integral part of, a vision of how the basic rights of Indigenous peoples are to be fulfilled. This fulfillment is framed in accordance with Indigenous peoples' own values and ways of life, through their own institutions, and with their full participation and consent. These provisions recognize that, without promoting the collective rights of Indigenous peoples, we cannot adequately promote those rights often viewed as individual rights, such as the right to live free from violence.

5. Implementing a Vision of Indivisible Human Rights

To understand more clearly how such a vision of human rights might play out in the lives of Indigenous peoples in Canada, let us take the example of the right to housing. The ICESCR recognizes "the right of everyone to an adequate standard of living for himself and his family, including adequate food, clothing and housing, and to the continuous improvement of living conditions."[23] In his 2008 report to the Human Rights Council, the then UN Special Rapporteur on adequate housing as a component of the right to an adequate standard of living and on the right to non-discrimination in this context, Miloon Kothari, defined the human right to adequate housing as "the right of every woman, man, youth and child to gain and sustain a safe and secure home and community in which to live in peace and dignity."[24] The Special Rapporteur adopted a holistic interpretation of the right to adequate housing, "stressing the indivisibility of human rights, without which the right to adequate housing loses its meaning."[25]

In 2007, the Special Rapporteur carried out an official mission to Canada. During the visit, many housing activists expressed concern that federal, provincial, and territorial governments in Canada are not prepared to treat access to housing as a right, either for Indigenous peoples or non-Indigenous people. A recent Statistics Canada study concluded that Aboriginal people in Canada are almost four times as likely as non-Aboriginal people to live in a crowded dwelling, and three times as likely to live in a dwelling in need of major repairs.[26] Clearly, governments in Canada are not fulfilling their obligations to ensure access to safe, quality, affordable housing for all without discrimination. This has serious consequences for the enjoyment of a wide range of rights in addition to the right to adequate housing. Poorly built government housing compromises the health of everyone living there. A lack of access to adequate housing has critical impacts on the ability of Indigenous women to enjoy other rights, particularly their right to be free from violence.

During the Special Rapporteur's visit to Canada, the Native Women's Association of Canada and Amnesty International Canada worked with the National

Aboriginal Health Organization to host a workshop and forum on Indigenous women's experience of housing in Canada. Participants included Inuit, Métis, and First Nations women from many regions. They expressed their concern over the chronic shortage of adequate housing accessible to Indigenous peoples on reserves, in remote communities, and in urban centres. The great difficulty in finding adequate, affordable housing may increase women's dependence on their male partners. Workshop participants described how overcrowded housing increases the vulnerability of women and girls to violence and other abuse while denying them opportunities to flee to the shelter of other people's homes. They also described how inadequate access to safe, quality housing leads to the removal of their children by the child welfare system.

Emergency and short-term shelter for women fleeing violence is rarely available to Indigenous women. Those in rural areas or the north may have no access to such shelter in their own communities. Those in urban areas have limited access owing to high demand by both Indigenous and non-Indigenous women. In addition, they are often unable to find shelters that offer culturally appropriate services.

The absence of matrimonial property provisions in the *Indian Act* has created a legislative gap whereby Indigenous men and women may be denied adequate legal protection in disputes arising over a couple's home or land that they have lived on or benefited from during their relationship. Without such protection, women experiencing the breakdown of their marital relationship, violence at home, or the death of a partner often lose their homes on reserve. In 2006, the government of Canada met with the Assembly of First Nations and the Native Women's Association of Canada about this inequality. In March 2008, the federal government unilaterally introduced Bill C-47, the *Family Homes on Reserve and Matrimonial Interests or Rights Act*.[27] It was re-introduced in February 2009,[28] and the 2010 throne speech mentioned the promise again. This legislation did not provide for the non-legislative measures identified as critical by the Native Women's Association of Canada. As the Native Women's Association of Canada observed in its submission to the UN Human Rights Council's Universal Periodic Review of Canada,

Equality rights for Aboriginal women include both their individual equality rights and their rights as members of their nations. NWAC is concerned that inadequate protection of the collective dimensions of their equality rights could lead to the diminishment of Aboriginal women's rights. Furthermore, legislation alone will create the perception among Canadians that another step has been taken to secure equality for Aboriginal women when the reality will be that little has changed. Aboriginal women have learned through their own experiences . . . that this is a recipe for disaster. Legal rights must be accessible and enforceable to be meaningful. NWAC is continuing to call for concrete measures to ensure that the non-legislative measures recommended by Aboriginal women are in fact implemented.[29]

Furthermore, at the meeting with the Special Rapporteur, Indigenous women from all regions and backgrounds described housing that is simply not appropriate to their cultures and ways of life. Inuit women described government-built housing that provided no place for butchering game. Other women described housing that could not accommodate extended families. In addition to the right to housing itself, the housing crisis facing Indigenous peoples in Canada violates a wide range of other rights, including the right to health, culture and tradition, self-determination, women's right to safety, and children's right to a safe and appropriate environment to grow up in.

In a preliminary note to the Human Rights Council on his mission to Canada, the Special Rapporteur recognized that "[o]vercrowded and inadequate housing conditions, as well as difficulties to access basic services, including water and sanitation, are major problems for Aboriginal peoples."[30] The Special Rapporteur was "disturbed" about the impact of the "unduly paternalistic" policies of the federal and provincial governments, which he believed "compromise the right to self-determination and have deeply affected housing and living conditions."[31] Despite Canada's erroneous claims that the *Declaration* "has no legal effect in Canada,"[32] the Special Rapporteur made it clear that implementation of the *Declaration* is one of the necessary components of fulfilling the right to housing for Indigenous peoples.[33]

If Canada were to live up to the vision of human rights found in the *Declaration*, it would have to approach Indigenous peoples' housing needs in a fundamentally different way. These needs would be met in a manner consistent with and supportive of Indigenous peoples' cultures and traditions, and with the specific needs of the most vulnerable members of Indigenous societies. Critical issues such as safe housing would be addressed in all regions of the country, whether in urban, rural, or remote locations. Perhaps most importantly, Indigenous peoples' housing rights would need to be understood as inseparable from the right to self-determination. In concrete terms, this would mean that Indigenous peoples would play a central role in all decisions over the design and delivery of housing solutions, and Indigenous women would need to be full participants in such processes.

This is one example of the holistic vision for the fulfillment of individual and collective rights promoted by the *Declaration*. But it is a long way from reality. Successive Canadian governments have demonstrated reluctance to apply a rights-based framework to ensuring the security of Indigenous women. Factors that are critical to the quality of life and survival of peoples and cultures, such as housing, health care, and land rights, are enjoyed at the discretion of government and have a lower priority than other economic and political considerations.

In short, we are a long way from achieving a vision of the world in which Indigenous peoples and individuals are able to enjoy the full range of human rights.

6. Conclusion: Making Rights a Reality

Indigenous peoples and representative organizations and human rights groups need to continue to be vigilant in asserting and advancing these rights, and in identifying concrete ways in which systems, policies, programs, and laws must be restructured to give meaning to the holistic set of rights contained in the *Declaration*.

Indigenous peoples' own governments and institutions have a critical role to play in making the rights recognized by the *Declaration* a reality. Not only must they pressure states to implement the *Declaration*, they must set a positive example by ensuring that their own policies, programs, and laws reflect and incorporate the principles and provisions of the *Declaration*. The symposium hosted by the Assembly of First Nations, the British Columbia Assembly of First Nations, the First Nations Summit and the Union of British Columbia Indian Chiefs on "Implementing the *United Nations Declaration on the Rights of Indigenous Peoples*" held in February 2008 is one example of this proactive approach being taken by Indigenous nations and representative organizations to assume this responsibility.

The work of advancing the *Declaration* should not depend on Indigenous peoples alone. In the long struggle to advance the *Declaration*, alliances between Indigenous peoples and groups in civil society have played a critical role in building state understanding of its provisions and support for its adoption. These alliances need to be maintained and expanded to bring public pressure on governments to address the needs of Indigenous peoples on a comprehensive rights basis.

As Beverley Jacobs, past President of the Native Women's Association of Canada, stated:

This Declaration holds the promise of a world in which our rights as peoples are viewed as equal to all others peoples. It is at this foundational level that we need to re-write history if we are to address the day-to-day inequalities and human rights violations facing Indigenous women as individuals.

Our lives are witness to the international legal principle that all rights are inter-related, indivisible and interdependent. The fact is that there is a growing recognition of the need to recognize and respect the rights of Indigenous peoples in Canada — one that is supported by the UN Special

Rapporteur on the situation of human rights and fundamental freedoms of indigenous people, Rodolfo Stavenhagen and the UN High Commissioner of Human Rights, Ms. Louise Arbour and many others. . . . It is this recognition that we call on all of you to help foster by taking concrete steps to implement the Declaration.[34]

The *Declaration* and other international human rights instruments affirm that the human rights of Indigenous women are indivisible, interrelated and interdependent – as are all human rights. It is everyone's responsibility to ensure that these rights are realized.

CHAPTER ELEVEN

More than Words

Promoting and Protecting the Rights of Indigenous Children with International Human Rights Instruments

◯

Mary Ellen Turpel-Lafond[*]

1. INTRODUCTION

Recognizing that, in all countries in the world, there are children living in exceptionally difficult conditions, and that such children need special consideration. . . .

Preamble, *Convention on the Rights of the Child*

Canada has a history of championing human rights in the international community. It signed and ratified the *Convention on the Rights of the Child (Convention)*[1] in 1991 and most recently signed the *Convention on the Rights of Persons with Disabilities*.[2] But Canada's national and international human rights commitment came into question when it voted against the adoption of the *United Nations Declaration on the Rights of Indigenous Peoples*.

In 1994, I had the opportunity to comment on the first draft declaration on the rights of Indigenous peoples. I recommended that

Canada must be seen, especially in light of its constitutional obligations to Aboriginal peoples, to behave honourably at the international level and in a fashion which ensures the broadest possible recognition of Indigenous peoples' rights and status for Indigenous peoples in Canada and around the world.[3]

Canada's refusal to accept international declarative principles to guide new national policies to assist in improving the well-being of Indigenous people, espe-

---

* I would like to thank Karen Ameyaw, LL.B., who provided research support and assisted with the preparation of this chapter.

cially Indigenous children, is disappointing. We must build on the high expectations and optimism following Prime Minister Harper's apology for residential
school policies[4] to move forward national Indigenous social policy in a positive
direction. The *Declaration* is a valuable starting point in understanding and addressing the inequities Indigenous children face.

Determinants of health, safety, and well-being for Indigenous children fall well
below the national averages for Canadian children, and remain one of the most
significant human rights challenges that Canadians must address. The United
Nations Children's Fund (UNICEF) observes that

> indigenous children consistently number among the most marginalized
> groups in society and are frequently denied the enjoyment of their rights,
> including the highest attainable standard of health, education, protection
> and participation in decision-making processes that are relevant to their
> lives.[5]

Over 25,000 Indigenous children are in state guardianship, or "in care" in Canada, a number that rivals the number of children enrolled in residential schools at
the height of that policy in the 1940s.[6] In many provincial jurisdictions, such as
the western Canadian provinces of Manitoba, Saskatchewan, Alberta, and British Columbia, more than half of all the children in the child welfare system are
Indigenous children,[7] and the trends suggest upward growth of that cohort in
state guardianship or out of the parental home. The Committee on the Elimination of Discrimination against Women in its most recent observations regarding
Canada expressed concern at the "disproportionately high number of aboriginal
children ... being taken into State custody":

> The Committee recommends that the State party take all necessary measures
> to address the issue of the separation of aboriginal children from their parents.
> In this regard, the State party should give particular attention to contributing
> factors such as poverty, lack of housing, violence and drug abuse.[8]

I believe it is valuable to explore how international human rights instruments, in
particular the *Convention* and the *Declaration*, can work in concert to support new
and more successful approaches to promoting and protecting the rights of Indigenous children in Canada, and provide a more effective and appropriate social
policy framework to support their health, safety, and well-being. Relying solely
on international instruments will not affect social policy development, and time
has demonstrated the domestic limitations of the *Convention* in addressing com-

plex issues for Indigenous children. Corporal punishment, for example, has been upheld by the highest court in Canada, despite articles in the *Convention* that oppose it.[9] International standards nevertheless play a vital role in advocacy, interpreting domestic law, and focusing political will to support better outcomes for Indigenous children.

Part 2 of this chapter will set out the context of Indigenous children in Canada. Parts 3 and 4 will provide an overview of the *Declaration* and the *Convention* and their implications for Indigenous children. Part 5 will discuss the ways that we can better meet the many unfinished challenges stemming from these two human rights instruments. Establishing a national Children's Commissioner, adhering more strictly to the reporting mechanism of the *Convention*, engaging in focused and co-ordinated advocacy, respecting rights of Indigenous peoples to self-determination in Indigenous child welfare, and promoting the meaningful participation of children in decision-making are important strategies to achieve progress with respect to the rights of Indigenous children.

2. Indigenous Children in Canada

The 2006 Census showed that the population of people who identified themselves as Aboriginal, Métis, or Inuit (hereafter referred to as Indigenous) had surpassed one million people.[10] Indigenous populations are increasing not only in Canada but also in New Zealand, Australia, and the United States.[11] According to the 2006 Census, Indigenous children are a growing proportion of all children, particularly in the territories and in the provinces of Saskatchewan and Manitoba.[12] The Census revealed that children and youth aged 24 and under made up 48 per cent of the Indigenous population in Canada, but only 31 per cent of the non-Indigenous population.[13]

Children represent the future, and their health and well-being is important. It is also crucial for Canada to reflect on our capacity and ability to achieve our ideals as a democratic nation with core values of equality and support for all children. Indigenous children depend on a strong social system for their development and to sustain and transmit their values, culture, and language. Indigenous children are often in a vulnerable position, owing to factors beyond their control. They may not be certain of the continuation of their parents' culture and language. Intergenerational poverty and social exclusion experienced by their families may mean that they do not begin their lives at the same starting point as other children. Their parents do not always have the means or access to services to improve their life circumstances. Yet Indigenous children play a vibrant and important role in their families and communities. They are considered "the custodians of a multitude of cultures, languages, beliefs and knowledge systems."[14] This custodial role has been disrupted, challenged, and harmed by historical and contemporary actions that have strained ties that Indigenous children have to their communities and family.

The removal of Indigenous children from their families and communities and the creation of residential schools are two of many examples of the ways Indigenous communities have been altered and unsettled by the harmful policies of another era. Indigenous children, removed in large numbers and placed in non-Indigenous homes and families or removed to residential schools, were separated from their families, culture, language, tradition, and identity. When states did not value Indigenous cultures, or advanced policies of assimilation (such as the residential schools policy), it was considered to be in the "best interests of the child"[15] to remove them from their cultural and familial context to bring them into the "mainstream" European settler culture.[16] Imposed standards of what was in the "best interest of a child" did not value Indigenous cultures or the rights of Indigenous people to decide the best interests of their own children.

Vestiges of these state acts and the injurious impacts of the colonial system in many state systems, including Canada, continue to affect Indigenous communities, family structures, and children. In Canada, the intergenerational trauma stemming from these policies, coupled with other destabilizing forces, has resulted in immense changes for Indigenous families and communities. The strength of social systems of support to assist in creating enriching and culturally appropriate environments for Indigenous children has not been a major focus of state investment or concern. This means that, by default, Indigenous children often receive the least support and attention necessary under mainstream state policies.

The impact of socioeconomic disadvantage and exclusion are pervasive. The former United Nations Special Rapporteur on the situation of human rights and fundamental freedoms of indigenous people acknowledged that indicators of socio-economic conditions for Indigenous peoples are "unacceptably lower" than those of non-Indigenous Canadians.[17]

To be an Indigenous child in Canada correlates with poverty-related barriers, including "income, education and culture, employment, health, housing, being taken into care and justice."[18] The disparities among Indigenous and non-Indigenous children and youth are alarming, especially in the key determinants of health. A greater proportion of young Indigenous children live in low-income families in contrast to non-Indigenous children.[19] Further, nearly half (49 per cent) of off-reserve First Nations children under six years of age living in the provinces were in low-income families in 2006, compared with 18 per cent of non-Aboriginal children.[20]

In the area of education, gaps are clear. A recent study concluded that, although Indigenous student outcomes are better in provincial than in on-reserve schools, a large gap exists between the performance of Indigenous and non-Indigenous students in most schools across Canada.[21] In British Columbia, more than half the children in care are not ready to learn when they enter kindergarten, even though that province has one of the strongest education systems in Canada. A joint report released in 2007 by the Representative for Children and Youth and the Provincial Health Officer examined a cohort of over 30,000 children in state care, over a period of seven years. The average graduation rate from high school in British Columbia is approximately 78 per cent, and is one of the highest in Canada. The report found, however that children in care graduate at the rate of 21 per cent, and Indigenous children in care graduate at the rate of 16 per cent.[22] Such "[d]isproportionately low Aboriginal rates of completion for secondary and post-secondary education can be traced to many factors, including systemic racism, socio-economic factors, lack of funding/resources and inadequate Aboriginal control or input into education."[23]

Jurisdictional conflicts over who pays for services present additional barriers for Indigenous people living on reserve lands. The Department of Indian and Northern Affairs Directive 20-1 funding formula provides support based on the number of children in care, and is undergoing renewal with a possible emphasis on enhanced financial supports for prevention. The Office of the Representative for Children and Youth monitors the Aboriginal program and service area in British Columbia and is aware of significant work underway to replace the Directive with a new policy and funding regime which would permit broader prevention activities in relation to child welfare. In 2009, the Office began reviewing all Aboriginal governance and service delivery systems for children and the policy foundations for supports to agencies, including those delegated to Aboriginal entities for service delivery under provincial legislation.

Other funding issues are a source of jurisdictional disputes amongst different levels of governments.[24] Supports for children with special needs or complex health needs are not necessarily available on First Nations reserves.[25] In some cases, families and/or children have had to move off reserves and away from their communities to obtain support and better access to primary health care and secondary supports such as home care, assisted living, or specialized therapies. As the *Canadian Medical Association Journal* has stated, "[g]eography is no excuse for the ... inequitable distribution of wealth, such that advanced care exists only in the south and First Nations children, parents and communities endure psychological and cultural stress to access it."[26]

In many provinces in Canada, Indigenous children are over-represented in the child protection system. In British Columbia, studies show that an Indigenous child is about six times more likely to be taken into care than a non-Aboriginal child.[27] Indigenous children make up over half of the total number of children removed from their parents and placed by legal order into the care of the Ministry of Children and Family Development.[28] It is, as noted earlier, a national issue, and, by virtue of the profound disparities and colonial attitudes, a Canadian and international human rights concern.

The impacts are also experienced by Indigenous youth. In terms of health, "[h]igh rates of suicide among First Nations people, particularly among youth, are linked to social exclusion and disconnection from their traditions and culture."[29] Further, all jurisdictions have issues with respect to the over-representation of Indigenous people in their youth justice system. Indigenous youth made up one-quarter of all sentenced custody admissions in 2004-2005, yet they represent approximately five per cent of the total youth population. [30] The over-representation of Indigenous youth in the criminal justice system presents conditions that might elevate criminogenic risk rather than provide effective pro-social supports to adolescents to prevent them from coming back into the justice system. A patchwork of policies supports this trend, and systemic factors lead to ongoing problems.[31]

Despite numerous reports, publications, and calls to action to address the "appalling circumstances of Aboriginal children and youth in this country," the situation remains "fundamentally unchanged."[32] In 2007, the Assembly of First Nations (AFN) and the First Nations Child and Family Caring Society of Canada formally filed a complaint with the Canadian Human Rights Commission regarding the lack of equitable funding for First Nations child welfare.[33] Indigenous leaders in Canada have struggled to find a middle ground with governments and communities to engage in meaningful policy development to support better outcomes for their children. Existing political institutions seem ill-equipped to address these matters, which tend to be invisible and relegated to the concerns of a powerless population. The complaint has now proceeded to the hearing stage as Canada has twice refused mediation.[34] One remains optimistic that governments will work more coherently and effectively on improving the life chances for Indigenous children.

In Canada and other places in the world, addressing these harms requires the recognition that Indigenous children's best interests can be secured within the "context of revitalized Aboriginal families, communities and nations."[35] It also requires the ability to overcome the difficulties of "turning ideals into reality."[36] From the most basic level of their health, security, and well-being, to the capacity of their families and communities to protect and develop their languages and cultures, improving the situation of Indigenous children requires clear policy understanding and support. The lack of political will to commit to a reconciliation process that acknowledges the past and recognizes touchstones for change has impeded the creation of a collaborative and comprehensive approach to support Indigenous children from birth to adulthood.

It is regrettable that Canada has not yet endorsed the *Declaration*, because it arguably represents the most specific iteration of Indigenous children's human rights and thus a framework for a new beginning to address the inequities that continue to be disproportionately borne by Indigenous peoples. In particular, a new framework would allow for a more nuanced approach to resolving conflicts over the "best interests of the child" and the cultural security of the child.

3. The United Nations Declaration on the Rights of Indigenous Peoples

3A Background

On 13 September 2007, the United Nations General Assembly adopted the *Declaration*, which affirms the collective and individual rights of the world's 370 million Indigenous people. After over 20 years of negotiations and consultations with member states, representatives from Indigenous groups and human rights organizations, the *Declaration* became the "key instrument and tool for raising awareness on and monitoring progress of indigenous peoples' situations and the protection, respect and fulfillment of indigenous peoples' rights."[37] The *Declaration* represents a "test of commitment of States and the whole international community to protect, respect and fulfill indigenous peoples collective and individual human rights."[38]

Having the distinction of being the only human rights declaration drafted with rights-holders themselves as an integral part of the process, it has been described as reflecting "a growing international consensus concerning the content of the rights of indigenous peoples, as they have been progressively affirmed in domestic legislation, in international instruments, and in the practice of international human rights bodies."[39] Indigenous and human rights organizations agree that the "UN Declaration is an essential, universal human rights standard that is urgently needed to inspire and guide states and public institutions to address the marginalization and discrimination faced by Indigenous peoples around the world."[40] The *Declaration* is now part of the array of international human rights instruments which work to promote a safe international social order and vibrant civil societies.

3B Canada's Position: Differing Opinions

The *Declaration* was adopted by the General Assembly with a vote total of 144 in favour, four against, and 11 abstentions. Canada voted against it, having also voted against a previous draft in 2006 at the United Nations Human Rights Council. In its statement to the General Assembly, Canada cited its concerns with certain provisions, including those relating to lands and resources, free, prior, and informed consent, and self-government. Canada regarded the provisions on lands, territories, and resources as "overly broad and unclear and . . . susceptible of a wide variety of interpretations . . . possibly putting into question matters that have already been settled by treaty in Canada."[41]

Voting against the *Declaration*, Canada's representative indicated that Canada was disappointed with both the text's substance and the process leading to its adoption, but would "continue to take effective action, at home and abroad, to promote and protect the rights of indigenous peoples based on our existing human rights obligations and commitments."[42] It may be that "effective action" would be weakened by not endorsing the *Declaration*, as a key use of the *Declaration* is to interpret the rights and obligations contained in existing human rights instruments, including those Canada that has ratified. Interpretation is a dynamic process, and the *Declaration* may allow for a fuller consideration of experiences, norms, and aspirations in resolving disputes in domestic law or policy.[43]

Significant efforts were made to encourage Canada to support the *Declaration*. The House of Commons Standing Committee on Aboriginal Affairs and Northern Development recommended that the government pledge its support for the *Declaration*.[44] An open letter sent on behalf of Indigenous and human rights organizations, including the AFN, the Native Women's Association of Canada, the Inuit Circumpolar Conference, the First Nations Summit, the British Columbia Assembly of First Nations, the Union of British Columbia Indian Chiefs, and Amnesty International urged Canada to "recognize that the Declaration is an essential step forward for the world's most vulnerable and frequently victimized peoples."[45]

Canada's decision to vote against the *Declaration*, along with Australia, New Zealand, and the United States, was met with disappointment both in the United Nations and domestically in Canada. The then UN High Commissioner for Human Rights, Canadian Louise Arbour, called it a "very surprising position for Canada to take after not only years (but) decades of progressive involvement on that issue."[46] The National Chief of the AFN stated that he was "gravely concerned that the Government of Canada chose to vote against the UN Declaration and, in effect, opposes fundamental human rights protections for Indigenous peoples."[47]

Over a hundred Canadian legal scholars and experts signed an open letter in which they concluded there was "[n]o credible legal rationale" for the adverse position adopted by the Canadian government toward the *Declaration*. Moreover, they stated that the *Declaration* provides a principled framework that promotes a vision of justice and reconciliation, and "[g]overnment claims to the contrary do a grave disservice to the cause of human rights and to the promotion of harmonious and cooperative relations."[48]

On 8 April 2008, the House of Commons passed a motion calling for "Parliament and the Government of Canada to fully implement the standards" contained in the *Declaration*.[49] This motion has not yet resulted in a change in the government's position. The government did not respond to a private member's bill that would have required it to "take all measures necessary to ensure that the laws of Canada are consistent with the *Declaration*."[50]

3c   Implications for Indigenous Children

Canada's reluctance to support the *Declaration* has resulted in delayed opportunities to improve the well-being of Indigenous children. In voting against the *Declaration*, Canada did not oppose or single out provisions relating to Indigenous children as matters of concern, yet the unfortunate result was that these articles have not yet been endorsed.

The *Declaration* contains several provisions that speak directly to the situation of Indigenous children. More than any other UN human rights instrument, the *Declaration* allows for a fuller appreciation of cultural and community attachment or security as a protective factor for the healthy development of children. This recognizes the strength of Indigenous peoples and cultures and the importance of the transmission of distinct languages, cultures, and kinship for the well-being of children. Indigenous peoples need to be supported to maintain their societies by having states acknowledge the positive role and human rights they possess to raise their children in their own unique language and culture and to sustain their attachment to their people when removed from the parental home.

The preamble of the *Declaration* links the well-being of Indigenous children to the strength and support of their families and communities: "*Recognizing in particular* the right of Indigenous families and communities to retain shared responsibility for the upbringing, training, education and well-being of their children, consistent with the rights of the child."

Further provisions in the *Declaration* support new policy development for better outcomes for Indigenous children, including article 7, which elaborates the collective right of Indigenous peoples to live in freedom, peace, and security as distinct peoples and not to be subjected to any act of genocide or other act of violence. It further acknowledges policies calling for the forcible removal of children as a human rights concern.[51]

In articles 14 and 15, the *Declaration* affirms the right of Indigenous peoples to establish and control their educational systems and institutions, providing education in their own languages, in a manner appropriate to their cultural methods of teaching and learning. Indigenous children have the right to all levels and forms of education witho ut discrimination. In conjunction with Indigenous peoples, states are to take effective measures to ensure that Indigenous children (including those living outside their communities) have access, when possible, to an education in their own culture and in their own language.[52]

Article 17(2) of the *Declaration* requires that specific measures be taken by states, in consultation and co-operation with Indigenous peoples, to protect Indigenous children from economic exploitation and from performing any work that is likely to be hazardous or to interfere with the child's education, or to be harmful to the child's health or physical, mental, spiritual, moral, or social development. In doing so, states are to take into account the special vulnerability of Indigenous children and the importance of education for their empowerment. In taking effective — and, where appropriate — special measures to ensure the continuing improvement of the economic and social conditions of Indigenous peoples, states are to pay special attention to the rights and special needs of Indigenous elders, women, youth, children, and persons with disabilities.[53] Indeed, the whole of the *Declaration* is to be interpreted and applied giving special consideration to the rights of Indigenous children and youth and their need for safety, security and well-being.[54]

The *Declaration* therefore affirms standards or guidelines that encourage new policy directions at a national level to create a better future for Indigenous children. It makes a valuable contribution to the dialogue on the rights of the child by acknowledging the strengths and rights of Indigenous peoples, and not just the past harm of failed policies. Efforts to improve the circumstances and opportunities for Indigenous children could arguably be strengthened by reading and applying the *Convention on the Rights of the Child* in a manner that is consistent with the *Declaration*.

4. THE CONVENTION ON THE RIGHTS OF THE CHILD

4A Background

The international effort on behalf of children's rights coalesced in a pinnacle of achievement with the entry into force of the *Convention on the Rights of the Child* in 1990. The *Convention* had moved from the stage of a declaration in 1959[55] to becoming a *Convention*, opened for signature, 30 years later in 1989. With 193 states parties, the *Convention on the Rights of the Child* is the most widely-ratified human rights treaty. Only the United States and Somalia have failed to ratify it. The *Convention* has been an invaluable tool in raising awareness and bringing attention to the plight of children, and the obstacles they face, on a national and global level.

Two optional protocols were developed supplementary to the *Convention*: the *Optional Protocol to the Convention on the Rights of the Child on the Involvement of Children in Armed Conflict*[56] and *Optional Protocol to the Convention on the Rights of the Child on the Sale of Children, Child Prostitution and Child Pornography.*[57] Canada ratified the optional protocols in 2000 and 2005, respectively.

The *Convention on the Rights of the Child* sets out the political, economic, social, and cultural rights of all children. It can be divided into eight themes:

1) general measures of implementation;

2) definition of the child;

3) general principles;

4) civil rights and freedoms;

5) family environment and alternative care;

6) basic health and welfare;

7) education, leisure and cultural activities; and

8) special protection measures, including children in situations of emergency, children in conflict with the law, children in situations of exploitation, and children belonging to a minority or an Indigenous group.[58]

4B   Implications for Indigenous Children

The majority of the provisions of the *Convention* are of general application — that is, they apply equally to all children. However, the *Convention* also refers specifically to Indigenous people in three articles. In article 17, states parties are to "[e]ncourage the mass media to have particular regard to the linguistic needs of the child who belongs to a minority group or who is indigenous." In article 29, states parties agree that the education of the child shall be directed to "[t]he preparation of the child for responsible life in a free society, in the spirit of understanding, peace, tolerance, equality of sexes, and friendship among all peoples, ethnic, national and religious groups and persons of indigenous origin."

Article 30 guarantees the rights of children to their language, culture, and religion:

> In those States in which ethnic, religious or linguistic minorities or persons of indigenous origin exist, a child belonging to such a minority or who is indigenous shall not be denied the right, in community with other members of his or her group, to enjoy his or her own culture, to profess and practise his or her own religion, or to use his or her own language.

This article reflects the importance of cultural safety for Indigenous children and families.

Under article 2, states are to "respect and ensure the rights set forth in the present Convention to each child within their jurisdiction without discrimination of any kind," and to "take all appropriate measures to ensure that the child is protected against all forms of discrimination or punishment." Although it does not mention Indigenous children specifically, this guarantee of rights without discrimination is vitally important for Indigenous children, as they are frequently unable to enjoy their rights in equality with non-Indigenous children.

Canada demonstrated a commitment to issues specific to Indigenous children in the development of the *Convention*, and registered two reservations and a statement of understanding when it signed. One reservation related to article 37(c) (regarding children deprived of their liberty), with Canada reserving "the right not to detain children separately from adults where this is not appropriate or feasible."[59] The other reservation pertained specifically to Indigenous children. Canada indicated that it reserved the right not to apply article 21 (relating to adoption) to the extent that it may "be inconsistent with customary forms of care among aboriginal peoples in Canada."[60] In making this reservation, Canada wanted to ensure that Indigenous customs with respect to adoption and placement of children would not be harmed by the application of the *Convention*.

Additionally, Canada made a statement of understanding to indicate that, in relation to the Indigenous peoples of Canada, the fulfillment of its obligations to "undertake all appropriate legislative, administrative, and other measures for the implementation of the rights recognized in the present Convention"[61]

> must take into account the provisions of article 30. In particular, in assessing what measures are appropriate to implement the rights recognized in the Convention for aboriginal children, due regard must be paid to not denying their right, in community with other members of their group, to enjoy their own culture, to profess and practice their own religion and to use their own language.[62]

Canada thus acknowledged the connections between Indigenous children and their communities and families. Unfortunately, it has not resulted in measurable changes to the situations Indigenous children face. Perhaps this can be attributed to the fact that the positive recognition of Indigenous peoples' existence as peoples was not by definition part of this *Convention*. In 2009, the *Convention on the Rights of the Child* celebrated its 20th anniversary, meaning that a generation of children has been born under its protections, and recognition that they are rights holders. Indigenous children have been prevented from enjoying these rights equally with their non-Indigenous peers.

5. We Can Do Better

5A Applying the Convention and the Declaration

While it is disappointing that Canada has not endorsed the *Declaration*, human rights commissions, social services and other agencies, Indigenous peoples, and the courts are free to find guidance in the *Declaration* in interpreting and promoting the rights of Indigenous children. The *Declaration* can also provide a framework for policy development and reconciliation. This will be strengthened when Canada endorses the *Declaration*.

As the Special Rapporteur on the situation of human rights and fundamental freedoms of indigenous people has observed, "the Declaration reflects and builds upon human rights norms of general applicability, as interpreted and applied by United Nations and regional treaty bodies."[63] The Committee on the Elimination of Racial Discrimination has already indicated that the *Declaration* should be used as a guide to interpret state party obligations under the *International Convention on the Elimination of All Forms of Racial Discrimination*.[64] In the same way, the articles of the *Declaration* can be used to build upon the application and interpretation of the *Convention on the Rights of the Child* as it applies to Indigenous children and their distinct communities. This is important because the *Convention* is generally concerned with individual rights. It is therefore limited in its ability to address issues faced by Indigenous children, given their broader human rights status as members of unique communities, or peoples.

This limitation has been addressed in recent years through work by the Committee on the Rights of the Child to better understand the circumstances of Indigenous children. A Day of General Discussion on the Rights of Indigenous Children was held by the Committee on the Rights of the Child in 2003. Following the Day of General Discussion, the Sub-Group on Indigenous Children and Young People was formed by Indigenous peoples' organizations as part of the NGO Group of the Committee. The Sub-group assisted the Committee to draft a General Comment on Indigenous Children and Young People to "give state parties clear directions on their obligations towards Indigenous children under the *Convention*."[65]

The Committee adopted the General Comment in January 2009. In the General Comment, the Committee "urges States parties to adopt a rights-based approach to indigenous children based on the Convention and other relevant international standards, such as ILO Convention No. 169 and the United Nations Declaration on the Rights of Indigenous Peoples."[66] This will further strengthen the interpretation and application of the *Convention* in a manner that is consistent with the rights of Indigenous children. A number of measures can be taken to significantly improve the lives of Indigenous children and promote their rights as affirmed by the *Convention* and the *Declaration*. None of these measures should wait until Canada formally endorses the *Declaration*, although this progressive step would significantly strengthen efforts toward implementing the following recommendations.

5B Establishing a National Children's Commissioner

Despite Canada's ratification of the *Convention*, it has been "effectively marginalized when it comes to its direct impact on children's lives."[67] One way to prioritize and engage our responsibilities to children is to establish an independent office of Parliament dedicated to examine child welfare issues nationally and monitor the implementation of the rights Canada endorsed in the *Convention*. Establishing such an office would be consistent with Canada's obligations to "undertake all appropriate legislative, administrative, and other measures for the implementation of the rights recognized" in the *Convention*.[68] Also, under article 38 of the *Declaration*, states are required to take appropriate measures, including legislative measures, to achieve the ends of the *Declaration*, in consultation and co-operation with Indigenous peoples. Given the unique federal responsibility in Canadian constitutional law for Indigenous peoples' status and rights, a National Commissioner could take a special focus in this area, evaluating the effectiveness of current policies and programs and making more visible to legislators and Canadians the needs and circumstances of Indigenous children and youth in Canada. It is evident that this focus is absent at the national level. The development of policy, legislation, and practices to support better outcomes for Indigenous children must receive dedicated focus.

UNICEF's global reseach on "Ombuds for Children" in different regions and countries has found a number of common characteristics of independent human rights institutions for children, including: the institution is established by legislation; independence, at both financial and political levels; pluralistic representation of the various elements of the civil society; the institution is geographically and physically accessible to children; the institution has a broad mandate, including powers to carry out investigations, monitor institutions where children spend time, advocate on behalf of children's rights, denounce children's rights violations, and raise awareness of the human rights of children among children and adults; child participation, efforts to promote respect for the views of children in all matters affecting them and to adapt the office for listening and communicating with children; and partnerships and co-operation with a wide range of actors at national, regional, and international levels.[69]

Scotland, England, and New Zealand are examples of countries that have appointed a national Children's Commissioner. The Children's Commissioner for England aims to "gives a voice to all children and young people, especially the disadvantaged and the vulnerable."[70] Scotland's Commissioner for Children and Young People has stated that the *Convention* is a "set of promises to do certain things to make life better for children and young people," and that the Commission's job is to "make sure those promises are kept."[71] The New Zealand Office of the Commissioner for Children "advocates for the best interests of all children and young people in New Zealand" and "looks to ensure all of their rights are respected and upheld."[72] Until April 2009, New Zealand had an Indigenous person, Dr. Cindy Kiro, as its Commissioner for Children.

A number of committees in Canada, including Parliamentary committees, have called for a national Children's Commissioner to be established.[73] This continues to be a major priority for the Canadian Council of Provincial Children's Advocates. A national Children's Commissioner would create the impetus for governments to prioritize children's issues and enable the *Convention* to be applied in a more pronounced manner. It would allow for a focused mandate on children and create partnerships and linkages amongst the different levels of government. A Children's Commissioner would endorse best practices, address national and regional issues, and co-ordinate monitoring and data collection for the "planning, policy design and implementation, and resource allocation"[74] that are essential to measure progress. The importance of monitoring is underscored by the authors of *Measuring and Monitoring Children's Well-being*:

> It is our assumption that children are a unique and distinct population group who need and deserve a unique policy or set of policies to promote their well-being. The best interest of the child may not only differ from that of the family or parents, but may even conflict with it. In order to shape appropriate and effective policies for children, a flow of data and information regarding their status, as well as the changes they experience and are facing, is also required.[75]

Being part of the federal level of government, a Children's Commissioner could provide important oversight and advocacy for better outcomes for Indigenous children, especially if he or she worked in tandem with provincial and territorial children's advocates. The Children's Commissioner should be encouraged to consider the provisions of the *Declaration* when evaluating the health, safety, and well-being of Indigenous children, including best practices.

5c Respecting the Right of Self-Determination in Indigenous Child Welfare

The *Declaration* affirms that Indigenous peoples have the right to self-determination,[76] and article 23 affirms, further, that Indigenous peoples "have the right to be actively involved in developing and determining health, housing and other economic and social programmes affecting them and, as far as possible, to administer such programmes through their own institutions."

These principles underlie recent efforts by Indigenous peoples to address the well-being of Indigenous children. Commenting on the AFN's human rights complaint, the National Chief remarked that

> we have the right to determine what is best for the future of our children. Our children must have an equal opportunity to grow-up with their families, in their communities, and in their culture. No First Nation child should have to forgo this opportunity as a result of poverty or an inability to access basic services.[77]

Respect for the right of Indigenous peoples to self-determination requires an acknowledgement that "Indigenous peoples are in the best position to make decisions that affect Indigenous children, youth, families, and communities."[78] This does not mean working in isolation, particularly as Indigenous children in Canada live in increasingly urban settings where collaboration by many levels of government and service providers is essential for positive outcomes.

There is growing evidence that there is increased "Aboriginal success in education where Aboriginal peoples are involved in determining Aboriginal education."[79] Self-determination through participation, design, and delivery of programs and services may support improved health outcomes, with studies showing that "cultural preservation and continuity, as well as living in communities with self-government, settled land claims, and access to self-managed education, health, cultural and policing services all have positive impacts on the health of the local population."[80] In particular, research in British Columbia has supported a finding that "communities with some level of self government and/or multiple community control factors present had the lowest rates of suicide."[81] Cultural safety and self-determination, therefore, seem to be significant factors in protecting and promoting the health and well-being of Indigenous people, especially children. Further work is required to fully understand (and support) the positive impact of cultural connection, transmission, and support for the health, safety, education, and well-being outcomes for Indigenous children and youth in Canada.

The Auditor General of Canada commented in her 2008 report that "[t]he overrepresentation of Aboriginal and First Nations children in care — and the indications that outcomes are poor — call for all parties involved in the child welfare system to find better ways of meeting these children's needs."[82] Such "better ways" need to include respect for the right of self-determination of Indigenous peoples, which can mean a degree of participation and control negotiated with other governments and authorities.

Typically, provincial child welfare legislation applies on reserve.[83] Nominal space has been made for Indigenous participation, governance, or child development practices. In British Columbia, efforts are under way to explore new models for the delivery of services to Aboriginal children and families. Delegation agreements have been signed "between the province and First Nations communities to return historic responsibilities for child protection and family support to Aboriginal communities."[84] These are still subject to provincial legislative authority and jurisdiction, but do point in the direction of Indigenous control. Indigenous jurisdiction over child welfare is recognized in the *Nisga'a Final Agreement*[85] and other agreements, but has not yet been exercised by the Indigenous governing body.

First Nations in British Columbia have engaged in significant planning activities toward taking responsibility for child and family wellness, including protection, support, and prevention programs. Some of these initiatives have sparked unique outreach activities, such as homecoming ceremonies reuniting Indigenous children with their home communities, families, and cultures.[86] Each of these initiatives gives expression to the voices, rights, and well-being of Indigenous children, and are to be encouraged.

It is fair to say that progress to date has been slow. The federal government has had limited involvement with Indigenous organizations at the national level in setting out a legal framework on a comprehensive set of outcomes measures to improve the well-being of children. Provincial governments have struggled to provide effective capacity and recognition to Aboriginal child services organizations.

Leading Canadian advocates have proposed that "[o]nly adequate and sustained resources will enable Indigenous communities to implement self-determination in child welfare."[87] Indeed, article 39 of the *Declaration* affirms that "Indigenous peoples have the right to have access to financial and technical assistance from States . . . for the enjoyment of the rights contained in this Declaration." Very limited discussion on how to move forward in this regard has occurred at the federal, provincial, or territorial level to date. Efforts to develop strategies to enable Indigenous communities to have concurrent or exclusive authority for child welfare and development, with appropriate funding and resources, must be encouraged, evaluated, and adequately supported within a human rights paradigm.

5D   Stricter Adherence to the Reportng Mechanism of the Convention

A Canadian Senate report has remarked that "Canada must begin to take its international human rights treaty obligations more seriously."[88] One particular area for improvement is Canada's compliance with the reporting mechanism under the *Convention*.

Article 44 of the *Convention* requir es states parties to report on their progress in implementing the *Convention*. States must submit reports two years after signing the *Convention* and every five years thereafter to the Committee on the Rights of the Child, an independent body that monitors the implementation of the *Convention* and its optional protocols. The reporting relationship works two ways: as the states submit reports, the committee can indicate its concerns and deliver recommendations.

There has been a considerable gap between Canada's reports. Canada has reported twice on its implementation of the *Convention*. The first report was submitted in June 1994 and outlined measures adopted up to 31 December 1992 by all governments in Canada.[89] The second report was submitted in May 2001 and covered the period from January 1993 to December 1997.[90] The next report was deferred after an exceptional measure was taken: in order to help Canada catch up with its reporting obligations so as to be in full compliance with the *Convention*, the committee invited Canada to submit its third and fourth periodic reports by 11 January 2009.[91] In November 2009, Canada submitted them both as a combined report, covering the period from January 1998 to December 2007.[92]

This delay in reporting means that we have an unclear picture of how the *Convention* is working in Canada. It also makes it difficult to measure progress and to examine what further action is required. Canada must be encouraged to meet its reporting obligations if it is to truly demonstrate its commitment to put children first.

5E   Focused and Co-ordinated Advocacy by NGOs and Indigenous Peoples' Organizations

The *Convention* was drafted with the input of non-governmental organizations, and they have continued to play a role in the reporting processes and monitoring of the implementation of the *Convention*.[93] In 2008, Canada engaged in consultations with non-governmental and Indigenous organizations in the preparation of the federal portion of Canada's report. Whether these consultations were adequate to reflect Canada's constitutional duties to consult Indigenous peoples in respect of major policy developments is a matter outside the scope of this paper, but one well worth considering. Those consultations, while nominal, were certainly better than none.

Non-governmental and Indigenous peoples' organizations can work together to highlight particular issues, challenges, and difficulties as well as push for new priorities and goals for Canadian social policy in support of vulnerable children. A number of organizations submit alternative reports directly to the committee in order to present a more accurate perspective as to Canada's progress in implementing the *Convention* and what still needs to be achieved to improve the lives of children.[94] It is often in these reports that the issues facing Indigenous children are identified, and this mechanism can therefore serve a valuable oversight function. It is essential that non-governmental and Indigenous peoples' organizations continue to co-ordinate their advocacy efforts to ensure that an accurate portrait of how Indigenous children are faring is presented to the committee. Non-governmental and Indigenous peoples' organizations may also begin looking to the provisions of the *Declaration* when commenting on Canada's progress in implementing the *Convention on the Rights of the Child*.

5F Ensuring the Meaningful Participation of Children

There are no greater stakeholders when considering issues affecting children than children themselves. Their voices and direct participation in decision-making processes affecting their rights and welfare must be strengthened. Efforts should be made to empower Indigenous children and prevent marginalization and discrimination. An excellent example of youth participation concerns the efforts of the students from the Attawapiskat Cree First Nation in fighting for the federal government to fulfill its responsibility to build a school in their isolated community on the James Bay coast. The students were moved into portable classrooms eight years ago when a diesel spill left their former school environment toxic.[95] The students sent notice to the federal government of their intention to send a report to the United Nations detailing the failure of the Department of Indian and Northern Affairs to build a school. It will be addressed in the upcoming review of Canada's obligations under the *Convention*.[96]

Article 12 of the *Convention* conveys the importance of the participation of children and the right of children to express their views freely in all matters affecting them.[97] For children to effectively participate, the dissemination of information is essential and their participation must be sought. This requires greater attention to the accessibility and availability of information. Canada has made few inroads in incr easing the participation of children at the national government level, and there has been uneven progress at the provincial and local government levels. Indigenous organizations and governments have youth councils in place, but clearly more should be done to build the participation of children and youth in the public process of governance, administration, and programming.

6. Conclusion

In response to Canada's last report, the Committee on the Rights of the Child expressed concerns about the "gap in life chances between Aboriginal and non-Aboriginal children," and the fact that "Aboriginal children continue to experience many problems, including discrimination in several areas, with much greater frequency and severity than their non-Aboriginal peers."[98] Now more than ever we have to ensure that international human rights instruments such as the *Convention on the Rights of the Child* and the *Declaration on the Rights of Indigenous Peoples* are more than words, aspirations, and possibilities, but that they have positive meaning and impacts in Canada and around the world.

We can more effectively support Indigenous children in Canada and elsewhere by embracing the principled, contextual, and normative framework provided by the *Declaration*. This builds on the *Convention* and other international human rights instruments which assist in resolving conflicts within and among states.

The act of endorsing the *Declaration* will not alone resolve the issues we face in Canada. However, it would assist to create a framework that brings us together to work with Indigenous children for a better, more respectful, and more fulfilling society, anchored by human rights and equality. This is sometimes referred to as reconciliation in Canada. The true test of reconciliation is not whether it is accepted at the national political table, but whether it supports better lives and opportunities for Indigenous children — supporting them to achieve everything they can both as individuals and as members of distinct communities and peoples. Until then, Indigenous children will continue to wait for words to turn into action.

Hopes and Challenges
on the Road Ahead

◯

Jackie Hartley, Paul Joffe,
and Jennifer Preston

On the day of the adoption of the *United Nations Declaration on the Rights of Indigenous Peoples*, Victoria Tauli-Corpuz, chair of the United Nations Permanent Forum on Indigenous Issues, called upon "governments, the UN system, Indigenous Peoples and civil society at large to rise to the historic task before us and make the UN Declaration on the Rights of Indigenous Peoples a living document for the common future of humanity."[1]

This collection contributes to this task by promoting further discussion and use of the *Declaration*. This dialogue is essential so that the human rights of Indigenous peoples are respected, protected, promoted, and fulfilled.

The authors in this collection demonstrate how the *Declaration* is being mainstreamed within the United Nations system and implemented by Indigenous peoples, states, and civil society. They illustrate the diverse ways that the *Declaration* can be further used to promote the rights of Indigenous peoples in domestic and international contexts.

However, much work lies ahead to ensure that the promise of the *Declaration* is fully and effectively realized.

A key challenge in this post-adoption era is to ensure that the rights affirmed by the *Declaration* are implemented at a domestic level. This will involve their being accepted and generally adhered to in society. It will also involve the inclusion of the rights in government policy and their incorporation in the legal system, through legislation or judicial interpretation — i.e., their social, political, and legal internalization.[2] In Canada and other states, we see these dynamics beginning to take place.

An important way to promote the internalization of the *Declaration* is to use it at every opportunity. As Kenneth Deer remarks in chapter one, "When rights are asserted, they grow." In the Australian context, Tom Calma, then the Aboriginal and Torres Strait Islander Social Justice Commissioner, commented that:

> One of the most effective ways that Indigenous Australians can use the *Declaration* is simply by referring to it as an applicable standard. This is because, as is the case with the *Universal Declaration of Human Rights*, the rights set out in the *Declaration* will be most effectively protected in Australia when they become a standard that is recognised and referred to by the community at large.[3]

Repeated use of the *Declaration* will ensure that it develops over time and gains wider acceptance, both internationally and domestically. As Norway has affirmed, "[t]he Declaration contextualizes all existing human rights for Indigenous Peoples and provides therefore the natural frame of reference for work and debate relating to the promotion of indigenous peoples rights."[4]

There are many ways that the *Declaration* can be used into the future.

It can guide the development of new relationships between Indigenous peoples and states. A significant example emanates from the Arctic. On 21 June 2009, Greenland achieved significantly enhanced self-government, changing its political relationship with Denmark.[5] Kuupik Kleist, Premier of Greenland, in his address to the UN Expert Mechanism on the Rights of Indigenous Peoples, underlined that "this new development in Greenland and in the relationship between Denmark and Greenland should be seen as a *de facto* implementation of the Declaration and, in this regard, hopefully an inspiration to others."[6] In addition to recognizing Greenlanders as a people under international law, the new *Act on Greenland Self-Government* recognizes Greenlandic as the official language.[7] Greenland's new status further includes the recognition of "Greenland's ownership and control of all natural resources."[8]

The *Declaration* encourages states to recognize Indigenous peoples. In June 2008, the Japanese legislature (Diet) unanimously adopted a resolution to recognize the Ainu as Indigenous people of Japan. The resolution, which drew upon the *Declaration*, is the first time Japan has recognized the Ainu as Indigenous. The resolution also called on the government to consider the opinions of a panel of expert advisors and, based on these opinions, advance Ainu policies and work toward establishing comprehensive measures.[9] The adoption of this resolution "can be seen as a logical consequence of Japan's vote in favour of the UN Declaration on the Rights of Indigenous Peoples."[10]

Similarly, the *Declaration* is being used as a standard to underpin engagement between Indigenous peoples, governments, corporations, and other third parties. Indigenous leaders and civil society are increasingly invoking the *Declaration* to assert the rights of Indigenous peoples in relation to resource development. In particular, the *Declaration* is being used to support efforts to encourage governments and resource companies to honour the right and principle of free, prior, and informed consent in their relationships with Indigenous peoples.[11]

A central purpose of the *Declaration* is to interpret Indigenous rights and state obligations. As illustrated by several authors in this collection, it can form a vital element of the "consistent advocacy" of Indigenous peoples to seek redress for rights violations, including violations of treaty rights.

The *Declaration* can fill in gaps in treaties, particularly historic treaties that often include less detail than contemporary treaties relating to lands, resources, governance, and other crucial matters. When used as a framework for interpreting Indigenous rights and state duties consistently with contemporary human rights standards and law, the *Declaration* can serve to ensure that treaties remain dynamic and lasting agreements.

The application of the *Declaration* by domestic courts as a tool to guide the interpretation of constitutions and legislation will also strengthen its normative significance and legal effect. The landmark case of *Cal and Coy* v. *Attorney General of Belize*, in which the Supreme Court of Belize referred to the *Declaration* in upholding the constitutional rights of the Maya people to lands and resources, provides an important example of how this can be achieved.[12]

The *Declaration* is also being used to support efforts to achieve greater protection for the rights of Indigenous peoples through constitutional and legislative reform.[13] In Bolivia, the *Declaration* was adopted at the national level as Law No. 3760 of 7 November 2007 and incorporated into the new constitution that was promulgated on 7 February 2009.[14]

As illustrated throughout this collection, the *Declaration* can be further used to advocate for a new approach to policy development — one that reflects the indivisibility and interconnectedness of human rights — leading to better outcomes for Indigenous people, including women and children.

International engagement will continue to be crucial in ensuring that the rights of Indigenous peoples are protected and promoted by states and human rights bodies. A challenge for the future is to ensure that the *Declaration* is firmly embedded in the work of the UN and regional bodies. Non-governmental and Indigenous peoples' organizations will play a major role in this process as they continue to use the standards affirmed in the *Declaration* to frame their engagement with a range of UN bodies and mechanisms. These include the UN treaty monitoring bodies, the

Human Rights Council, and the Permanent Forum on Indigenous Issues.

The Universal Periodic Review (UPR) of Canada before the Human Rights Council in February 2009 provides an example of how international mechanisms can draw attention to failures to endorse or implement the *Declaration*. In their submissions to the UPR, numerous Indigenous and human rights organizations highlighted Canada's failure to support the *Declaration* and how Canada's actions had violated the rule of law.[15] Many states subsequently raised the *Declaration* during the questioning of Canada and recommended that Canada change its position.[16] Certainly a number of states regard Canada's opposition as seriously tarnishing its human rights record.

The *Declaration* has also been repeatedly raised in other UPR sessions by states during the examination of other states.[17] This is an important way to hold states publicly accountable for their human rights performance, and it should be increasingly used in the future.

There is significant potential for the *Declaration* to be further mainstreamed in the work of international and regional bodies. The Office of the High Commissioner for Human Rights is firmly committed to implementing the *Declaration*.[18] In addition, several treaty monitoring bodies are already referring to the *Declaration* and its standards to interpret Indigenous rights and state obligations in existing treaties and conventions.[19] This presents opportunities for Indigenous peoples to raise the *Declaration* to support their arguments in complaints before international or regional bodies.

The *Declaration* is also being promoted internationally through the work of the Permanent Forum on Indigenous Issues, the Expert Mechanism on the Rights of Indigenous Peoples, and the Special Rapporteur on the situation of human rights and fundamental freedoms of indigenous people. In September 2009, members of these mechanisms jointly concluded:

> The United Nations Declaration on the Rights of Indigenous Peoples is the principal normative framework for the three United Nations mechanisms with a specific mandate regarding indigenous peoples' rights, and it should also constitute an important frame of reference for the United Nations treaty bodies and other relevant international and regional human rights mechanisms.[20]

They added that, in accordance with article 42 of the *Declaration*, the three mechanisms are required "to apply the Declaration universally, irrespective of the positions of individual States" on this instrument.[21]

In an example of the application of the *Declaration* by international bodies, the Permanent Forum organized a multi-agency mission in 2009 at the invitation of the governments of Bolivia and Paraguay to assess the forced labour, servitude, and land dispossession of Indigenous people.[22] The Permanent Forum used the *Declaration*,[23] together with diverse international treaties and domestic laws, in making recommendations on the state of slavery and related human rights violations affecting the Guarani people.

Regional human rights bodies in the Americas and Africa are also integrating the *Declaration* into their work. As described by authors in this collection, state and Indigenous representatives in the Organization of American States are negotiating a draft American Declaration on the Rights of Indigenous Peoples, using the *Declaration* as a baseline and minimum standard.

Further, in a landmark ruling the African Commission on Human and Peoples' Rights has affirmed in effect that the *Declaration* is applicable to all African states regardless of whether they voted in its favour at the General Assembly – and regardless of whether or not certain Indigenous rights are recognized as such in a state's constitutional and legal framework.[24]

Efforts will continue to encourage the states that voted against the *Declaration* to reconsider their positions, and those that abstained from the vote to publicly support it. As indicated in the Introduction, at the time of writing there is renewed hope that Canada, New Zealand, and the United States may endorse the *Declaration* in the future. Such support needs to occur without qualifications. The *Declaration* will grow in international prominence as further states choose to endorse it.

Any new endorsements will further reinforce the use of the *Declaration* as a standard in international and regional systems, consolidating international support for the rights of Indigenous peoples. In some instances, constructive pressure on domestic governments may prove necessary, so that they fulfill their international obligations to protect and promote the human rights of all peoples and individuals without discrimination.

Finally, the development of human rights learning and education programs will be vital for ensuring that the *Declaration* is widely understood, accepted, and applied.

The *ad hoc* coalition in Canada is continuing its educational work on several levels, developing materials, distributing the *Declaration* to academic institutions, and delivering presentations to a wide variety of audiences, from law conferences to community centres. This information-sharing is increasing grassroots awareness and engagement. The booklet version of the *Declaration* produced by the *ad hoc* coalition inspired the Greenland Home Rule Government to produce a similar version in both Danish and Greenlandic. The *Declaration* is also being produced in Indigenous and other languages throughout the world.[25]

State governments have a responsibility to support human rights education. The *Declaration* provides a framework for promoting awareness of the rights of Indigenous peoples in school curricula and through training for public servants, parliamentarians, and judges. Such education can help develop a culture of respect for the rights of Indigenous peoples at all levels of government and in the community generally.

As shown throughout this collection, the *Declaration* promotes justice and reconciliation. Its adoption heralded a new era in international human rights. As UN Secretary-General Ban Ki-moon emphasized:

> The Declaration is a visionary step towards addressing the human rights of indigenous peoples. It sets out a framework on which States can build or rebuild their relationships with indigenous peoples. The result of more than two decades of negotiations, it provides a momentous opportunity for States and indigenous peoples to strengthen their relationships, promote reconciliation and ensure that the past is not repeated.[26]

Undoubtedly, many more visionary steps must be taken to ensure that Indigenous peoples fully enjoy their human rights. This collection highlights the many ways that the *Declaration* is being realized and how implementation can be advanced in the future. Ultimately, the implementation of the *Declaration* can contribute to new relationships and a better future, founded on "the principles of justice, democracy, respect for human rights, equality, non-discrimination, good governance and good faith."[27]

United Nations Declaration on the Rights of Indigenous Peoples

Sixty-first session   **A/RES/61/295**

Agenda item 68

Resolution adopted by the General Assembly

[*without reference to a Main Committee (A/61/L.67 and Add.1)*]

61/295. United Nations Declaration on the Rights of Indigenous Peoples

The General Assembly,

Taking note of the recommendation of the Human Rights Council contained in its resolution 1/2 of 29 June 2006,[1] by which the Council adopted the text of the United Nations Declaration on the Rights of Indigenous Peoples,

Recalling its resolution 61/178 of 20 December 2006, by which it decided to defer consideration of and action on the Declaration to allow time for further consultations thereon, and also decided to conclude its consideration before the end of the sixty-first session of the General Assembly,

Adopts the United Nations Declaration on the Rights of Indigenous Peoples as contained in the annex to the present resolution.

107th plenary meeting
13 September 2007

Annex
United Nations Declaration on the Rights of Indigenous Peoples

The General Assembly,

Guided by the purposes and principles of the Charter of the United Nations, and good faith in the fulfilment of the obligations assumed by States in accordance with the Charter,

Affirming that indigenous peoples are equal to all other peoples, while recognizing the right of all peoples to be different, to consider themselves different, and to be respected as such,

Affirming also that all peoples contribute to the diversity and richness of civilizations and cultures, which constitute the common heritage of humankind,

Affirming further that all doctrines, policies and practices based on or advocating superiority of peoples or individuals on the basis of national origin or racial, religious, ethnic or cultural differences are racist, scientifically false, legally invalid, morally condemnable and socially unjust,

---

1 See Official Records of the General Assembly, Sixty-first Session, Supplement No. 53 (A/61/53), part one, chap. II, sect. A.

Reaffirming that indigenous peoples, in the exercise of their rights, should be free from discrimination of any kind,

Concerned that indigenous peoples have suffered from historic injustices as a result of, *inter alia*, their colonization and dispossession of their lands, territories and resources, thus preventing them from exercising, in particular, their right to development in accordance with their own needs and interests,

Recognizing the urgent need to respect and promote the inherent rights of indigenous peoples which derive from their political, economic and social structures and from their cultures, spiritual traditions, histories and philosophies, especially their rights to their lands, territories and resources,

Recognizing also the urgent need to respect and promote the rights of indigenous peoples affirmed in treaties, agreements and other constructive arrangements with States,

Welcoming the fact that indigenous peoples are organizing themselves for political, economic, social and cultural enhancement and in order to bring to an end all forms of discrimination and oppression wherever they occur,

Convinced that control by indigenous peoples over developments affecting them and their lands, territories and resources will enable them to maintain and strengthen their institutions, cultures and traditions, and to promote their development in accordance with their aspirations and needs,

Recognizing that respect for indigenous knowledge, cultures and traditional practices contributes to sustainable and equitable development and proper management of the environment,

Emphasizing the contribution of the demilitarization of the lands and territories of indigenous peoples to peace, economic and social progress and development, understanding and friendly relations among nations and peoples of the world,

Recognizing in particular the right of indigenous families and communities to retain shared responsibility for the upbringing, training, education and well-being of their children, consistent with the rights of the child,

Considering that the rights affirmed in treaties, agreements and other constructive arrangements between States and indigenous peoples are, in some situations, matters of international concern, interest, responsibility and character,

Considering also that treaties, agreements and other constructive arrangements, and the relationship they represent, are the basis for a strengthened partnership between indigenous peoples and States,

Acknowledging that the Charter of the United Nations, the International Covenant on Economic, Social and Cultural Rights[2] and the International Covenant on Civil and Political Rights, as well as the Vienna Declaration and Programme of Action,[3] affirm the fundamental importance of the right to self-determination of all peoples, by virtue of which they freely determine their political status and freely pursue their economic, social and cultural development,

---

2 See resolution 2200 A (XXI), annex.

3 A/CONF.157/24 (Part I), chap. III.

Bearing in mind that nothing in this Declaration may be used to deny any peoples their right to self-determination, exercised in conformity with international law,

Convinced that the recognition of the rights of indigenous peoples in this Declaration will enhance harmonious and cooperative relations between the State and indigenous peoples, based on principles of justice, democracy, respect for human rights, non-discrimination and good faith,

Encouraging States to comply with and effectively implement all their obligations as they apply to indigenous peoples under international instruments, in particular those related to human rights, in consultation and cooperation with the peoples concerned,

Emphasizing that the United Nations has an important and continuing role to play in promoting and protecting the rights of indigenous peoples,

Believing that this Declaration is a further important step forward for the recognition, promotion and protection of the rights and freedoms of indigenous peoples and in the development of relevant activities of the United Nations system in this field,

Recognizing and reaffirming that indigenous individuals are entitled without discrimination to all human rights recognized in international law, and that indigenous peoples possess collective rights which are indispensable for their existence, well-being and integral development as peoples,

Recognizing that the situation of indigenous peoples varies from region to region and from country to country and that the significance of national and regional particularities and various historical and cultural backgrounds should be taken into consideration,

Solemnly proclaims the following United Nations Declaration on the Rights of Indigenous Peoples as a standard of achievement to be pursued in a spirit of partnership and mutual respect:

Article 1
Indigenous peoples have the right to the full enjoyment, as a collective or as individuals, of all human rights and fundamental freedoms as recognized in the Charter of the United Nations, the Universal Declaration of Human Rights[4] and international human rights law.

Article 2
Indigenous peoples and individuals are free and equal to all other peoples and individuals and have the right to be free from any kind of discrimination, in the exercise of their rights, in particular that based on their indigenous origin or identity.

Article 3
Indigenous peoples have the right to self-determination. By virtue of that right they freely determine their political status and freely pursue their economic, social and cultural development.

Article 4
Indigenous peoples, in exercising their right to self-determination, have the right to autonomy or self-government in matters relating to their internal and local affairs, as well as ways and means for financing their autonomous functions.

---

4 Resolution 217 A (III).

Article 5

Indigenous peoples have the right to maintain and strengthen their distinct political, legal, economic, social and cultural institutions, while retaining their right to participate fully, if they so choose, in the political, economic, social and cultural life of the State.

Article 6

Every indigenous individual has the right to a nationality.

Article 7

1. Indigenous individuals have the rights to life, physical and mental integrity, liberty and security of person.

2. Indigenous peoples have the collective right to live in freedom, peace and security as distinct peoples and shall not be subjected to any act of genocide or any other act of violence, including forcibly removing children of the group to another group.

Article 8

1. Indigenous peoples and individuals have the right not to be subjected to forced assimilation or destruction of their culture.

2. States shall provide effective mechanisms for prevention of, and redress for:

(a) Any action which has the aim or effect of depriving them of their integrity as distinct peoples, or of their cultural values or ethnic identities;

(b) Any action which has the aim or effect of dispossessing them of their lands, territories or resources;

(c) Any form of forced population transfer which has the aim or effect of violating or undermining any of their rights;

(d) Any form of forced assimilation or integration;

(e) Any form of propaganda designed to promote or incite racial or ethnic discrimination directed against them.

Article 9

Indigenous peoples and individuals have the right to belong to an indigenous community or nation, in accordance with the traditions and customs of the community or nation concerned. No discrimination of any kind may arise from the exercise of such a right.

Article 10

Indigenous peoples shall not be forcibly removed from their lands or territories. No relocation shall take place without the free, prior and informed consent of the indigenous peoples concerned and after agreement on just and fair compensation and, where possible, with the option of return.

Article 11

1. Indigenous peoples have the right to practise and revitalize their cultural traditions and customs. This includes the right to maintain, protect and develop the past, present and future manifestations of their cultures, such as archaeological and historical sites, artefacts, designs, ceremonies, technologies and visual and performing arts and literature.

2. States shall provide redress through effective mechanisms, which may include restitution, developed in conjunction with indigenous peoples, with respect to their cultural, intellec-

tual, religious and spiritual property taken without their free, prior and informed consent or in violation of their laws, traditions and customs.

Article 12

1. Indigenous peoples have the right to manifest, practise, develop and teach their spiritual and religious traditions, customs and ceremonies; the right to maintain, protect, and have access in privacy to their religious and cultural sites; the right to the use and control of their ceremonial objects; and the right to the repatriation of their human remains.

2. States shall seek to enable the access and/or repatriation of ceremonial objects and human remains in their possession through fair, transparent and effective mechanisms developed in conjunction with indigenous peoples concerned.

Article 13

1. Indigenous peoples have the right to revitalize, use, develop and transmit to future generations their histories, languages, oral traditions, philosophies, writing systems and literatures, and to designate and retain their own names for communities, places and persons.

2. States shall take effective measures to ensure that this right is protected and also to ensure that indigenous peoples can understand and be understood in political, legal and administrative proceedings, where necessary through the provision of interpretation or by other appropriate means.

Article 14

1. Indigenous peoples have the right to establish and control their educational systems and institutions providing education in their own languages, in a manner appropriate to their cultural methods of teaching and learning.

2. Indigenous individuals, particularly children, have the right to all levels and forms of education of the State without discrimination.

3. States shall, in conjunction with indigenous peoples, take effective measures, in order for indigenous individuals, particularly children, including those living outside their communities, to have access, when possible, to an education in their own culture and provided in their own language.

Article 15

1. Indigenous peoples have the right to the dignity and diversity of their cultures, traditions, histories and aspirations which shall be appropriately reflected in education and public information.

2. States shall take effective measures, in consultation and cooperation with the indigenous peoples concerned, to combat prejudice and eliminate discrimination and to promote tolerance, understanding and good relations among indigenous peoples and all other segments of society.

Article 16

1. Indigenous peoples have the right to establish their own media in their own languages and to have access to all forms of non-indigenous media without discrimination.

2. States shall take effective measures to ensure that State-owned media duly reflect indigenous cultural diversity. States, without prejudice to ensuring full freedom of expression, should encourage privately owned media to adequately reflect indigenous cultural diversity.

Article 17

1. Indigenous individuals and peoples have the right to enjoy fully all rights established under applicable international and domestic labour law.

2. States shall in consultation and cooperation with indigenous peoples take specific measures to protect indigenous children from economic exploitation and from performing any work that is likely to be hazardous or to interfere with the child's education, or to be harmful to the child's health or physical, mental, spiritual, moral or social development, taking into account their special vulnerability and the importance of education for their empowerment.

3. Indigenous individuals have the right not to be subjected to any discriminatory conditions of labour and, *inter alia*, employment or salary.

Article 18

Indigenous peoples have the right to participate in decision-making in matters which would affect their rights, through representatives chosen by themselves in accordance with their own procedures, as well as to maintain and develop their own indigenous decision-making institutions.

Article 19

States shall consult and cooperate in good faith with the indigenous peoples concerned through their own representative institutions in order to obtain their free, prior and informed consent before adopting and implementing legislative or administrative measures that may affect them.

Article 20

1. Indigenous peoples have the right to maintain and develop their political, economic and social systems or institutions, to be secure in the enjoyment of their own means of subsistence and development, and to engage freely in all their traditional and other economic activities.

2. Indigenous peoples deprived of their means of subsistence and development are entitled to just and fair redress.

Article 21

1. Indigenous peoples have the right, without discrimination, to the improvement of their economic and social conditions, including, *inter alia*, in the areas of education, employment, vocational training and retraining, housing, sanitation, health and social security.

2. States shall take effective measures and, where appropriate, special measures to ensure continuing improvement of their economic and social conditions. Particular attention shall be paid to the rights and special needs of indigenous elders, women, youth, children and persons with disabilities.

Article 22

1. Particular attention shall be paid to the rights and special needs of indigenous elders, women, youth, children and persons with disabilities in the implementation of this Declaration.

2. States shall take measures, in conjunction with indigenous peoples, to ensure that indigenous women and children enjoy the full protection and guarantees against all forms of violence and discrimination.

Article 23

Indigenous peoples have the right to determine and develop priorities and strategies for exercising their right to development. In particular, indigenous peoples have the right to be actively involved in developing and determining health, housing and other economic and social programmes affecting them and, as far as possible, to administer such programmes through their own institutions.

Article 24

1. Indigenous peoples have the right to their traditional medicines and to maintain their health practices, including the conservation of their vital medicinal plants, animals and minerals. Indigenous individuals also have the right to access, without any discrimination, to all social and health services.

2. Indigenous individuals have an equal right to the enjoyment of the highest attainable standard of physical and mental health. States shall take the necessary steps with a view to achieving progressively the full realization of this right.

Article 25

Indigenous peoples have the right to maintain and strengthen their distinctive spiritual relationship with their traditionally owned or otherwise occupied and used lands, territories, waters and coastal seas and other resources and to uphold their responsibilities to future generations in this regard.

Article 26

1. Indigenous peoples have the right to the lands, territories and resources which they have traditionally owned, occupied or otherwise used or acquired.

2. Indigenous peoples have the right to own, use, develop and control the lands, territories and resources that they possess by reason of traditional ownership or other traditional occupation or use, as well as those which they have otherwise acquired.

3. States shall give legal recognition and protection to these lands, territories and resources. Such recognition shall be conducted with due respect to the customs, traditions and land tenure systems of the indigenous peoples concerned.

Article 27

States shall establish and implement, in conjunction with indigenous peoples concerned, a fair, independent, impartial, open and transparent process, giving due recognition to indigenous peoples' laws, traditions, customs and land tenure systems, to recognize and adjudicate the rights of indigenous peoples pertaining to their lands, territories and resources, including those which were traditionally owned or otherwise occupied or used. Indigenous peoples shall have the right to participate in this process.

Article 28

1. Indigenous peoples have the right to redress, by means that can include restitution or, when this is not possible, just, fair and equitable compensation, for the lands, territories and resources which they have traditionally owned or otherwise occupied or used, and which have been confiscated, taken, occupied, used or damaged without their free, prior and informed consent.

2. Unless otherwise freely agreed upon by the peoples concerned, compensation shall take the form of lands, territories and resources equal in quality, size and legal status or of monetary compensation or other appropriate redress.

Article 29

1. Indigenous peoples have the right to the conservation and protection of the environment and the productive capacity of their lands or territories and resources. States shall establish and implement assistance programmes for indigenous peoples for such conservation and protection, without discrimination.

2. States shall take effective measures to ensure that no storage or disposal of hazardous materials shall take place in the lands or territories of indigenous peoples without their free, prior and informed consent.

3. States shall also take effective measures to ensure, as needed, that programmes for monitoring, maintaining and restoring the health of indigenous peoples, as developed and implemented by the peoples affected by such materials, are duly implemented.

Article 30

1. Military activities shall not take place in the lands or territories of indigenous peoples, unless justified by a relevant public interest or otherwise freely agreed with or requested by the indigenous peoples concerned.

2. States shall undertake effective consultations with the indigenous peoples concerned, through appropriate procedures and in particular through their representative institutions, prior to using their lands or territories for military activities.

Article 31

1. Indigenous peoples have the right to maintain, control, protect and develop their cultural heritage, traditional knowledge and traditional cultural expressions, as well as the manifestations of their sciences, technologies and cultures, including human and genetic resources, seeds, medicines, knowledge of the properties of fauna and flora, oral traditions, literatures, designs, sports and traditional games and visual and performing arts. They also have the right to maintain, control, protect and develop their intellectual property over such cultural heritage, traditional knowledge, and traditional cultural expressions.

2. In conjunction with indigenous peoples, States shall take effective measures to recognize and protect the exercise of these rights.

Article 32

1. Indigenous peoples have the right to determine and develop priorities and strategies for the development or use of their lands or territories and other resources.

2. States shall consult and cooperate in good faith with the indigenous peoples concerned through their own representative institutions in order to obtain their free and informed consent prior to the approval of any project affecting their lands or territories and other resources, particularly in connection with the development, utilization or exploitation of mineral, water or other resources.

3. States shall provide effective mechanisms for just and fair redress for any such activities, and appropriate measures shall be taken to mitigate adverse environmental, economic, social, cultural or spiritual impact.

Article 33

1. Indigenous peoples have the right to determine their own identity or membership in accordance with their customs and traditions. This does not impair the right of indigenous individuals to obtain citizenship of the States in which they live.

2. Indigenous peoples have the right to determine the structures and to select the membership of their institutions in accordance with their own procedures.

Article 34
Indigenous peoples have the right to promote, develop and maintain their institutional structures and their distinctive customs, spirituality, traditions, procedures, practices and, in the cases where they exist, juridical systems or customs, in accordance with international human rights standards.

Article 35
Indigenous peoples have the right to determine the responsibilities of individuals to their communities.

Article 36
1. Indigenous peoples, in particular those divided by international borders, have the right to maintain and develop contacts, relations and cooperation, including activities for spiritual, cultural, political, economic and social purposes, with their own members as well as other peoples across borders.

2. States, in consultation and cooperation with indigenous peoples, shall take effective measures to facilitate the exercise and ensure the implementation of this right.

Article 37
1. Indigenous peoples have the right to the recognition, observance and enforcement of treaties, agreements and other constructive arrangements concluded with States or their successors and to have States honour and respect such treaties, agreements and other constructive arrangements.

2. Nothing in this Declaration may be interpreted as diminishing or eliminating the rights of indigenous peoples contained in treaties, agreements and other constructive arrangements.

Article 38
States in consultation and cooperation with indigenous peoples, shall take the appropriate measures, including legislative measures, to achieve the ends of this Declaration.

Article 39
Indigenous peoples have the right to have access to financial and technical assistance from States and through international cooperation, for the enjoyment of the rights contained in this Declaration.

Article 40
Indigenous peoples have the right to access to and prompt decision through just and fair procedures for the resolution of conflicts and disputes with States or other parties, as well as to effective remedies for all infringements of their individual and collective rights. Such a decision shall give due consideration to the customs, traditions, rules and legal systems of the indigenous peoples concerned and international human rights.

Article 41
The organs and specialized agencies of the United Nations system and other intergovernmental organizations shall contribute to the full realization of the provisions of this Decla-

ration through the mobilization, *inter alia*, of financial cooperation and technical assistance. Ways and means of ensuring participation of indigenous peoples on issues affecting them shall be established.

Article 42

The United Nations, its bodies, including the Permanent Forum on Indigenous Issues, and specialized agencies, including at the country level, and States shall promote respect for and full application of the provisions of this Declaration and follow up the effectiveness of this Declaration.

Article 43

The rights recognized herein constitute the minimum standards for the survival, dignity and well-being of the indigenous peoples of the world.

Article 44

All the rights and freedoms recognized herein are equally guaranteed to male and female indigenous individuals.

Article 45

Nothing in this Declaration may be construed as diminishing or extinguishing the rights indigenous peoples have now or may acquire in the future.

Article 46

1. Nothing in this Declaration may be interpreted as implying for any State, people, group or person any right to engage in any activity or to perform any act contrary to the Charter of the United Nations or construed as authorizing or encouraging any action which would dismember or impair, totally or in part, the territorial integrity or political unity of sovereign and independent States.

2. In the exercise of the rights enunciated in the present Declaration, human rights and fundamental freedoms of all shall be respected. The exercise of the rights set forth in this Declaration shall be subject only to such limitations as are determined by law and in accordance with international human rights obligations. Any such limitations shall be non-discriminatory and strictly necessary solely for the purpose of securing due recognition and respect for the rights and freedoms of others and for meeting the just and most compelling requirements of a democratic society.

3. The provisions set forth in this Declaration shall be interpreted in accordance with the principles of justice, democracy, respect for human rights, equality, non-discrimination, good governance and good faith.

APPENDIX II

May 1, 2008
Open Letter

UN Declaration on the Rights of Indigenous Peoples

Canada Needs to Implement this New Human Rights Instrument

On September 13, 2007, the United Nations General Assembly adopted the *UN Declaration on the Rights of Indigenous Peoples* by an overwhelming vote of 144-4. The UN Secretary-General, other prominent international leaders, and human rights experts hailed this historic event as a victory for the human rights of the world's most disadvantaged and victimized peoples.

There are over 370 million Indigenous people worldwide. Indigenous peoples urgently require international affirmation and protection of their human rights. Their rights are routinely trampled by national governments, even when these rights are entrenched in law.

Canada was one of only four states that opposed the *Declaration*. Government ministers characterize the *Declaration* as incompatible with Canada's Constitution and the Canadian Charter of Rights and Freedoms. They state that the *Declaration* affirms only the collective rights of Indigenous peoples and fails to balance individual and collective rights or the rights of Indigenous and non-Indigenous peoples. No credible legal rationale has been provided to substantiate these extraordinary and erroneous claims.

We, the undersigned, have researched and worked in the fields of Indigenous rights and/or constitutional law in Canada. We are concerned that the misleading claims made by the Canadian government continue to be used to justify opposition, as well as impede international cooperation and implementation of this human rights instrument.

The *Declaration* contains some of the most comprehensive balancing provisions that exist in any international human rights instrument. Article 46 of the *UN Declaration* states that every provision must be interpreted "in accordance with the principles of justice, democracy, respect for human rights, equality, non-discrimination, good governance and good faith". These are the core principles and values of not only Canada's Constitution, but also the international system that Canada has championed.

Further, seventeen provisions in the *Declaration* address individual rights. The *UN Declaration* also states that the rights of Indigenous peoples may be limited when strictly necessary "for the purpose of securing due recognition and respect for the rights and freedoms of others." This approach allows for both flexibility and balance.

In response to Canada's position, the UN High Commissioner for Human Rights and former Supreme Court of Canada Justice, Louise Arbour, publicly expressed her "astonishment" and "profound disappointment." The *Declaration* provides a principled framework that promotes a vision of justice and reconciliation. In our considered opinion, it is consistent with the Canadian Constitution and Charter and is profoundly important for fulfilling their promise. Government claims to the contrary do a grave disservice to the cause of human rights and to the promotion of harmonious and cooperative relations.

As a member of the UN Human Rights Council, Canada has a duty to "uphold the highest standards" of human rights for all. This mandate is guided by principles of impartiality, objectivity and non-selectivity. Elimination of politicization of human rights is a vital objective. For Canada to act otherwise is prejudicial to Indigenous peoples' human rights. It undermines Canada's credibility and international role.

September 13, 2007 was a shameful day for Canada but a tremendous achievement for the world's Indigenous peoples and the international system. It is time for the government of Canada to cease publicizing its misleading claims and, together with Indigenous peoples, actively implement this new human rights instrument.

SIGNED BY

Prof. Jennie Abell, Director, Institute of Women's Studies, University of Ottawa

Merle C. Alexander, Barrister and Solicitor

Prof. Sharry Aiken, Faculty of Law, Queen's University

Warren Allmand, former Attorney General, Minister of Indian Affairs and President of Rights and Democracy

Prof. Kirsten Anker, Faculty of Law, McGill University

Prof. Rachel Ariss, Department of Sociology, Lakehead University

Prof. Constance Backhouse, Faculty of Law, University of Ottawa

Prof. Michael Barutciski, Glendon School of Public Affairs, York University

Prof. Nigel Bankes, Faculty of Law, University of Calgary

Tom Berger, Barrister and Solicitor

Debra Hanuse, Barrister and Solicitor

Veryan Haysom, Barrister and Solicitor

Prof. Sa'ke'j Henderson, Research Director, Four Direction Council, Research Director, Native Law Centre of Canada

Prof. Shin Imai, Director, Intensive Program on Aboriginal Lands, Resources and Governments, Faculty of Law, Osgoode Hall, York University

Barbara Jackman, Barrister and Solicitor

Prof. Michael Jackson, Faculty of Law, University of British Columbia

Paul Joffe, Barrister and Solicitor

Roger Jones, Law and Policy Consultant

Prof. Jennifer Koshan, Faculty of Law, University of Calgary

Lois Leslie, Barrister and Solicitor

Prof. Linda Kreitzer, Faculty of Social Work, University of Calgary

Professeur Émérite, Jean-Paul Lacasse, Faculté de droit, Université d'Ottawa

Professeure Emérite Andrée Lajoie, Faculté de droit, Université de Montréal

Prof. Lucie Lamarche, Chaire Gordon F Henderson en droits de la personne / Gordon F. Henderson Human Rights Chair, Université d'Ottawa

Professeur François J. Larocque, Directeur du programme national / National Program Director, Faculté de droit, Université d'Ottawa

Chief Wilton Littlechild, former United Nations Permanent Forum member

Prof. Jennifer Llewellyn, Faculty of Law, Dalhousie University

Prof. Roderick Macdonald, Faculty of Law, McGill University

Prof. A. Wayne MacKay C.M., Faculty of Law, Dalhousie University

Prof. Audrey Macklin, Faculty of Law, University of Toronto

Prof. Joseph Eliot Magnet, Faculty of Law, University of Ottawa

Louise Mandell, Barrister and Solicitor

Prof. Egla Martinez, Institute of Interdisciplinary Studies / Human Rights, Institute of Women's Studies, Carleton University

Prof. Maxine V. H. Matilpi, Director, Academic and Cultural Support Program, Faculty of Law, University of Victoria

Prof. June McCue, Faculty of Law, University of British Columbia

Prof. Kent McNeil, Faculty of Law, Osgoode Hall, York University

Prof. Errol P. Mendes, Faculty of Law, University of Ottawa

John Merritt, Barrister and Solicitor

Loretta Michelin, Director of Legal Services, Nunatsiavut Government

Prof. Patricia Monture, Department of Sociology, University of Saskatchewan

Maria Morellato, Barrister and Solicitor

Nancy A. Morgan, Barrister and Solicitor

Prof. Bradford W. Morse, Faculty of Law, University of Ottawa

Alex Neve, Secretary General, Amnesty International Canada (English-Speaking Branch).

Professeur Pierre Noreau, Faculté de droit, Université de Montréal

John Olthuis, Barrister and Solicitor

Arthur Pape, Barrister and Solicitor

Professeure Sylvie Paquerot, École d'études politiques, Université d'Ottawa

Laurie Pelly, Barrister and Solicitor

Bruce Porter, Director, Social Rights Advocacy Centre

Prof. Dianne Pothier, Faculty of Law, Dalhousie University

Prof. Emeritus Richard J. Preston, Faculty of Anthropology, McMaster University

Prof. Janna Promislow, Faculty of Law, Osgoode Hall, York University

Owen Rees, Barrister and Solicitor

Prof. Ben Richardson, Faculty of Law, Osgoode Hall, York University

Professeur Guy Rocher, Centre de recherche en droit public, Université de Montréal

Allan Rock, former MP and Ambassador to the United Nations

Prof. Sanda Rodgers, Faculty of Law, University of Ottawa

Prof. Rémi Savard, Département d'anthropologie, Université de Montréal

Prof. William A. Schabas, Director, Irish Centre for Human Rights, National University of Ireland, Galway

Prof. Craig Martin Scott, Director, Nathanson Centre on Transnational Human Rights, Crime and Security, Faculty of Law, Osgoode Hall, York University

Prof. Elizabeth Sheehy, Faculty of Law, University of Ottawa

Prof. Peter Showler, Director, The Refugee Forum, Human Rights Research and Education Centre, University of Ottawa

Prof. Brian Slattery, Faculty of Law, Osgoode Hall, York University

Richard Spaulding, Barrister and Solicitor

Prof. Joanne St. Lewis, Faculty of Law, University of Ottawa

Hon. Mary Ellen Turpel-Lafond, British Columbia Representative for Children and Youth

Lorne Waldman, Barrister and Solicitor

Prof. Rosemary Cairns Way, Faculty of Law, Common Law, University of Ottawa

Michael (Jerry) Wetzel, Barrister and Solicitor

Prof. Christiane Wilke, Faculty of Law, Carleton University

Peigi Wilson, Barrister and Solicitor

Gary Yabsley, Barrister and Solicitor

Maxwell Yalden, former Canadian Human Rights Commissioner and member of the United Nations Human Rights Committee

Prof. Norman Zlotkin, College of Law, University of Saskatchewan

UN Declaration on the Rights of Indigenous Peoples

Supportive Statements Worldwide

United Nations

The Declaration is a visionary step towards addressing the human rights of indigenous peoples. It sets out a framework on which States can build or rebuild their relationships with indigenous peoples. . . . [I]t provides a momentous opportunity for States and indigenous peoples to strengthen their relationships, promote reconciliation and ensure that the past is not repeated.

UN Secretary-General Ban Ki-moon,
International Day of the World's Indigenous People, 9 Aug. 2008

— — —

I look forward to further steps towards universal acceptance of this significant human rights instrument. . . . My Office is committed to be a frontline advocate of universal acceptance and implementation of the Declaration. . . . Indeed, these rights are, and will remain, a priority area for OHCHR.

Navanethem Pillay, UN High Commissioner for Human Rights, Geneva, 10 Aug. 2009

— — —

The Declaration . . . has been 20 years in the making. Its contents are drawn from the experiences of thousands of indigenous representatives who have shared their anguish and their hopes. . . . As we stand at the brink of this historic decision by the General Assembly, it is the time to call upon member states of the United Nations to join as one and adopt the Declaration and thereby establish a universal framework for indigenous peoples' rights, social justice and reconciliation.

Message of Louise Arbour and Rodolfo Stavenhagen, 7 Aug. 2007

— — —

The United Nations Declaration on the Rights of Indigenous Peoples represents an authoritative common understanding, at the global level, of the minimum content of the rights of indigenous peoples, upon a foundation of various sources of international human rights law.

Special Rapporteur S. James Anaya, Human Rights Council, 11 Aug. 2008

— — —

. . . the Expert Mechanism has an important role in promoting the rights affirmed in the Declaration, and in mainstreaming them into the Human Rights Council's overall efforts to promote and protect all human rights.

Expert Mechanism on the Rights of Indigenous Peoples, 1 Oct. 2008

— — —

Mandate-holders agreed that the effective implementation of the Declaration constituted a major challenge ahead, and decided to strengthen their efforts in that regard.

Meeting of rapporteurs/representatives, independent experts and chairpersons of working groups of the special procedures of the Human Rights Council, Geneva, 23-27 June 2008

Specialized Agencies

The Inter-Agency Support Group on Indigenous Peoples' Issues hails the adoption of the Declaration on the Rights on Indigenous Peoples by the General Assembly.... The Declaration sends out a clear message to the entire international community, reaffirming the human rights of the world's indigenous peoples. This landmark action of the United Nations bears political, legal, symbolic and moral significance....

Inter-Agency Support Group on Indigenous Issues,
Statement on the United Nations Declaration on the Rights of Indigenous Peoples, Sept. 2007

— — —

With the adoption of the Declaration, the UN has taken a major step forward in the promotion and protection of indigenous and tribal peoples' rights throughout the world.... The ILO welcomes the adoption of [the Declaration] and is committed to promoting it.

Information note for ILO staff and partners, distributed at the Permanent Forum on Indigenous Issues, New York, April 2008

— — —

... the new Declaration echoes the principles of the UNESCO Universal Declaration on Cultural Diversity (2001) and related Conventions — notably the 1972 World Heritage Convention, the 2003 Convention for the Safeguarding of the Intangible Cultural Heritage, and the 2005 Convention on the Protection and Promotion of the Diversity of Cultural Expressions. Each of these recognizes the pivotal role of indigenous peoples as custodians of cultural diversity and biodiversity.

Koïchiro Matsuura, Director-General of UNESCO
International Day of the World's Indigenous People, 9 Aug. 2008

— — —

... the World Bank welcomes the adoption of the "United Nations Declaration on the Rights of Indigenous Peoples" by the United Nations General Assembly.... The Declaration asks that the organs and specialized agencies of the UN system (of which the World Bank is one) and other intergovernmental organizations contribute to the full realization of the Declaration's provisions ...

World Bank Statement
Permanent Forum on Indigenous Issues, New York, 21 April 2008

— — —

UN Human Rights Treaty Monitoring Bodies

[T]he Committee ... recommends that the declaration be used as a guide to interpret the State party's obligations under the Convention relating to indigenous peoples.

Committee on the Elimination of Racial Discrimination: United States of America,
9 May 2008

— — —

... the Committee regrets the change in the position of [Canada] in the Human Rights Council and the General Assembly.... The Committee recommends that the State party support the immediate adoption of the United Nations Declaration on the Rights of Indigenous Peoples ...

> *Committee on the Elimination of Racial Discrimination: Canada*, 25 May 2007

In 2007, the United Nations General Assembly adopted the Declaration on the Rights of Indigenous Peoples which provides important guidance on the rights of indigenous peoples, including specific reference to the rights of indigenous children in a number of areas.

> Committee on the Rights of the Child, *Indigenous children and their rights under the Convention*, General Comment No. 11, 30 Jan. 2009

— — —

The Committee ... encourages the State party to continue with its efforts to promote and implement the principles of the United Nations Declaration on the Rights of Indigenous Peoples.

> *Committee on Economic, Social and Cultural Rights: Nicaragua*, 28 Nov. 2008

— — —

Regional Human Rights Bodies

The African Commission is confident that the Declaration will become a very valuable tool and a point of reference for the African Commission's efforts to ensure the promotion and protection of indigenous peoples' rights on the African continent.

> Communique on the United Nations Declaration on the Rights of Indigenous Peoples, Brazzaville, Republic of Congo, 28 Nov. 2007

— — —

The Inter-American Commission on Human Rights (IACHR) ... Rapporteurship hopes that the recently approved UN Declaration will facilitate the prompt approval of the OAS Declaration so that the rights of indigenous peoples of the Americas can be recognized and protected.

> "Inter-American Commissioner on Human Rights Rapporteurship Applauds Approval of UN Declaration on Rights of Indigenous Peoples," 18 Sept. 2007

— — —

Non-Governmental Organizations

Adoption of the Declaration sends a clear message to the international community that the rights of Indigenous Peoples are not separate from or less than the rights of others, but are an integral and indispensable part of a human rights system dedicated to the rights of all.

> Joint Statement by Amnesty International, Friends World Committee for Consultation, International Federation of Human Rights Leagues, International Service for Human Rights, and Rights & Democracy, 14 Sept. 2007

— — —

It is . . . most fitting that this historic first session of the Council has the opportunity to propose to the General Assembly for adoption one of the most urgently needed and long overdue standards for the recognition and protection of human rights, the draft United Nations Declaration on the Rights of Indigenous Peoples.

Joint Statement by over 40 Human Rights NGOs, Geneva, 27 June 2006

– – –

Indigenous Peoples

The Declaration is a framework for States to link and integrate with the Indigenous Peoples, to initiate new and positive relations but this time without exclusion, without discrimination and without exploitation. . . . These rights in the Declaration are already recognised in international law, but they are rights which have been denied to Indigenous Peoples everywhere.

Les Malezer, Chair of the Indigenous Peoples' Caucus, Statement to the UN General Assembly, New York, 13 Sept. 2007

– – –

With the passage of the Declaration we herald the dawning of a new era for relations between pacific Indigenous Peoples and States, as well as UN agencies and specialized bodies. An era which we believe can now be established on a strong human rights foundation. The passage of the Declaration affirms the fundamental principle that human rights are universal and that the Indigenous Peoples and cultures of the Pacific are entitled to the rights and fundamental freedoms which have for so long been withheld.

Pacific Regional Caucus Statement, 13 Sept. 2007

– – –

[The UN Declaration] will be an instrument and tool which we will use to raise the awareness of the society at large on our rights and to make governments address the situation of indigenous peoples who have long been suffering from injustice, discrimination and marginalization. It will be an instrument that will be used [to] enhance further the empowerment of Indigenous Peoples.

Asia Indigenous Peoples Caucus on the Occasion of the Adoption of the UN Declaration on the Rights of Indigenous Peoples, 13 Sept. 2007

– – –

Les Peuples Autochtones doivent interpréter la déclaration comme une dynamique de reconnaissance des Droits des Peuples Autochtones qui viennent d'être inclus dans la grande famille des Droits reconnu par la charte des nations unies. Cet acte moral ne constitue pas un règlement définitif des violations des droits des Peuples Autochtones mais plutôt un pas qui favorise et ouvre les voies pour des règlements pacifiques de nos situations.

African Indigenous Caucus, Regional Statement, New York, 13 Sept. 2007

– – –

The Inuit Circumpolar Council and Sami Council welcome this momentous occasion. For the first time, the world community has proclaimed a universally applicable human rights instrument in order to end centuries of marginalisation and discrimination, and to affirm that Indigenous peoples are peoples, equal in dignity and rights with all other peoples.

Statement of the Arctic Region, 13 Sept. 2007

The Declaration recognizes our collective histories, traditions, cultures, languages, and spirituality. It is an important international instrument that supports the activities and efforts of Indigenous peoples to have their rights fully recognized, respected and implemented by state governments.

Phil Fontaine, "AFN National Chief applauds today's passage of the UN Declaration on the Rights of Indigenous Peoples — Recognizing 30 years of work in the making," 13 Sept. 2007

— — —

. . . the *UN Declaration* is a triumph of achievement — a cause for great celebration. It is a contribution to justice and humanity. The international human rights system is being strengthened. . . . The *Declaration* is the most comprehensive international instrument addressing the rights of Indigenous peoples. . . . As distinct peoples, we now have a principled international legal framework that affirms our human rights.

Grand Chief Matthew Mukash, Grand Council of the Crees (Eeyou Istchee), 26 Sept. 2007

— — —

What a tremendous day. It's all over now and we have in our hands a Declaration we helped construct and one on which we can proudly stand. Notwithstanding Canada's "NO" vote they will have to be accountable against the Declaration's standards. It cannot pick and choose the human rights it wants. We should all be proud in our collective achievement. I was proud to be a part of our tremendous effort and achievement!

Grand Chief Edward John, Co-Coordinator of the North American Regional Indigenous Peoples Caucus, New York, 13 Sept. 2007

— — —

. . . we remain shocked and angered at Canada's refusal to support this important international human rights instrument.

Grand Chief Steward Phillip, President, Union of BC Indian Chiefs, 13 Sept. 2007

— — —

The 13th of Sept. 2007 will be remembered as an international human rights day for the Indigenous Peoples of the world, a day that the United Nations and its Member States, together with Indigenous Peoples, reconciled with past painful histories and decided to march into the future on the path of human rights. Unfortunately this is a bittersweet victory for Indigenous Peoples in this country. . . . Canada will have to work very hard to redeem itself and its position as an international leader of the protection of Human Rights.

Quebec Native Women's Association, Press Release, 14 Sept. 2007

— — —

The Declaration on the Rights of Indigenous Peoples will serve as a comprehensive international human rights instrument for Indigenous women, men and youth around the world. . . . The adoption of the Declaration will allow Indigenous women and their families to infuse local human rights struggles with the power of international law and hold their governments accountable to international human rights standards.

International Indigenous Women's Forum, 13 Sept. 2007

— — —

Although the challenge ahead is huge, the recognition of the rights of Indigenous Peoples by the United Nations is truly a cause for celebration. . . .

Anselmo Lee, Asia Forum of Human Rights and Development, "A Milestone Achieved: the Declaration on the Rights of Indigenous Peoples is adopted by the United Nations General Assembly," 14 Sept. 2007

– – –

No one is rejoicing here in Manipur, in the northeastern territories of India, as many people began a fast yesterday against a racist military law that has seen thousands of indigenous persons held without charge, assaulted, killed, maimed, disappeared, tortured, sexually abused or extra-judicially executed since 1958 till today. While the present scenario is bleak for the surviving indigenous peoples, even critical for many, the declaration comes to us this autumn as a long overdue fresh wind with an elusive promise.

Roy Laifungbam, Centre for Organisation Research & Education, Indigenous Peoples' Centre for Policy and Human Rights in India's Eastern Himalayan Territories, Manipur, India, 16 Sept. 2007

– – –

States

The need for legal protection of indigenous peoples' rights . . . is at the top of the international agenda. The recent adoption of the United Nations Declaration on the Rights of Indigenous Peoples after 20 long years of delay provides confirmation of this fact; the Declaration is an instrument for legal, administrative and policy reform for the nations of the world.

Peru, Information provided to the UN Permanent Forum on Indigenous Issues, 12 Feb. 2008

– – –

The Government of Bolivia . . . granted legal status to the United Nations Declaration on the Rights of Indigenous Peoples by the adoption of Act No. 3760 of 7 Nov. 2007. . . . Bolivia has therefore taken the lead in the field of indigenous rights, since it is the first country in the world to have taken this measure.

Bolivia, Information provided to the UN Permanent Forum on Indigenous Issues, 11 Feb. 2008

– – –

The Declaration constitutes one of the most significant achievements in this field of human rights, and we are confident that it will advance the rights and ensure the continued development of indigenous peoples around the world. The EU was encouraged by the wide support to the Declaration from Indigenous peoples' representatives, as well as the large number of States. . . . The challenge before us now, is to make sure that the indigenous peoples will in fact enjoy the rights recognised in the Declaration.

Portugal (on behalf of the European Union), Human Rights Council, Oral Statement, Geneva, 26 Sept. 2007

– – –

The recent adoption by the General Assembly, by an overwhelming majority, of the UN Declaration on the Rights of Indigenous Peoples will provide a new and comprehensive framework for the Special Rapporteur in pursuing the realization of the rights of indigenous peoples, numbering over 315 million around the world, constituting one of the world's most vulnerable groups. Indeed, the adoption of the Declaration requires the continuation of the mandate of the Special Rapporteur, with a view to promote its implementation . . .

Egypt (on behalf of the African Group),
Human Rights Council, Oral Statement, Geneva, 26 Sept. 2007

– – –

The Declaration contextualizes all existing human rights for Indigenous Peoples and provides therefore the natural frame of reference for work and debate relating to the promotion of indigenous peoples rights. . . . In a Norwegian context, . . . it strengthens knowledge and conscience about existing rights and thereby strengthens the implementation of indigenous rights.

Norway, Expert Mechanism on the Rights of Indigenous Peoples, Geneva,
Oral Statement, 12 Aug. 2009

– – –

The Declaration has been endorsed by both Government and Parliament of Greenland and it has raised expectations of citizens and interest groups. We need to take a closer look at our own compliance with this important (human) rights instrument.

Greenland (Delegation of Denmark), Expert Mechanism on the
Rights of Indigenous Peoples, Geneva, 11 Aug. 2009

– – –

Today, Australia joins the international community to affirm the aspirations of all Indigenous peoples. . . . The decades of work culminated in a landmark document . . . that reflects and pays homage to the unique place of Indigenous peoples and their entitlement to all human rights as recognised in international law. . . . Today, Australia gives our support to the Declaration. . . .

Government of Australia (Jenny Macklin, Minister for Families, Housing, Community
Services and Indigenous Affairs), Canberra, 3 April 2009

– – –

Domestic Human Rights Bodies

The passage of the Declaration on the Rights of Indigenous Peoples on Sept. 13, 2007 marked a milestone for the world's indigenous peoples, and for the United Nations. . . . The Commission will look to the Declaration for inspiration in our own work.

Canadian Human Rights Commission, Public Statement, 15 Feb. 2008

.. by supporting the UN Declaration, Canada would be affirming its commitment to the rights of its own indigenous peoples, many of whom have become increasingly alienated by the seeming inaction of governments in response to their plight. . . . Canada's otherwise respected human rights position would be sullied by continuing efforts to oppose the Declaration and slow down the General Assembly's approval of it.

> Barbara Hall, Chief Commissioner, Ontario Human Rights Commission,
> Letter to Prime Minister Stephen Harper, 9 Aug. 2007

The Human Rights Commission today welcomed the adoption of the Declaration on the Rights of Indigenous Peoples by the United Nations General Assembly. This is an important milestone internationally in the recognition of the rights of indigenous peoples . . . the Commission is sorry that the New Zealand government felt unable to support the adoption of the Declaration over a few outstanding issues . . .

> Chief Human Rights Commissioner Rosslyn Noonan and Race Relations Commissioner
> Joris de Bres, New Zealand Human Rights Commission, "Indigenous Rights Declaration
> to guide Commission work," New Zealand, 14 Sept. 2007

There is a clear role for National Human Rights Institutions in implementing the UN Declaration on the Rights of Indigenous Peoples at the national level. . . . Of most relevance are articles 38 (relating to the taking of appropriate measures to implement the Declaration) and Article 40 (which relates to access to conflict resolution procedures and the provision of effective remedies).

> Australian Human Rights Commission, Expert Mechanism on the
> Rights of Indigenous Peoples, Geneva, 11 Aug. 2009

Parliament of Canada

That the government endorse the United Nations Declaration on the Rights of Indigenous Peoples as adopted by the United Nations General Assembly on 13 Sept. 2007 and that Parliament and Government of Canada fully implement the standards contained therein.

> House of Commons, Canada, *Motion*, adopted 8 April 2008
> (Conservative MPs dissented)

Opposition Parties

Stephen Harper's government has failed in its duty by voting against the adoption of the Declaration. . . . The Conservative government is moving backwards on the Aboriginal question and is once again isolated on the international scene. It's deplorable.

> Bloc Québécois, "The United Nations Adopts the Declaration on the Rights of
> Indigenous Peoples without Canada's Support," 13 Sept. 2007

Today's vote marks the first time Canada has opposed a major human rights document. By arguing against the text it helped draft, and ultimately trying to defeat it, Canada has lost credibility among the community of nations concerned about the protection of human rights.

Liberal Party, "Harper Government failed Canada with UN Vote," 13 Sept. 2007

— — —

Canada had an opportunity to show the world it still has some relevance in international affairs as a catalyst to create agreement, instead of blocking action. . . . voting in favour of the Declaration on Indigenous Peoples Rights would have been a confirmation of our history of conciliation and compromise and a signal that Canada intends to honour its obligations to indigenous peoples.

New Democratic Party, "NDP appalled by Canada's vote against
UN declaration on Indigenous peoples' rights," 29 June 2006

NOTES

INTRODUCTION

1 General Assembly, *Official Records*, UN GAOR, 61st Sess., 108th plen. mtg., UN Doc. A/61/PV.108 (2007) at 11 (statement on behalf of the President of the General Assembly, Sheikha Haya Rashed Al-Khalifa).

2 The *United Nations Declaration on the Rights of Indigenous Peoples* is annexed to GA Res. 61/295, UN GAOR, 61st Sess., Supp. No. 49, Vol. III, UN Doc. A/61/49 (2008) 15. See Appendix 1 of this volume.

3 *Ibid.*, art. 43. In regard to the injustices suffered by Indigenous peoples and the urgent need for remedial action, see generally United Nations (Department of Economic and Social Affairs), *State of the World's Indigenous Peoples* (New York: United Nations, 2009): www.un.org/esa/socdev/unpfii/documents/SOWIP_web.pdf.

4 *Ibid.*, preambular paras. 7 and 22.

5 UN records indicate a recorded vote of 143 States in favour of the resolution on the adoption of the *Declaration*. Montenegro subsequently advised that it had intended to vote in favour of the resolution. General Assembly, *Official Records*, UN GAOR, 61st Sess., 107th plen. mtg., UN Doc. A/61/PV.107 (2007) at 19.

6 The Hon. Jenny Macklin, MP, "Statement on the United Nations Declaration on the Rights of Indigenous Peoples" (Delivered at Parliament House, Canberra, 3 April 2009): www.jennymacklin.fahcsia.gov.au/internet/jennymacklin.nsf/content/un_declaration_03apr09.htm.

7 Human Rights Council, *Report of the Working Group on the Universal Periodic Review: New Zealand*, UN Doc. A/HRC/12/8 (4 June 2009) at para. 15. In regard to the US, see Haider Rizvi, "US: Obama Urged to Sign Native Rights Declaration," *Inter Press Service* (6 May 2009): www.ipsnews.net/news.asp?idnews=46742.

8 Colombia, "Gobierno anuncia respaldo unilateral a la Declaración de Naciones Unidas sobre los Derechos de los Pueblos Indígenas" (21 April 2009): http://web.presidencia.gov.co/sp/2009/abril/21/10212009.html. In regard to Samoa, see United Nations General Assembly, News Release, GA/SHC/3954, "Implementing Declaration on Indigenous Rights will bring 'Historical Justice,' Develop Stronger, Democratic, Multicultural Societies, Third Committee Told" (19 Oct. 2009): www.un.org/News/Press/docs/2009/gashc3954.doc.htm.

9 Victoria Tauli-Corpuz, "Statement of Victoria Tauli-Corpuz, Chair of the UN Permanent Forum on Indigenous Issues on the Occasion of the Adoption of the UN Declaration on the Rights of Indigenous Peoples" (Delivered to the United Nations General Assembly, New York, 13 Sept. 2007): www.un.org/esa/socdev/unpfii/documents/Declaration_ip_vtc.doc.

10 *Convention on the Rights of the Child*, 20 Nov. 1989, 1577 U.N.T.S. 3 (entered into force 2 Sept. 1990).

11 Michael Dodson (on behalf of the UN Permanent Forum on Indigenous Issues), "Statement" (Delivered at Parliament House, Canberra, 3 April 2009): www.un.org/esa/socdev/unpfii/documents/Australia_endorsement_UNDRIP_Michael_Dodson_statement.pdf.

12 Canada, *A Stronger Canada. A Stronger Economy. Now and for the Future: Speech from the Throne to Open the Third Session of the Fortieth Parliament of Canada: March 3, 2010* (2010) at 19: www.speech.gc.ca/grfx/docs/sft-ddt-2010_e.pdf.

13 Assembly of First Nations *et al.*, "Canada's endorsement of the *UN Declaration* must be consistent with human rights" (Joint Statement, 18 Mar. 2010).

CHAPTER ONE

1 See Russell Means (with Marvin J. Wolf), *Where White Men Fear to Tread: The Autobiography of Russell Means* (New York: St. Martin's Press, 1995). Wounded Knee is also the site where, in 1890, the US Seventh Cavalry attacked and killed as many as 300 Lakota men, women, and children: see Dee Brown, *Bury My Heart At Wounded Knee: An Indian History of the American West* (New York: Holt, Rinehart & Winston, 1970) at 439 - 445.

2 This history is documented in *Akwesasne Notes, Basic Call to Consciousness* (Summertown, Tenn.: Native Voices, 2005).

3 Common article 1, *International Covenant on Civil and Political Rights*, 19 Dec. 1966, 999 U.N.T.S. 171 (entered into force 23 Mar. 1976) [ICCPR], and *International Covenant on Economic, Social and Cultural Rights*, 19 Dec. 1966, 993 U.N.T.S. 3 (entered into force 3 Jan. 1976) [ICESCR].

4 *Study of the problem of discrimination against indigenous populations*, ESC Res. 1982/34, UN ESCOR, 1982, Supp. No. 1, UN Doc. E/1982/82, 26 at 26 - 27.

5 Commission on Human Rights, *Study of the Problem of Discrimination against Indigenous Populations: Final Report (last part) submitted by the Special Rapporteur, Mr. José R. Martinez-Cobo*, UN Doc. E/CN.4/Sub.2/1983/21/Add.8 (30 Sept. 1983) at para. 627.

6 *Draft United Nations declaration on the rights of indigenous peoples*, UN Sub-Commission on Prevention of Discrimination and Protection of Minorities Res. 1994/45, in Commission on Human Rights, *Report of the Sub-Commission on Prevention of Discrimination and Protection of Minorities on its Forty-Sixth Session*, UN Doc. E/CN.4/1995/2, E/CN.4/Sub.2/1994/56 (28 Oct. 1994) 103.

7 *Establishment of a working group of the Commission on Human Rights to elaborate a draft declaration in accordance with paragraph 5 of General Assembly res olution 49/214*, ESC Res. 1995/32, UN ESCOR, 1996, Supp. No. 1, UN Doc. E/1995/95, 44.

8 Commission on Human Rights, *Report of the working group established in accordance with Commission on Human Rights resolution 1995/32 of 3 March 1995 on its eleventh session*, UN Doc. E/CN.4/2006/79 (22 Mar. 2006).

9 *Ibid.* at para. 25.

10 *Ibid.* at para. 28: the chairperson-rapporteur "indicated that his revised proposals would include all the language provided by the facilitators as it constituted a basis for provisional agreement. He also indicated that he would make proposals regarding articles that were still pending, based on the discussions held during the sessions."

11 *Human Rights Council*, GA Res. 60/251, 60th Sess., UN GAOR, Supp. No. 49, Vol. III, UN Doc A/60/49 (2007) 2.

12 The text submitted by the chairperson-special rapporteur was adopted by the Human Rights Council by resolution: see *Working group of the Commission on Human Rights to elaborate a draft declaration in accordance with paragraph 5 of General Assembly resolution 49/214 of 23 December 1994*, HRC Res. 1/2, GAOR, 61st Sess., Supp. No. 53, UN Doc. A/61/53 (2006) 18.

13 The Commission on Human Rights, the parent of the WGDD, disappeared during the reorganization of the Human Rights system. Anything below the Commission on Human Rights, such as the Sub-Commission, the WGIP, no longer exists.

14 See African Group, "Draft Aide Memoire: African Group: United Nations Declaration on the Rights of Indigenous People" (9 Nov. 2006): www.iwgia.org/graphics/ Synkron-Library/Documents/InternationalProcesses/DraftDeclaration/AfricanGrou pAideMemoireOnDeclaration.pdf.

15 *Working group of the Commission on Human Rights to elaborate a draft declaration in accordance with paragraph 5 of General Assembly resolution 49/214 of 23 December 1994*, GA Res. 61/178, GAOR, 61st Sess., Supp. No. 49, Vol. I, UN Doc. A/61/49 (2007) 417.

16 See, e.g., Indigenous Peoples' Caucus, "UN Declaration on the Rights of Indigenous Peoples: African Group of States' Proposed Revised Text: A Model for Discrimination and Domination": www.treatycouncil.org/PDFs/UN%20Decl%20-%20African%20Gr 36BDE5.pdf.

17 Paul Martin, quoted in Allan Woods, "Former PM makes rare appearance to bash Tory aboriginal policy," *CanWest News Service* (4 Oct. 2006): www.canada.com/topics/news/ politics/story.html?id=1939366f-3ea5-4b4a-be81-36625c229e7f&k=62909&p=1.

18 See ICCPR and ICESCR, *supra* note 3, common art. 1.

19 The Hon. Jenny Macklin, MP, "Statement on the United Nations Declaration on the Rights of Indigenous Peoples" (Delivered at Parliament House, Canberra, 3 April 2009): www.jennymacklin.fahcsia.gov.au/internet/jennymacklin.nsf/content/un_dec- laration_03apr09.htm.

20 General Assembly, *Official Records*, UN GAOR, 61st Sess., 107th Plen. Mtg., UN Doc. A/61/PV.107 (2007) at 21 (Statement of the United Kingdom, delivered by Ms Pierce).

21 *Ibid.* at 12.

22 *Draft United Nations declaration on the rights of indigenous peoples*, *supra* note 6, annex (art. 7).

23 See, e.g., *Declaration of San José*, UNESCO Doc. FS 82/WF.32 (1982), Meeting of Experts on Ethno-Development and Ethnocide in Latin America, Final Report, San José, Costa Rica (7-11 Dec. 1981): "Ethnocide means that an ethnic group is denied the right to enjoy, develop and transmit its own culture and its own language, whether collectively or individually. This involves an extreme form of massive violation of human rights and, in particular, the right of ethnic groups to respect for their cultural identity, as established by numerous declarations, covenants and agreements of the United Nations and its Specialised Agencies, as well as various regional intergovernmental bodies and numerous non-governmental organisations."

24 William A. Schabas, *Genocide in International Law* (Cambridge: Cambridge University Press, 2000) at 223. See also *Prosecutor v. Krstic* (*Srebrenica-Drina Corps*), IT-98-33, Judgment (2 Aug. 2001) at para. 580 (International Criminal Tribunal for the former

Yugoslavia, Trial Chamber I): "[W]here there is physical or biological destruction there are often simultaneous attacks on the cultural and religious property and symbols of the targeted group as well, attacks which may legitimately be considered as evidence of an intent to physically destroy the group."

25 Bartolomé Clavero, *Genocide or Ethnocide, 1933–2007: How to Make, Unmake and Remake Law with Words* (Milan, Italy: Giuffrè Editore, 2008) at 225.

CHAPTER TWO

1 *Study of the problem of discrimination against indigenous populations*, ESC Res. 1982/34, UN ESCOR, 1982, Supp. No. 1, UN Doc E/1982/82, 26.

2 *Programme of activities for the International Decade of the World's Indigenous People*, GA Res. 50/157, UN GAOR, 50th Sess. Supp. No. 49, Vol. I, UN Doc. A/50/49 (1996) 219 at 221 (Annex, para. 6).

3 *Draft United Nations declaration on the rights of indigenous peoples*, UN Sub-Commission on Prevention of Discrimination and Protection of Minorities Res. 1994/45, in Commission on Human Rights, *Report of the Sub-Commission on Prevention of Discrimination and Protection of Minorities on its Forty-Sixth Session*, UN Doc. E/CN.4/1995/2, E/CN.4/Sub.2/1994/56 (28 Oct. 1994) 103.

4 *Establishment of a working group of the Commission on Human Rights to elaborate a draft declaration in accordance with paragraph 5 of General Assembly resolution 49/214*, ESC Res. 1995/32, UN ESCOR, 1996, Supp. No. 1, UN Doc. E/1995/95, 44.

5 Commission on Human Rights, *Information provided by States: Draft Declaration on the Rights of Indigenous Peoples: Amended Text: Denmark, Finland, Iceland, New Zealand, Norway, Sweden and Switzerland*, UN Doc. E/CN.4/2004/WG.15/CRP.1 (6 Sept. 2004).

6 Commission on Human Rights, *Report of the working group established in accordance with Commission on Human Rights resolution 1995/32 of 3 March 1995 on its eleventh session*, UN Doc. E/CN.4/2006/79 (22 Mar. 2006) at Annex I [Commission on Human Rights, *Report of the working group*].

7 *Working group of the Commission on Human Rights to elaborate a draft declaration in accordance with paragraph 5 of General Assembly resolution 49/214 of 23 December 1994*, HRC Res. 1/2, GAOR, 61st Sess., Supp. No. 53, UN Doc. A/61/53 (2006) 18.

8 *Working group of the Commission on Human Rights to elaborate a draft declaration in accordance with paragraph 5 of General Assembly resolution 49/214 of 23 December 1994*, GA Res. 61/178, GAOR, 61st Sess., Supp. No. 49, Vol. I, UN Doc. A/61/49 (2007) 417.

9 African Group, "Draft Aide Memoire: African Group: United Nations Declaration on the Rights of Indigenous People" (9 Nov. 2006): www.iwgia.org/graphics/Synkron-Library/Documents/InternationalProcesses/DraftDeclaration/AfricanGroupAideMemoireOnDeclaration.pdf.

10 Commission on Human Rights, *Report of the Special Rapporteur on the situation of human rights and fundamental freedoms of indigenous people, Mr. Rodolfo Stavenhagen*, UN Doc. E/CN.4/2006/78 (16 Feb. 2006) at para. 83.

11 *United Nations Declaration on the Rights of Indigenous Peoples*, preambular para. 20. See Appendix 1.

12 *Ibid.*, preambular para. 2.

13 *Ibid.*, art. 2.

14 *International Covenant on Civil and Political Rights*, 19 Dec. 1966, 999 U.N.T.S. 171 (entered into force 23 Mar. 1976).

15 *International Covenant on Economic, Social and Cultural Rights*, 19 Dec. 1966, 993 U.N.T.S. 3 (entered into force 3 Jan. 1976).

16 Commission on Human Rights, *Report of the working group, supra* note 6 at 21, 22 (Proposal on article 3 by Australia, New Zealand, United States of America).

17 *Indigenous issues*, GA Res. 63/161, UN GAOR, 63d Sess., Supp. No. 49, Vol. I, UN Doc. A/63/49 (2009) 370.

18 United Nations General Assembly, Press Release, GA/SHC/3954, "Implementing Declaration on Indigenous Rights Will Bring 'Historical Justice', Develop Stronger, Democratic, Multicultural Societies, Third Committee Told" (19 Oct. 2009): www.un.org/News/Press/docs/2009/gashc3954.doc.htm.

19 *International Convention on the Elimination of All Forms of Racial Discrimination*, 7 Mar. 1966, 660 U.N.T.S. 195 (entered into force 4 Jan. 1969).

20 *Convention on the Rights of the Child*, 20 Nov. 1989, 1577 U.N.T.S. 3 (entered into force 2 Sept. 1990).

21 General Assembly, *Draft Programme of Action for the Second International Decade of the World's Indigenous People: Report of the Secretary General,* UN Doc. A/60/270 (18 Aug. 2005) [General Assembly, Draft Programme of Action]. This draft was adopted by the General Assembly: *Programme of Action for the Second International Decade of the World's Indigenous People,* GA Res 60/142, UN GAOR, 60th Sess., Supp. No. 49, Vol. 1, UN Doc. A/60/49 (2006) 344.

22 General Assembly, *Draft Programme of Action, ibid.* at para. 98.

23 *Ibid.*

24 *Ibid.* at para. 85.

25 *Ibid.* at para. 95.

26 *Declaration*, arts. 40 and 27.

27 *Ibid.*, preambular para. 14.

28 *Ibid.*, art. 37.

29 See Andrea Carmen, "The *United Nations Declaration on the Rights of Indigenous Peoples*, Treaties and the Right to Free, Prior, and Informed Consent: A Framework for Harmonious Relations and New Processes for Redress," chap. 8 in this volume.

30 *Declaration*, preambular para. 20.

31 *Programme of Action for the Second International Decade of the World's Indigenous People,* *supra* note 21 at 345.

32 *Declaration*, preambular para. 19.

33 General Assembly, *Draft Programme of Action, supra* note 21 at para. 9.

34 *Ibid.* at para. 56; *Programme of activities for the International Decade of the World's Indigenous People, supra* note 2 at 221.

35 *Convention (No. 169) Concerning Indigenous and Tribal Peoples in Independent Countries,* 27 June 1989, ILO Official Bulletin, Vol. 72, Ser. A, No. 2, 59 (entered into force 5 Sept. 1991).

36 Commonwealth of Australia, House of Representatives, *Parliamentary Debates,* 13 Feb. 2008, 167 (Prime Minister Kevin Rudd).

37 The Hon. Jenny Macklin, MP, "Statement on the United Nations Declaration on the Rights of Indigenous Peoples" (Delivered at Parliament House, Canberra, 3 April 2009): www.jennymacklin.fahcsia.gov.au/internet/jennymacklin.nsf/content/un_declaration_03apr09.htm.

38 *Ibid.*

39 Australian Human Rights Commission, Media Release, "United we stand — Support for United Nations Indigenous Rights Declaration a watershed moment for Australia" (3 April 2009): www.humanrights.gov.au/about/media/media_releases/2009/21_09.html.

40 Martin Luther King, Jr., "I See the Promised Land (1968)" in Martin Luther King, Jr. & James M. Washington, *I Have a Dream: Writings and Speeches that Changed the World* (San Francisco: Glenview: ScottForesman, 1992) 193 at 203.

CHAPTER THREE

1 *United Nations Declaration on the Rights of Indigenous Peoples,* art. 43. See Appendix 1.

2 Secretary-General, Press Release, SG/SM/11715 HR/4957 OBV/711, "Protect, Promote Endangered Languages, Secretary-General Urges in Message for International Day of World's Indigenous People" (23 July 2008): www.un.org/News/Press/docs/2008/sgsm11715.doc.htm.

3 "Canada Criticized over UN Aboriginal Rights Vote" *Canadian Press* (22 Oct. 2007): www.ctv.ca/servlet/ArticleNews/story/CTVNews/20071022/aboriginal_rights_071022/20071022/.

4 Amnesty International Canada, *Canada and the International Protection of Human Rights: An Erosion of Leadership? An Update to Amnesty International's Human Rights Agenda for Canada* (Dec. 2007) at 5.

5 *An Act to Provide for the Government of British Columbia, 1858* (U.K.), 21 & 22 Vic, c 99.

6 Governor James Douglas, *Proclamation* (14 Feb. 1859).

7 *Constitution Act, 1982,* being Schedule B to the *Canada Act 1982* (U.K.), 1982, c. 11.

8 *R. v. Van der Peet* [1996] 2 S.C.R. 507 at para. 36.

9 *Delgamuukw* v. *British Columbia,* [1997] 3 S.C.R. 1010. at para. 166.

10 Commission on Human Rights, *Report of the Special Rapporteur on the situation of human rights and fundamental freedoms of indigenous people, Mr. Rodolfo Stavenhagen,* UN Doc. E/CN.4/2006/78 (16 Feb. 2006) at para. 83.

11   Committee on the Elimination of Racial Discrimination (CERD), *Concluding observations of the Committee on the Elimination of Racial Discrimination: Canada*, UN Doc. CERD/C/CAN/CO/18 (25 May 2007) at para. 22. [CERD, Concluding Observations: Canada.]

12   Jack Woodward, "Rejection of the 'Postage Stamp' Approach to Aboriginal Title: The Tsilhqot'in Nation Decision" at 1.2.7, in The Continuing Legal Education Society of British Columbia, *Aboriginal Law:* Tsilhqot'in *v.* BC: *Materials prepared for the Continuing Legal Education Society Seminar, Aboriginal Law:* Tsilhqot'in *v.* British Columbia, *Vancouver, 2008* (Vancouver: The Continuing Legal Education Society of British Columbia, 2008).

13   *Tsilhqot'in Nation* v. *British Columbia* (2007) BCSC 1700 at para. 1373. [*Tsilhqot'in Nation*]

14   *Ibid.*

15   *Ibid.* at para. 1376.

16   *Ibid.* at para. 1357.

17   *Delgamuukw, supra* note 9 at paras. 186, 207. See also *Tsilhqot'in Nation, supra* note 13 at paras. 1338-1382.

18   British Columbia Treaty Commission, *Annual Report* (2009) at 9.

19   The Tsawwassen First Nation Final Agreement (TFNFA) was ratified on 25 July 2007. Legislation to give it effect received Royal Assent in BC on 22 Nov. 2007 and federally on 26 June 2008. The TFNFA came into effect on 3 April 2009. The Maa-nulth First Nations Final Agreement (MFNFA) was ratified in a series of votes in July and October 2007. Legislation to give effect to the MFNFA received Royal Assent in BC on 29 Nov. 2007 and federally on 18 June 2009: www.gov.bc.ca/arr/treaty/final.html.

20   See, e.g., First Nations Summit, "Framework for 'Advancing Recognition & Reconciliation' & 'Improving the Lives of First Nations People' in British Columbia" (Sept. 2005).

21   See TFNFA, *supra* note 19 at chap. 2, clauses 11-14, 17; MFNFA, *supra* note 19 at clauses 1.11.1-1.11.4, 1.11.7.

22   See, e.g., James Bay and Northern Quebec Agreement (1975).

23   See, e.g., CERD, *Consideration of Reports, Comments and Information Submitted by States Parties under Article 9 of the Convention: Seventeenth and eighteenth periodic reports of Canada*, UN Doc. CERD/C/SR.1790 (28 Feb. 2007) at para. 46.

24   See, e.g., Human Rights Committee, *Concluding observations of the Human Rights Committee: Canada*, UN Doc. CCPR/C/79/Add.105 (7 April 1999) at para. 8; Commission on Human Rights, *Report of the Special Rapporteur on the situation of human rights and fundamental freedoms of indigenous people, Rodolfo Stavenhagen: Addendum: Mission to Canada*, UN Doc. E/CN.4/2005/88/Add.3 (2 Dec. 2004) at paras 20, 99; Committee on Economic, Social and Cultural Rights, *Concluding observations of the Committee on Economic, Social and Cultural Rights: Canada*, UN Doc. E/C.12./CAN/CO/4, E/C.12/CAN/CO/5 (22 May 2006) at para. 16; CERD, *Concluding observations: Canada, supra* note 11 at para. 22.

25   British Columbia Treaty Commission, *supra* note 18 at 33.

26 *Declaration*, art. 39.

27 *Haida Nation* v. *British Columbia (Minister of Forests)*, [2004] 3 S.C.R. 511 at para. 20.

28 *Ibid.*

29 *Supra* note 13 at para. 1338.

30 *Declaration*, preambular para. 24.

31 Human Rights Council, *Report of the Special Rapporteur on the situation of human rights and fundamental freedoms of indigenous people, S. James Anaya*, UN Doc. A/HRC/9/9 (11 Aug. 2008) at para. 46.

32 *Declaration*, art. 2.

33 *Ibid.*

34 *Ibid.*, art. 1.

35 *Ibid.*, art. 46 (3).

36 *Ibid.*, arts. 3, 4.

37 *Ibid.*, art. 19.

38 *Ibid.*, arts. 26, 25.

39 *Ibid.*, art. 26(3); see also art. 27.

40 *Ibid.*, art. 28(1).

41 *Ibid.*, arts. 8, 11, 12, 13.

42 *Ibid.*, art. 22.

43 *House of Commons Debates*, No. 110 (11 June 2008) at 6850 (Right Hon. Stephen Harper).

44 *Report of the Royal Commission on Aboriginal Peoples*, vol. 1 (Ottawa: Canada Communication Group, 1996) at 365.

45 *An Act to amend the Indian Act*, S.C. 1919-20, c.50, s. 1, amending *Indian Act*, R.S.C. 1906, c. 81.

46 Kristen Thompson, "Apology to Aboriginals Draws Tears" *Metro* (12 June 2008) 1.

47 *House of Commons Debates, supra* note 43 at 6854 (Hon. Jack Layton).

48 *Ibid.* at 6854 (Gilles Duceppe).

49 Romeo Saganash, "Keynote Address" (Delivered at the Faculty of Law, Common Law Section, University of Ottawa, 2 Sept. 2008) at 6.

50 *Declaration*, art. 8(1).

51 *Ibid.*, art. 7(2).

52 First Nations Summit, "Support and Endorsement of the United Nations Declaration on the Rights of Indigenous Peoples," Resolution #0907.35 (28 Sept. 2007).

53 "'All Our Relations': A Declaration of the Sovereign Indigenous Nations of British Columbia" (29 Nov. 2007), annexed to British Columbia Assembly of First Nations, First Nations Summit, and Union of British Columbia Indian Chiefs, News Release, "First Nations of British Columbia Issue Declaration Affirming Aboriginal Title" (30 Nov. 2007): www.fns.bc.ca/pdf/FNLC_NR_re1107Declaration.pdf.

54 *Ibid.*

55 First Nations Summit, "First Nations Summit Support for Declaration of Unity and Protocol," Resolution #0906.08 (29 Sept. 2006).

56 Kaska Nation, Tsay Keh Dene and Carrier Sekani Tribal Council, Press Release, "Peace and Friendship Treaty Signed" (7 Oct. 2008): www.cstc.bc.ca/news/text/330/12/peace+ and+friendship+treaty+signed?.

57 Representative for Children and Youth, *2007 Progress Report on the Implementation of the Recommendations of the BC Children and Youth Review ("Hughes Review")* (26 Nov. 2007) at 21: www.rcybc.ca/Groups/Our%20Reports/2007%20Hughes%20Progress%20 Report.pdf.

58 *Convention on the Rights of the Child,* 20 Nov. 1989, 1577 U.N.T.S. 3 (entered into force 2 Sept. 1990).

59 "Walking Together to Keep Indigenous Children at the Centre: Declaration of Commitment" (25 Jan. 2008).

60 "One Heart, One Mind: Statement of Solidarity & Cooperation" (23 July 2008).

61 "Recognition and Reconciliation Protocol on First Nations Children, Youth and Families" (30 Mar. 2009): www.mcf.gov.bc.ca/publications/Recognition_Reconciliation_Protocol.pdf.

62 First Nations Leadership Council, "BC First Nations Energy Action Plan" (7 June 2007) at 15.

63 First Nations Leadership Council, "BC First Nations Forestry & Land Stewardship Action Plan" (16 May 2008) at 5.

CHAPTER FOUR

1 *Charter of the United Nations,* preamble.

2 *Ibid.,* art. 1(3).

3 *Ibid.,* art. 4.

4 Permanent Mission of Guatemala, "Voluntary Pledges and Commitments of Guatemala to the Promotion and Protection of Human Rights" (1 May 2006): www.un.org/ga/60/elect/hrc/guatemala.pdf.

5 *Draft United Nations declaration on the rights of indigenous eoples,* Sub-Commission on Prevention of Discrimination and Protection of Minorities Res. 1994/45, in Commission on Human Rights, *Report of the Sub-Commission on Prevention of Discrimination and Protection of Minorities on its Forty-Sixth Session,* UN Doc. E/CN.4/1995/2, E/CN.4/Sub.2/1994/56 (28 Oct. 1994) 103.

6 *International Covenant on Civil and Political Rights,* 19 Dec. 1966, 999 U.N.T.S. 171 (entered into force 23 Mar. 1976) and *International Covenant on Economic, Social and Cultural Rights,* 19 Dec. 1966, 993 U.N.T.S. 3 (entered into force 3 Jan. 1976).

7 *Working group of the Commission on Human Rights to elaborate a draft declaration in accordance with paragraph 5 of General Assembly resolution 49/214 of 23 December 1994,* HRC Res 1/2, GAOR, 61st Sess., Supp. No. 53, UN Doc. A/61/53 (2006) 18.

8   African Group, "Draft Aide Memoire: African Group: United Nations Declaration on the Rights of Indigenous People" (9 Nov. 2006) at para. 3.1: www.iwgia.org/graphics/ Synkron-Library/Documents/InternationalProcesses/DraftDeclaration/AfricanGrou pAideMemoireOnDeclaration.pdf.

9   *Working group of the Commission on Human Rights to elaborate a draft declaration in accordance with paragraph 5 of General Assembly resolution 49/214 of 23 December 1994*, GA Res. 61/178, GAOR, 61st Sess., Supp. No. 49, Vol. I, UN Doc. A/61/49 (2007) 417.

10 General Assembly, *Official Records*, UN GAOR, 61st Sess., 108th Plen. Mtg., UN Doc. A/61/PV.108 (2007) at 8 – 9 (Statement of Guatemala, delivered by Mr. Briz Gutiérrez).

11 *The right to development*, GA Res. 62/161, UN GAOR, 62d Sess., Supp. No. 49, Vol. I, UN Doc. A/62/49 (2008) 396 at 400 (para. 32.). This resolution was presented by Cuba as President of the Movement of Non-Aligned Countries and adopted.

12 *The right to food*, GA Res. 62/164, UN GAOR, 62d Sess., Supp. No. 49, Vol. I, UN Doc. A/62/49 (2008) 405 at 408 (para 12). This was also a resolution presented by Cuba and adopted.

13 *Implementation of the outcome of the World Summit for Social Development and of the twenty-fourth special session of the General Assembly*, GA Res. 62/131, UN GAOR, 62d Sess., Supp. No. 49, Vol. I, UN Doc. A/62/49 (2008) 320 at 322 (para. 20).

14 *Global efforts for the total elimination of racism, racial discrimination, xenophobia and related intolerance and the comprehensive implementation of and follow-up to the Durban Declaration and Programme of Action*, GA Res. 62/220, UN GAOR, 62d Sess., Supp. No. 49, Vol. I, UN Doc. A/62/49 (2008) 435 at 438 (para. 25). This resolution was presented by the Group of 77 (G-77) and China, and was adopted.

15 *Rights of the child*, GA Res. 62/141, UN GAOR, 62d Sess., Supp. No. 49, Vol. I, UN Doc. A/62/49 (2008) 349 at 350 (preambular para. 8).

16 *United Nations Development Fund for Women*, GA Res. 62/135, UN GAOR, 62d Sess., Supp. No. 49, Vol. I, UN Doc. A/62/49 (2008) 331 at 333 (para. 21).

17 *Violence against women migrant workers*, GA Res. 62/132, UN GAOR, 62d Sess., Supp. No. 49, Vol. I, UN Doc. A/62/49 (2008) 324 at 324 – 325 (preambular para. 11). See also *Intensification of efforts to eliminate all forms of violence against women*, GA Res. 62/133, UN GAOR, 62d Sess., Supp. No. 49, Vol. I, UN Doc. A/62/49 (2008) 327 at 327 (preambular para. 4).

18 *Improvement of the situation of women in rural areas*, GA Res. 62/136, UN GAOR, 62d Sess., Supp. No. 49, Vol. I, UN Doc. A/62/49 (2008) 334 at 334 (preambular para. 5).

19 *Cooperatives in social development*, GA Res. 62/128, UN GAOR, 62d Sess., Supp. No. 49, Vol. I, UN Doc. A/62/49 (2008) 316.

20 *Human rights and cultural diversity*, GA Res. 62/155, UN GAOR, 62d Sess., Supp. No. 49, Vol. I, UN Doc. A/62/49 (2008) 384.

21 *Policies and programmes involving youth: youth in the global economy — promoting youth participation in social and economic development*, GA Res. 62/126, UN GAOR, 62d Sess., Supp. No. 49, Vol. I, UN Doc. A/62/49 (2008) 305.

22 *Implementation of the World Programme of Action concerning Disabled Persons: realizing the Millennium Development Goals for persons with disabilities*, GA Res.62/127, UN GAOR, 62d Sess., Supp. No. 49, Vol. I, UN Doc. A/62/49 (2008) 314.

23 *Human Rights and indigenous peoples: Mandate of the Special Rapporteur on the situation of human rights and fundamental freedoms of indigenous people*, HRC Res. 6/12, UN GAOR, 63d Sess., Supp. No. 53, UN Doc. A/63/53 (2008) 22 at 22 (para. 1(g)).

24 "Statement by Professor James Anaya, Special Rapporteur on the Situation of the Human Rights and Fundamental Freedoms of Indigenous Peoples" (Delivered to the 8th Session of the United Nations Permanent Forum on Indigenous Issues, New York, 20 May 2008) at 2.

25 *Second International Decade of the World's Indigenous People*, GA Res. 59/174, UN GAOR, 59th Sess., Supp. No. 49, Vol. 1, UN Doc. A/59/49 (2005) 344 at 344 (para. 2).

26 *Indigenous issues*, GA Res. 63/161, UN GAOR, 63d Sess., Supp. No, 49, Vol. 1, UN Doc. A/63/49 (2009) 370 at 371 (para. 2).

27 United Nations General Assembly, Press Release, GA/SHC/3954, "Implementing Declaration on Indigenous Rights Will Bring 'Historical Justice', Develop Stronger, Democratic, Multicultural Societies, Third Committee Told" (19 Oct. 2009): www.un.org/News/Press/docs/2009/gashc3954.doc.htm.

28 Permanent Forum on Indigenous Issues, "IASG / Inter-Agency Support Group on Indigenous Issues": www.un.org/esa/socdev/unpfii/en/iasg.html.

29 Permanent Forum on Indigenous Issues, *Report of Inter-Agency Support Group on Indigenous Issues*, UN Doc. E/C.19/2008/6 (5 Feb. 2008) at 11.

30 United Nations Development Group, *United Nations Development Group Guidelines on Indigenous Peoples' Issues* (Feb. 2008): www2.ohchr.org/english/issues/indigenous/docs/guidelines.pdf.

31 *Ibid.* at 10.

32 Permanent Forum on Indigenous Issues, *Inter-agency Support Group (IASG) on indigenous peoples: Special meeting on United Nations Declaration on the Rights of Indigenous Peoples: Palais des Nations: Geneva, 26 and 27 February 2008*, UN Doc. E/C.19/2008/CRP.7 (27 Mar. 2008) at 3.

33 *Ibid.* at 8.

34 Organization of American States, Working Group to Prepare the Draft American Declaration on the Rights of Indigenous Peoples, *Report of the Chair on the Meeting for Reflection on the Meetings of Negotiations in the Quest for Points of Consensus (Washington, D.C., United States — November 26-28, 2007)*, OEA/Ser.K/XVI, GT/DADIN/doc.321/08 (14 Jan. 2008) at 3.

35 Inter-American Commission on Human Rights, Press Release, No. 51/07, "IACHR Rapporteurship Applauds Approval of UN Declaration on Rights of Indigenous Peoples" (18 Sept. 2007): www.cidh.oas.org/Comunicados/English/2007/51.07eng.htm.

36 *Universal Declaration of Human Rights*, GA Res. 217(III), UN GAOR, 3d Sess., UN Doc. A/810 (1948) 71 at 71 (preambular para. 1).

1   Victoria Tauli-Corpuz, "Statement of Victoria Tauli-Corpuz, Chair of the UN Permanent Forum on Indigenous Issues on the Occasion of the Adoption of the UN Declaration on the Rights of Indigenous Peoples" (Delivered to the United Nations General Assembly, New York, 13 Sept. 2007): www.un.org/esa/socdev/unpfii/documents/Declaration_ip_vtc.doc.

2   *United Nations Declaration on the Rights of Indigenous Peoples,* preambular para. 7. See Appendix 1.

3   *Ibid.*, art. 43.

4   "Statement Attributable to the Spokesperson for the Secretary-General on the Adoption of the *Declaration on the Rights of Indigenous Peoples*" (New York, 13 Sept. 2007): www.un.org/apps/sg/sgstats.asp?nid=2733.

5   Portugal (on behalf of the European Union), "Special Rapporteur on the situation of human rights and fundamental freedoms of indigenous people" (Statement delivered to the Human Rights Council, 6th Sess., 18th Mtg., Geneva, 26 Sept. 2007).

6   Egypt (on behalf of the African Group), "African Statement on the mandate of the Special Rapporteur on the situation of human rights and fundamental freedoms of Indigenous People" (Statement Delivered to the Human Rights Council, 6th Sess., 18th Mtg., Geneva, 26 Sept. 2007).

7   Letter from Minister of Indian Affairs and Northern Development, Chuck Strahl, to Assembly of First Nations National Chief Phil Fontaine (10 Dec. 2007).

8   Letter from Minister of Indian Affairs and Northern Development, Chuck Strahl, to Assembly of First Nations National Chief Phil Fontaine (28 Mar. 2008).

9   Chuck Strahl, "Address" (Delivered at Luncheon Hosted by Canada's Permanent Mission to the United Nations, New York, 1 May 2008): www.ainc-inac.gc.ca/ai/mr/spch/2008/may0108-eng.asp.

10   Robin Bajer, "Canada loses face internationally in voting against indigenous rights," *Lawyers Weekly* (19 Sept. 2008) 12.

11   Beverley McLachlin, "Aboriginal Rights: International Perspectives" (Speech delivered at the Order of Canada Luncheon, Canadian Club of Vancouver, 8 Feb. 2002).

12   Human Rights Council, *Report of the Special Rapporteur on the situation of human rights and fundamental freedoms of indigenous people, Rodolfo Stavenhagen,* UN Doc. A/HRC/6/15 (15 Nov. 2007) at para. 64. See also Committee on the Rights of the Child, *General Comment No. 11 (2009): Indigenous children and their rights under the Convention,* UN Doc. CRC/C/GC/11 (12 Feb. 2009) at para. 82: "the Committee urges States parties to adopt a rights-based approach to indigenous children based on the Convention [on the Rights of the Child] and other relevant international standards, such as ILO Convention No. 169 and the United Nations Declaration on the Rights of Indigenous Peoples."

13 United Nations Development Group, *United Nations Development Group Guidelines on Indigenous Peoples' Issues* (Feb. 2008) at 24: www2.ohchr.org/english/issues/indigenous/docs/guidelines.pdf. The Guidelines were drafted by a group of UN organizations and specialized agencies under the aegis of the Inter-Agency Support Group on Indigenous Peoples' Issues.

14 See, e.g., James Youngblood Henderson, Marjorie L. Benson & Isobel M. Findlay, *Aboriginal Tenure in the Constitution of Canada* (Toronto: Carswell, 2000) at 447; Paul Joffe, "Assessing the *Delgamuukw* Principles: National Implications and Potential Effects in Québec" (2000) 45 McGill L.J. 155 at 182; Cynthia Price Cohen, ed., *Human Rights of Indigenous Peoples* (Ardsley, NY: Transnational, 1998); Mary Ellen Turpel, "Indigenous Peoples' Rights of Political Participation and Self-Determination: Recent International Legal Developments and the Continuing Struggle for Recognition" (1992) 25 Cornell Int'l L. J. 579; Raidza Torres, "The Rights of Indigenous Populations: The Emerging International Norm" (1991) 16 Yale J. Int'l L. 127.

15 Irwin Cotler, "Human Rights Advocacy and the NGO Agenda" in Irwin Cotler & F. Pearl Eliadis, eds., *International Human Rights Law: Theory and Practice* (Montreal: Canadian Human Rights Foundation, 1992) 63 at 66.

16 Canadian Human Rights Commission, *"Still A Matter of Rights": A Special Report of the Canadian Human Rights Commission on the Repeal of Section 67 of the Canadian Human Rights Act* (Ottawa: Minister of Public Works and Government Services, 2008) at 8: www.chrc-ccdp.ca/proactive_initiatives/smr_tqd/toc_tdm-en.asp.

17 *Institution-building of the United Nations Human Rights Council*, HRC Res. 5/1, UN GAOR, 62d Sess., Supp. No. 53, UN Doc. A/62/53 (2007) 48 at 62 (Annex, V(C)).

18 Office of the High Commissioner for Human Rights, "OHCHR Fact Sheet: The *UN Declaration on the Rights of Indigenous Peoples*": www2.ohchr.org/english/issues/indigenous/docs/IntDay/IndigenousDeclarationeng.pdf.

19 Letter from Assembly of First Nations National Chief Phil Fontaine to the Minister of Indian Affairs and Northern Development, Chuck Strahl (30 Jan. 2007), Annex, at 8.

20 *Concluding observations of the Committee on Economic, Social and Cultural Rights: Canada*, UN Doc. E/C.12/1/Add.31 (10 Dec. 1998) at para. 18. See also *Concluding Observations of the Committee on the Elimination of Racial Discrimination: Canada*, UN Doc. CERD/C/61/CO/3 (23 Aug. 2002) at para. 17.

21 Dalee Sambo, "Indigenous Peoples and International Standard-Setting Processes: Are State Governments Listening?" (1993) 3 Transnat'l L. & Contemp. Probs. 13 at 31.

22 Paul Joffe & Mary Ellen Turpel, *Extinguishment of the Rights of Aboriginal Peoples: Problems and Alternatives*, A study prepared for the Royal Commission on Aboriginal Peoples, vol. 2 (1995) ch. 8, at 322 *et seq.*, which concludes that extinguishment is incompatible with human rights and other norms.

23 *2005 World Summit Outcome*, GA Res. 60/1, UN GAOR, 60th Sess., Supp. No. 49, Vol. I, UN Doc. A/60/49 (2006) 3 at 18 (para. 119): "all human rights, the rule of law and democracy ... are interlinked and mutually reinforcing and ... they belong to the universal and indivisible core values and principles of the United Nations."

24 Stephen J. Toope, "Legal and Judicial Reform through Development Assistance: Some Lessons" (2003) 48 McGill L.J. 357 at 387-388.

25 *R. v. Demers* [2004] 2 S.C.R. 489 at para. 79 [*Demers*].

26 *Report of the Royal Commission on Aboriginal Peoples*, vol. 3 (Ottawa: Canada Communication Group, 1996) at 5: "Current social problems are in large part a legacy of historical policies of displacement and assimilation, and their resolution lies in recognizing the authority of Aboriginal people to chart their own future within the Canadian federation." See also Committee on Economic, Social and Cultural Rights, *General Comment No. 14 (2000): The right to the highest attainable standard of health*, UN Doc. E/C.12/2000/4 (11 Aug. 2000) at para. 27: "The Committee notes that, in indigenous communities, the health of the individual is often linked to the health of the society as a whole and has a collective dimension."

27 Canadian Medical Association, *Bridging the Gap: Promoting Health and Healing for Aboriginal Peoples in Canada* (Ottawa: Canadian Medical Association, 1994) at 14.

28 Rodolfo Stavenhagen, *The Ethnic Question: Conflicts, Development, and Human Rights*, (Tokyo: United Nations Univ. Press, 1990) at 105: "Indigenous peoples are aware of the fact that unless they are able to retain control over their land and territories, their survival as identifiable, distinct societies and cultures is seriously endangered."

29 "Message of Louise Arbour, United Nations High Commissioner for Human Rights and Rodolfo Stavenhagen, Special Rapporteur on the situation of human rights and fundamental freedoms of indigenous people, on the occasion of the International Day of the World's Indigenous Peoples" (Geneva, 7 Aug. 2007): www.un.org/esa/socdev/unpfii/documents/Message_OHCHR07_en.doc.

30 *International Year of Human Rights Learning*, GA Res. 62/171, UN GAOR, 62d Sess., Supp. No. 49, Vol. 1, UN Doc. A/62/49 (2008) 420 at 420 (preambular para. 9).

31 Paul Joffe & Willie Littlechild, "Administration of Justice and How to Improve it: Applicability and Use of International Human Rights Norms" in Commission on First Nations and Métis Peoples and Justice Reform, *Final Report: Submissions to the Commission*, vol. 2 (Saskatoon: Saskatchewan Commission on First Nations and Métis Peoples and Justice Reform, 2004) section 12 at 12-25 – 12-26: www.justicereformcomm.sk.ca/volume2/15section12.pdf.

32 General Assembly, *Draft Programme of Action for the Second International Decade of the World's Indigenous People: Report of the Secretary-General*, UN Doc. A/60/270 (18 Aug. 2005) at para. 47 [General Assembly, *Draft Programme of Action*]. This draft was adopted by the General Assembly: *Programme of Action for the Second International Decade of the World's Indigenous People*, GA Res. 60/142, UN GAOR, 60th Sess., Supp. No. 49, Vol. I, UN Doc. A/60/49 (2006) 344.

33 See, e.g., Permanent Forum on Indigenous Issues, *Information received from the United Nations system and other intergovernmental organizations: United Nations Children's Fund*, UN Doc. E/C.19/2008/4/Add.1 (23 Jan. 2008) at para. 3.

34 Committee on the Elimination of Racial Discrimination, *Concluding observations of the Committee on the Elimination of Racial Discrimination: Canada*, UN Doc. CERD/C/CAN/CO/18 (25 May 2007) at para. 27.

35 In regard to the vote, see *House of Commons Debates*, No. 074 (8 April 2008) at 4656. The text of the motion is reproduced in *House of Commons Debates*, No. 073 (7 April 2008).

36 *Haida Nation* v. *British Columbia (Minister of Forests)*, [2004] 3 S.C.R. 511 at paras. 16 and 17 [*Haida Nation*].

37 *Taku River Tlingit First Nation* v. *British Columbia (Project Assessment Director)*, [2004] 3 S.C.R. 550 at para. 24 [*Taku River Tlingit First Nation*].

38 *R.* v. *Badger*, [1996] 1 S.C.R. 771 at para. 41 [*Badger*].

39 *Taku River Tlingit First Nation*, *supra* note 37 at para. 25.

40 *Mikisew Cree First Nation* v. *Canada (Minister of Canadian Heritage)*, [2005] 3 S.C.R. 388 at para. 54.

41 *Haida Nation*, *supra* note 36 at para. 61: "On questions of law, a decision-maker must generally be correct. . . . To the extent that the issue is one of pure law, and can be isolated from the issues of fact, the standard is correctness."

42 Chuck Strahl, quoted in Steven Edwards, "Tories defend 'no' in native rights vote" *The [Montreal] Gazette* (14 Sept. 2007) A16.

43 See *Declaration* at preambular paras. 4 and 22; arts. 1, 2, 6, 7, 8, 9, 14, 17, 21, 22, 24, 33, 40, 44 and 46.

44 Letter from the Permanent Missions of Canada, Colombia, New Zealand, and the Russian Federation to the President of the United Nations General Assembly (13 Aug. 2007), attaching a "Non-Paper on Proposed Amendments."

45 GA Res. 217(III), UN GAOR, 3d Sess., UN Doc. A/810 (1948) 71.

46 *International Covenant on Civil and Political Rights*, 19 Dec. 1966, 999 U.N.T.S. 171 (entered into force 23 Mar. 1976) [ICCPR]; *International Covenant on Economic, Social and Cultural Rights*, 19 December 1966, 993 U.N.T.S. 3 (entered into force 3 Jan. 1976) [ICESER].

47 For example, in Latin America, a number of states constitutions provide that all subsurface resources are the property of the state: see, e.g., Committee on the Elimination of Racial Discrimination, *Concluding observations of the Committee on the Elimination of Racial Discrimination: Suriname*, UN Doc. CERD/C/64/CO/9 (28 April 2004) at para. 11. This type of argument has been used to dispossess Indigenous peoples of their resource rights. In Canada, it could open the door to further specious constitutional arguments by the government for severely limiting or denying Indigenous peoples' human rights.

48 *House of Commons Debates*, No. 045 (21 June 2006) at 2719 (Hon. Jim Prentice).

49 Indian and Northern Affairs Canada (INAC), "Canada's Position: United Nations Draft Declaration on the Rights of Indigenous Peoples - June 29, 2006." The document was mounted on the Indian Affairs web site by 28 Sept. 2006, and then back-dated to three months earlier, so as to appear that the information was available at the time of the vote on the *Declaration* at the Human Rights Council on 29 June 2006.

50 Edwards, *supra* note 42.

51 *Reference re Same-Sex Marriage* [2004] 3 S.C.R. 698 at para. 51.

52 Gloria Galloway, "Back UN on native rights, Ottawa urged" *The Globe and Mail* (8 June 2007) A1.

53 INAC, "Canada's Position," *supra* note 49.

54 World Conference on Disaster Reduction, *Hyogo Framework for Action, 2005-2015: Building the Resilience of Nations and Communities to Disasters: World Conference on Disaster Reduction, 18-22 January 2005, Kobe, Hyogo, Japan* (undated) at para. 18: www.unisdr.org/eng/hfa/docs/Hyogo-framework-for-action-english.pdf.

55 Permanent Missions of Canada *et al., supra* note 44.

56 Working Group on Indigenous Populations, *Principal Theme: "Utilization of Indigenous Peoples' Lands by Non-Indigenous Authorities, Groups or Individuals for Military Purposes": Note by the Secretariat,* UN Doc. E/CN.4/Sub.2/AC.4/2006/2 (14 June 2006) at para. 44.

57 *House of Commons Debates,* No. 083 (21 Nov. 2006) at 5147 (Hon. Jim Prentice).

58 Joffe & Littlechild, *supra* note 31 at 12-12 – 12-14: "Their treaties often entail a wide range of human rights considerations. Whether in general or specific terms, Indigenous peoples' treaties constitute an elaboration of arrangements relating to the political, economic, social, cultural or spiritual rights and jurisdictions of the Indigenous peoples concerned. These treaties also often include important dimensions relating to the collective and individual security of Indigenous peoples and individuals."

59 *Declaration,* preambular paras. 8 and 15.

60 See also *ibid.,* art. 37(2): "Nothing in this Declaration may be interpreted as diminishing or eliminating the rights of indigenous peoples contained in treaties, agreements and other constructive arrangements."

61 *Badger, supra* note 38 at para. 41, Cory J.: "First, it must be remembered that a treaty represents an exchange of solemn promises between the Crown and the various Indian nations. It is an agreement whose nature is sacred."

62 Prentice, *supra* note 48.

63 *Indian Act,* R.S.C. 1927, c. 98, s. 141.

64 Jim Prentice, "Address" (Delivered at Assembly of First Nations 27th Annual General Assembly, Vancouver, BC, 13 July 2006): www.ainc-inac.gc.ca/ai/mr/spch/2006/af27-eng.asp.

65 See *Applicability of the Obligation to Arbitrate under Section 21 of the United Nations Headquarters Agreement of 26 June 1947,* Advisory Opinion [1988] I.C.J. Rep. 12 at 34 (para. 57), which confirmed that "the fundamental principle of international law [is] that international law prevails over domestic law."

66 See also *Media Rights Agenda and Constitutional Rights Project v. Nigeria,* African Commission on Human and Peoples' Rights, Communications 105/93, 128/94, 130/94, 152/96 (1998) at para. 66: "To allow national law to have precedent over the international law of the [African] Charter would defeat the purpose of the rights and freedoms enshrined in the Charter. International human rights standards must always prevail over contradictory national law."

67 *House of Commons Debates,* No. 073 (7 April 2008) at 4567 [Rod Bruinooge].

68 INAC, "Canada's Position," *supra* note 49.

69 Bruinooge, *supra* note 67.

70 *Delgamuukw* v. *British Columbia*, [1997] 3 S.C.R. 1010 at para. 144 [*Delgamuukw*]: "In order to establish a claim to aboriginal title, the aboriginal group asserting the claim must establish that it occupied the lands in question at the time at which the Crown asserted sovereignty over the land subject to the title."

71 Indian and Northern Affairs Canada, *Comprehensive Claims (Modern Treaties) in Canada: March 1996*: www.ainc-inac.gc.ca/pr/info/trty_e.html: "The traditional use and occupancy of the territory must have been sufficient to be an established fact at the time of assertion of sovereignty by European nations."

72 Strahl (10 Dec. 2007), *supra* note 7 at 1.

73 Permanent Missions of Canada *et. al.*, *supra* note 44.

74 S. James Anaya, *Indigenous Peoples in International Law*, 2d ed. (Oxford: Oxford University Press, 2004) at 150: "Self-government is the overarching political dimension of ongoing self-determination."

75 Permanent Missions of Canada *et. al.*, *supra* note 44.

76 "Tangible heritage" refers to both cultural and natural heritage of outstanding universal value. "Tangible cultural heritage" may include monuments and structures of an architectural or archaeological nature; buildings; sites and human-made elements with cultural significance. See, e.g., *Convention Concerning the Protection of the World Cultural and Natural Heritage*, 23 Nov. 1972, 1037 U.N.T.S. 151 (entered into force 17 Dec. 1975) art. 1.

77 *Convention for the Safeguarding of the Intangible Cultural Heritage*, 17 Oct. 2003, 2368 U.N.T.S. 3 (entered into force 20 April 2006) art. 2: "For the purposes of this Convention, 1. The 'intangible cultural heritage' means the practices, representations, expressions, knowledge, skills — as well as the instruments, objects, artefacts and cultural spaces associated therewith — that communities, groups and, in some cases, individuals recognize as part of their cultural heritage."

78 See, e.g., Committee on Economic, Social and Cultural Rights, *Concluding observations of the Committee on Economic, Social and Cultural Rights: Canada*, UN Doc. E/C.12/CAN/CO/4, E/C.12/CAN/CO/5 (22 May 2006) at para. 67: "The Committee recommends that the State party undertake the adoption and implementation of concrete plans, with relevant benchmarks and time frames . . . in the area of intellectual property for the protection and promotion of ancestral rights and traditional knowledge of Aboriginal peoples."

79 *Convention on the Protection and Promotion of the Diversity of Cultural Expressions*, 20 Oct. 2005 (entered into force 18 Mar. 2007), preamble.

80 Indian and Northern Affairs Canada, "Update Paper: United Nations Declaration on the Rights of Indigenous Peoples" (10 Jan. 2008): www.ainc-inac.gc.ca/ap/ia/pubs/updir/updir-eng.asp.

81 Canada, "Statement by Ambassador Paul Meyer, Head of Delegation, Working Group on the Draft Declaration on the Rights of Indigenous Peoples to the 1st Session of the Human Rights Council" (Delivered to the Human Rights Council, 1st Sess., 21st Mtg., Geneva, 29 June 2006) [Canada, "Statement by Ambassador Paul Meyer"].

82 See "Non-Paper, United Nations Declaration on the Rights of Indigenous Peoples: Summary of Key Areas of Concerns" (28 June 2007) in Hilario G. Davide, Jr., "Supplement to the Report of the Facilitator on the Draft Declaration on the Rights of Indigenous Peoples" (20 July 2007) Annex I. This "non-paper" was submitted by Canada and six other states (Australia, Colombia, Guyana, New Zealand, the Russian Federation, and Suriname) to a closed meeting of the UN General Assembly hosted by Ambassador Davide. The non-paper indicates that not all of these states shared all of the concerns raised therein.

83 Permanent Forum on Indigenous Issues, *Information received from the United Nations system and other intergovernmental organizations: World Intellectual Property Organization*, UN Doc. E/C.19/2007/3/Add.14 (22 Mar. 2007) at para. 3.

84 "Message from Mr. Koïchiro Matsuura, Director-General of UNESCO, on the occasion of the International Day of the World's Indigenous People, 9 Aug. 2008": www.un.org/esa/socdev/unpfii/en/news_internationalday2008.html.

85 *Declaration*, arts. 10, 11(2), 19, 28(1), 29(2) and 32(2).

86 *Convention (No. 169) Concerning Indigenous and Tribal Peoples in Independent Countries*, 27 June 1989, ILO Official Bulletin Vol. 72, Ser. A, No. 2, 59 (entered into force 5 Sept. 1991), art. 4: "1. Special measures shall be adopted as appropriate for safeguarding the persons, institutions, property, labour, cultures and environment of the peoples concerned. 2. Such special measures shall not be contrary to the freely-expressed wishes of the peoples concerned." See also *Centre for Minority Rights Development (Kenya) and Minority Rights Group International on behalf of Endorois Welfare Council v. Kenya* (2009) African Commission on Human and Peoples' Rights, Communication No. 276/2003 (not yet reported) at para. 291: "... the African Commission is of the view that any development or investment projects that would have a major impact within the Endorois territory, the State has a duty not only to consult with the community, but also to obtain their free, prior, and informed consent, according to their customs and traditions."

87 *Cal v. Attorney General of Belize and Minister of Natural Resources and Environment; Coy v. Attorney General of Belize and Minister of Natural Resources and Environment* (18 Oct. 2007); Claims No. 171 & 172 of 2007 (Consolidated), (Supreme Court of Belize) at para. 136(d).

88 Committee on the Elimination of Racial Discrimination, *General Recommendation on the rights of indigenous peoples* [General Recommendation No. XXIII], at para. 5, in General Assembly, *Report of the Committee on the Elimination of Racial Discrimination*, UN GAOR, 52d Sess., Supp. No. 18, UN Doc. A/52/18 (1997) 122 (Annex V): "The Committee especially calls upon States parties to recognise and protect the rights of indigenous peoples to own, develop, control and use their communal lands, territories and resources and, where they have been deprived of their lands and territories traditionally owned or otherwise inhabited or used without their free and informed consent, to take steps to return these lands and territories." See also Human Rights Committee, *Concluding observations of the Human Rights Committee: Nicaragua*, UN Doc. CCPR/C/NIC/CO/3 (12 Dec. 2008) at para. 21.

89 Commission on Human Rights, *Report of the Special Rapporteur on the situation of human rights and fundamental freedoms of indigenous people, Mr. Rodolfo Stavenhagen, submitted pursuant to Commission resolution 2005/51, Addendum: Progress report on prepara-*

tory work for the study regarding best practices carried out to implement the recommendations contained in the annual reports of the Special Rapporteur, UN Doc. E/CN.4/2006/78/Add.4 (26 Jan. 2006) at para. 11.

90   United Nations Development Group, *supra* note 13 at 25: "The principle of free, prior and informed consent is an integral part of the human rights-based approach."

91   Permanent Forum on Indigenous Issues, *Ongoing priorities and themes: Note by the Secretariat,* UN Doc. E/C.19/2006/8 (26 Mar. 2006) at para. 10(c): "In the context of the Millennium Development Goals, free, prior and informed consent should apply not only to land development initiatives, but to all development initiatives focused on improving the lives of indigenous peoples."

92   *Case of the Saramaka People* v. *Suriname* (2007), Preliminary Objections, Merits, Reparations, and Costs, Inter-Am. Ct. H.R. (Ser. C) No. 172, at para. 134 (the *Declaration* was cited in this case: at para. 131).

93   General Assembly, *Draft Programme of Action, supra* note 32 at para. 47.

94   Strahl (10 Dec. 2007), *supra* note 7 at 1.

95   *Haida Nation, supra* note 36 at para. 24.

96   This meeting was the 14th Conference of Parties of the *United Nations Framework Convention on Climate Change* [4 June 1992, 1771 U.N.T.S. 107 (entered into force 21 Mar. 1994)].

97   Victoria Tauli-Corpuz, Press Statement, "International Human Rights Day 2008: A Sad Day for Indigenous Peoples" (10 Dec. 2008): http://unfccc.int/resource/docs/2008/sbsta/eng/l23.pdf.

98   Bill Curry and Martin Mittelstaedt, "Ottawa's stand at talks hurting native rights, chiefs say," *Globe and Mail* (12 Dec. 2008) A10.

99   Previously, as Minister of Indian Affairs and Northern Development, Jim Prentice played a leading role in the Conservative government's strategy to oppose the *Declaration* at home and abroad.

100   Human Rights Council, *Report of the Office of the United Nations High Commissioner for Human Rights on the relationship between climate change and human rights,* UN Doc. A/HRC/10/61 (15 Jan. 2009) at para. 53: "The United Nations Declaration on the Rights of Indigenous Peoples sets out several rights and principles of relevance to threats posed by climate change." See also Permanent Forum on Indigenous Issues, *Conference on Indigenous Peoples and Climate Change, Copenhagen, 21-22 February 2008: Meeting Report: Submitted by the International Work Group for Indigenous Affairs (IWGIA),* UN Doc. E/C.19/2008/CRP. 3 (10 Mar. 2008) at para. 4: "For indigenous peoples around the world, climate change brings different kinds of risks, brings threats to cultural survival and undermines indigenous human rights. The consequences of ecosystem changes have implications for the use, protection and management of wildlife, fisheries, and forests, affecting the customary uses of culturally and economically important species and resources."

101   Human Rights Council, *Report of the Special Rapporteur on the situation of human rights and fundamental freedoms of indigenous people, S. James Anaya,* UN Doc. A/HRC/9/9 (11 Aug. 2008) at para. 77 [Human Rights Council, *Report of the Special Rapporteur, S. James Anaya*].

102 Permanent Forum on Indigenous Issues, *Report on the seventh session (21 April - 2 May 2008)*, UN ESCOR, 2008, Supp. No. 23, UN Doc. E/2008/43, E/C.19/2008/13, at para.18.

103 IUCN, "Implementing the United Nations Declaration on the Rights of Indigenous Peoples," Resolution 4.052, adopted by the IUCN World Conservation Congress, 4th Session, Barcelona, Spain, 5-14 Oct. 2008: intranet.iucn.org/webfiles/doc/ IUCNPolicy/Resolutions/2008_WCC_4/English/RES/Res_4_052_Implementing_ the_UN_Decl.pdf.

104 Kyung-wha Kang, "Climate Change and Human Rights" (Address to the Conference of the Parties to the United Nations Framework Convention on Climate Change and its Kyoto Protocol, 3-14 Dec. 2007, Bali, Indonesia): www.unhchr.ch/huricane/ huricane.nsf/o/013DC0FAA475EC87C12573B10074796A?opendocument.

105 Permanent Forum on Indigenous Issues, *Information received from the United Nations system and other intergovernmental organizations: Office of the United Nations High Commissioner for Human Rights*, UN Doc. E/C.19/2008/4/Add.14 (15 Feb. 2008) at para. 31.

106 Development Group, *supra* note 13 at 18.

107 "*UN Declaration on the Rights of Indigenous Peoples*: Canada Needs to Implement This New Human Rights Instrument" (1 May 2008): www.cfsc.quaker.ca/pages/ documents/UNDecl-Expertsign-onstatementMay1.pdf. See Appendix 11.

108 See, e.g., *Halfway River First Nation* v. *British Columbia (Ministry of Forests)*, [1999] 4 C.N.L.R. 1 at para. 160 (quoted with approval by Binnie J in *Mikisew Cree First Nation, supra* note 40 at para. 64): "The Crown's duty to consult imposes on it a positive obligation to reasonably ensure that aboriginal peoples are provided with all necessary information in a timely way so that they have an opportunity to express their interests and concerns, and to ensure that their representations are seriously considered and, wherever possible, demonstrably integrated into the proposed plan of action."

109 *Charter of the United Nations*, art. 1(3).

110 *Demers, supra* note 25 at para. 79.

111 *Human Rights Council*, GA Res. 60/251, UN GAOR , 60th Sess., Supp. No. 49, Vol. III, UN Doc. A/60/49 (2007) 2 at 4 (para. 9).

112 *Ibid.* at para. 2.

113 *Ibid.* preamble at para. 5.

114 Assembly of First Nations *et al.*, *Closing the Implementation Gap: Indigenous Peoples and Human Rights in Canada: A forum to follow up on the 2004 mission to Canada by the United Nations Special Rapporteur on the situation of human rights and fundamental freedoms of indigenous people, Rodolfo Stavenhagen, University of Ottawa, October 2-3, 2006* (2008) at 23 (recommendation 5): www.cfsc.quaker.ca/pages/documents/closingtheimplementati ongap.pdf; and Assembly of First Nations, "Call for the Removal of Canada as a Member of the United Nations Human Rights Council," Resolution No. 38/2007 (adopted by consensus), Special Chiefs' Assembly, 11-13 Dec. 2007, Ottawa, Canada.

115 General Assembly, *Report of the United Nations High Commissioner for Human Rights*, UN GAOR, 61st Sess., Supp. No. 36, UN Doc. A/61/36 (2006) at para. 52.

116 *2005 World Summit Outcome, supra* note 23 at 3 (para. 9).

117 General Assembly, *In larger freedom: Towards development, security and human rights for all: Report of the Secretary-General*, UN Doc. A/59/2005 (21 Mar. 2005) at para. 17.

118 Canada, "Statement to the Human Rights Council on the Mandate of the UN Special Rapporteur on the situation of the human rights and fundamental freedom of indigenous people" (Delivered to the Human Rights Council, 6th Sess., 18th Mtg., Geneva, 26 Sept. 2007).

119 Amnesty International Canada, *Canada and the International Protection of Human Rights: An Erosion of Leadership? An Update to Amnesty International's Human Rights Agenda for Canada* (Dec. 2007) at 7-8.

120 Alex Neve, "Shame on Canada for Opposing the UN Indigenous Peoples Declaration" *The Lawyers Weekly* (6 June 2008) 5.

121 INAC, "Update Paper," *supra* note 80.

122 Human Rights Council, *Report of the Special Rapporteur, S. James Anaya, supra* note 101 at para. 86: "[t]he declaration does not attempt to bestow indigenous peoples with a set of special or new human rights, but rather provides a contextualized elaboration of general human rights principles and rights as they relate to the specific historical, cultural and social circumstances of indigenous peoples."

123 *Ibid.* at para. 63; see also para. 86.

124 See Committee on the Elimination of Racial Discrimination, *Concluding observations of the Committee on the Elimination of Racial Discrimination: United States of America*, UN Doc. CERD/C/USA/CO/6 (8 May 2008) at para. 29: "While noting the position of the State party with regard to the United Nations Declaration on the Rights of Indigenous Peoples (A/RES/61/295), the Committee finally recommends that the declaration be used as a guide to interpret the State party's obligations under the Convention relating to indigenous peoples." In regard to interpreting the *Convention on the Rights of the Child*, see Committee on the Rights of the Child, *General Comment No. 11, supra* note 12. In this General Comment, the *Declaration* is referred to in paragraphs 10; 29, note 12; 45; 52; 58, note 26; 66, note 30; and 82.

125 Organization of American States, Working Group to Prepare the Draft American Declaration on the Rights of Indigenous Peoples, *Report of the Chair on the Meeting for Reflection on the Meetings of Negotiations in the Quest for Points of Consensus (Washington, D.C., United States — November 26-28, 2007)*, OEA/Ser.K/XVI, GT/DADIN/doc.321/08 (14 Jan. 2008) at 3.

126 John H. Currie, Craig Forcese & Valerie Oosterveld, *International Law: Doctrine, Practice, and Theory* (Toronto: Irwin Law, 2007) at 130. See also *Military and Paramilitary Activities in and against Nicaragua (Nicaragua* v. *United States)*, Merits, [1986] I.C.J. Rep. 14. *Opinio juris* refers to a sense of legal duty that motivates states to adhere to a particular state practice. See Section 4(B).

127 Kenneth Abbott & Duncan Snidal, "Hard and Soft Law in International Governance" in Charlotte Ku & Paul F. Diehl, eds., *International Law: Classic and Contemporary Readings*, 3d ed. (Boulder, Colo.: Lynne Rienner, 2009) 21 at 22-23.

128 Anthea Roberts, "Traditional and Modern Approaches to Customary International Law: A Reconciliation" in Ku & Diehl, *ibid.* 49 at 68: "While hard law that is always enforced may be preferable to soft law, the choice in areas such as human rights is often between soft law and no law."

129 See, e.g., Dinah Shelton, "Editor's Concluding Note: The Role of Non-binding Norms in the International Legal System" in Dinah Shelton, ed., *Commitment and Compliance: The Role of Non-Binding Norms in the International Legal System* (Oxford/New York: Oxford University Press, 2003) 554 at 555: "In the field of human rights, soft law usually preceded hard law in the past, helping to build consensus on the norms. . . . The situation has changed now that the 'easy' topics on which there was widespread consensus have been completed and there are fewer treaties being concluded on the global level. Instead, the United Nations increasingly adopts declarations without subsequent treaties."

130 See Charlotte Ku & Paul F. Diehl, "Filling in the Gaps: Extrasystemic Mechanisms for Addressing the Imbalances Between International Legal Operating and Normative Systems" in Ku & Diehl, *supra* note 127, 163 at 178.

131 Dinah Shelton, "Introduction: Law, Non-Law and the Problem of 'Soft Law'" in Shelton, *supra* note 129, 1 at 10, 14. See also Christine Chinkin, "Normative Development in the International Legal System," in Shelton, *supra* note 129, 21 at 36.

132 Christine Chinkin, "The Challenge of Soft Law: Development and Change in International Law" (1989) 38 Int'l and Comp. L.Q. 850 at 850.

133 Mauro Barelli, "The Role of Soft Law in the International Legal System: The Case of the United Nations Declaration on the Rights of Indigenous Peoples" (2009) 58 ICLQ 957 at 983.

134 Letter from Indian Affairs Minister, Jim Prentice, to Assembly of First Nations National Chief Phil Fontaine (20 Sept. 2006), Annex at 6.

135 *Nicaragua v. United States, supra* note 126 at para. 175. Similarly, see Malcolm N. Shaw, *International Law*, 4th ed. (Cambridge: Cambridge University Press, 1997) at 76.

136 Shaw, *ibid.* at 75.

137 Antonio Cassese, *International Law*, 2d ed. (Oxford: Oxford University Press, 2005) at 156.

138 Rosalyn Higgins, *Problems and Process: International Law and How We Use It* (Oxford: Clarendon Press, 1994) at 34.

139 *Nicaragua v. United States, supra* note 126 at para. 186.

140 For a broad description of such normative processes, see S. James Anaya & Robert A. Williams, Jr., "The Protection of Indigenous Peoples' Rights over Lands and Natural Resources Under the Inter-American Human Rights System" (2001) 14 Harv. H. Rts J. 33 at 53-55.

141 Smita Narula, "The Right to Food: Holding Global Actors Accountable Under International Law" (2006) 44 Colum. J. Transnat'l L. 691 at 787: "Declarations provide additional evidence of state practice and, in some circumstances, *opinio juris.*"

142 *Ibid.* at 779.

143 William A. Schabas & Stéphane Beaulac, *International Human Rights and Canadian Law: Legal Commitment, Implementation and the Charter*, 3d ed. (Toronto: Carswell, 2007) at 68.

144 Human Rights Council, *Report of the Special Rapporteur, S. James Anaya, supra* note 101 at para. 41

145 Ian Brownlie, *Principles of Public International Law*, 5th ed. (Oxford: Clarendon Press, 1998) at 515.

146 Mark W. Janis, *An Introduction to International Law*, 2d ed. (Boston: Little, Brown & Company, 1993) at 65: "Probably no rule better fits the definition of a norm of *jus cogens* than *pacta sunt servanda*, for it is essential to the theory of both conventional and customary international law that contracts between states be legally binding." The relevant provisions in the *Declaration* are preambular paras. 8 and 14, and art. 37.

147 Brownlie, *supra* note 145 at 515: "The least controversial examples of [peremptory norms] are the prohibition of the use of force, the law of genocide, the principle of racial non-discrimination, crimes against humanity, and the rules prohibiting trade in slaves and piracy." The relevant provisions in the *Declaration* regarding the prohibition of racial discrimination are: preambular paras. 5, 9, 18, 22 and arts. 1, 2, 8(2)(e), 9, 14, 15(2), 16(1), 17(3), 21(1), 24(1), 29(1), 46(2) and 46(3).

148 Robert McCorquodale, "Self-Determination: A Human Rights Approach" (1994) 43 Int'l & Comp. L.Q. 857 at 858: "This right [of self-determination] has been declared in other international treaties and instruments, is generally accepted as customary international law and could even form part of *jus cogens*." See also *Reference re Secession of Québec* [1998] 2 S.C.R. 217 at para. 114: "The existence of the right of a people to self-determination is now so widely recognized in international conventions that the principle has acquired a status beyond 'convention' and is considered a general principle of international law." The relevant provisions in the *Declaration* regarding self-determination are preambular paras. 1, 16 and 17, and arts. 3 and 4.

149 In relation to Indigenous peoples and the right of self-determination in identical art. 1 of the ICCPR and ICESER, see Human Rights Committee, *Concluding observations of the Human Rights Committee: Canada*, UN Doc. CCPR/C/79/Add.105 (7 April 1999) at para. 8: "the Committee emphasizes that the right to self-determination requires, *inter alia*, that all peoples must be able to freely dispose of their natural wealth and resources and that they may not be deprived of their own means of subsistence (art. 1, para. 2)." In the *Declaration*, explicit provisions on subsistence are arts. 3 and 20(1).

150 Brownlie, *supra* note 145 at 515. The relevant provision in the *Declaration* is art. 7.

151 *Charter of the United Nations*, art. 1(3); see also arts. 55(c) and 56. The relevant provisions in the *Declaration* are preambular para. 1 and arts. 38 and 42. See also Office of the High Commissioner for Human Rights & International Bar Association, *Human Rights in the Administration of Justice: A Manual on Human Rights for Judges, Prosecutors and Lawyers*, Professional Training Series No. 9 (New York: United Nations, 2003) at 10: www.ohchr.org/Documents/Publications/training9chapter1en.pdf: "It is . . . beyond doubt that basic human rights obligations form part of customary international law."

152 *Charter of the United Nations*, art. 2(2). See Shaw, *supra* note 135 at 81: "Perhaps the most important general principle, underpinning many international legal rules is that of good faith." This principle is contained in the *Declaration* at preambular para. 1.

153 Louise Arbour, "National Human Rights Institutions as Catalysts for Change" (Keynote address delivered to the Canadian Human Rights Commission, Ottawa, 22 Oct. 2007), at 3: www.chrc-ccdp.ca/whats_new/default-en.asp?id=438&content_type=2. See also Shaw, *supra* note 135 at 213. The relevant provisions in the *Declaration* are arts. 22(2) and 44.

154 This legal capacity is not limited to Canadian courts. See generally Human Rights Council, *Report of the Special Rapporteur, S. James Anaya, supra* note 101 at para. 54: "Even if not empowered to directly apply the Declaration, domestic courts may and should use the Declaration as an interpretive guide in applying provisions of domestic law."

155 *Reference re Public Service Employee Relations Act (Alta.)*, [1987] 1 S.C.R. 313 at 348.

156 Schabas & Beaulac, *supra* note 143 at 87: "the distinction ... between ratified and un-ratified instruments has generally been ignored. Canadian judges rarely, if ever, consider international law sources by taking into account whether they have a legally binding effect on Canada. Instead, they tend to consider all sources of international law as 'relevant and persuasive'."

157 For a lengthy list of examples where Canadian courts have referred to declarations, see *ibid.* at 136, note 90.

158 Human Rights Council, *Report of the Expert Mechanism on the Rights of Indigenous Peoples on its Second Session, Geneva: 10–14 August 2009*, UN Doc. A/HRC/12/32 (8 Sept. 2009) at para. 78 (Expert John Henriksen): "individual provisions cannot be interpreted nor implemented in isolation as the articles of the Declaration are inter-connected, and connected to other international human rights instruments." See also Mary Ann Glendon, "*Propter Honoris Respectum*: Knowing the Universal Declaration of Human Rights" (1998) 73 Notre Dame L. Rev. 1153 at 1174: "By isolating each part from its place in an overall design, that now-common misreading of the Declaration promotes misunderstanding and facilitates misuse."

159 Gibran van Ert, *Using International Law in Canadian Courts* (The Hague: Kluwer Law International, 2002) at 30, note 78: "a General Assembly resolution may represent customary international law. While such resolutions are generally not binding, they may in some cases be declaratory of customary international law."

160 Anne F. Bayefsky, *International Human Rights Law: Use in Canadian Charter of Rights and Freedoms Litigation* (Toronto: Butterworths, 1992) at 17. See also Schabas & Beaulac, *supra* note 143 at 77: "Customary international law may be applied by Canadian courts without any need for an express legislative act, unless there is a clear conflict with statute law or common law."

161 Bayefsky, *ibid.* at 20. Professor Bayefsky adds at 20–21: "There is a presumption at common law that Parliament and the legislatures do not intend to act in breach of international law, either customary or conventional. Concomitantly ... there is an interpretive presumption, applicable in the context of construing the Charter, that Parliament and the legislatures intend to fulfil Canada's international obligations."

162 Currie, Forcese & Oosterveld, *supra* note 126 at 141.

163 Jonathan I. Charney, "The Persistent Objector Rule and the Development of Customary International Law" (1985) 56 B.Y.I.L. 1 at 19.

164 See Cassese, *supra* note 137 at 163, where it is indicated that the only explicit contention in favour of this doctrine is set out in two *obiter dicta* of the ICJ in *Asylum Case (Colombia v. Peru)* [1950] I.C.J. Rep. 266 at 277–78 and *Fisheries Case (U.K. v. Norway)*, [1951] I.C.J. Rep. 116 at 131, and in the pleadings of the UK and Norway in *Fisheries.*

165 Charney, *supra* note 163 at 16.

166 *Ibid.* at 22.

167   Cassese, *supra* note 137 at 163.

168   Ted L. Stein, "The Approach of the Different Drummer: The Principle of the Persistent Objector in International Law" (1985) 26 Harv. Int'l L.J. 457 at 463.

169   Holning Lau, "Rethinking the Persistent Objector Doctrine in International Human Rights Law" (2005) 6 Chicago J. Int'l L. 495 at 501.

170   *Ibid.* At 503, Lau further states, "Principles of consent are not violated because that state already consented to the universality of human rights. Requesting an exception would be in violation of its original consent to universalism."

171   Brian Adeba, "Aboriginal Rights Treaty Should Have Been Signed" *Embassy* (4 Oct. 2006) 1.

172   See Canada, "Statement by Ambassador Paul Meyer," *supra* note 81.

173   INAC, "Canada's Position," *supra* note 49.

174   *Human Rights Council, supra* note 111 at 4 (para. 9).

175   *Ibid.* at 3 (para. 2). See also *2005 World Summit Outcome, supra* note 23 at 18 (para. 120).

176   Permanent Forum on Indigenous Issues, *Report of the Inter-Agency Support Group on Indigenous Issues,* UN Doc. E/C.19/2008/6 (5 Feb. 2008) at para. 10: "The Support Group pledges to advance the spirit and letter of the Declaration within our agencies' mandates and to ensure that the Declaration becomes a living document throughout our work." As of 2008, the IASG is made up of 31 agencies, including the World Health Organization, the International Labour Organization, the United Nations Development Programme, UNICEF, the Secretariat of the Convention on Biological Diversity (SCBD), the World Bank, and the World Intellectual Property Organization.

177   United Nations Secretary-General, Press Release, "Secretary-General, in Video Message, says Indigenous Permanent Forum Assumes New Role in Translating Declaration on Indigenous Peoples' Rights into 'Living' Text," SG/SM/11524, HR/4945 (21 April 2008): www.un.org/News/Press/docs/2008/sgsm11524.doc.htm.

178   Permanent Forum on Indigenous Issues, *Report on the seventh session, supra* note 102 at paras. 61, 131, and 132.

179   Claudia Parsons, "Canada slammed at U.N. over indigenous rights" (1 May 2008): http://ca.reuters.com/article/domesticNews/idCAN0134751220080501 (quoting Victoria Tauli-Corpuz, chair of the Permanent Forum on Indigenous Issues): "Canada used to have a good image on indigenous rights and played a leadership role in drafting the declaration. . . . The change of government, however, changed the situation in a totally different direction. . . . Now, [Ms. Tauli-Corpuz] said, Canada's reputation was 'very bad'." See also Rachel Brett, *Righting Historic Wrongs: First Session of the UN Human Rights Council (19-30 June 2006)* (2006) at 4: www.quno.org/geneva/pdf/humanrights/RightingHistoricWrongs200606.pdf: "*Canada's Shame:* Short-term political expediency seems to have been the basis for Canada's change of position from supporting to opposing the draft declaration — encouraged by Australia, New Zealand and the USA."

1   The creation of the WGIP was authorized by the Economic and Social Council: *Study of the problem of discrimination against indigenous populations*, ESC Res. 1982/34, UN ESCOR, 1982, Supp. No. 1, UN Doc. E/1982/82, 26. The WGIP worked on the draft declaration from 1985-93. A draft was approved and subsequently submitted to the Sub-Commission on Prevention of Discrimination and Protection of Minorities, which unanimously approved the text. The Sub-Commission text was then forwarded to the Commission on Human Rights. See *Draft United Nations declaration on the rights of indigenous peoples*, Sub-Commission on Prevention of Discrimination and Protection of Minorities Res. 1994/45, in Commission on Human Rights, *Report of the Sub-Commission on Prevention of Discrimination and Protection of Minorities on its Forty-Sixth Session*, UN Doc. E/CN.4/1995/2, E/CN.4/Sub.2/1994/56 (28 Oct. 1994) 103.

2   *Establishment of a working group of the Commission on Human Rights to elaborate a draft declaration in accordance with paragraph 5 of General Assembly resolution 49/214*, ESC Res. 1995/32, UN ESCOR, 1996, Supp. No. 1, UN Doc. E/1995/95, 44. The WGDD met at least annually from 1995 until Jan. 2006.

3   *2005 World Summit Outcome*, GA Res. 60/1, UN GAOR, 60th Sess., Supp. No. 49, Vol. I, UN Doc. A/60/49 (2006) 3 at 24 (para. 172).

4   United Nations, Press Release, SG/SM/7318, "Partnership with Civil Society Necessity in Addressing Global Agenda, Says Secretary-General in Wellington, New Zealand Remarks" (29 Feb. 2000): www.un.org/News/Press/docs/2000/20000229.sgsm7318.doc.html.

5   José Alvarez, *International Organizations as Law-Makers* (New York: Oxford University Press, 2005) at 611.

6   Steve Charnovitz, "Nongovernmental Organizations and International Law" in Charlotte Ku & Paul F. Diehl, eds., *International Law: Classic and Contemporary Readings*, 3d ed. (Boulder, Colo.: Lynne Rienner, 2009) 117 at 117.

7   *An Act to Establish the International Centre for Human Rights and Democratic Development*, S.C. 1988, c. 64. It is not an NGO, but works closely with NGOs.

8   The Quakers work globally through their world body, the Friends World Committee for Consultation (FWCC), which has had NGO status with ECOSOC since 1948. The Quaker UN offices in Geneva and New York work under the auspices of the FWCC. National Service Committees such as the CFSC work in liaison with FWCC. The work on the *Declaration* was mandated by the FWCC and carried out mainly by the CFSC.

9   For several years the Indigenous Peoples' Caucus was united on the position that there would be no changes to the text approved by the WGIP and subsequently approved by the Sub-Commission. This is often referred to as the "Sub-Commission text." See Kenneth Deer, "Reflections on the Development, Adoption, and Implementation of the *UN Declaration on the Rights of Indigenous Peoples*," chap. 1 in this volume.

10 See, e.g., *Declaration on the Right and Responsibility of Individuals, Groups and Organs of Society to Promote and Protect Universally Recognized Human Rights and Fundamental Freedoms*, art. 18(2), annexed to GA Res. 53/144. UN GAOR, 53d Sess., Supp. No. 49, Vol. I, UN Doc A/53/49 (1999) 269: "Individuals, groups, institutions and non-govern-

mental organizations have an important role to play and a responsibility in safeguarding democracy, promoting human rights and fundamental freedoms and contributing to the promotion and advancement of democratic societies, institutions and processes." This human rights instrument is often referred to as the *UN Declaration on Human Rights Defenders*.

11   *Universal Declaration of Human Rights*, GA Res. 217(III), UN GAOR, 3d Sess., UN Doc. A/810 (1948) 71 at 71 (preambular para. 1): "recognition of the inherent dignity and of the equal and inalienable rights of all members of the human family is the foundation of freedom, justice and peace in the world."

12   Charnovitz, *supra* note 6 at 125.

13   See, e.g., Grand Council of the Crees (Eeyou Istchee) *et al.*, "Assessing the International Decade: Urgent Need to Renew Mandate and Improve the U.N. Standard-Setting Process on Indigenous Peoples' Human Rights," Joint Submission to the Office of the High Commissioner for Human Rights, Geneva (Mar. 2004).

14   See Paul Joffe, "Canada's Opposition to the *UN Declaration*: Legitimate Concerns or Ideological Bias?" Chap. 5 in this volume.

15   Amnesty International Canada *et al.*, *Advancing the Human Rights of Indigenous Peoples, A Critical Challenge for the International Community: Voices from a forum at the 61st session of the United Nations Commission on Human Rights 13 April 2005* (Oct. 1995): www.cfsc.quaker.ca/pages/documents/CHRforumE.pdf.

16   For example, Friends World Committee for Consultation (Quakers) *et al.*, "Human Rights of Indigenous Peoples are a Global Priority" (Joint statement to the 61st session of the Commission on Human Rights, 3 Mar. 2005): www.cfsc.quaker.ca/pages/documents/FWCC-CHRe.pdf; Letter from Amnesty International *et al.* to the Bureau of the Commission on Human Rights (21 Mar. 2006): www.cfsc.quaker.ca/pages/documents/LetterGeneva.pdf (supporting the text as presented at the end of the WGDD).

17   See especially *Charter of the United Nations*, art. 1(3): "To achieve international cooperation . . . in promoting and encouraging respect for human rights and for fundamental freedoms for all without distinction as to race, sex, language, or religion"; and art. 2(2): "All Members . . . shall fulfill in good faith the obligations assumed by them in accordance with the present Charter." See also art. 55(c): ". . . based on respect for the principle of equal rights and self-determination of peoples, the United Nations shall promote . . . c. universal respect for, and observance of, human rights and fundamental freedoms for all without distinction"; and art. 56: "All Members pledge themselves to take joint and separate action in co-operation with the Organization for the achievement of the purposes set forth in Article 55."

18   The *Declaration* was adopted by the Human Rights Council by resolution: *Working group of the Commission on Human Rights to elaborate a draft declaration in accordance with paragraph 5 of General Assembly resolution 49/214 of 23 December 1994*, HRC Res. 1/2, GAOR, 61st Sess., Supp. No. 53, UN Doc. A/61/53 (2006) 18.

19   *Working group of the Commission on Human Rights to elaborate a draft declaration in accordance with paragraph 5 of General Assembly resolution 49/214 of 23 December 1994*, GA Res. 61/178, GAOR, 61st Sess., Supp. No. 49, Vol. I, UN Doc. A/61/49 (2007) 417.

20 In response to initial concerns raised by African states, see, e.g., Indigenous Peoples of Africa Coordinating Committee (IPACC), *United Nations Declaration on the Rights of Indigenous Peoples* — 'Draft Aide Memoire' of the African Group: A Brief Commentary" (16 Jan. 2007): www.iwgia.org/graphics/Synkron-Library/Documents/InternationalProcesses/DraftDeclaration/IPACCCommentaryToAideMemoire.doc; and *"U.N. Declaration on the Rights of Indigenous Peoples* — The Human Rights and Development Response: African States Support for the Declaration is Just and Crucial" (15 Jan. 2007). IPACC leaders were also involved in the International Work Group for Indigenous Affairs: www.iwgia.org/graphics/Synkron-Library/Documents/InternationalProcesses/DraftDeclaration/ResponseNoteToAideMemoire_EN.pdf.

21 "Notes for an Address by the Honourable Peter MacKay, Minister of Foreign Affairs and Minister of the Atlantic Canada Opportunities Agency, to the Democracy Council's Dialogue on Canada's Approach to Democratic Development" (Delivered at Ottawa, 15 Feb. 2007) at 2.

22 Canada, "Opening Statement: John Sims, Deputy Minister of Justice" (Delivered to the United Nations Human Rights Council, Working Group on the Universal Periodic Review, 4th Sess., 3 Feb. 2009).

23 Working Group on the Universal Periodic Review, *National Report Submitted in Accordance with Paragraph 15 (A) of the Annex to Human Rights Council Resolution 5/1: Canada,* UN Doc. A/HRC/WG.6/4/CAN/1 (5 Jan. 2009): http://lib.ohchr.org/HRBodies/UPR/Documents/Session4/CA/A_HRC_WG6_4_CAN_1_E.pdf.

24 *Institution-building of the United Nations Human Rights Council,* HRC Res. 5/1, UN GAOR, 62d Sess., Supp. No. 53, UN Doc. A/62/53 (2007) 48 at 50 (Annex, para. 15(a)) See also Human Rights Council, *Report of the Special Rapporteur on the situation of human rights defenders, Margaret Sekaggya,* UN Doc. A/HRC/10/12 (12 Feb. 2009) at para. 98: "The Special Rapporteur considers national consultations crucially important for human rights defenders, in order for their views and concerns to be properly reflected in the national report which forms one of the bases of the UPR process."

25 The text of the motion is contained in House of Commons, Standing Committee on the Status of Women, "Third Report (United Nations Declaration on the Rights of Indigenous Peoples)," 39th Parl., 2d Sess. (Presented to the House on 13 Feb. 2008). Concurred in by the House on 8 April 2008: *House of Commons Debates,* No. 074 (8 April 2008) at 4656.

26 "*UN Declaration on the Rights of Indigenous Peoples:* Canada Needs to Implement This New Human Rights Instrument" (1 May 2008): www.cfsc.quaker.ca/pages/documents/UNDecl-Expertsign-onstatementMay1.pdf. See Appendix II.

27 Assembly of First Nations *et al.,* Press Release, "Legal scholars and experts urge Canadian government to abandon 'erroneous' and 'misleading' opposition to *UN Declaration on the Rights of Indigenous Peoples*" (1 May 2008): www.cfsc.quaker.ca/pages/documents/pressstatementreopenletterMay08-2.pdf.

28 Human Rights Council, *Report of the Working Group on the Universal Periodic Review: Canada,* UN Doc. A/HRC/11/17 (5 Oct. 2009).

29 Norway, "UPR — Canada" (Statement delivered to the Human Rights Council, Working Group on the Universal Periodic Review, 4th Sess., 3 Feb. 2009).

30 Paul Joffe, "Global Implementation of the *UN Declaration on the Rights of Indigenous Peoples* – and Canada's Increasing Isolation" (Sept. 2009): www.cfsc.quaker.ca/pages/documents/UNDeclaration-2ndAnniversary-ReportFINAL-Sep2009.pdf.

31 Assembly of First Nations *et al.*, News Release, "UN Declaration on the Rights of Indigenous Peoples: Canadian government isolated as global implementation moves ahead" (12 Sept. 2009): www.cfsc.quaker.ca/pages/documents/UNDeclaration-2ndAnniversary-NewsRelease-Sep1209.pdf.

32 *UN Declaration on Human Rights Defenders, supra* note 10, art. 2(1); see also art. 3.

33 Carsten Smith, *International expert group meeting on the role of the United Nations Permanent Forum on Indigenous Issues in the implementation of article 42 of the United Nations Declaration on the Rights of Indigenous Peoples, 14-16 January 2009, New York: Comments on Article 42 as legal basis for a Declaration "treaty body,"* UN Doc. PFII/2009/EGM1/5 (undated) at 3: www.un.org/esa/socdev/unpfii/documents/EGM_Art_42_Smith.doc.

34 *Ibid.*: "the voting of the General Assembly, which proves that a great majority of the international community stands behind the Declaration, is a significant factor when determining its legal strength."

35 The English version is available at: www.cfsc.quaker.ca/pages/documents/United Nations Small.pdf.

36 Steven Edwards, "Native rights declaration inconsistent with legal tradition: Strahl" *National Post* (13 Sept. 2007): www.canada.com/nationalpost/news/story.html?id=23df9769-3423-4f43-b828-a755725c2719&k=23677: "The rights of non-native Canadians would have been threatened had the government not opposed an indigenous rights declaration that the United Nations overwhelmingly approved on Thursday, Indian Affairs Minister Chuck Strahl said. The Universal Declaration of Indigenous Peoples' Rights is inconsistent with Canadian legal tradition, and signing on to it would have given native groups an unfair advantage, the minister said in an interview in advance of the UN General Assembly vote."

37 Jim Brown, "UN human rights czar lashes Canada for vote against native rights" (22 Oct. 2007): www.thestar.com/article/269221.

38 Commission on Human Rights, *Report of the Special Rapporteur on the situation of human rights and fundamental freedoms of indigenous people, Rodolfo Stavenhagen:, Addendum: Mission to Canada*, UN Doc. E/CN.4/2005/88/Add.3 (2 Dec. 2004).

39 Assembly of First Nations *et al.*, *Closing the Implementation Gap: Indigenous Peoples and Human Rights in Canada: A forum to follow up on the 2004 mission to Canada by the United Nations Special Rapporteur on the situation of human rights and fundamental freedoms of indigenous people, Rodolfo Stavenhagen, University of Ottawa, October 2-3, 2006* (2008): www.cfsc.quaker.ca/pages/documents/closingtheimplementationgap.pdf.

40 International Centre for Human Rights and Democratic Development *et al.*, *The UN Special Rapporteur: Indigenous Peoples Rights: Experiences and Challenges* (Copenhagen, 2007). Available to download in English, Spanish, and French at: www.iwgia.org/sw29919.asp.

41 Antonio Cassese, *International Law* (Oxford: Oxford University Press, 2001) at 374.

42 World Conference on Human Rights, *Vienna Declaration and Programme of Action,* UN Doc. A/CONF.157/23 (12 July 1993) at 5 (para. 5) (adopted 25 June 1993).

43 Victoria Tauli-Corpuz, "The Concept of Indigenous Peoples at the International Level: Origins, Development and Challenges" in Christian Erni, ed., *The Concept of Indigenous Peoples in Asia: A Resource Book* (Copenhagen/Chang Mai: International Work Group for Indigenous Affairs/Asian Indigenous Peoples Pact Foundation, 2008) 77 at 97.

44 Amnesty International *et al.*, "Adoption of the United Nations Declaration on the Rights of Indigenous Peoples: Joint Statement by International Non-Governmental Organizations" (13 Sept. 2007): www.cfsc.quaker.ca/pages/documents/NGOstatement091307.pdf.

CHAPTER SEVEN

1 For background on Wounded Knee, see Kenneth Deer, "Reflections on the Development, Adoption, and Implementation of the *UN Declaration on the Rights of Indigenous Peoples,*" chapter 1 in this volume.

2 *Convention (No. 107) Concerning the Protection and Integration of Indigenous and Other Tribal and Semi-Tribal Populations in Independent Countries*, 26 June 1957, 328 U.N.T.S. 247 (entered into force 2 June 1959).

3 See "The Treaties at Fort Carlton and Pitt, Number Six" in Alexander Morris, *The Treaties of Canada with The Indians of Manitoba and the North-West Territories Including the Negotiations on which They Were Based* (Toronto: Belfords, Clarke & Co., 1880; reprinted Saskatoon, Sask.: Fifth House Publishers, 1991), appendix at 351 *et seq.* and "Adhesions to Treaty Number Six" at 360 *et seq.*

4 *R. v. Secretary of State for Foreign and Commonwealth Affairs, Ex parte Indian Association of Alberta*, [1982] 2 All E.R. 118.

5 "Extracts from the Report of the Meeting of Experts on the Revision of the Indigenous and Tribal Populations Convention, 1957 (No. 107) (Geneva, 1-10 September 1986)" in International Labour Office, *Partial revision of the Indigenous and Tribal Populations Convention, 1957 (No. 107)*, Report VI (1) (Geneva: International Labour Office, 1987) appendix 1 at para. 46: "The Meeting is unanimous in concluding that the integrationist language of Convention No. 107 is outdated, and that the application of this principle is destructive in the modern world. ... [Integration] had become a destructive concept, in part at least because of the way it was understood by governments."

6 *Convention (No. 169) Concerning Indigenous and Tribal Peoples in Independent Countries*, 27 June 1989, ILO Official Bulletin Vol. 72, Ser. A, No. 2, 59 (entered into force 5 Sept. 1991).

7 Manuela Tomei and Lee Swepston, *Indigenous and Tribal Peoples: A Guide to ILO Convention No. 169* (Geneva: International Labour Organization, 1996) at 7.

8 *Declaration*, preambular para. 15: "[T]reaties, agreements and other constructive arrangements, and the relationship they represent, are the basis for a strengthened partnership between indigenous peoples and States." See Appendix 1.

9 *Ibid.*, art. 7(2): "Indigenous peoples have the collective right to live in freedom, peace and security as distinct peoples."

10 *Ibid.*, art. 43: "The rights recognized herein constitute the minimum standards for the survival, dignity and well-being of the indigenous peoples of the world." Art. 37 affirms our right to "the recognition, observance and enforcement of treaties . . . and to have States honour and respect such treaties."

11 *Report of the Royal Commission on Aboriginal Peoples*, vol. 2(1) (Ottawa: Canada Communication Group, 1996) at 175.

12 Human Rights Council, *Report of the Office of the United Nations High Commissioner for Human Rights on the relationship between climate change and human rights*, UN Doc. A/HRC/10/61 (15 Jan. 2009) at para. 39.

13 Deer, *supra* note 1.

14 Commission on Human Rights, *Study on treaties, agreements and other constructive arrangements between States and indigenous populations: Final report by Miguel Alfonso Martínez, Special Rapporteur*, UN Doc. E/CN.4/Sub.2/1999/20 (22 June 1999) at para. 322(c).

15 Commission on Human Rights, *Report of the seminar on treaties, agreements and other constructive arrangements between States and indigenous peoples (Geneva, 15-17 December 2003)*, UN Doc. E/CN.4/Sub.2/AC.4/2004/7 (1 June 2004); Commission on Human Rights, *Indigenous Issues: Note by the secretariat*, UN Doc. E/CN.4/2004/111 (2 Jan. 2004) (Conclusions and recommendations of the Seminar on Treaties, Agreements and Other Constructive Arrangements between States and Indigenous Peoples, held in Geneva 15-17 December 2003). For documents relating to the second expert seminar on treaties held on 14-17 Nov. 2006 in the Samson Cree Nation of the Maskwacîs Cree territory in Alberta, Canada, see: www.treatycouncil.org/new_page_524122421222.htm.

16 Commission on Human Rights, *Report of the meeting of experts to review the experience of countries in the operation of schemes of internal self-government for indigenous peoples: Nuuk, Greenland, 24 – 28 September 1991*, UN Doc. E/CN.4/1992/42 (25 Nov. 1991) at 12 (Conclusions and Recommendations): "Autonomy and self-government can be built on treaties, constitutional recognition or statutory provisions recognizing indigenous rights. Further, it is necessary for the treaties, conventions and other constructive arrangements entered into in various historical circumstances to be honoured, in so far as such instruments establish and confirm the institutional and territorial basis for guaranteeing the right of indigenous peoples to autonomy and self-government."

17 Commission on Human Rights, *Report of the Special Rapporteur on the situation of human rights and fundamental freedoms of indigenous people, Mr. Rodolfo Stavenhagen: Addendum: Conclusions and recommendations of the expert seminar on indigenous peoples and the administration of justice*, UN Doc. E/CN.4/2004/80/Add.4 (27 Jan. 2004).

18 World Health Organization, *Report of the International Consultation on the Health of Indigenous Peoples: Geneva, 23 - 26 November 1999*, Doc. No. WHO/HSD/00.1 (2000).

19 Commission on Human Rights, *Report of the Special Rapporteur on the situation of human rights and fundamental freedoms of indigenous people, Rodolfo Stavenhagen: Addendum: Conclusions and Recommendations of the Expert Seminar on Indigenous Peoples and Education*, UN Doc. E/CN.4/2005/88/Add.4 (15 Dec. 2004).

20 *Establishment of a working group of the Commission on Human Rights to elaborate a draft declaration in accordance with paragraph 5 of General Assembly resolution 49/214*, ESC Res. 1995/32, UN ESCOR, 1996, Supp. No. 1, UN Doc. E/1995/95, 44.

21 *Declaration*, preambular para. 15.

22 *Draft United Nations declaration on the rights of indigenous peoples*, Sub-Commission on Prevention of Discrimination and Protection of Minorities Res. 1994/45, in Commission on Human Rights, *Report of the Sub-Commission on Prevention of Discrimination and Protection of Minorities on its Forty-Sixth Session*, UN Doc. E/CN.4/1995/2, E/CN.4/Sub.2/1994/56 (28 Oct. 1994) 103 at 114 (Annex, art. 36).

23 See *Tee-Hit-Ton Indians v. United States*, 348 U.S. 272 at 289-290: "Every American schoolboy knows that the savage tribes of this continent were deprived of their ancestral ranges by force and that, even when the Indians ceded millions of acres by treaty in return for blankets, food and trinkets, it was not a sale but the conquerors' will that deprived them of their land."

24 Commission on Human Rights, *Indigenous Issues: Note by the secretariat, supra* note 15 at para. 2.

25 *Ibid.*

26 Barack Obama, Speech on the occasion of his visit to the Crow Tribe in Montana (19 May 2008): videos.billingsgazette.com/p/video?id=1888836.

27 "Remarks by the First Lady at the U.S. Department of the Interior" (9 Feb. 2009): www.whitehouse.gov/the_press_office/RemarksbytheFirstLadyattheUSDepartmentof theInterior/.

28 Government of Canada, *Analysis of Principles, Processes and the Essential Elements of Modern Treaty-Making — The Canadian Experience*, UN Doc. HR/GENEVA/TSIP/ SEM/2003/BP.9 (undated) at 13-14 (Background paper, prepared by the Government of Canada for the Expert Seminar on Treaties, Agreements and Other Constructive Arrangements between States and Indigenous Peoples, 15-17 Dec. 2003).

29 Land Claims Agreements Coalition (LCAC), *Universal Periodic Review of Canada: Submission of the Land Claims Agreements Coalition (LCAC) to the United Nations Human Rights Council* (8 Sept. 2008) at paras 1, 3: http://lib.ohchr.org/HRBodies/UPR/ Documents/Session4/CA/LCAC_CAN_UPR_S4_2009_LandClaimsAgreements-Coalition_JOINT.pdf?.

30 *R. v. Badger*, [1996] 1 S.C.R. 771 at para. 41, Cory J.: "it must be remembered that a treaty represents an exchange of solemn promises between the Crown and the various Indian nations. It is an agreement whose nature is sacred."

31 *Ermineskin Indian Band and Nation v. Canada* [2009] SCC 9 (Fed. C.A.).

32 Permanent Forum on Indigenous Issues, *Report of the international expert group meeting on the role of the Permanent Forum on Indigenous Issues in the implementation of article 42 of the United Nations Declaration on the Rights of Indigenous Peoples*, UN Doc. E/C.19/ 2009/2 (4 Feb. 2009) at para. 51.

33 Wilton Littlechild, (Presentation to the UN Expert Group Meeting on the Implementation of Article 42 of the United Nations Declaration on the Rights of Indigenous Peoples, 14-16 Jan. 2009) UN Doc. PFII/2009/EGM1/8 (undated) at 3-4.

1   Commission on Human Rights, *Indigenous Issues: Note by the secretariat*, UN Doc. E/CN.4/2004/111 (2 Jan. 2004) at para. 3 (Conclusions and recommendations of the Seminar on Treaties, Agreements and Other Constructive Arrangements between States and Indigenous Peoples, held in Geneva, 15-17 Dec. 2003).

2   *International Convention on the Elimination of All Forms of Racial Discrimination*, 7 Mar. 1966, 660 U.N.T.S. 195 (entered into force 4 Jan. 1969) [ICERD].

3   Committee on the Elimination of Racial Discrimination (CERD), *Concluding observations of the Committee on the Elimination of Racial Discrimination: United States of America*, UN Doc. CERD/C/USA/CO/6 (8 May 2008) at para. 29.

4   General Assembly, *The situation of human rights and fundamental freedoms of indigenous people: Note by the Secretary-General*, UN Doc. A/59/258 (12 Aug. 2004) at para. 18. (Report of the Special Rapporteur on the situation of human rights and fundamental freedoms of indigenous people).

5   *United States* v. *Sioux Nation*, 518 F.2d 1298 at 1302 (1975), cited in *United States* v. *Sioux Nation of Indians*, 448 U.S. 371 at 388 (1980).

6   *Ibid.* (1975).

7   *Indian Claims Commission Act of 1946*, Pub. L. No. 726, ch. 959, 60 Stat. 1049. See also Patrick W. Wandres, " Indian Land Claims: *Sherrill* and the Impending Legacy of the Doctrine of Laches" (2006) 31 Am. Indian L. Rev. 131 at 135: "It soon became apparent that the Act failed to meet the expectations of either tribes or of Congress. . . . In the early 1970s, President Nixon declared that the termination policy under the Indian Claims Commission Act was a failure."

8   Nell Jessup Newton, "Indian Claims in the Courts of the Conqueror" (1992) 41 Am. U.L. Rev. 753 at 784.

9   *Mary and Carrie Dann* v. *United States* (2002) Inter-Am. Comm., H.R. Report No. 75/02, Case 11.140 [*Dann* v. *US*].

10   *Ibid.* at para. 54.

11   See *ibid.* at para. 85, which describes the observations provided by the United States.

12   See *ibid.* at para. 43. This approach of maintaining dispossessions is similar to the "settlement" process used by the ICC and the US government with regard to the claims of the Sioux Nation for treaty violations and land theft. Tribes of the Sioux Nation continue to affirm to this day that the Black Hills are not for sale. In 1980, the US Supreme Court awarded the tribes of the Sioux Nation $146 million for the taking of the Black Hills and land east of the Black Hills (including interest). They have refused to accept the money, which remains in the bank untouched. With interest, the amount has reached over $860 million. See, e.g., Tim Giago, "The Black Hills: A Case of Dishonest Dealings," *Huffington Post* (3 June 2007): www.huffingtonpost.com/tim-giago/the-black-hills-a-case-o_b_50480.html; Commission on Human Rights, *Study on treaties, agreements and other constructive arrangements between States and indigenous populations: Final report by Miguel Alfonso Martínez, Special Rapporteur*, UN Doc. E/CN.4/Sub.2/1999/20 (22 June 1999) at para. 276 [*Martínez Report*]; and International Indian Treaty Council *et al.*, "Examination of the United States 4th, 5th, and 6th Periodic Reports of

April, 2007: Racial Discrimination Against Indigenous Peoples in the United States," Consolidated Indigenous Shadow Report, submission to the Committee on the Elimination of Racial Discrimination (Jan. 2008) at 37 - 38.

13   *Dann* v. *US, supra* note 9 at para. 139. At para. 113, the Inter-American Commission added that the processes of the ICC had been criticized over the years, including "this fact that the ICC Act permitted an individual or small group of Indians to present a claim on behalf of a whole tribal group without requiring proof of the consent of that tribe, the absence of rules permitting the intervention of interested persons in the proceedings before the ICC, and the narrowing of the ICC jurisdiction to award only monetary compensation and accordingly to preclude claimants from recovering lands." See also Caroline L. Orlando, "Aboriginal Title Claims in the Indian Claims Commission: *United States* v. *Dann* and its Due Process Implications" (1986) 13 B.C. Envir. Aff. L. Review 215 at 241.

14   CERD, E*arly Warning and Urgent Action Procedure: Decision 1(68): United States of America*, UN Doc. CERD/C/USA/Dec/1 (11 April 2006) at para. 6.

15   Minority Rights Group International, *World Directory of Minorities and Indigenous Peoples — New Zealand: Maori* (2008): www.unhcr.org/refworld/docid/49749cd8c.html.

16   Craig Coxhead, "Where are the Negotiations in the Direct Negotiations of Treaty Settlements?" [2002] Waikato L. Rev. 2: www.nzlii.org/nz/journals/WkoLRev/2002/2.html.

17   *Vienna Convention on the Law of Treaties*, 23 May 1969, 1155 U.N.T.S. 331 (entered into force 27 Jan. 1980), preamble: "the principles of free consent and of good faith and the *pacta sunt servanda* rule ["treaties must be kept"] are universally recognized." In Canada, see *Haida Nation* v. *British Columbia (Minister of Forests)*, [2004] 3 S.C.R. 511 at para. 19: "The honour of the Crown also infuses the processes of treaty making and treaty interpretation. In making and applying treaties, the Crown must act with honour and integrity, avoiding even the appearance of 'sharp dealing'. . . ."

18   Working Group on Indigenous Populations (WGIP), *Principal Theme: Indigenous Peoples and their Right to Development, Including their Right to Participate in Development Affecting Them: Note by the secretariat*, UN Doc. E/CN.4/Sub.2/AC.4/2001/2 (20 June 2001) at para. 30. The WGIP further states, at para 30: "Of major importance to sustainable development and the protection of the environment is the principle of precaution. This principle acknowledges the complexity of interactions between cultural and biological communities, and thus the inherent uncertainty of effects due to genetic, ethno-biological and other research and development activities. ... The importance of the active participation of indigenous peoples in the early planning stages of development, including the establishment of local criteria for environmental, social and cultural impact studies, is paramount to successful developmental processes."

19   *Vienna Convention on the Law of Treaties, supra* note 17, art. 54.

20   *Martínez Report, supra* note 12 at para 279.

21   The WGDD was established by the Commission on Human Rights in 1995: *Establishment of a working group of the Commission on Human Rights to elaborate a draft declaration in accordance with paragraph 5 of General Assembly Resolution 49/214*, ESC Res. 1995/32, UN ESCOR, 1995, Supp. No. 1, UN Doc. 1995/95, 44.

22 *United Nations Declaration on the Rights of Indigenous Peoples*, art 3. See Appendix 1.

23 *Ibid.*, art. 1.

24 *International Covenant on Economic, Social and Cultural Rights*, 19 Dec. 1966, 993 U.N.T.S. 3 (entered into force 3 Jan. 1976) [ICESCR].

25 *International Covenant on Civil and Political Rights*, 19 Dec. 1966, 999 U.N.T.S. 171 (entered into force 23 Mar. 1976) [ICCPR].

26 ICERD, *supra* note 2.

27 *Declaration*, preambular para. 15.

28 See *Declaration*, preambular paras 8, 10, 14, 15, 16, 17, 19; arts 3, 10, 11, 19, 20, 23, 26, 28, 29, 32, 37.

29 Craig Mokhiber, Officer in Charge, New York Office of the High Commissioner for Human Rights, "Declaration is a Historic Document, out of a Historic Process" (Panel presentation, United Nations, New York, 26 Oct. 2006): www.ipcaucus.net/ Mokhiber.html.

30 *Convention (No. 169) Concerning Indigenous and Tribal Peoples in Independent Countries*, 27 June 1989, ILO Official Bulletin, Vol. 72, Ser. A, No. 2, 59 (entered into force 5 Sept. 1991), art. 4.

31 *Ibid.*, art. 16(2).

32 *Ibid.*, art. 7(1).

33 *Ibid.*, arts 2, 6, 16, 27, 33.

34 *Ibid.*, art. 6(2).

35 The Second Decade commenced 1 Jan. 2005: *Second International Decade of the World's Indigenous People*, GA Res. 59/174, UN GAOR, 59th Sess., Supp. No. 49, Vol. 1, UN Doc. A/59/49, (2005) 344.

36 General Assembly, *Draft Programme of Action for the Second International Decade of the World's Indigenous People: Report of the Secretary-General*, UN Doc. A/60/270 (18 Aug. 2005) at para. 9. The draft was adopted by the General Assembly: *Programme of Action for the Second International Decade of the World's Indigenous People*, GA Res 60/142, UN GAOR, 60th Sess., Supp. No. 49, Vol. 1, UN Doc. A/60/49 (2006) 344.

37 CERD, *General Recommendation on the rights of indigenous peoples* [General Recommendation No. XXIII], at para. 4(d), in *Report of the Committee on the Elimination of Racial Discrimination*, UN GAOR, 52d Sess., Supp. No. 18, UN Doc. A/52/18 (1997) 122 (Annex V).

38 CERD, *supra* note 3 at para. 29.

39 *Ibid.*

40 *Report of the Committee on the Elimination of Racial Discrimination: Fifty-eighth session (6–23 March 2001); Fifty-ninth session (30 July–17 August 2001)*, UN GAOR, 56th Sess., Supp. No. 18, UN Doc A/56/18 (2001) at para. 400.

41 *Ibid.*

42 *Committee on Economic, Social and Cultural Rights: Report on the Twenty-Fifth, Twenty-Sixth and Twenty-Seventh Sessions,* UN ESCOR, 2002, Supp. No. 2, UN Doc. E/2002/22, E/C.12/2001/17, para. 761.

43 *Ibid.* at para. 782.

44 *Committee on Economic, Social and Cultural Rights: Report on the Thirty-Second and Thirty-Third Sessions,* UN ESCOR, 2005, Supp. No. 2, UN Doc. E/2005/22, E/C.12/2004/9, at para. 278.

45 Human Rights Committee, *Views: Communication No. 1457/2006,* UN Doc. CCPR/C/95/D/1457/2006 (24 April 2009), Annex at para. 7.6 (*Poma v. Peru*).

46 See, e.g., Commission on Human Rights, *Indigenous peoples' permanent sovereignty over natural resources: Final report of the Special Rapporteur, Erica-Irene A. Daes,* UN Doc. E/CN.4/Sub.2/2004/30 (13 July 2004); The 2nd Global Consultation on the Right to Food and Food Security for Indigenous Peoples, *Cultural Indicators for Food Security, Food Sovereignty and Sustainable Development: Conclusions and Recommendations* (undated): www.treatycouncil.org/PDFs/Conclusions%202nd%20Global%20Consultatio n.pdf; Commission on Human Rights, *Expanded working paper submitted by Mrs. Antoanella-Iulia Motoc and the Tebtebba Foundation offering guidelines to govern the practice of Implementation of the principle of free, prior and informed consent of indigenous peoples in relation to development affecting their lands and natural resources,* UN Doc. E/CN.4/Sub.2/AC.4/2005/WP.1 (14 July 2005); Permanent Forum on Indigenous Issues, *Report of the International Workshop on Methodologies regarding Free, Prior and Informed Consent and Indigenous Peoples,* UN Doc. E/C.19/2005/3 (17 Feb. 2005).

47 United Nations Development Group, *United Nations Development Group Guidelines on Indigenous Peoples' Issues* (Feb. 2008) at 25: www2.ohchr.org/english/issues/indigenous/docs/guidelines.pdf. These guidelines were drafted by a group of United Nations organizations and specialized agencies under the aegis of the Inter-Agency Support Group on Indigenous Peoples' Issues.

48 Commission on Human Rights, *Report of the Special Rapporteur on the situation of human rights and fundamental freedoms of indigenous people, Mr. Rodolfo Stavenhagen, submitted pursuant to Commission resolution 2005/51: Addendum: Progress report on preparatory work for the study regarding best practices carried out to implement the recommendations contained in the annual reports of the Special Rapporteur,* UN Doc. E/CN.4/2006/78/Add.4 (26 Jan. 2006) at para. 11.

49 World Commission on Dams, *Dams and Development: A new framework for decision-making: The Report of the World Commission on Dams* (London: Earthscan, 2000) at 112.

50 Extractive Industries Review, *Striking a Better Balance: The Final Report of the Extractive Industries Review,* vol. I (Dec. 2003) at 21.

51 *Case of the Saramaka People v. Suriname,* (2007), Preliminary Objections, Merits, Reparations, and Costs, Inter-Am. Ct. H.R. (Ser. C) No. 172, at para. 137.

52 *Dann v. US, supra* note 9 at para. 130.

53 *Ibid.* at para. 131. See also *Maya Indigenous Communities of the Toledo District v. Belize* (2004) Inter-Am. Comm. H.R. Report No. 40/04, Case 12.053; *Case of the Mayagna (Sumo) Awas Tingni Community v. Nicaragua* (2001), Inter-Am. Ct. H.R. (Ser. C) No. 79.

54 *Martínez Report, supra* note 12 at para. 307.

55 *Ibid.*

56 *Ibid.* at para. 308.

57 *Ibid.* at para. 309.

58 *Declaration*, arts. 27, 40.

59 *Ibid.*

60 *Ibid.*

61 *Ibid.*, art. 40.

62 *Ibid.*

63 *Ibid.*, art. 27.

64 *Ibid.*, arts 27, 28.

65 *Ibid.*, art. 28.

CHAPTER NINE

1 Commission on Human Rights, *Report on the United Nations Seminar on the effects of racism and racial discrimination on the social and economic relations between indigenous peoples and States: Geneva, Switzerland, 16-20 January 1989*, UN Doc. E/CN.4/1989/22 (8 Feb. 1989) at para. 40(b): "The concepts of 'terra nullius', 'conquest' and 'discovery' as modes of territorial acquisition are repugnant, have no legal standing, and are entirely without merit or justification to substantiate any claim to jurisdiction or ownership of indigenous lands and ancestral domains, and the legacies of these concepts should be eradicated from modern legal systems."

2 The doctrine of discovery is described in *Johnson* v. *McIntosh*, 21 U.S. (8 Wheat.) 543 (1823) at 573-574, by Chief Justice Marshall of the United States Supreme Court: "[D]iscovery gave title to the government . . . by whose authority, it was made, against all other European governments. . . . The exclusion of all other Europeans, necessarily gave to the nation making the discovery the sole right of acquiring the soil from the natives, and establishing settlements upon it. . . . [T]he rights of the original inhabitants were, in no instance, entirely disregarded; but were necessarily, to a considerable extent, impaired. They were admitted to be the rightful occupants of the soil, with a legal as well as just claim to retain possession of it, and to use it according to their own discretion; but . . . their power to dispose of the soil at their own will, to whomsoever they pleased, was denied by the original fundamental principle, that discovery gave exclusive title to those who made it."

3 See, e.g., James Crawford, *The Creation of States in International Law* (Oxford: Clarendon Press, 1979) at 182: "a necessary condition for valid acquisition of nearly all inhabited territory was the consent of the native chiefs or peoples involved."

4 *Declaration*, preambular para. 4. See Appendix 1.

5 *Ibid.*, art. 26.

6 *Ibid.*, art. 28.

7   See, e.g., "Message of Louise Arbour, United Nations High Commissioner for Human Rights and Rodolfo Stavenhagen, Special Rapporteur on the situation of human rights and fundamental freedoms of indigenous people, on the occasion of the International Day of the World's Indigenous Peoples" (Geneva, 7 Aug. 2007): www.un.org/esa/socdev/unpfii/documents/Message_OHCHR07_en.doc: "the Declaration . . . establish[es] a universal framework for indigenous peoples' rights, social justice and reconciliation." See also United Nations Development Group, *United Nations Development Group Guidelines on Indigenous Peoples' Issues* (Feb. 2008) at 10: www2.ohchr.org/english/issues/indigenous/docs/guidelines.pdf: "the United Nations Declaration . . . recognizes the rights of indigenous peoples on a wide range of issues and provides a universal framework for the international community and States."

8   *Declaration*, art. 43.

9   Commission on Social Determinants of Health, *Closing the gap in a generation: Health equity through action on the social determinants of health*, Final Report (Geneva: World Health Organization, 2008) at 36.

10 *Declaration*, preambular para. 7.

11 Craig Mokhiber, Officer in Charge, New York Office of the High Commissioner for Human Rights, "Declaration is a Historic Document, out of a Historic Process" (Panel presentation, United Nations, New York, 26 Oct. 2006): www.ipcaucus.net/Mokhiber.html: "The Declaration is not just a re-statement of existing rights, although it does not create any new rights. It is a remarkably clear articulation of the nature of the obligations and entitlements that attach to those pre-existing rights in the case of Indigenous Peoples."

12 Human Rights Council, *Report of the Special Rapporteur on the situation of human rights and fundamental freedoms of indigenous people, S. James Anaya*, UN Doc. A/HRC/9/9 (11 Aug. 2008) at para. 40 [Human Rights Council, *Report of the Special Rapporteur, S. James Anaya*].

13 *Declaration*, preambular para. 22.

14 Commission on Human Rights, *supra* note 1 at para. 40(d). See also *Delgamuukw v. British Columbia*, [1997] 3 S.C.R. 1010 at para. 115: "A further dimension of aboriginal title is the fact that it is held communally. Aboriginal title cannot be held by individual aboriginal persons; it is a collective right to land held by all members of an aboriginal nation."

15 United Nations Development Programme, *Human Development Report 2004: Cultural liberty in today's diverse world* (New York: UNDP, 2004) at 68: "the lack of legal recognition of collective rights violates individual rights." See also *Case of Mayagna (Sumo) Awas Tingni Community v. Nicaragua* (2001), Inter-Am. Ct. H.R. (Ser. C) No. 76, at para. 148: "[A]rticle 21 of the [*American Convention on Human Rights*] protects the right to property in a sense which includes, among others, the rights of members of the indigenous communities within the framework of communal property"; and *Case of Moiwana Village v. Suriname*, (2005) Inter-Am. Ct. H.R. (Ser. C) No. 124 at para. 135: "[T]he Court concludes that Suriname violated the right of the Moiwana community members to the communal use and enjoyment of their traditional property."

16 International Indigenous Women's Forum (FIMI), *Mairin Iwanka Raya: Indigenous Women Stand Against Violence: A Companion Report to the United Nations Secretary-General's Study on Violence Against Women* (New York: FIMI, 2006) at 15.

17 S. James Anaya, *Indigenous Peoples in International Law*, 2d ed. (Oxford: Oxford University Press, 2004) at 7.

18 *International Covenant on Civil and Political Rights*, 19 Dec. 1966, 999 U.N.T.S. 171 (entered into force 23 Mar. 1976) [ICCPR]; and *International Covenant on Economic, Social and Cultural Rights*, 19 Dec. 1966, 993 U.N.T.S. 3 (entered into force 3 Jan. 1976) [ICESER].

19 Art. 1(3) of ICCPR and ICESCR.

20 GA Res. 217(III), UN GAOR, 3d Sess., UN Doc. A/810 (1948) 71 [UDHR].

21 Richard Falk, "Foreword" in Maivan Clech Lâm, *At the Edge of the State: Indigenous Peoples and Self-Determination* (Ardsley, NY: Transnational Publishers, 2000) at xiii.

22 *Institution-building of the United Nations Human Rights Council*, HRC Res. 5/1, UN GAOR, 62d Sess., Supp. No. 53, UN Doc. A/62/53 (2007) 48, Annex (adopted 18 June 2007 without a vote).

23 General Assembly, *Official Records*, UN GAOR 61st Sess., 107th Plen. Mtg., UN Doc. A/61/PV.107 (13 Sept. 2007) at 21 (Statement by United Kingdom (delivered by Ms Pierce)) : "since equality and universality are the fundamental principles underpinning human rights, we do not accept that some groups in society should benefit from human rights that are not available to others. With the exception of the right to self-determination, we therefore do not accept the concept of collective human rights in international law." See also United States Mission to the United Nations, "Observations of the United States with respect to the Declaration on the Rights of Indigenous Peoples" (13 Sept. 2007): "Collective Rights: There was discussion within the Working Group regarding whether or not the collective indigenous rights set forth in the declaration were collective human rights.... [A]s has always been the case, human rights are universal and apply in equal measure to all individuals. This principle is fundamental to international human rights, and means that one group cannot have human rights that are denied to other groups within the same nation-state."

24 Letter from Assembly of First Nations National Chief Phil Fontaine to Minister of Indian Affairs, Chuck Strahl (30 Jan. 2008), Annex at para. 26.

25 Letter from Minister of Indian Affairs, Jim Prentice, to Assembly of First Nations National Chief Phil Fontaine (20 Sept. 2006), Annex, at para. 12.

26 Discriminating against or otherwise undermining Indigenous peoples' human rights is not consistent with the *Charter of the United Nations*. As indicated in its first preambular paragraph, the *Declaration* is "[g]uided by the purposes and principles of the Charter of the United Nations." One of the core purposes of the UN and its member states is to uphold the "principle of equal rights and self-determination of peoples" (*Charter of the United Nations*, art. 1(2)). Another key purpose is to "achieve international cooperation ... in promoting and encouraging respect for human rights ... for all without distinction as to race, sex, language, or religion" (*Charter of the United Nations*, art. 1(3)). Art. 55(c) of the *Charter* elaborates on this purpose in the human rights context based on respect for the "principle of equal rights and self-determination of peoples."

27 Indigenous peoples' collective rights are regularly considered by such international and regional human rights bodies as the UN Human Rights Council, the Human Rights Committee, the Committee on Economic, Social and Cultural Rights, the Committee on the Elimination of Racial Discrimination, the Inter-American Commission on Human Rights, and the Inter-American Court of Human Rights.

28 See, e.g., *Mary and Carrie Dann* v. *United States* (2002) Inter-Am. Comm. H.R. Report No. 75/02, Case 11.140, at para. 125 [*Dann* v. *US*]: "In particular, a review of pertinent treaties, legislation and jurisprudence reveals the development over more than 80 years of particular human rights norms and principles applicable to the circumstances and treatment of indigenous peoples. Central to these norms and principles is a recognition that ensuring the full and effective enjoyment of human rights by indigenous peoples requires consideration of their particular historical, cultural, social and economic situation and experience."

29 Canadian Human Rights Commission, *"Still A Matter of Rights": A Special Report of the Canadian Human Rights Commission on the Repeal of Section 67 of the Canadian Human Rights Act* (Ottawa: Minister of Public Works and Government Services, 2008) at 8.

30 *Declaration*, art. 46(2).

31 *Ibid.*, art. 46(3).

32 Committee on Economic, Social and Cultural Rights, *General Comment No. 14 (2000): The right to the highest attainable standard of health*, UN Doc. E/C.12/2000/4 (11 Aug. 2000) at para. 27.

33 *American Convention on Human Rights*, 22 Nov. 1969, O.A.S.T.S. No. 36, 1144 U.N.T.S. 144 (entered into force 18 July 1978), art. 21.

34 *Case of Sawhoyamaxa* v. *Paraguay* (2006), Judgment, Inter-Am. Ct. H.R. (Ser. C) No. 146, at para. 120.

35 *Convention (No. 169) Concerning Indigenous and Tribal Peoples in Independent Countries*, 27 June 1989, ILO Official Bulletin, Vol. 72, Ser. A, No. 2, 59 (entered into force 5 Sept. 1991) [ILO Convention No. 169].

36 International Labour Organization, "ILO standards and the UN Declaration on the Rights of Indigenous Peoples: Information note for ILO staff and partners" (undated) at 2. This document was distributed at the Permanent Forum on Indigenous Issues, 7th Sess. (April 2008).

37 Human Rights Council, *Report of the Special Rapporteur, S. James Anaya, supra* note 12 at para. 43.

38 Examples include the UN Working Group on Indigenous Populations, the Second International Decade of the World's Indigenous People, and the UN Special Rapporteur on the situation of human rights and fundamental freedoms of indigenous people.

39 Russel Lawrence Barsh, "Indigenous Peoples in the 1990s: From Object to Subject of International Law?" (1994) 7 Harvard Hum. Rts. J. 33 at 58.

40 *Declaration*, art. 41.

41 James (Sa'ke'j) Youngblood Henderson, "The Status of Indian Treaties in International Law" in *Aboriginal Rights and International Law: Proceedings of the 1993 Conference of the Canadian Council on International Law* (Ottawa: Canadian Council on International Law, 1993) 126 at 132.

42 In regard to treaties of peace and friendship, see Gundmundur Alfredsson, "The Right of Self-Determination and Indigenous Peoples" in Christian Tomuschat, ed., *Modern Law of Self-Determination* (Boston: Martinus Nijhoff, 1993) 41 at 47: "These agreements were of an international character until the international status of one of the parties was eliminated by way of unilateral acts of the other party, sometimes by legislation, sometimes by the courts, often by force, and as a rule without indigenous consent." See also Timo Koivurova, "The Draft Nordic Saami Convention: Nations Working Together" (2008) 10 International Community Law Review 279 at 279: "During the time of first encounters between indigenous peoples and settler populations, some of the European states concluded international treaties between themselves and the respective indigenous peoples. . . . Unfortunately, many of these international treaties soon became 'domesticated' by the settlers, that is, the treaties were not seen as regulating the legal relation on the international plane, but domestic laws took over and subjected indigenous peoples to the rule of the settlers."

43 For further discussion of the international character of Indigenous peoples' treaties, see Paul Joffe & Willie Littlechild, "Administration of Justice and How to Improve it: Applicability and Use of International Human Rights Norms" in Commission on First Nations and Métis Peoples and Justice Reform, *Final Report: Submissions to the Commission*, vol. 2 (Saskatoon: Saskatchewan Commission on First Nations and Métis Peoples and Justice Reform, 2004) section 12 at 12-14 – 12-23: www.justicereformcomm.sk.ca/volume2/15section12.pdf.

44 Anaya, *supra* note 17 at 189.

45 *Declaration*, art. 40.

46 See, e.g., *Declaration*, preambular para. 15 and art. 36. See also Peter Hogg & Mary Ellen Turpel, "Implementing Aboriginal Self-Government: Constitutional and Jurisdictional Issues" (1995) 74 Can. Bar Rev. 187 at 190: "[T]he rights which Aboriginal peoples enjoy in Canadian law are inherent to their own history and experience as the first peoples. Many treaties concluded between Aboriginal peoples and the Crown also demonstrate that Aboriginal peoples exercised their rights of self-government by structuring their relations with governments in Canada on the basis of consent and mutual recognition."

47 *R. v. Badger*, [1996] 1 S.C.R. 771 at 793 [*Badger*].

48 Robert A. Williams, Jr., *Like a Loaded Weapon: The Rehnquist Court, Indian Rights, and the Legal History of Racism in America* (Minneapolis: University of Minnesota Press: 2005) at xvi.

49 *Declaration*, preambular para. 8.

50 James (Sa'ke'j) Youngblood Henderson, *Indigenous Diplomacy and the Rights of Peoples: Achieving UN Recognition* (Saskatoon: Purich , 2008) at 97: "Failure to respect the status and significance of treaties would be inconsistent with the Crown's constitutional fiduciary obligations — as well as the principles of good faith, honour of the Crown, and trust that are associated with such obligations and with the process of treaty making itself. Indigenous treaties serve as a benchmark for measuring fairness and justice."

51 Ted Moses, "Renewal of the Nation" in Gudmundur Alfredsson & Maria Stavropoulou, eds., *Justice Pending: Indigenous Peoples and Other Good Causes, Essays in Honour of Erica-Irene A. Daes* (The Hague: Martinus Nijhoff, 2002) 57 at 65.

52 In regard to the Aboriginal and treaty rights of the Western Shoshone, see, e.g., *Dann v. US, supra* note 28 at para. 124: "in determining the claims currently before it, the Commission considers that this broader corpus of international law includes the developing norms and principles governing the human rights of indigenous peoples. As the following analysis indicates, these norms and principles encompass distinct human rights considerations relating to the ownership, use and occupation by indigenous communities of their traditional lands. Considerations of this nature in turn controvert the State's contention that the Danns' complaint concerns only land title and land use disputes and does not implicate issues of human rights."

53 Joffe & Littlechild, *supra* note 43 at 12-14.

54 *Declaration*, art. 7(1).

55 *Ibid.*, art. 7(2).

56 *Edwards v. A.-G. Canada*, [1930] A.C. 124 (P.C.) at 136. See also *Hunter v. Southam Inc.*, [1984] 2 S.C.R. 145 at 155 [*Hunter*]: "A constitution . . . is drafted with an eye to the future. . . . Once enacted, its provisions cannot easily be repealed or amended. It must, therefore, be capable of growth and development over time to meet new social, political and historical realities often unimagined by its framers. The judiciary is the guardian of the constitution and must, in interpreting its provisions, bear these considerations in mind."

57 See, e.g., *Case of the Mayagna (Sumo) Awas Tingni Community v. Nicaragua, supra* note 15 at para. 146: "human rights treaties are live instruments whose interpretation must adapt to the evolution of the times and, specifically, to current living conditions." See also *Canada (A.G.) v. Mossop*, [1993] 1 S.C.R. 554 at 621, L'Heureux-Dubé J.: "concepts of equality and liberty which appear in human rights documents are not bounded by the precise understanding of those who drafted them. Human rights codes are documents that embody fundamental principles, but which permit the understanding and application of these principles to change over time."

58 See James (Sa'ke'j) Youngblood Henderson, *Treaty Rights in the Constitution of Canada* (Toronto: Carswell, 2007) at 1045-1046: "filling gaps in the old treaties in accordance with human rights covenants" should be a goal in addressing constitutional reform.

59 *Reference re Secession of Québec*, [1998] 2 S.C.R. 217 at para. 53. The Court is quoting *Reference re Remuneration of Judges of the Provincial Court of Prince Edward Island*, [1997] 3 S.C.R. 3 (*Provincial Judges Reference*) at para. 104.

60 Since Indigenous peoples are distinct peoples and not simply minorities, it is more appropriate to consider the protection of existing Aboriginal and treaty rights as a separate constitutional principle. Similarly, see Claude-Armand Sheppard, "The Cree Intervention in the Canadian Supreme Court Reference on Québec Secession: A Subjective Assessment" (1999) 23 Vermont L. Rev. 845 at 856.

61 *Reference re Secession of Québec, supra* note 59 at para. 82. See also para. 80: "[T]he protection of minority rights is itself an independent principle underlying our constitutional order." In *R. v. Marshall (No. 2)*, [1999] 3 S.C.R. 533 at para. 45, the obligation in s. 35 of the *Constitution Act, 1982* to protect Aboriginal and treaty rights is referred to as a "national commitment"; and in *R. v. Powley*, [2003] 2 S.C.R. 207 at para. 45: "Section 35 reflects a new promise: a constitutional commitment."

62 *Declaration*, art. 40.

63 UDHR, *supra* note 20, art. 8; ICCPR, *supra* note 18, art. 2(3); *International Convention on the Elimination of All Forms of Racial Discrimination*, 7 Mar. 1966, 660 U.N.T.S. 195 (entered into force 4 Jan. 1969) art. 6; and *American Convention on Human Rights, supra* note 33, art. 8.

64 Sub-Commission on the Promotion and Protection of Human Rights, *Indigenous peoples and their relationship to land: Final working paper prepared by the Special Rapporteur, Mrs. Erica-Irene A. Daes*, E/CN.4/Sub.2/2001/21 (11 June 2001) at para. 49.

65 US, *Cong. Rec.*, vol. 139, no. 147, S14880, 103d Congress, First Session, 27 Oct. 1993.

66 African Commission on Human and Peoples' Rights (ACHPR) and International Work Group for Indigenous Affairs, *Report of the African Commission's Working Group of Experts on Indigenous Populations/Communities, submitted in Accordance with the "Resolution on the Rights of Indigenous Populations/Communities in Africa"* (Somerset, NJ: Transaction, 2005) at 24: "The famous fake treaties signed between the British and Maasai in 1904 and 1911 to evict the Maasai from their best land to make room for colonial settlers have never been settled."

67 *James Bay and Northern Québec Agreement and Complementary Agreements*, 1997 Edition (Québec: Les Publications du Québec, 1996).

68 With the subsequent adoption of the *Constitution Act, 1982*, being Schedule B to the *Canada Act 1982* (U.K.), 1982, c.11, the "existing aboriginal and treaty rights of the aboriginal peoples of Canada" were "recognized and affirmed" in s. 35(1). See also s. 35(3): "For greater certainty . . . 'treaty rights' includes rights that now exist by way of land claims agreements or may be so acquired."

69 Dalee Sambo, "Indigenous Peoples and International Standard-Setting Processes: Are State Governments Listening?" (1993) 3 Transnat'l L. & Contemp. Probs. 13 at 31-32.

70 Human Rights Committee, *Concluding observations of the Human Rights Committee: Canada*, UN Doc. CCPR/C/79/Add.105 (7 April 1999) at para. 8.

71 Sub-Commission on Prevention of Discrimination and Protection of Minorities, *The Right to Self-Determination: Implementation of United Nations Resolutions*, UN Doc. E/CN.4/Sub.2/405/Rev.1 (1980) at para. 59: "[H]uman rights can only exist truly and fully when self-determination also exists. Such is the fundamental importance of self-determination as a human right and as a prerequisite for the enjoyment of all the other rights and freedoms." See also Kurt Mills, *Human Rights in the Emerging Global Order:*

A New Sovereignty? (New York: St. Martin's Press, 1998) at 83: "... while self-determination is required for the development and enjoyment of human rights, human rights are also a precondition for communal self-determination. They cannot be divorced from each other. In this sense, self-determination is a human right along with civil, political, and economic rights which, taken as a whole, describe and guarantee the rights of human existence."

72 *Agreement Concerning a New Relationship Between Le Gouvernement du Quebec and the Crees of Quebec,* entered into in Waskaganish, Quebec, 7 Feb. 2002.

73 *Ibid.*, preambular para. 1.

74 *Declaration,* preambular para. 15.

75 Matthew Coon Come, "The Cree-Quebec relationship is at a crossroads" *Montreal Gazette* (13 Nov. 2009) at A23. He added, "[p]lans cannot be imposed because there must be trust, respect and accommodation. Otherwise social conflict, mistrust and litigation will result. When we signed the Paix des Braves, we hoped we could consign tired approaches and negative instincts to the past."

76 See *Declaration,* art. 44: "All the rights and freedoms recognized herein are equally guaranteed to male and female indigenous individuals."

77 *Grand Chief Michael Mitchell* v. *Canada* [2003], Admissibility, Inter-Am. Comm. H.R., Report No. 74/03, Petition 790/01, at para. 37.

78 Eric Heinze, "Beyond Parapraxes: Right and Wrong Approaches to the Universality of Human Rights Law" (1994) 12 Neth. Q. H. R. 369 at 381.

79 *Hunter, supra* note 56 at 155.

80 *Reference re Public Service Employee Relations Act (Alberta),* [1987] 1 S.C.R. 313 at 348. This same passage has been cited with approval in subsequent cases: see, e.g., *United States of America* v. *Burns,* [2001] 1 S.C.R. 283 at para. 80. See also *McIvor* v. *Canada (Registrar, Indian and Northern Affairs),* [2007] 3 C.N.L.R. 72 (B.C.S.C.) at para. 184, where the *Burns* case is cited on this same point.

81 *Haida Nation* v. *British Columbia (Minister of Forests),* [2004] 3 S.C.R. 511 at para. 16 [*Haida Nation*].

82 *Ibid.* at para. 17.

83 *Ibid.* at para. 32.

84 *Tzeachten First Nation* v. *Canada (Attorney General),* 2007 BCCA 133, at para. 47.

85 *Ibid.* at para. 91.

86 See also *R.* v. *Kapp,* 2008 SCC 41 at para. 6; *Taku River Tlingit First Nation* v. *British Columbia (Project Assessment Director)* [2004] 3 S.C.R. 550; *Delgamuukw* v. *British Columbia,* [1997] 3 S.C.R. 1010 at para. 115 [*Delgamuukw*]; and *Badger, supra* note 47 at para. 41.

87 *Little Salmon/Carmacks First Nation* v. *Yukon (Minister of Energy, Mines and Resources),* [2008] Y.J. No. 55, at para. 58. The appeal of this case was heard by the Supreme Court of Canada in Nov. 2009.

88   See, e.g., *Petition to the Inter-American Commission on Human Rights submitted by the Hul'qumi'num Treaty Group against Canada* (10 May 2007). This petition has been determined to be admissible and is now registered as Case No. 12.734 by the Inter-American Commission on Human Rights: see *Hul'qumi'num Treaty Group* v. *Canada* [2009] Admissibility, Inter-Am. Comm. H.R., Report No. 105/09.

89   Land Claims Agreements Coalition (LCAC), *Universal Periodic Review of Canada: Submission of the Land Claims Agreements Coalition (LCAC) to the United Nations Human Rights Council* (8 Sept. 2008) at para. 19: lib.ohchr.org/HRBodies/UPR/Documents/Session4/CA/LCAC_CAN_UPR_S4_2009_LandClaimsAgreementsCoalition_JOINT.pdf.

90   Standing Senate Committee on Aboriginal Peoples, *Honouring the Spirit of Modern Treaties: Closing the Loopholes* (May 2008) at vii: www.parl.gc.ca/39/2/parlbus/commbus/senate/com-e/abor-e/rep/rep05may08-e.pdf.

91   General Assembly, *The situation of human rights and fundamental freedoms of indigenous people: Note by the Secretary-General*, UN Doc. A/59/258 (12 Aug. 2004) at para. 18. (Report of the Special Rapporteur on the situation of human rights and fundamental freedoms of indigenous people).

92   *Ibid.* at para. 20.

93   *Ibid.*

94   *Case of the Saramaka People* v. *Suriname* (2007), Preliminary Objections, Merits, Reparations, and Costs, Inter-Am. Ct. H.R. (Ser. C) No. 172, at para. 131.

95   *Cal* v. *Attorney General of Belize and Minister of Natural Resources and Environment; Coy* v. *Attorney General of Belize and Minister of Natural Resources and Environment* (18 Oct. 2007) Claims No. 171 & 172 of 2007 (Consolidated), (Supreme Court of Belize) at para. 131.

96   *Haida Nation*, *supra* note 81 at para. 24.

97   *Delgamuukw*, *supra* note 86 at para. 168.

98   *Declaration*, preambular para. 6.

99   *Sparrow* v. *The Queen*, [1990] 1 S.C.R. 1075.

100   *Ibid.* at 1112. At 1114: "If a valid legislative objective is found, the analysis proceeds to the second part of the justification issue. Here, we refer back to the guiding interpretive principle … That is, the honour of the Crown is at stake in dealings with aboriginal peoples. The special trust relationship and the responsibility of the government vis-à-vis aboriginals must be the first consideration in determining whether the legislation or action in question can be justified. . . ." At 1119, the court noted that further questions might also arise depending on the circumstances of the inquiry: "These include the questions of whether there has been as little infringement as possible in order to effect the desired result; whether, in a situation of expropriation, fair compensation is available; and, whether the aboriginal group in question has been consulted with respect to the conservation measures being implemented. . . . We would not wish to set out an exhaustive list of the factors to be considered in the assessment of justification."

101   *R.* v. *Côté*, [1996] 3 S.C.R. 139 at para. 33, Lamer C.J.

102   *Badger*, *supra* note 47 at para. 75.

103   *Ibid.* at para. 82.

104 Peter W. Hogg, *Constitutional Law of Canada*, 4th ed. (looseleaf) (Toronto: Carswell, 1997) at 27-42, n. 1480.

105 Ruth Sullivan, *Sullivan on the Construction of Statutes*, 5th ed. (Markham, Ont.: Lexis-Nexis Canada, 2008) at 525.

106 *Declaration*, preambular para. 15.

107 *Ibid.*, preambular paras. 18 and 24.

108 *R. v. Sundown*, [1999] 1 S.C.R. 393 at para. 46, Cory J.

109 Permanent Forum on Indigenous Issues, *Information received from the United Nations system and other intergovernmental organizations: Office of the United Nations High Commissioner for Human Rights*, UN Doc. E/C.19/2008/4/Add.14 (15 Feb. 2008) at para. 31.

110 World Conference on Human Rights, *Vienna Declaration and Programme of Action*, UN Doc. A/CONF.157/23 (12 July 1993) at 5 (para. 5) (adopted 25 June 1993).

111 United Nations Secretary-General, "Human Rights: The Common Language of Humanity," in World Conference on Human Rights, *The Vienna Declaration and Program of Action June 1993*, UN DPI/1394-39399-August 1993-20 M.

112 *Charter of the United Nations*, arts. 1(3), 2(2), 55(c) and 56.

113 Permanent Forum on Indigenous Issues, *Report of the Inter-Agency Support Group on Indigenous Issues on the special theme: "Territories, lands and natural resources,"* UN Doc. E/C.19/2007/2/Add.1 (19 Mar. 2007) at para. 3(a).

114 *Human rights and indigenous peoples: Mandate of the Special Rapporteur on the situation of human rights and fundamental freedoms of indigenous people*, HRC Res. 6/12, UN GAOR, 63d Sess., Supp. No. 53, UN Doc. A/63/53 (2008) 22 at 22 (para. 1(g)).

115 Human Rights Council, *Report of the Special Rapporteur on the situation of human rights and fundamental freedoms of indigenous people, Rodolfo Stavenhagen*, UN Doc. A/HRC/6/15 (15 Nov. 2007) at para. 6.

116 *Expert mechanism on the rights of indigenous peoples*, HRC Res. 6/36, UN GAOR, 63d Sess., Supp. No. 53, UN Doc. A/63/53 (2008) 67. ;

117 "Statement by John Henriksen, Chairperson-Rapporteur" (Expert Mechanism on the Rights of Indigenous Peoples, 1st Sess., Geneva, 1 Oct. 2008) at 5.

118 Permanent Forum on Indigenous Issues, *Report on the seventh session (21 April - 2 May 2008)*, UN ESCOR, 2008, Supp. No. 23, UN Doc. E/2008/43, E/C.19/2008/13, at para. 132.

119 African Commission on Human and Peoples' Rights, "Communiqué on the United Nations Declaration on the Rights of Indigenous Peoples" (28 Nov. 2007).

120 See Organization of American States, Working Group to Prepare the Draft American Declaration on the Rights of Indigenous Peoples, *Report of the Chair on the Meeting for Reflection on the Meetings of Negotiations in the Quest for Points of Consensus (Washington, D.C., United States – November 26-28, 2007)*, OR OEA/Ser.K/XVI, GT/DADIN/doc.321/08 (14 Jan. 2008) at 3.

121 "Opening Remarks Ms. Navanethem Pillay, United Nations High Commissioner for Human Rights to the 2nd session of the Expert Mechanism on the Rights of Indigenous Peoples" (Delivered at the United Nations, Geneva, 10 Aug. 2009): www.unhchr.ch/huricane/huricane.nsf/view01/0A1A8D39C55CE3F9C125760E00304 246?opendocument.

122 Liberal Party of Canada, "Statement by Liberal Leader Michael Ignatieff on the United Nations Declaration on the Rights of Indigenous Peoples" (10 Dec. 2009): www.liberal.ca/en/newsroom/media-releases/17090_statement-by-liberal-leader-michael-ignatieff-on-the-united-nations-declaration-on-the-rights-of-indigenous-peoples.

123 The text of the motion is reproduced in *House of Commons Debates*, No. 074 (7 April 2008).

CHAPTER TEN

1 Victoria Tauli-Corpuz, "Statement of Victoria Tauli-Corpuz, Chair of the UN Permanent Forum on Indigenous Issues on the Occasion of the Adoption of the UN Declaration on the Rights of Indigenous Peoples" (Delivered to the United Nations General Assembly, New York, 13 Sept. 2007): www.un.org/esa/socdev/unpfii/documents/Declaration_ip_vtc.doc.

2 *Declaration*, arts. 3, 26, 12, 13, 2, 7, and 22, respectively. See Appendix 1.

3 *Lovelace* v. *Canada*, Communication No. 24/1977 (views adopted 30 July 1981) in *Report of the Human Rights Committee*, UN GAOR, 36th Sess., Supp. No. 40, UN Doc. A/36/40 (1981) 166.

4 *Bernard Ominayak, Chief of the Lubicon Lake Band* v. *Canada*, Communication No. 167/1984 (views adopted 26 Mar. 1990) in *Report of the Human Rights Committee*, UN GAOR, 45th Sess., Supp. No. 40, Vol. II, UN Doc. A/45/40 (1990) 1.

5 *International Covenant on Civil and Political Rights*, 19 Dec. 1966, 999 U.N.T.S. 171 (entered into force 23 Mar. 1976) [ICCPR]; *International Covenant on Economic, Social and Cultural Rights*, 19 Dec. 1966, 993 U.N.T.S. 3 (entered into force 3 Jan. 1976) [ICESCR].

6 In October 2005, the Human Rights Committee called on Canada to "gather accurate statistical data throughout the country on violence against Aboriginal women": *Concluding observations of the Human Rights Committee: Canada*, UN Doc. CCPR/C/CAN/CO/5 (20 April 2006) at para. 23. For an analysis of the persistent gaps in reporting by police and the justice system, see Rebecca Kong and Karen Beattie, *Collecting Data on Aboriginal People in the Criminal Justice System: Methods and Challenges* (Ottawa: Minister of Industry, 2005).

7 Indian and Northern Affairs Canada, *Aboriginal Women: A Demographic, Social and Economic Profile* (1996).

8 Maire Gannon & Karen Mihorean, "Criminal Victimization in Canada, 2004" (2005) 25(7) *Juristat* 1 at 8.

9 Native Women's Association of Canada. *Voices of Our Sisters In Spirit: A Report to Families and Communities*, 2d ed. (2009): www.nwac-hq.org/en/documents/NWAC_VoicesofOurSistersInSpiritII_March2009FINAL.pdf. It is likely that there are additional cases that have yet to be identified or made public.

10 Douglas A. Brownridge, "Male Partner Violence against Aboriginal Women in Canada — An Empirical Analysis" (2003) 18 *Journal of Interpersonal Violence* 65.

11 Amnesty International, *Stolen Sisters: A Human Rights Response to Discrimination and Violence Against Indigenous Women in Canada* (2004): www.amnesty.ca/stolensisters/amr2000304.pdf.

12 For an analysis of cultural bias against Indigenous women in Canadian society and Canada's failure to protect Indigenous women from violence, see *ibid*.

13 Committee on the Elimination of Discrimination against Women, *Concluding observations of the Committee on the Elimination of Discrimination against Women: Canada*, UN Doc. CEDAW/C/CAN/CO/7 (7 Nov. 2008) at para 44.

14 See, e.g., Human Rights Council, *Report of the Working Group on the Universal Periodic Review: Canada*, UN Doc. A/HRC/11/17 (5 Oct. 2009) at para 86.

15 Amnesty International, *No More Stolen Sisters: The Need for a Comprehensive Response to Discrimination and Violence against Indigenous Women in Canada* (2009) at 4: www.amnesty.ca/amnestynews/upload/AMR200122009.pdf.

16 *Ibid*. at 26.

17 World Conference on Human Rights, *Vienna Declaration and Programme of Action*, UN Doc.A/CONF.157/23 (12 July 1993) at 5 (para. 5).

18 *House of Commons Debates*, No. 083 (21 Nov. 2006) at 5147. (Hon. Jim Prentice).

19 See, e.g., International Indigenous Women's Forum (FIMI), *Mairin Iwanka Raya: Indigenous Women Stand Against Violence: A Companion Report to the United Nations Secretary-General's Study on Violence Against Women* (New York: FIMI, 2006).

20 *International Convention on the Elimination of All Forms of Racial Discrimination*, 7 Mar. 1966, 660 U.N.T.S. 195 (entered into force 4 Jan. 1969).

21 *Convention on the Elimination of All Forms of Discrimination against Women*, 18 Dec. 1979, 1249 U.N.T.S. 13 (entered into force 3 Sept. 1981).

22 *Inter-American Convention on the Prevention, Punishment, and Eradication of Violence against Women (Convention of Belem do Para)*, 9 June 1994, 33 I.L.M. 1534 (entered into force 5 Mar. 1995).

23 ICESCR, *supra* note 5, art. 11(1).

24 Human Rights Council, *Report of the Special Rapporteur on adequate housing as a component of the right to an adequate standard of living, and on the right to non-discrimination in this context, Miloon Kothari*, UN Doc. A/HRC/7/16 (13 Feb. 2008) at para. 4.

25 *Ibid*.

26 Statistics Canada, *Aboriginal Peoples in Canada in 2006: Inuit, Métis and First Nations, 2006 Census* (Ottawa: Minister of Industry, 2008) at 16.

27 Bill C-47, *An Act Respecting Family Homes Situated on First Nation Reserves and Matrimonial Interests or Rights in or to Structures and Lands Situated on Those Reserves*, 2d Sess., 39th Parl., 2008.

28 Bill C-8, *An Act Respecting Family Homes Situated on First Nation Reserves and Matrimonial Interests or Rights in or to Structures and Lands Situated on Those Reserves*, 2d Sess., 40th Parl., 2009.

29 Native Women's Association of Canada, *Submission of the Native Women's Association of Canada Regarding the Universal Periodic Review of Canada by the Human Rights Council, September 8, 2008* (2008) at 3: www.nwac-hq.org/en/documents/NWACUPRSubm issionSeptember808Final.pdf (emphasis in original).

30 Human Rights Council, *Report of the Special Rapporteur on adequate housing as a component of the right to an adequate standard of living, and on the right to non-discrimination in this context, Miloon Kothari: Addendum: Preliminary note on the mission to Canada (9 to 22 October 2007)*, UN Doc. A/HRC/7/16/Add.4 (28 Feb. 2008) at para. 15.

31 *Ibid.* at para. 14.

32 General Assembly, *Official Records*, UN GAOR, 61st Sess., 107th Plen. Mtg., UN Doc. A/61/PV.107 (2007) at 13 (Statement of Canada, delivered by Mr. McNee).

33 UN Special Rapporteur on adequate housing as a component of the right to an adequate standard of living and on the right to non-discrimination in this context, Miloon Kothari, press conference, (Ottawa, 22 Oct. 2007).

34 Beverley Jacobs, "A Roadmap for Rights and Reconciliation: Canadian Implementation of the *UN Declaration on the Rights of Indigenous Peoples*" (Address delivered to a parliamentary breakfast briefing, Ottawa, 29 Jan. 2008) at 4, 5: www.nwac-hq.org/en/documents/SpeechJanuary29-08.pdf.

CHAPTER ELEVEN

1 *Convention on the Rights of the Child*, 20 Nov. 1989, 1577 U.N.T.S. 3 (entered into force 2 Sept. 1990) (Convention).

2 GA Res. 61/106, UN GAOR, 61st Sess., Supp. No. 49, Vol. I, UN Doc. A/61/49 (2008) 65, Annex I (opened for signature 30 Mar. 2007, entered into force 3 May 2008).

3 Mary Ellen Turpel, "UN Draft Declaration on the Rights of Indigenous Peoples: Commentaries" (1994) 1 C.N.L.R. 50 at 51.

4 *House of Commons Debates*, No. 110 (11 June 2008) at 6849 (Right Hon. Stephen Harper).

5 UNICEF, "Ensuring the Rights of Indigenous Children" (2003) *Innocenti Digest*, No.11 at 2: www.unicef.at/fileadmin/medien/pdf/Digest11_FINALEnglish.pdf.

6 Cindy Blackstock and Marlyn Bennett, *National Children's Alliance Policy Paper on Aboriginal Children* (Ottawa: National Children's Alliance, 2003) at 6: www.nationalchildre nsalliance.com/nca/pubs/2003/Aboriginal_Children-Blackstock_%20Bennett.pdf.

7   See, e.g., Representative for Children and Youth, *2007 Progress Report on the Implemen-tation of the Recommendations of the BC Children and Youth Review ("Hughes Review")* (26 Nov. 2007) at 21: www.rcybc.ca/Groups/Our%20Reports/2007%20Hughes%20Pro gress%20Report.pdf [RCY, *2007 Progress Report*].

8   Committee on the Elimination of Discrimination Against Women, *Concluding obser-vations of the Committee on the Elimination of Discrimination against Women: Canada*, UN Doc. CEDAW/C/CAN/CO/7 (7 Nov. 2008) at paras. 45-46.

9   *Canadian Foundation for Children, Youth and the Law v. Canada (Attorney General)*, [2004] 1 S.C.R. 76. See further Committee on the Rights of the Child, *General Comment No. 8 (2006): The right of the child to protection from corporal punishment and other cruel or degrading forms of punishment (arts. 19; 28, para. 2; and 37, inter alia)*, UN Doc. CRC/C/ GC/8 (2 Mar. 2007).

10   Statistics Canada, *Aboriginal Peoples in Canada in 2006: Inuit, Metis and First Na-tions, 2006 Census* (Ottawa: Minister of Industry, 2008) at 9: www12.statcan.ca/census-recensement/2006/as-sa/97-558/pdf/97-558-XIE2006001.pdf. Note that census results on Indigenous populations tend to underestimate their numbers in Canada, particu-larly since many Indigenous people choose not to participate in such processes.

11   *Ibid.* at 10.

12   Statistics Canada, *Aboriginal Children's Survey 2006: Family, Community and Child Care* (Ottawa: Minister of Industry, 2008) at 6, 9: www.statcan.gc.ca/pub/89-634-x/89-634-x2008001-eng.pdf [Statistics Canada, *Aboriginal Children's Survey 2006*].

13   Statistics Canada, *Aboriginal Peoples, supra* note 10 at 14.

14   UNICEF, "Ensuring the Rights of Indigenous Children," *supra* note 5 (on back cover).

15   See, e.g., Marlee Kline, "Child Welfare Law, 'Best Interests of the Child' Ideology, and First Nations" (1992) 30 Osgoode Hall L.J. 375.

16   See, e.g., Brian Rice and Anna Snyder, "Reconciliation in the Context of a Settler Soci-ety: Healing the Legacy of Colonialism in Canada" in Marlene Brant Castellano, Lin-da Archibald & Mike DeGagné, eds., *From Truth to Reconciliation: Transforming the Legacy of Residential Schools* (Ottawa: Aboriginal Healing Foundation, 2008) 45 at 53: "Belief in the superiority of European culture and Christianity, dominant for centuries in Europe and North America, is not as prevalent today as in the past. Nevertheless, Canadian society perpetuates stereotypes of Aboriginal people that justify Canadian domination and help to alleviate any sense of guilt or responsibility for Aboriginal op-pression."

17   Commission on Human Rights, *Report of the Special Rapporteur on the situation of human rights and fundamental freedoms of indigenous people, Rodolfo Stavenhagen: Addendum: Mission to Canada*, UN Doc. E/CN.4/2005/88/Add.3 (2 Dec. 2004) at para. 33.

18   National Council of Welfare, "First Nations, Métis and Inuit Children and Youth: Time to Act" (2007) *National Council of Welfare Reports, vol. 127 at 7*: www.ncwcnbes.net/ documents/researchpublications/ResearchProjects/FirstNationsMetisInuitChildrenA ndYouth/2007Report-TimeToAct/ReportENG.pdf.

19   Statistics Canada, *Aboriginal Children's Survey 2006, supra* note 12 at 6.

20   *Ibid.* at 16.

21 John Richards *et al.*, "Understanding the Aboriginal/ Non-Aboriginal Gap in Student Performance: Lessons From British Columbia" (2008) *CD Howe Institute Commentary*, No 276: www.cdhowe.org/pdf/commentary_276.pdf.

22 *Ibid.* at 26.

23 National Council of Welfare, *supra* note 18 at 59.

24 See, e.g., First Nations Child and Family Caring Society of Canada, *Wen:de — We are Coming to the Light of Day* (Ottawa: First Nations Child and Family Caring Society of Canada, 2005) at 179.

25 The First Nations Child and Family Caring Society of Canada spearheaded efforts to promote the adoption of "Jordan's Principle" in resolving healthcare jurisdictional disputes involving First Nations children. See, e.g., First Nations Child and Family Caring Society of Canada, "Joint Declaration of Support for Jordan's Principle": www.fncfcs.com/more/jordansPrinciple.php. See also Indian and Northern Affairs Canada, "Backgrounder — Implementation of Jordan's Principle in Saskatchewan": www.ainc-inac.gc.ca/ai/mr/nr/s-d2009/bk000000451-eng.asp: "Jordan's Principle honours the memory of Jordan River Anderson, a young boy from Manitoba's Norway House Cree Nation, who was born with a rare neuromuscular disorder and required care from multiple service providers. He became the centre of a jurisdictional funding dispute which prevented him from leaving the hospital to receive care in a family home."

26 Noni MacDonald and Amir Attaran, "Jordan's Principle, Governments' Paralysis" (2007) 177 CMAJ 321 at 321: www.cmaj.ca/cgi/content/full/177/4/321. Note that the federal and the Manitoba governments have reached an agreement on "Jordan's Principle" in resolving jurisdictional disputes involving First Nations children. See "Manitoba, Ottawa come to agreement on 'Jordan's Principle": www.cbc.ca/health/story/2008/09/05/jordans-principle.html. However, advocates still express concerns that the federal and provincial governments have failed to live up to their obligations: Dan Lett, "Jordan's Principle remains in limbo" (2008) 179 CMAJ 12 at 1256: www.ecmaj.ca/cgi/content/full/179/12/1256.

27 Office of the Auditor General of British Columbia, *Management of Aboriginal Child Protection Services: Ministry of Children and Family Development* (Victoria: Office of the Auditor General of British Columbia, 2008) at 2: www.bcauditor.com/include/view_file.asp?id=10&type=publication.

28 RCY, *2007 Progress Report, supra* note 7 at 21.

29 Chief Public Health Officer, *The Chief Public Health Officer's Report on the State of Public Health in Canada 2008* (Ottawa: Minister of Health, 2008) at 53: www.phac-aspc.gc.ca/publicat/2008/cpho-aspc/pdf/cpho-report-eng.pdf.

30 Donna Calverely, "Youth custody and community services in Canada, 2004/2005" (2007) *Juristat*, vol. 27(2): www.statcan.ca/english/freepub/85-002-XIE/85-002-XIE2007002.pdf.

31 See Representative for Children and Youth & Office of the Provincial Health Officer, *Kids, Crime and Care: Joint Special Report: Health and Well-Being of Children in Care: Youth Justice Experiences and Outcomes* (2009).

32 National Council of Welfare, *supra* note 18 at 7.

33 Assembly of First Nations, News Release, "Canadian Human Rights complaint on First Nations child welfare filed today by Assembly of First Nations and First Nations Child and Family Caring Society of Canada" (23 Feb. 2007): www.afn.ca/article.asp?id=3374 [Assembly of First Nations, "Canadian Human Rights complaint"].

34 Assembly of First Nations, News Release, "National Chief Praises decision regarding Human Rights Complaint on Child Welfare" (16 Oct. 2008): www.newswire.ca/en/releases/archive/October2008/16/c6561.html.

35 *Report of the Royal Commission on Aboriginal Peoples*, vol. 3 (Ottawa: Canada Communication Group, 1996) at 52.

36 *Ibid.*

37 Victoria Tauli-Corpuz, "Statement of Victoria Tauli-Corpuz, Chair of the UN Permanent Forum on Indigenous Issues on the Occasion of the Adoption of the UN Declaration on the Rights of Indigenous Peoples" (Delivered to the United Nations General Assembly, New York, 13 Sept. 2007): www.un.org/esa/socdev/unpfii/documents/Declaration_ip_vtc.doc.

38 *Ibid.*

39 United Nations, Press Release, "Adoption of Declaration on Rights of Indigenous Peoples a historic moment for human rights UN Expert Says" (14 Sept. 2007): www.unhchr.ch/huricane/huricane.nsf/view01/2F9532F220D85BD1C125735600493F0B?opendocument.

40 Assembly of First Nations *et al.*, Press Release, "Legal scholars and experts urge Canadian government to abandon 'erroneous' and 'misleading' opposition to *UN Declaration on the Rights of Indigenous Peoples*" (1 May 2008): www.cfsc.quaker.ca/pages/documents/pressstatementreopenletterMay08-2.pdf.

41 General Assembly, *Official Records*, UN GAOR, 61st Sess, 107th Plen. Mtg., UN Doc. A/61/PV.107 (2007) at 13 (Statement of Canada, delivered by Mr. McNee).

42 *Ibid.*

43 For example, in *R. v. C.D*; *R. v. C.D.K.*, [2005] 3 S.C.R. 668, the Court referenced article 37(b) of the *Convention* to reinforce an objective of the *Youth Criminal Justice Act*, S.C. 2002, c. 1. to restrict the use of arrest, detention, or imprisonment for young persons. In *R. v. D.B.*, [2008] 2 S.C.R. 3, the Court found that the legal principle of a presumption of diminished moral culpability for young persons was consistent with article 40 of the *Convention*.

44 House of Commons, Standing Committee on Aboriginal Affairs and Northern Development, "Second Report of the Committee (United Nations Draft Declaration on the Rights of Aboriginal Peoples)" (Presented to the House on 14 June 2006); House of Commons, Standing Committee on Aboriginal Affairs and Northern Development, "Fourth Report of the Committee (United Nations Declaration on the Rights on Indigenous Peoples)," 39th Parl., 1st Sess (Presented to the House on 20 Nov. 2006).

45 Letter from Phil Fontaine *et al.* to the Right Hon. Stephen Harper (9 Aug. 2007): www.amnesty.ca/resource_centre/news/view.php?load=arcview&article=4025&c=Resource+Centre+News.

46 "Canada Criticized over UN Aboriginal Rights Vote" *Canadian Press* (22 Oct. 2007): www.ctv.ca/servlet/ArticleNews/story/CTVNews/20071022/aboriginal_rights_071022/20071022?hub=Canada.

47 Assembly of First Nations, News Release, "AFN National Chief applauds today's passage of the UN Declaration on the Rights of Indigenous Peoples – Recognizing 30 years of work in the making" (13 Sept. 2007): www.afn.ca/article.asp?id=3772.

48 "*UN Declaration on the Rights of Indigenous Peoples:* Canada Needs to Implement this New Human Rights Instrument": www.cfsc.quaker.ca/pages/documents/UNDecl-Expertsign-onstatementMay1.pdf. See Appendix 1.

49 House of Commons, Standing Committee on the Status of Women, "Third Report (United Nations Declaration on the Rights of Indigenous Peoples)," 39th Parl., 2d Sess. (Presented to the House on 13 Feb. 2008). Concurred in by the House on 8 April 2008: *House of Commons Debates*, No. 074 (8 April 2008) at 4656.

50 C-569, *An Act to Ensure that the Laws of Canada are Consistent with the United Nations Declaration on the Rights of Indigenous Peoples*, 2d Sess., 39th Parl., 2008: www2.parl.gc.ca/HousePublications/Publication.aspx?DocId=3591320&Language=e&Mode=1&File=24.

51 *Declaration*, art. 7(2). See Appendix 1.

52 *Ibid.*, art 14(3).

53 *Ibid.*, art. 21(2).

54 *Ibid.*, art. 22(1).

55 *Declaration on the Rights of the Child*, GA Res. 1386(XIV), UN GAOR, 14th Sess., Supp. No. 16, UN Doc. A/4354 (1960) 19.

56 25 May 2000, 39 I.L.M. 1285 at 1286 (entered into force 12 Feb. 2002).

57 25 May 2000, 39 I.L.M. 1285 at 1290 (entered into force 18 Jan. 2002).

58 *General Guidelines Regarding the Form and Content of Initial Reports to be Submitted by States Parties under Article 44, Paragraph 1(a), of the Convention*, UN Doc. CRC/C/5 (30 Oct. 1991) at paras. 8-24.

59 United Nations Treaty Collection, "Convention on the Rights of the Child: Declarations and Reservations: Canada": http://treaties.un.org/Pages/ViewDetails.aspx?src=TREATY&mtdsg_no=IV-11&chapter=4&lang=en.

60 *Ibid.*

61 *Convention, supra* note 1, art. 4.

62 *Supra* note 59.

63 Human Rights Council, *Report of the Special Rapporteur on the situation of human rights and fundamental freedoms of indigenous people, S. James Anaya*, UN Doc. A/HRC/9/9 (11 Aug. 2008) at para. 85.

64 Committee on the Elimination of Racial Discrimination, *Concluding observations of the Committee on the Elimination of Racial Discrimination: United States of America*, UN Doc. CERD/C/USA/CO/6 (8 May 2008) at para. 29.

65 Judith Rae and the Sub Group on Indigenous Children and Youth, *Indigenous Children: Rights and Reality*, (Ottawa: First Nations Child and Family Caring Society, 2006) at 30.

66 Committee on the Rights of the Child, *General Comment No. 11 (2009): Indigenous children and their rights under the Convention*, UN Doc. CRC/C/GC/11 (12 Feb. 2009) at para. 82.

67 Standing Senate Committee on Human Rights, "Children: The Silenced Citizens: Effective Implementation of Canada's International Obligations with Respect to the Rights of Children" (April 2007) at ix: www.parl.gc.ca/39/1/parlbus/commbus/senate/Com-e/huma-e/rep-e/rep10apr07-e.htm#_Toc164844427.

68 *Convention, supra* note 1, art. 4.

69 UNICEF Innocenti Research Centre, "Global Research on Ombuds for Children: What is an Ombuds for Children?": www.unicef-irc.org/knowledge_pages/resource_pages/ombuds/.

70 See Department for Children, Schools and Families, "Children's Commissioner for England: Secretary of State Foreword": www.childrens-commissioner.co.uk/html/stateForeword.html.

71 See Scotland's Commissioner for Children and Young People, "About SCCYP": www.sccyp.org.uk/webpages/about_sccyp.php.

72 Office of the Children's Commissioner, "About the Office of the Children's Commissioner": www.occ.org.nz/aboutus/about_the_office_of_the_childrens_commissioner.

73 See, e.g., Standing Senate Committee on Human Rights, *supra* note 67, recommendation 20.

74 UNICEF, "Ensuring the Rights of Indigenous Children," *supra* note 5 at 20.

75 Asher Ben-Arieh *et al*, eds., *Measuring and Monitoring Children's Well-Being*, Social Indicators Research Series, Vol. 7 (Dordrecht: Kluwer Academic Publishers, 2001) at 6.

76 *Declaration*, art. 3.

77 Assembly of First Nations, "Canadian Human Rights complaint," *supra* note 33.

78 Cindy Blackstock *et al.*, *Reconciliation in Child Welfare: Touchstones of Hope for Indigenous Children, Youth and Families* (Ottawa: First Nations Child & Family Caring Society of Canada, 2006) at 10: fncfcs.com/docs/Touchstones_of_Hope.pdf.

79 National Council of Welfare, *supra* note 18 at 59.

80 Chief Public Health Officer, *supra* note 29 at 53.

81 *Ibid.*

82 *Report of the Auditor General of Canada to the House of Commons*, Chap. 4: First Nations Child and Family Services Program — Indian and Northern Affairs Canada (Ottawa: Office of the Auditor General of Canada, 2008) at 3: www.oag-bvg.gc.ca/internet/docs/aud_ch_oag_200805_04_e.pdf.

83 See Marlyn Bennett, "First Nations Fact Sheet: A General Profile on First Nations Child Welfare in Canada" (undated): www.fncaringsociety.com/docs/FirstNationsFS1.pdf.

84 British Columbia, Ministry of Children and Family Development, "Delegated Child & Family Service Agencies": www.mcf.gov.bc.ca/about_us/aboriginal/delegated/index.htm.

85 See, e.g., Nisga'a Final Agreement, chap. 11, clauses 89-99. See also Tsawwassen First Nation Final Agreement, chap. 16, clauses 55-76; Maa-Nulth First Nations Final Agreement, clauses 13.15 – 13.18; *Sechelt Indian Band Self-Government Act*, S.C. 1986, c. 27; and Spallumcheen First Nation By-Law, described in Bennett, *supra* note 83 at 4.

86 Shaun Thomas, "Haida Children Return to Haida Gwaii for Coming Home Camp" *The Northern View* (2 Sept. 2008).

87 Blackstock *et al.*, *supra* note 78 at 10.

88 Standing Senate Committee on Human Rights, *supra* note 67 at ix.

89 Committee on the Rights of the Child, *Consideration of Reports Submitted by States Parties under Article 44 of the Convention: Initial reports of States parties due in 1994: Addendum: Canada*, UN Doc. CRC/C/11/Add.3 (28 July 1994).

90 Committee on the Rights of the Child, *Consideration of Reports Submitted by States Parties under Article 44 of the Convention: Second periodic reports of States parties due in 1999: Canada*, UN Doc CRC/C/83/Add.6 (12 Mar. 2003).

91 Committee on the Rights of the Child, *Consideration of Reports Submitted by States Parties under Article 44 of the Convention: Concluding observations: Canada*, UN Doc. CRC/C/15/Add.215 (27 Oct. 2003) at para. 62 [Committee on the Rights of the Child, *Concluding observations: Canada*].

92 Canada, *Convention on the Rights of the Child: Third and Fourth Reports of Canada: Covering the period January 1998 – December 2007* (20 Nov. 2009): www2.ohchr.org/english/bodies/crc/docs/AdvanceVersions/CRC-C-CAN-3_4.pdf.

93 Lisa Woll, "Organizational Responses to the Convention on the Rights of the Child: International Lessons for Child Welfare Organizations" (2001) 80 Child Welfare 668 at 670.

94 See Canadian Coalition for the Rights of Children, "Monitoring": http://rightsofchildren.ca/monitoring.

95 Ontario Public School Boards Association, News Release, "Attawapiskat Human Rights Youth Forum" (25 Nov. 2008): www.newswire.ca/en/releases/archive/November2008/25/c3903.html.

96 New Democratic Party, News Release, "Attawapiskat School Battle Nominated for International Children's Peace Prize" (8 Aug. 2008): www.charlieangus.net/newsitem.php p?id=349&PHPSESSID=f912e92488e0c0d10ca81a6cb8ec2ae4.

97 See further UNICEF, "Fact Sheet: The Right to Participation": www.unicef.org/crc/files/Right-to-Participation.pdf; Committee on the Rights of the Child, *General Comment No. 12 (2009): The right of the child to be heard*, UN Doc. CRC/C/GC/12 (20 July 2009).

98 Committee on the Rights of the Child, *Concluding observations: Canada*, *supra* note 91 at paras. 58-59.

1   Victoria Tauli-Corpuz, "Statement of Victoria Tauli-Corpuz, Chair of the UN Permanent Forum on Indigenous Issues on the Occasion of the Adoption of the UN Declaration on the Rights of Indigenous Peoples" (Delivered to the United Nations General Assembly, New York, 13 Sept. 2007): www.un.org/esa/socdev/unpfii/documents/Declaration_ip_vtc.doc.

2   See Harold Hongju Koh, "How Is International Human Rights Law Enforced?" (1999) 74 Indiana L.J. 1397 at 1413- 1414.

3   Aboriginal and Torres Strait Islander Social Justice Commissioner, *Social Justice Report 2008* (2009) at 35: www.humanrights.gov.au/social_justice/sj_report/sjreport08/index.html.

4   Norway, "Statement (Agenda Item 4)" (Delivered to the Expert Mechanism on the Rights of Indigenous Peoples, 2d Sess, Geneva, 12 Aug. 2009).

5   *Act on Greenland Self-Government*: http://uk.nanoq.gl/sitecore/content/Websites/uk,-d-,nanoq/Emner/Government/~/media/F74BAB3359074B29AAB8C1E12AA1ECFE.ashx.

6   Greenland (Delegation of Denmark), "Statement by Mr. Kuupik Kleist, Premier of Greenland" (Delivered to the Expert Mechanism on the Rights of Indigenous Peoples, 2d Sess., Geneva, 11 Aug. 2009) at 2.

7   *Act on Greenland Self-Government*, *supra* note 5, preamble, s. 20.

8   Greenland, *supra* note 6 at 3. See also *Act on Greenland Self-Government*, *supra* note 5, ss. 2, 4, 7.

9   Kanako Uzawa & Kelly Dietz, "Japan" in Kathrin Wessendorf, ed., *The Indigenous World 2009* (Copenhagen: The International Work Group for Indigenous Affairs, 2009) 270 at 280.

10   Kathrin Wessendorf & Lola Garcia-Alix, "Editorial" in Wessendorf, *ibid.*, 10 at 11.

11   See, e.g., "Concerns about Mining Act revisions" (2009) 36(10) *Wawatay Online*: www.wawataynews.ca/archive/all/2009/5/14/Concerns-about-Mining-Act-revisions_16625; Viviane Weitzner, "Bucking the Wild West — Making Free, Prior and Informed Consent Work" (Speech to the Prospector and Developer's Association of Canada Annual Convention, 3 Mar. 2009): www.nsi-ins.ca/english/pdf/PDAC_FPIC_%20panel_%20feb_%202009.pdf.

12   *Cal* v. *Attorney General of Belize and Minister of Natural Resources and Environment*; *Coy* v. *Attorney General of Belize and Minister of Natural Resources and Environment* (18 Oct. 2007) Claims No. 171 & 172 of 2007 (Consolidated) (Supreme Court of Belize) at paras. 131-33.

13   In relation to such efforts in Australia, see Aboriginal and Torres Strait Islander Social Justice Commissioner, *supra* note 3 at ch. 2 ; Australian Human Rights Commission, *Submission to the National Human Rights Consultation* (2009): www.humanrights.gov.au/legal/submissions/2009/200906_NHRC.html.

14   See Permanent Forum on Indigenous Issues, *Information received from Governments: Bolivia*, UN Doc. E/C.19/2009/4/Add.2 (24 Feb. 2009) at paras. 26, 57.

15　See, e.g., Grand Council of the Crees (Eeyou Istchee) *et al., Joint Submission to the United Nations Human Rights Council in regard to the Universal Periodic Review Concerning Canada* (Sept. 2008): http://lib.ohchr.org/HRBodies/UPR/Documents/Session4/CA/JS4_EI_CAN_UPR_S4_2009_GrandCounciloftheCreesEeyouIstchee_Etal_JOINT.pdf.

16　See Human Rights Council, *Report of the Working Group on the Universal Periodic Review: Canada,* UN Doc. A/HRC/11/17 (5 Oct. 2009) at paras. 29, 23, 24, 30, 48, 50, 76.

17　See Human Rights Council, *Report of the Working Group on the Universal Periodic Review: New Zealand,* UN Doc. A/HRC/12/8 (4 June 2009) at paras. 30, 33, 36, 46, 48 and 50; *Report of the Working Group on the Universal Periodic Review: Colombia,* UN Doc. A/HRC/10/82 (9 Jan. 2009) at para. 58; and *Report of the Working Group on the Universal Periodic Review: Russian Federation,* UN Doc. A/HRC/11/19 (5 Oct. 2009) at para. 81.

18　See, e.g., "Opening Remarks Ms. Navanethem Pillay, United Nations High Commissioner for Human Rights, to the 2nd session of the Expert Mechanism on the Rights of Indigenous Peoples" (Delivered at the *Palais des Nations,* Geneva, 10 Aug. 2009): www.unhchr.ch/huricane/huricane.nsf/view01/0A1A8D39C55CE3F9C125760E00304 246?opendocument.

19　See Committee on the Rights of the Child, *General Comment No. 11* (2009): *Indigenous children and their rights under the Convention,* UN Doc. CRC/C/GC/11 (12 Feb. 2009) at para. 82; Committee on Economic, Social and Cultural Rights, *Concluding observations of the Committee on Economic, Social and Cultural Rights: Nicaragua,* UN Doc. E/C.12/NIC/CO/4 (28 Nov. 2008) at para. 35; Committee on the Elimination of Racial Discrimination, *Concluding observations of the Committee on the Elimination of Racial Discrimination: Fiji,* UN Doc. CERD/C/FJI/CO/17 (16 May 2008) at para. 13; Committee on the Elimination of Racial Discrimination, *Concluding observations of the Committee on the Elimination of Racial Discrimination: United States of America,* UN Doc. CERD/C/USA/CO/6 (8 May 2008) at para. 29.

20　Human Rights Council, *Report of the Special Rapporteur on the situation of human rights and fundamental freedoms of indigenous people, James Anaya: Addendum: Conclusions and Recommendations of the International Expert Seminar on the Role of United Nations Mechanisms with a Specific Mandate Regarding the Rights of Indigenous Peoples,* UN Doc. A/HRC/12/34/Add.7 (1 Sept. 2009), Annex, at para. 5.

21　*Ibid.* at para. 6.

22　Permanent Forum on Indigenous Issues, *Mission of the United Nations Permanent Forum on Indigenous Issues to Bolivia: Recommendations and Summary of Report,* UN Doc. E/C.19/2010/6 (18 Jan. 2010); Permanent Forum on Indigenous Issues, *Mission of the United Nations Permanent Forum on Indigenous Issues to Paraguay: Recommendations and Summary of Report,* UN Doc. E/C.19/2010/5 (18 Jan. 2010).

23　Relevant provisions of the *Declaration* included, *inter alia,* arts. 17 (Indigenous labour rights and State obligations); 26 (right to lands, territories and resources); and 28 (right to redress for land dispossessions).

24　*Centre for Minority Rights Development (Kenya) and Minority Rights Group International on behalf of Endorois Welfare Council* v. *Kenya* (2009) African Commission on Human and Peoples' Rights, Communication No. 276/2003 (not yet reported) at paras. 155, 204.

25 Copies of the *Declaration* translated into the six official languages of the UN and other languages are available at www.un.org/esa/socdev/unpfii/en/declaration.html.

26 Secretary-General, Press Release, SG/SM/11715 HR/4957 OBV/711, "Protect, Promote Endangered Languages, Secretary-General Urges in Message for International Day of World's Indigenous People" (23 July 2008): www.un.org/News/Press/docs/2008/sgsm11715.doc.htm.

27 *Declaration*, art. 46(3).

poverty 40; Indigenous peoples' experience of 74, 135: children 170-72, 183; women 158, 160

principled framework 152; absence of 72, 143-44; *UN Declaration* as 12, 52, 136, 141-42, 176, 188

property: right to 30, 123, 128, 131-32, 137, 139, 165. *See also* intellectual property rights

racism 46, 53, 54, 65, 135-36, 137, 173

reconciliation 49-52, 53; Canada and 71, 94, 147-48, 151, 174; *UN Declaration* to promote 12, 15, 47-8, 54, 176, 181, 188, 194

redress: in regard to land 40, 52, 56, 72, 121, 127, 133; right to 30, 120, 125, 130; for treaty violations 122-23, 132-34; *UN Declaration* as framework for 127, 132-34, 136, 163, 191

residential schools 28, 53-54, 170, 172; Harper's apology for 53, 58, 170

resource development 121-23, 191; extractive industries 121-22, 130, 131, 148

restitution: opposition to 30, 50; *UN Declaration* on right to 29, 30, 40, 121, 127, 133-34

Royal Commission on Aboriginal Peoples (RCAP) 53, 114

Royal Proclamation, 1763 138

Russia 24, 25, 26, 33

Second International Decade of the World's Indigenous People 37, 66-67, 134; Programme of Action (POA) for 42-43, 44-45, 75, 82, 128-29

self-determination: collective right of 15, 27, 72, 74, 114, 126, 160; denial of right of 72, 74, 137; in Indigenous child welfare 171, 184-85; as inherent right 56, 57, 72, 980, 114, 115, 120, 141, 144; right of 12, 19, 39, 40, 55-56, 114, 129-30, 114, 160-61; and secession concerns 36, 63; in *UN Declaration, which see*

self-government 114, 184; Canada's objection to 92-93, 176; right to 39, 80-81

slavery 193

sovereignty: Indigenous 51, 55-56, 120, 147; objections to 30, 48

Special Rapporteur 38, 82; on adequate housing 164-65; Canada objecting to 85-86, 90; on discrimination 20, 143; on FPIC 121-22, 130; and the "implementation gap" 37, 44, 107-08; national situation 41-42, 172; promotion of *UN Declaration* 66-67, 72, 83, 137, 140, 153, 181, 192; on treaties 132-33, 148-49

spirituality: rights to 128-29, 139, 149; and treaties 142; affirmed in *UN Declaration* 40, 52, 83, 109, 136

Stavenhagen, Rodolfo 37, 99-100, 130, 153, 168, 208

Strahl, Chuck 77

Stolen Sisters 158-59

Supreme Court of BC 49

Supreme Court of Belize 149, 191

Contributors

CRAIG BENJAMIN works for Amnesty International Canada as the co-ordinator of an ongoing campaign in support of the human rights of Indigenous peoples. One of the key projects in this campaign is the 2004 report, *Stolen Sisters: Discrimination and Violence against Indigenous Women in Canada*. He represented Amnesty International in both Geneva and New York during the final years of negotiation on the *United Nations Declaration on the Rights of Indigenous Peoples*, and continues to collaborate with Indigenous peoples' organizations and human rights groups to promote the implementation of the *Declaration* and other human rights standards in Canada.

ANDREA CARMEN is a member of the Yaqui Indian Nation and executive director of the International Indian Treaty Council. She has many years of experience working with Indigenous communities from North, Central, and South America, and the Pacific. A founding member of the Indigenous Initiative for Peace with Nobel laureate Rigoberta Menchu, she has participated as a human rights observer and mediator in crisis situations in the US, Chiapas, Mexico, and Ecuador. Andrea was one of the first Indigenous representatives to formally address the UN General Assembly and the first Indigenous woman to serve as rapporteur for a UN expert seminar. During 2006–2009, she served as the North America Regional Indigenous Caucus Co-coordinator.

KENNETH DEER is the Secretary of the Mohawk Nation at Kahnawake. The former publisher/managing editor of *The Eastern Door*, an award-winning paper serving the Mohawk community of Kahnawake, he was involved in the development of the *United Nations Declaration on the Rights of Indigenous Peoples* beginning in 1987. He is a member of the Indigenous Information and Communications Technology (ICT) Task Force, which was created after the World Summit on the Information Society in Tunis in 2005. Kenneth is involved in the Indigenous Portal, a web site that provides a focal point for Indigenous content, owned and operated by Indigenous people for Indigenous people.

PHIL FONTAINE, former National Chief of the Assembly of First Nations, is a member of the Sagkeeng First Nation in Manitoba. He took a leading role in the Indian residential school settlement, lobbied for the *Declaration on the Rights of Indigenous Peoples*, and helped negotiate a fair and just process for the settlement of specific land claims. He has previously served as Manitoba Regional Chief for the Assembly of First Nations and Grand Chief of the Assembly of Manitoba Chiefs. He is the recipient of seven honorary degrees and the Order of Manitoba.

JACKIE HARTLEY is a Policy and Research Officer with the Australian Human Rights Commission. Jackie previously worked as a Policy Analyst with the First Nations Summit. She holds a Master of Laws from the Indigenous Peoples' Law and Policy Program, University of Arizona, as well as a Bachelor of Arts (Hons.) and a Bachelor of Laws from the University of New South Wales, where she was awarded the University Medal in History. She has taught Australian history and public law at the University of New South Wales, and is a member of the editorial panel of the *Australian Indigenous Law Review*. The views expressed in the jointly authored Introduction and Conclusion are her personal views and not those of the Australian Human Rights Commission.

PAUL JOFFE is an attorney who, since 1974, has specialized in human rights and other issues relating to Indigenous peoples at the international and domestic level. For over two decades, he has been involved in international standard-setting processes, including those relating to the *United Nations Declaration on the Rights of Indigenous Peoples*, the draft American Declaration on the Rights of Indigenous Peoples, and the *Indigenous and Tribal Peoples Convention, 1989*. In 1998, he was involved in the Québec secession referendum, acting on behalf of the Grand Council of the Crees (Eeyou Istchee) before the Supreme Court of Canada. He is a member of the Québec and Ontario bars.

GRAND CHIEF EDWARD JOHN (Akile Ch'oh) is a hereditary chief of Tl'azt'en Nation and member of the First Nations Summit's political executive. A former tribal chief of the Carrier Sekani Tribal Council, a former Minister of Child and Family Services for the Province of British Columbia, and a former member of the National Aboriginal Economic Development Board of Canada, he also served as an elected councillor and then chief of Tl'azt'en Nation. He was a member of the tripartite British Columbia Claims Task Force which recommended the establishment of the independent BC Treaty Commission to facilitate negotiations among First Nations, Canada, and British Columbia. He holds a Bachelor of Arts from the University of Victoria, a Bachelor of Laws from the University of British Columbia and an honorary doctorate of laws from the University of Northern British Columbia.

CHIEF WILTON LITTLECHILD was the first Treaty Indian in Alberta to graduate with a law degree and the first Treaty Indian elected to the Canadian Parliament. As a parliamentarian, he served on several senior committees in the House of Commons and was a parliamentary delegate to the United Nations. At the international level, he organized a coalition of Indigenous Nations that sought and gained consultative status with the United Nations Economic and Social Council. He served as a member of the United Nations Permanent Forum on Indigenous

Issues as the North America representative from 2002–2007, and has served as chair of the Saskatchewan Justice Commission. Having been appointed Honorary Chief for the Maskwacîs Cree and International Chief for Treaty 6, he was elected as Regional Chief for Alberta in 2006. In 2009, he was named as a Commissioner for the Truth and Reconciliation Commission.

LES MALEZER is from the Butchulla/Gubbi Gubbi peoples of southeast Queensland, Australia, the traditional owners of Fraser Island and the Sunshine Coast/ Mary River region. As chair of the Global Indigenous Peoples Caucus, he co-ordinated the campaign for the adoption of the *United Nations Declaration on the Rights of Indigenous Peoples* in 2006 and 2007. He is chair of the Foundation for Aboriginal and Islander Research Action (FAIRA), well-known for its role in land rights and cultural heritage protection. He has held senior positions in Indigenous policy development in the Queensland and Australian governments, as well as elected positions as regional representative for Aboriginal communities, including Secretary General for the National Aboriginal Conference, and Executive Assistant to the chair of the Aboriginal and Torres Strait Islander Commission.

CÉLESTE MCKAY is a Métis woman from Manitoba. She holds a Bachelor of Social Work from the University of Manitoba, an LLB from the University of Victoria, and an LLM from the University of Ottawa that focused on the international human rights of Canadian Indigenous women. She has worked in the areas of human rights, policy, research, and advocacy, primarily on behalf of Indigenous women's organizations. She is currently the Director of Human Rights and International Affairs for the Native Women's Association of Canada.

JENNIFER PRESTON is the Program Coordinator for Aboriginal Affairs for the Canadian Friends Service Committee (Quakers). Educated at McMaster University, Hamilton (BA (Hons.), and the University of Guelph (MA), she has been a lecturer in Canadian Studies at the University of Waterloo. Her work in recent years has focused on international Indigenous rights, specifically the *United Nations Declaration on the Rights of Indigenous Peoples*. She was involved in the lobbying to ensure the successful adoption of the *Declaration* at the United Nations in both Geneva and New York, and has worked with Indigenous and state representatives as well as human rights organizations in various regions of the world. Her work is now focusing on implementation of the *Declaration*.

ROMEO SAGANASH studied at Université du Québec in Montreal where he obtained his law degree in 1989. He has since been involved in numerous organizations dealing with Cree and Aboriginal issues, including the Cree Nation Youth Council (as founding president), Creeco Inc., and the James Bay Eeyou Corporation. For over twenty years, including his tenure as Deputy Grand Chief of the Grand Council of the Crees of Eeyou Istchee (People's Land), he represented the Cree Nation at national and international conferences dealing with environmental and constitutional issues, self-government, international law, and human rights. Trilingual in Cree, English, and French, he has since 1993 worked in Waswanipi and Quebec City as Director of Quebec Relations and International Affairs for the Grand Council of the Crees.

CONNIE TARACENA is currently Minister Counsellor for the mission of Guatemala to the United Nations, representing Guatemala in the General Assembly's Third Committee (Social, Humanitarian and Cultural Affairs). Her career has included senior diplomatic positions with embassies to the Russian Federation, Sweden, Belgium, the Netherlands, Luxembourg and the European Union, the United States, and Colombia. She holds two master's degrees, one in international politics from the Universite Libre de Bruxelles, and one in political sciences from the Pontificia Universidad Javeriana, in Bogota, Colombia.

MARY ELLEN TURPEL-LAFOND is British Columbia's first Representative for Children and Youth, appointed for a five-year term in 2006. On leave from the Saskatchewan Provincial Court, she was involved in the administration of the court in relation to access to justice, judicial independence projects, technology, and public outreach. She has also worked as a criminal law judge in youth and adult courts, which led her to work at developing partnerships to better serve the needs of young people in the justice system, particularly sexually exploited children and youth, and children and youth with disabilities. Prior to her judicial appointment, she practiced law in Nova Scotia and Saskatchewan, and was a tenured professor of law at Dalhousie University.